D1154718

342.437
St34c

CZECHO/SLOVAKIA

Ethnic CONFLICT,
Constitutional FISSURE,
Negotiated BREAKUP

ERIC STEIN

With a Foreword by Lloyd Cutler

Ann Arbor

THE UNIVERSITY OF MICHIGAN PRESS

Copyright © by the University of Michigan 1997
All rights reserved
Published in the United States of America by
The University of Michigan Press
Manufactured in the United States of America
♾ Printed on acid-free paper

2000   1999   1998   1997   4   3   2   1

No part of this publication may be reproduced, stored in a retrieval system, or transmitted in any form or by any means, electronic, mechanical, or otherwise, without the written permission of the publisher.

A CIP catalog record for this book is available from the British Library.

Library of Congress Cataloging-in-Publication Data
Stein, Eric.
    Czecho/Slovakia : ethnic conflict, constitutional fissure,
negotiated breakup / Eric Stein ; with a foreword by Lloyd Cutler.
       p.   cm.
    Includes bibliographical references and index.
    ISBN 0-472-10804-2
    1. Constitutional history—Czechoslovakia.   2. Federal government—
Czechoslovakia—History.   3. Nationalism—Czechoslovakia—History.
4. Czechoslovakia—Ethnic relations.   5. Constitutional history—
Czech Republic.   6. Constitutional history—Slovakia.   I. Title.
KJP2101.S74   1997
342.437′029—dc21   97-8586
                                                                              CIP

Once more to my wife
Virginia

CAIApr27/98

ALLEGHENY COLLEGE LIBRARY

Contents

Foreword

I first met Václav Havel in the summer of 1989 at his country cottage outside Prague when our former ambassador to Czechoslovakia, William Luers, and his wife Wendy took us along on a visit to the Havels. Even then—only four months before the Velvet Revolution—Havel thought it would take at least five years before the Communist regime would fall.

Shortly after the Velvet Revolution in 1989 and Havel's election to the presidency, he asked me to put together a group of American and West European constitutional scholars to advise on the drafting of a new Czecho-Slovak constitution. One of our first recruits was Eric Stein. With his extensive background in European and American law, his Czech origins and his knowledge of the language, he proved to be one of our most valuable and influential assets.

The constitution we helped to draft was a federal constitution for the sovereign state of Czecho-Slovakia, a federation of two republics. For a federation of states, two is the worst possible number, because each necessarily has *de facto* veto power over the other. In the outcome, the two states could not agree on the federal aspects of the new constitution, and they split apart by mutual agreement, but without a Yugoslav-style ethnic war. Nevertheless, both states adopted those parts of the draft constitution relating to a Bill of Rights, an independent judiciary, and other indispensable elements of the rule of law. Eric Stein played a substantial role in the drafting process.

The book Stein has written about his experience is an engrossing, unique exploration of failed federalism against the background of an ethnic conflict and in the context of complex societal, political and economic transformations.

Lloyd N. Cutler
Member of the D.C. Bar,
Counsel to the President of the
United States (1979–80, 1994)

Acknowledgments

Drawing on my notes and a fallible memory, I list in the back of this book more than sixty persons whom I interviewed, often more than once, in the course of my research. I want to acknowledge their help with a sincere sense of gratitude and with apologies for any omission.

As the manuscript progressed, I have received indispensable comments from Ivo Bárta, LLM, Judge Vojtěch Cepl Jr., Prof. Jon Elster, Prof. JUDr. Viktor Knapp, JUDr. Peter Kresák, Doc. JUDr. Jozef Moravčík, Charles Myers, Prof. Dr. Petr Piťha, Dr. Paweł Lutomski, Prof. Herman Schwartz, JUDr. Vladimír Sládeček, Doc. JUDr. Luboš Tichý, and last but not least Ing. Václav Žák to whom I am particularly indebted for his sustained interest and assistance. My colleagues at Michigan, Professors Robert Axelrod, Alfred F. Conard, Tom Green, Don Herzog, Richard Pildes, Sallyanne Payton, Terrance Sandalow, and J. David Singer, also read the drafts, and I want to thank them for their observations.

Ivo Bárta, Vassil Breskovski, Filip Hanzlík, and Peter Schwartz, students at the University of Michigan Law School, provided competent research assistance. Marek Vojáček, a law student at the Charles University, has done an astute sleuth's job of checking citations in Prague.

I am particularly obligated to the outstanding reference staff of the University of Michigan Law Library, lead by Barbara Vaccaro, for their devoted and efficient service. Similarly, I want to acknowledge the friendly cooperation of Ms. Dolečková and Karfiková, Information Specialists in the former Library of the Federal Assembly of the Czech and Slovak Federative Republics, and of Ms. Šuchmová, Černíková, Vacková, and Vrbová in the Library of the Czech Republic Parliament.

Shelly Christian-Sherman and Linda Schubert have done expert computer work on the manuscript.

I received generous financial support from the research funds of the University of Michigan Law School, administered by the committee headed by Professor Yale Kamisar and Professor Joel Seligman. The IREX Foundation financed one of my study visits to the area.

Parts of the book were published earlier in more or less modified versions in the New Europe Law Review, American Journal of International Law,

Michigan Journal of International Law, and in a Festschrift für Ernst-Joachim Mestmäcker (NOMOS Verlagsges, Baden-Baden, Germany, 1996), Essays in Honor of Henry G. Schermers (Nijhoff Pub., Dordrecht, 1994) and in W. F. Ebbke and D. F. Vagts, Democracy, Market Economy, and the Law (Verlag Recht und Wirtschaft, Heidelberg, 1995), Festschrift für Günther Winkler (Springer Verlag, Wien/New York, 1997), American Journal of Comparative Law, Columbia Journal of Transnational Law.

Lloyd Cutler and Herman Schwartz (with the financial help of the Bass family) are responsible for my return to Central Europe and to that extent share the credit or blame for the enterprise.

My wife Virginia read every word of the successive versions with infinite patience and critical imagination.

Preface

I was born and raised in Czechoslovakia and graduated from the Charles University Law Faculty in Prague. On the raw morning of March 15, 1939, I awoke at the usual hour in the barracks of the 28th Prague Infantry Regiment where I was doing my military service. Looking out of the window, I saw the courtyard below teeming with gray uniforms and vehicles. The Czech officer on night duty did not bother to wake us before the arrival of the advance unit of the German army of occupation. I was directed to accompany a German non-commissioned officer with an escort on his search for concealed weapons in the barracks. Whenever we encountered a portrait of President Beneš, the Germans smashed it to smithereens. That was my last act of army duty. I was told to go home. I left the country not long thereafter for the United States, another legal training, another (the U.S.) army, and some nine fascinating years in the U.S. Department of State.

I revisited Prague 43 years later, in 1982—arriving by one of those baffling coincidences that defy explanation—one day before the fiftieth reunion of my high school (gymnasium) class, which was attended by 15 of the 21 graduates. Their compelling stories took me through the Nazi occupation, the wartime, the brief return of the "second" democratic Republic in 1945–48, the Communist takeover of 1948, the Stalin-directed trials of leading Communists in the early 1950s, the "Prague spring" of 1968, and the subsequent re-Stalinization after the invasion by Warsaw Pact forces. Of all the gymnasium graduates, those who had chosen law had fared worst. The most talented one, because he came from a long established bourgeois family of lawyers, ended up as a lowly clerk in a government corporation after a stint at a construction site. Another found refuge in the transportation department of the Prague General Prosecutor's Office after returning, in 1945, from a concentration camp. One Law Faculty graduate, a convinced Communist since his adolescent days, became a successful documentary filmmaker but after 1968 was reduced to dubbing foreign films into Czech. Still another made a meager living as a "black market" purveyor of legal advice. A promising classics scholar was dismissed from his posts at the university and academy because of his kinship with the finance minister in the First Republic; his mother took him as a young boy to the funeral of the minister—the only connection with this relative. He ruined his eyesight working in a sandpit.

I returned again in 1985 and left with a firm determination never to come back to a country so grievously torn from its Western roots by a regime that, although it no longer relied on physical torture or faith in an ideology, reposed on a demoralizing combination of assured economic security (at the price of a low living standard) and pervasive surveillance. Although almost everyone criticized the government in private, there were few outward signs of dissent beyond reports of the courageous few, some 1,200 in number, who signed the Charter 77. That document, authored principally by Václav Havel in 1977, exhorted the Communist government to abide by its international obligations for the protection of human rights.

In the closing years of the Communist regime, a handful of American lawyers established contact with Czech and Slovak dissidents and provided them with a variety of support. Professor Herman Schwartz of the American University in Washington, D.C., went to Prague under the auspices of Helsinki Watch to monitor the criminal trial of Václav Havel and wrote a brief on his behalf.

In a startling turn of events, the same dissidents became leading actors in the government that emerged from the November 1989 revolution. It was not surprising for these leaders to suggest, building on the previous contacts, that the Americans provide assistance in the preparation of a new federal constitution by making available Western constitutional experiences from which the country had been cut off for 40 years. In response to this suggestion, a small international advisory group was organized and I was asked to become a member. This call—for better or for worse—made me return to Central Europe despite my earlier vow never to come back, and it was the origin of this book.

Abbreviations

ABAJ	*American Bar Association Journal*
AM. J. POL. SCI.	*American Journal of Political Science*
AM. POL. SCI. REV.	*American Political Science Review*
AM. U. J'L OF INT'L L. AND POLICY	*American University Journal of International Law and Policy*
CAN. J. POL. SCI.	*Canadian Journal of Political Science*
ČD	*Český deník*
CDA	Civic Democratic Alliance
CDM	Christian Democratic Movement
CDP	Civic Democratic Party
CDU–CPP	Christian Democratic Union–Czech People's Party
CF	Civic Forum
CM	Civic Movement
NC	National Council
CNC	Czech National Council
ČNR	Česká národní rada
CONSTITUTIONS OF THE COUNTRIES	Albert P. Blaustein and Gilbert H. Flanz (eds.), *Constitutions of the Countries of the World* (Oceana Pub., Dobbs Ferry, N.Y.)
ČTK, ČSTK	Reports in the English language provided by the Czechoslovak News Agency, ČTK National News Wire, available on Lexis Nexis
EAST EUR. CONST. REV.	*East European Constitutional Review*
EUROPE (n.s)	*Europe, Agence Press, Luxemburg (new series), English edition*
F.A. PRINT	Federal Assembly Print

GA. J. INT'L & COMP. L. *Georgia Journal of International and Comparative Law*

GG Grundgesetz, Basic Law of the Federal Republic of Germany

HN *Hospodářské noviny* daily

I.L.M. *International Legal Materials*

INT'L AFF. *International Affairs*

LD *Lidová demokracie*

LN *Lidové noviny*

LSU Liberal Social Union

MDS Movement for Democratic Slovakia

MFD *Mladá fronta Dnes*

MICH. J. INT'L L. *Michigan Journal of International Law*

MICH. L. REV. *Michigan Law Review*

MICH. Q. REV. *Michigan Quarterly Review*

NEDĚLNÍ LN *Nedělní Lidové noviny*

NEW EUR. L. REV. *New Europe Law Review*

NO *Národná obroda*

N.Y. REV. OF BOOKS *New York Review of Books*

N.Y. TIMES *New York Times*

ÖJZ *Österreichische Juristische Zeitung*

ODS Občanská demokratická strana

PAV Public against Violence

PDL Party of the Democratic Left

PO *Právný obzor*

POL. SCI. Q. *Political Science Quarterly*

REV. INT'L STUD. *Review of International Studies*

RFE/RL RES. REP. Radio Free Europe–Radio Liberty, Inc., *Research Report on Eastern Europe* (Munich, F.R.G.)

RP *Rudé právo*

SB. *Sbírka zákonů České a Slovenské Federativní Republiky* [Collection of Laws of the Czech and Slovak Federative Republic]; or *Sbírka zákonů České republiky* [Collection of Laws of the Czech Republic]

SB. Z. A N. *Sbírka zákonů a nařízení Cěskoslovenské republiky* [Collection of Laws and Ordinances of the Czechoslovak Republic]

SDL	Strana demokratické levice
SNC	Slovak National Council
SNP	Slovak National Party
SNR	Slovenská národná rada
SP	*Slobodný piatok*
SS	*Svobodné slovo*
U. Chi. L. Rev.	*University of Chicago Law Review*
Yale J. Int'l L.	*Yale Journal of International Law*
Wash. L. Rev.	*Washington Law Review*
Zb.	*Zbierka zákonov Slovenskej republiky* [Collection of Laws of the Slovak Republic]

A Framework

1. The Questions

I have written this book in the twilight of my professional career. It is in one respect a record of an episode in the ageless learning process, a story of a lawyer's brush with contemporary nationalism, and his effort to grasp the elusive underpinning of that complex phenomenon. It centers on the clusters of people in former Czechoslovakia because of strong personal reasons—and also because I thought that the failed search for a constitutional framework in that country, one of the troubled "ethno-territorial"[1] groupings in Western and Eastern Europe, merited an inquiry.

I began writing on this subject in late 1990, about a year after the "negotiated revolution" of November 1989.[2] In a rare moment of their history, the Czechs and Slovaks were in a position to determine their future course freely and without outside dictation. It was my hope, if not expectation, that they would write a new federal constitution based on constitutionalism, democracy, and a free economy as vowed by Václav Havel, a leading dissenter from the old regime and the first post-Communist president of the country. By mid-1991, the common state was given a fifty-fifty chance by those privy to the constitutional negotiations. The prospect of its survival plunged when an apparent agreement reached in February 1992 was rejected in the Presidium of the Slovak National Council and it was further reduced by the outcome of the national elections of June 1992. The federation was terminated on December 31, 1992.

---

1. Robert J. Thompson and Joseph R. Rudolf Jr., "The Ebb and Flow of Ethnoterritorial Politics in the Western World," in J.R. Rudolf Jr. and R.J. Thompson (eds.), Ethnoterritorial Politics, Policy, and the Western World 1, 2 (Lynne Rienner Pub., Boulder and London, 1989), using "ethnoterritorial" to indicate "various political movements and conflicts that are derived from a group of people . . . having some identifiable geographic base within the boundaries of an existing political system."

2. President Havel prefers the term "negotiated revolution" to "velvet revolution," a term allegedly invented by Rita Klímová, the first ambassador to Washington of the now defunct Czech and Slovak Federative Republic. The revolutions in Hungary and Poland, for instance, were just as "velvety" as in former Czechoslovakia.

The book is idiosyncratic and more personal than is commonly expected from an academic study. It is written from a point of view determined largely by my experience. Without a point of view, the story would amount to a heap of unrelated happenings. Václav Havel's role is a thread running through the account. This might create a false impression of his actual influence on the course of events. In fact, the leader's clarion call faded into the voice of a Greek chorus at an early stage. Wherever possible I have the principal actors speak in their own words, but I make no pretense of "nonjudgmental" objectivity. For one thing, it is impossible to exhaust the mass of available sources so that the selection process, even with the best of intentions, is more or less arbitrary. Moreover, some of the crucial materials relating to the final phases of the negotiations are still sealed. Second, I do not delude myself into believing that I could completely transcend my biases, no matter how hard I tried. I have heard it said that a fact becomes history only when set in a chronological context. For that reason, subject to some exceptions, my study follows chronological order.

Within these parameters, the book should throw some light on a number of issues of more general import even though it cannot offer any complete answers:

— What is the source of ethnic conflicts? Is it, in the words of the American sociologist Donald L. Horowitz, "cultural differences," "ignorance or realistic divergence of interests"?[3] What is the impact of the structure and the individual actors on efforts to reach a settlement of such conflicts?

— What are the prospects for democratic multiethnic policies in an ethnically divided grouping? Why do territorially based ethnic groups choose secession or consensual separation even at the price of a substantial loss, and what makes for peaceful rather than violent separation? Is there anything new to be said about the immanent dilemma that has baffled international lawyers and diplomats, between assertions of self-determination up to secession on one hand and the integrity and "sovereignty" of states on the other? What, if any, is the role of the international community in the self-determination process and what forms for the expression of the wishes of "the peoples" are required or appropriate? Do differences in the perception of "sovereignty" or "international personality" matter?

— What institutional form offers the most promise to contain a specific ethnic conflict in given circumstances: a federation (the American or modern German variant), a "confederation," or a more complex arrange-

---

3. Donald L. Horowitz, Ethnic Groups in Conflict xii (University of California Press, Berkeley, Los Angeles, London, 1985). In this section I rely heavily on this important treatise.

ment with confederate and powersharing ("consociation") elements? Why do federations generally prosper in the West but wane not only in Africa and Asia but in Central-Eastern-Southern Europe as well? More specifically, does federalism fail in multiethnic societies in which the component units consist of different ethnic groups organized on a territorial basis? Would some of the multiethnic Western federations (Belgium, Canada) hold if exposed to a multilayered shock comparable to the 1988–91 revolutions and transformations?

— Is there a need for novel, more flexible regimes that would satisfy the demand of "a people" for self-determination, particularly in terms of participation in the international arena, and thus avoid a further fragmentation of the international system? Or is such a fragmentation a natural— and desirable—way toward a world (or specifically Europe) of "regions" and more or less loose functional associations?

— What particular features characterize the interaction between constitution making and the political, economic, and societal transformation to a democratic, market economy system in an atmosphere of ethnic tension?

— Why are there such striking differences in attitudes toward the scope and the degree of flexibility of constitutional documents and the role of constitutions in a society?

— Can an ethnic conflict be bridged by constitution writing? In what way are post-Communist constitutional negotiations influenced by the institutions, the emergent political party system, special interest groups, the churches and religious organizations, the interests of the elites, personal ambitions of the leaders, mass media, public opinion, international developments, and legal experts? What are the respective roles of the executive and legislatures? How do these negotiations interact with the action on "quasi-constitutional issues" such as electoral legislation, status of central banks, and regulation of media?[4] What is the role of symbols such as the name of the country and its flag? What is the impact of legal training and thinking? Does "law" matter?

— Does an analysis of the tactics and strategies offer some insights for a methodology of negotiations?

— What is the impact on the negotiations of foreign consultation, foreign institutional models, and the comparative legal method? Can a foreign lawyer free himself from the bias of his cultural and educational background so as to be able to offer useful advice?

---

4. Jon Elster, "Making Sense of Constitution-Making," 1 EAST EUR. CONS. REV. 15, 17 (1992).

2. Some Thoughts on Nationalism and Ethnic Conflict

"Ethnicity is one of those forces that is community-building in moderation, community-destroying in excess."[5] Ethnic violence since World War II has claimed millions of lives.[6]

I cannot deal here with the deluge of contemporary literature on ethnicity and ethnic-based nationalism. These writings consist primarily of empirical case studies and cannot be said to have "yet wholly met the aspiration of positivist ideals of social science"[7] by offering a persuasive general theory. My modest purpose here is to include a few basic thoughts combed from this literary bounty in order to broaden the context of this study.

Anthony D. Smith defines modern nationalism as "an ideological move-ment, for the attainment and maintenance of self-government and indepen-dence on behalf of a group, some of whose members conceive it to constitute an actual or potential 'nation' like others."[8] Scholars disagree on the sources of ethnic nationalism, a dispute that is of some relevance to the understanding of the Czech and Slovak situation. Ernest Gellner, the eminent sociologist of Czech extraction, sees nationalism "as the playing out of forces inherent in the switch from agrarian to industrial society . . . meshed in with other great changes."[9] Others challenge this "prevalent view" on the ground that it fails to explain the emergence of nationalism before industry.[10]

---

5. Donald L. Horowitz, *supra* note 3, at xiii. For Pierre Trudeau, nationalism is by its nature intolerant, discriminating, and in the end totalitarian.

6. Harold R. Isaacs, Idols of the Tribe: Group Identity and Political Changes 3 (Harper and Row, New York, 1975).

7. John McGary and Brendan O'Leary, "Introduction: The Macro-Political Regulation of Ethnic Conflict," in John McGary and Brendan O'Leary (eds.), The Politics of Ethnic Conflict Regulation 1, 3 (Routledge, London, New York, 1993); Benedict Anderson, Imagined Com-munities: Reflections on the Origin and Spread of Nationalism 3 (Verso, London, New York, 1983).

8. Anthony D. Smith, Theories of Nationalism 171 (Harper and Row, New York, Evan-ston, San Francisco, London, 1971). In a similar vein, with reference to Ernest Gellner, stressing the congruences of political and national units as distinguishing modern nationalism "from other and less demanding forms of national and group identification," Eric J. Hobsbawm, Nations and Nationalism since 1780: Programme, Myth, Reality 9 (2d ed., Cambridge U. Press, Cambridge, New York, Melbourne, 1992). *See also* John Breuilly, Nationalism and the State 2 (2d ed., U. of Chicago Press, Chicago, 1993).

9. Ernest Gellner, "Nationalism Reconsidered and E.H. Carr," 18 REV. OF INT'L. STUDIES (Great Britain) 285, 293 (1992), apparently modifying his view under the influence of E.H. Carr. Previously he saw "the switch to industrial society" as the *sole* factor. *See* Ernest Gellner, Nations and Nationalism, *passim* (Cornell University Press, Ithaca and London, 1983): "The transition from one kind of high culture to the other is visible outwardly as the coming of nationalism" (at 142).

10. John A. Hall, "Nationalism Classified and Explained," 122 DAEDALUS 1, 5 (No. 3,

It is the German ethnic nationalism that developed in the late eighteenth and early nineteenth centuries that is of particular relevance to this study. As part of the European *risorgimento* movement, it evolved not from the nobility (as in England, France, or Russia) but from the intellectuals, and it appeared in three phases: from the "scholarly interest" (study of language, culture, history), to "patriotic agitation," to "the rise of mass national movement."[11] It reached the final stage of a political program in reaction to the Napoleonic invasion and was fed by the sense of envy and inferiority toward the "advanced" nations of France and England.[12]

German romantic nationalism received "its ultimate form" in Nazism, which cannot be explained solely as a reaction to the defeat in World War I and Versailles.[13] It has been suggested, moreover, that Marxism as well is a "metamorphosed German nationalism," economized and internationalized by Karl Marx. There was, however, no direct road from German nationalism to Nazism, and its link with Marxism is questioned.[14]

A development similar to nineteenth-century German nationalism with an emphasis on common language as the highest value occurred among the Czech and later also among the Slovak elites. Their "reawakening," marked by the revival of the long suppressed local vernacular and the folk culture, turned into

---

1993). Czech history demonstrates an explosion of nationalism along with religious zeal as early as the beginning of the fifteenth century. One view sees the origin of modern nationalism in sixteenth century English nobility. Liah Greenfeld, "Transcending the Nation's Worth," 122 DAEDALUS 47, 49 (no. 3, 1993). But John Breuilly, referring to Burke, sees "something akin to nationalism" emerging in England at the end of the eighteenth century only. John Breuilly, Nationalism and the State 87 (2d ed., U. of Chicago Press, Chicago, 1994). See also Liah Greenfeld, Nationalism: Five Roads to Modernity 14 (Harvard U. Press, Cambridge, Mass., 1992). What about "the struggles for cultural and religious self-expression and national survival of the Hellenes and the Hebrews in the Greek classics and in the Bible?" Uri Ra'anan, "The National State Fallacy," in Joseph V. Montville (ed.), Conflict and Peacemaking in Multilateral Societies 5, 9 (Lexington Books, Lexington, Mass., Toronto, 1990). Anthony D. Smith distinguishes the ancient forms of "ethnocentric" nationalism from the modern "polycentric" nationalism. Anthony D. Smith, Theories of Nationalism, *supra* note 8, 158–64.

11. Miroslav Hroch, Social Preconditions of National Revival in Europe (transl. by Ben Fowkes) 23 (Cambridge Univ. Press, Cambridge, London, New York, 1985).

12. Liah Greenfeld, DAEDALUS, *supra* note 10, 52, 56.

13. John A. Hall, DAEDALUS, *supra* note 10, 12.

14. Liah Greenfeld, DAEDALUS, *supra* note 10, 56. See Tony Judt, "The New Old Nationalism," N.Y. REV. OF BOOKS, Mar. 26, 1994, p. 44, 48: "Greenfeld does add a twist of her own when she suggests that Karl Marx was not only heir to many of the moods and metaphors of German pietists and romantic thought but was in essence, a German nationalist himself, sharing similar feelings of *ressentiment* and with equally millenarian visions of individual authenticity to be achieved through fusion with the whole, and collective fulfillment attained through violent, apocalyptic conflict. This seems to me to go a little too far." The original Marxist thought drew on a rational, enlightened, and universalist approach to history rather than on nationalism. See also Anthony D. Smith, Theories of Nationalism, *supra* note 8, 4–5.

a revolutionary movement against Austrian rule and Germanization in the Czech lands and Magyar oppression in Slovakia and it culminated in the destruction of the Hapsburg multinational state. The Czechoslovak Republic, itself a "multinational" entity, was only one of the many new states that emerged from the ruins of the Austro-Hungarian, Ottoman, and Russian empires after World War I, "the greatest of all wars of nationalism."[15] In one jaundiced view,

> the new units set up in 1918 had all the defects of those alleged prison-houses of nations (or should one say nurseries of nations and nationalism) which they replaced, plus some additional ones of their own. They were just as minority-haunted, but they were smaller, unhallowed by age and often without experienced leaders, while the minorities whose irredentism they had to face included members of previously dominant cultural groups [e.g., the Germans and Hungarians], unused to subordination and well placed to resist it. The weakness of this system soon became manifest: in the age of Hitler and Stalin, it collapsed with very little resistance. . . ."[16]

This picture, although realistic in rough outline, is painted with too broad a brush, disregarding the substantial differences between the newly born states. I shall have more to say specifically on the viability of Czechoslovakia.

Decolonization after World War II in the wake of the liquidation of the British, French, and German empires is seen as a second wave of "triumphant nationalism." The collapse of the Soviet Union and communism as a viable system initiated a third wave of proliferation of political units with massacres and massive displacement of populations to which the peaceful divorce in Czechoslovakia is a startling exception. A benign view of this dénouement is that under certain conditions the intensity of ethnic conflict may abate, not enough to allow a continuation of the conflicting groups in a single state but still enough to allow a civilized separation through a process conforming (more or less) to the prevailing common constitutional order.

3. Sources of Ethnic Conflict

Some believe that cultural differences engender ethnic conflict, stressing cultural divergence, the limitations of cross-cultural contacts, lack of shared

---

15. William Pfaff, The Wrath of Nations 28 (Simon and Schuster, New York, 1993).

16. E.H. Carr paraphrased by Ernest Gellner, "Nationalism Reconsidered and E.H. Carr," 18 REV. OF INT'L STUD. 285, 288 (Great Britain) (1992). See also Zdeněk Pinc, "The Idea of the Czechoslovak State: History, Theory, and Political Reality," 10 CZECHOSLOVAK AND CENTRAL EUROPE JOURNAL 36 (1991).

values, absence of a "common will," and incompatible institutional systems and belief patterns.[17]

Although nationalism originated as a reaction to structural contradictions of the society, it concerns primarily an affirmation of national identity and dignity against those who deny it and reflects a sense of anxiety, humiliation, envy, and *"ressentiment."*[18] According to Horowitz, "[t]he sources of ethnic conflict are not to be found solely in the psychology of group juxtaposition, but they cannot be understood without a psychology, an explanation that takes account of the emotional concomitants of group traits and interactions."[19]

Economic factors, although often present in an ethnic conflict, are not the primary source. Even Adam Smith, the author of the *Wealth of Nations* and a father of the discipline of economics, considered "place" or status to be "the cause of all the tumult and bustle, all the rapine and injustice, which avarice and ambition have introduced into this world."[20] Nor can ethnic conflict be explained by class politics or class analysis of politics. "Ethnic groups and social classes rarely overlap perfectly; ethnic affiliations generally seem to elicit more passionate loyalty than do class allegiances. . . ."[21]

I shall return to these propositions as my story of the attempt to save the Czechoslovak state unfolds. They must be kept in mind before a judgment is rendered as to the responsibility for its failure. Although I do not embrace the postmodernist superrelativist pose denying the very idea of reality or truth, I am aware that any effort to depict a segment of the seamless band of history can, in the best of worlds, succeed only partially, with the picture remaining incomplete and subject to revision.[22]

4. On Negotiation for a Constitution: General Criteria

One may conjure up a continuum on which each of the infinite number of negotiating situations are ranged according to the simplicity/complexity factor: at one pole a two-party, monolithic, single issue negotiation for a sales contract in a fixed, stable setting "in the shadow of the law"; and at the other pole a multiparty, international negotiation with multiple political, economic, and

---

17. J.S. Furnivall and M.G. Smith, quoted in Donald Horowitz, *supra* note 3, 135–37. The term *culture* in a broad sense sums up "beliefs, norms, institutions and traditional ways of 'doing things' in a society." Staffan Zetterholm, "Introduction" in Staffan Zetterholm (ed.), National Cultures and European Integration—Exploratory Essays on Cultural Diversity and Common Policy 21 (Berg, Oxford/Providence, RI, 1994).

18. Liah Greenfeld, Nationalism, *supra* note 10, 15.

19. Donald L. Horowitz, Ethnic Groups in Conflict, *supra* note 3, 181–82.

20. Adam Smith, The Theory of Moral Sentiments 57 (ed. D.D. Raphael and L.A. Macfie, Liberty Classics, Indianapolis, 1982).

21. Donald L. Horowitz, *supra* note 3, 105–6.

22. *See generally* Gertrude Himmelfarb, On Looking into the Abyss, Untimely Thoughts on Culture and Society (A.A. Knopf, New York, 1994).

security issues conducted within the loose international system with minimal constraints (such as the United Nations conferences on the establishment of the International Atomic Energy Agency or on the Law of the Sea).[23]

I think of the Czech and Slovak negotiations for a constitution as a bargaining process for a contract, not in the sense of classic, primordial, social contract theorists such as Hobbes, Locke, and Rousseau but as a strategic bargaining over the allocation of expected benefits and costs focused "on the actual conditions on which real contracts are negotiated"[24] and leading to an agreement ultimately embodied in the new constitution. However appealing, the contractual analogy must not be allowed to conceal the specificity of the situation due to at least two factors: one was the direct and pervasive role of governmental institutions, and the other was due to the fact that the bargaining went to the very existence of a political community and ultimately appeared to both parties as not susceptible to settlement by compensation or "splitting the difference."[25]

Howard Raiffa lists a series of "strategic elements" that may serve as determinants of the simplicity/complexity factor but also as helpful parameters for the specific analysis of the Czech and Slovak negotiation process.[26] These "elements" are as follows.

Number and nature of negotiating parties. A three-party negotiation among the Czech-Slovak Federation and the two component Republics turned, as we shall see, into a two-party process. However, rather than "monolithic," each party delegation consisted of alliances engaged in complex internal negotiations among its members for a consensus on a common stand. As in any contractual context, the discussion reflected a mixture of complementary and opposed interests on the entire spectrum of constitutional issues, including genuine institutional concerns, personal and group interests, and ambitions of the individual elite actors. The confrontation between parties and within the delegations was complicated by the changing political scene, which raised the problem of the legitimacy of the negotiators and their preliminary agreements. Paradoxically, the final, crucial decision was made by two "monolithic" individuals acting almost alone on behalf of the two parties.

---

23. Bernhard G. Bechhofer and Eric Stein, "Atoms for Peace: The New International Atomic Energy Agency," 55 MICH. L. REV. 747 (1957); René-Jean Dupuy and Daniel Vignes, A Handbook on the Law of the Sea, vol. 1, 163–244 (Martinus Nijhoff, Dordrecht, Boston, Lancaster, 1991); Harold Karan Jacobson and Eric Stein, Diplomats, Scientists, and Politicians: The United States and Nuclear Test Ban Negotiations (Univ. of Michigan Press, Ann Arbor, 1966).

24. Douglas D. Heckathorn and Steven M. Maser, "Bargaining and Constitutional Contracts," 31 AM. J. POL. SCI. 142, 144, and generally (1987).

25. Dankwart A. Rustow, "Transition to Democracy: Toward a Dynamic Model," 3 COMPARATIVE POLITICS 337, 359 (April 1970).

26. Howard Raiffa, The Art and Science of Negotiation 11–19 (Harvard University Press, Cambridge, 1982).

One or more issues. The multiple issues comprised within the three principal constitutional sectors—allocation of powers between the Federation and the Republics, the bill of rights, and the structure of federal institutions—were discussed in different settings involving in part different groups of representatives of the parties and different institutions, adding to the complexity.

Requirement for the agreement to be legally binding and ratified by others. The legal nature of the agreement between the two Republics and the requirement of its ultimate ratification by the Republic legislatures proved to be major contentious items, with the first one contributing to the final breakup.

The possibility for the parties to break off negotiations and not arrive at an agreement. At the outset of the negotiations, a break appeared inacceptable: while seeking their own "pay-offs" on the basic issue of distribution of powers, the parties were prepared to cooperate in a solution that would preserve the common state. Over time, however, that pattern changed, ending ultimately with the breakup.

Existence of a formal time constraint. The hope of the principal actors was that the new constitutions for both the Federation and the Republics would be adopted by the first freely elected federal legislature, whose term, however, was limited to two years. This expectation proved highly unrealistic, and the successive deadlines were disregarded. The failure to agree within the publicly set time limitations increased the sense of impatience and frustration, which was a factor particularly on the Czech side in the final outcome.

Private or public negotiations. "Secret" discussions are said to provide mutual trust building and a willingness to compromise. An effort was made to keep the Czech-Slovak negotiations secret with scant information given in official communiqués and varied, often conflicting interpretations offered by the participants. The negotiators ran the risk of being disavowed when the agreement reached in private was brought to their principals and made public.

"Favors" to be repaid and linkage to other bargains. The Slovaks were acutely aware of past constitutional arrangements designed to give them an "equal voice" in decision making, all of which failed to change the "Prago-centrist" system; they expected the Czechs to "come across" this time. There was a linkage with budgetary negotiations. In the final stage, an agreement on the breakup was linked to the difficult division of federal property and the choice of constitutional procedures.

Tactics, including a threat of breaking off. The conventional bargaining techniques included appeals to the common good, ethical, rational and legal principles, concealment and misrepresentation, moves to squeeze concessions out of the other side by offering minimal concessions, and finally warnings and threats.[27] The Czech bargaining position was notably stronger not only be-

---

27. Douglas D. Heckathorn and Steven M. Maser, "Bargaining and Constitutional Contracts," 31 Am. J. Pol. Sci. 142, 159 (1987). *See also* Jon Elster, "Constitutionalism in Eastern

cause of its demographic and economic superiority but also because of the skill and experience of the Czech side—a factor complicating the negotiations. Pursuing the so-called bulldozer tactic, negotiators concentrated in each session on issues that appeared tractable, "sweeping" the other items ahead for future consideration. A fatal flaw was the unavailability or unwillingness to consider factual data such as the size of the past transfers of resources from the Czech Republic to Slovakia.

One-time bargaining or anticipated repetitions. It is said that continuing interaction makes the emergence of cooperation possible.[28] This proposition may have applied to the earlier phases of negotiations when ignorance of each other's motivations posed a psychological barrier and when the Czechs in particular began to learn about the depth of Slovak feeling.

The use of the services of "an intervenor." Foreign governments and international institutions, while mostly neutral in public, privately urged prompt agreement on a new federal constitution. President Havel, although associated with one of the parties, assumed the role of "facilitator" or "mediator" or "intervenor," but his position turned precarious at a relatively early stage.

Europe: An Introduction," 58 U. CHI. L. REV. 447, 449 (1991).

28. Robert Axelrod, "The Emergence of Cooperation among Egoists," 75 AM. POL. SCI. REV. 306, 307 (1981).

Prologue

I

The Setting

1. Constitution Makers and Foreign Advisors

a. The Actors

I observed the early negotiations for a new Czech-Slovak constitution from the vantage point of the international advisory group I mentioned in the preface.[1] The first object of the consultations was the draft federal constitution prepared under the direction of the then procurator general of the Czech Republic, Dr. Pavel Rychetský, an intelligent lawyer. In 1970, Dr. Rychetský had been dismissed by the Communist regime from his assistantship at the Charles University Law Faculty in the course of the "normalization" following the suppression of the 1968 "Prague spring." Thereafter he worked as a lawyer with various organizations. He was one of the original signatories of Charter 77[2] and published samizdat materials opposing the regime. He came forth as a major figure in the Civic Forum, which spearheaded the "velvet" revolution[3] of November 1989. With its Slovak counterpart, Public against Violence, that movement emerged from the first free elections of June 1990 as the strongest political force in the Federation. At that time Dr. Rychetský became senior

---

1. The group was brought together by Lloyd Cutler, the quintessential Washington attorney and counsel to presidents, along with Professor Herman Schwartz of the American University College of Law, and it included judges, academics, and politicians from the United States, the Western federal states, France, and the United Kingdom. The financing was provided by Mr. and Mrs. Sid Bass and the Charter 77 Foundation of New York. The original group included, among non-Americans, former Prime Minister Pierre Trudeau of Canada; Prof. Dr. Helmut Steinberger, Director of the Max Planck Institute for Foreign Public and International Law, Heidelberg, Germany; Prof. Vernon Bogdanor, Oxford University, United Kingdom; Prof. Francis Delpérée, Catholic University, Louvain-la-Neuve, Belgium; Prof. Roger Errera, member of the Conseil d'Etat, Paris, France; Prof. Dr. Herbert Hausmaninger, University of Vienna; and Prof. Gilles Petitpierre, University of Geneva, member of the Swiss Federal Parliament. Working papers prepared by the following members of the group were published in Czech translation in the review PRÁVNÍK: H. Schwartz, Laurence H. Tribe, F. Delpérée, and E. Stein (issue no. 1 of 1991); Vicki C. Jackson (no. 2 of 1991); V. Pěchota, Martin Garbus, and A.E. Dick Howard (no. 4 of 1991); and Albert J. Rosenthal, Charles Fried, and Nigel Wright (no. 5 of 1991).

2. See *supra* preface.

3. See *supra,* "A Framework," 1, note 2.

deputy prime minister of the federal government in charge of federal legislation and relations with the legislative bodies.

Another prominent member of the Czech and Slovak group that was
organized to work with the international counterpart was Dr. Zdeněk Jičínský,
an austere, somewhat melancholy man with a neatly trimmed goatee, deputy
chairman of the Federal National Assembly. A law professor by profession, he
had been another victim of the post-1968 "re-Stalinization." After his expulsion from the Communist Party and the Prague Law Faculty, Professor Jičínský, having refused a laborer's job, was employed in an insurance organization, only to be dismissed again because of signing Charter 77. After the
revolution, he was expected to head the important committee of the Federal
Assembly responsible for drafting the new constitution, but he was not reelected, reputedly because of his prominent role in the drafting of the 1960
"socialist" constitution.

The deputy federal prime minister, Dr. Ján Čarnogurský, a Slovak lawyer
in his midforties, was disbarred under the old regime for criticizing the government in the course of defending religious dissidents in criminal trials. He
worked for a time as a chauffeur, became unemployed when his wife was
pregnant with a fourth child, and was jailed for his dissident activities.[4] He
went from the prison directly to join the new leadership. It was Dr. Čarnogurský, courteous, "low key," and somewhat reserved, who articulated the
mission of our group in the first press conference: to provide a rational, impartial perspective as a necessary corrective in a tense and emotional atmosphere.
Another Slovak, František Mikloško, a dissenter and intimate friend of Ján
Čarnogurský, went from the Institute of Technical Cybernetics to repairing
mountain roads and tending furnaces. As an early leader of Public against
Violence with close connections to Catholic Church circles, he became the
pivotal chairman of the Slovak National Council.[5] He was the counterpart in
the constitutional negotiations of Dr. Dagmar Burešová, about whom I shall
have more to say later on.

There were two principal expert spokesmen: on the Slovak side the jovial,
rotund, red-cheeked Karol Plank, professor of civil law at the Comenius University in Bratislava, chair of the Slovak Supreme Court, and chair of the
federal Commission of Experts for the Preparation of the Federal Constitution.
He, too, suffered briefly in the post-1968 "normalization" but was not removed
from his teaching position. On the Czech side was Professor Plank's deputy on

---

4. Marián Leško, L'udia a l'udkovia z politickej elity [People and Little People of the
Political Elite] 17, 18 (Perex a.s., Bratislava?, 1993). For a full-page portrait of J. Čarnogurský, see
MFD, May 27, 1992, p. 7.

5. Marián Leško, *ibid.*, 9–10.

the Expert commission, Professor Jiří Boguszak of the Charles University Law Faculty and Czechoslovak Academy of Sciences, a clever, flexible, and articulate lawyer.

b. The Stage

The international and Czech-Slovak groups met for the first time in April 1990 in Salzburg, Austria, at the baroque castle built in the 1830s by the ruling Archbishop Firmian; it now serves as the seat of the American Salzburg Seminar.[6] After two days of meetings, we all traveled under the benevolent command of the Czecho-Slovak ambassador to the United States, Rita Klímová, by bus to Prague. At the frontier, we saw the remnants of the barbed wire barriers. As we proceeded, we were struck by the sharp contrast between the prosperous Austrian countryside and the run-down Czech villages.

The meetings continued in an estate outside Prague originally built in the early fourteenth century by a Czech nobleman, Jan of Rokycany, held for a time by the Hapsburg General Wallenstein, and presently owned and beautifully restored by the government. The haunting past that lurked pervasively near the surface emerged poignantly when Professor Jičínský recalled that in the cellars under this very building the police of the former regime held and interrogated its political prisoners. Yet postrevolutionary euphoria and hope for the future were in the air.[7]

The international group returned to Prague in January 1991, the night before the unleashing of Operation Desert Storm. The government, press, and, by all indications, the people were remarkably united in support of the Allied action: "A small country like ours can feel a bit less lonely on this planet," a taxi driver told me. Alas, I thought, there was no oil in his land. This was also before the unchecked Bosnian disaster.[8] In the modernist building of the

---

6. Two elegant, silver-haired ladies were prominent among the guests from Prague: they were the granddaughters of President T.G. Masaryk, who survived the anti-Masaryk campaign of the Communist regime. In a private talk they confessed to being taken aback by what they felt were the strong Slovak nationalist attitudes that emerged in the discussions; they had not encountered any such feelings among the Slovaks during the regular vacations of the extended presidential family in Slovakia.

7. After the first conference, more papers were written, and small meetings of specialists on basic human rights, emergency presidential powers, and the judiciary were arranged in Prague.

8. In August 1992, the "tireless, articulate and bitter spokesman for the beleaguered Sarajevo government" said: "Bosnia has sent a very clear message to other small nations that they cannot count on principles. They should forget democracy and free market, and arm themselves first. In Eastern Europe and the former Soviet Union, the message is that there is a new era of turmoil and vulnerability in the world . . . and nations should be better prepared for it." N.Y. TIMES, Aug. 20, 1992, p. A4.

ALLEGHENY COLLEGE LIBRARY

Charles University Law Faculty on the banks of the river Vltava, we assembled in the vast faculty room, an inner sanctum that I, as a student, had never dreamed of entering. We also held meetings in the Prime Minister's Building, which had been a student dormitory in my day, and in the cozy Ministry of Justice of the Czech Republic where we met with the minister and members of the judiciary. Shortly thereafter, the minister, Dr. Leon Richter, accused in the media of links to the Secret Police, resigned only to be fully exonerated many months later in a judicial proceeding.[9] We met also in the Hrzánský Palace, a delightful baroque structure in the romantic castle area. There, at the very entry, visitors were faced with a large mural declaring "With the Soviet Union for all times."

In the presidential wing of the castle we were received by the chancellor, "Prince Karl von Schwarzenberg, the chairman of the International Helsinki Federation, with tweed jacket and Sherlock Holmes pipe,"[10] a picture of an Oxford don except for the elegant cowboy boots. A scion of an ancient Austro-Hungarian nobility that was closely identified with the First Czechoslovak Republic, he aided the Czech dissidents at some personal risk. His ancestor, Prince Felix Schwarzenberg, was the first Austrian prime minister after the 1848 revolution, a pillar of the conservative court party, and "Richelieu" to the youthful Emperor Franz Josef I.[11] When I mentioned that as a student at Charles University I had participated in a Roman Law seminar with a Schwarzenberg, he pointed to a photograph of his father.[12] In the newly independent Czech Republic, the prince and his family regained the ownership of vast estates in southern Bohemia that had been confiscated by the Communist regime.

The next joint meeting, which threw some light on the impact of foreign advice, took place in June of 1991 in Bratislava, the capital of Slovakia, at the request of Dr. Čarnogurský, by then prime minister of the Slovak Republic and head of the Christian Democratic movement.[13] In the following months and years, I remained in professional and personal contact with the principal personalities, and we shall follow their destiny as my story unfolds.

2. A Lesson in Self-Knowledge

Having been trained in two different legal systems and having spent a lifetime in international activities, I thought of myself—more or less consciously—as a

9. LN, Dec. 15, 1992, p. 3.

10. Timothy Garton Ash, The Magic Lantern: The Revolution of '89 Witnessed in Warsaw, Budapest, Berlin, and Prague 118 (Random House, New York, 1990).

11. Otto Urban, František Josef I, 35, 37 (Ed. Archiv, vol. 67. MfD, Praha, 1991).

12. I was told subsequently that it was apparently his uncle, rather than father, who was my fellow student.

13. A brief summary of the record of this conference is included as annex I to this book.

cosmopolite in Henry James's sense of a person to whom "one set of customs" (and laws) seems "about as provincial as another."[14] To my astonishment, I found myself faced with not one but two strong biases that stood in the way of my understanding of the Czecho-Slovak reality.

First, having been raised under the First Czechoslovak Republic of 1918, I was subliminally wedded to that unitary democratic system, the only one existing in my memory. At the Bratislava meeting, Slovak Prime Minister Čarnogurský urged the constitution makers to "draw on the best" from the experience in the East as well as in the West, and he made it clear that our group was expected to offer technical expert advice rather than political solutions. Quite inappropriately, I found myself, in the presence of a Slovak TV crew, making an impassioned defense of the 1920 Constitution.[15]

The second bias, with an intensity that equally surprised me, was due to my identification with American life and law and, more importantly, my deep conviction of the unique rationality of the Constitution of the United States. This stimulated interesting but at times misleading analogies. I was by no means alone in this quandary.[16] It took several months of conscious effort and face-to-face exposure to the local environment to bring the double bias under a measure of control.

A closely related but separate factor was my indoctrination in American thinking about democratic federalism in general. The traditional discourse among constitutional lawyers, not only in the United States but in other mature federations, centers on an analysis of constitutional texts and of problems arising from the "living law" as it evolves from these texts. Political scientists dealing with federalism also often follow the formalistic pattern of legal thought. They assume the existence of given conditions that make a federalist system possible, desirable, or indispensable and do not inquire into the nature of these conditions. They do not distinguish conditions that enable an existing federal system to continue functioning in a changing environment from conditions that enable a new federal system to come into being in the first place. "The temptation is to make functional theories to do double duty as genetic theories."[17]

After some time, I became aware that the American approach to federalism must be reconsidered when it comes to a situation such as that in the Czech and Slovak state. In the next section, I outline a simple conceptual framework

---

14. Leon Edel, Henry James: A Life 121 (Harper and Row, New York, 1985).

15. *Infra,* Annex I, text at note 31.

16. Henry J. Reske, "U.S. Constitution Unpopular," ABAJ, Dec. 1991, 28–29; Herman Schwartz, "Innocents and Experience," 1 EAST EUR. CONST. REV. 26 (1992).

17. Dankwart A. Rustow, "Transitions to Democracy: Toward a Dynamic Model," 3 COM-PARATIVE POLITICS 337, 341 (Apr. 1970) (referring to the distinction between how a democratic system comes into existence and an existing democracy can best be preserved).

that has helped me—after some trials and tribulations—to comprehend better the problems faced by the constitution makers in that country, including the chances for transferability of foreign institutions into indigenous structures.

3. On Asymmetric Federation—and Beyond

In a "theoretical speculation" on elements of federalism, an American political scientist distinguished an ideal *symmetric* federal system, in which the interests of the component units in relation to the center as well as to each other would be identical, and an ideal *asymmetric* system. In the latter, "each component unit would have about it a unique feature or set of features which would separate in important ways, its interests from those of any other [component unit] or the system considered as a whole"[18] (situation of "latent secession" or "secession potential").[19]

The interests in question are predicated upon equality or disparity in the aggregate conditions of the respective units. These may be grouped into environmental factors (size, location and character of the territory, climate, population), social factors (ethnic origin, language, religion, history, tradition, economy, law, social groupings), and political factors (the political system).

One may conjure up a continuum between the two opposite ideal models in which the position of a given federal state would depend on the degree to which the interests of the units coincide or diverge. "[H]armony or conflict within a federal system can be thought of as a function of the symmetrical or asymmetrical pattern prevailing within the system." In general, "real" federal

---

18. Charles D. Tarlton, "Symmetry and Asymmetry as Elements of Federalism: A Theoretical Speculation," 27 J. OF POLITICS 861, 869 (1965). In an asymmetric system, "it would be difficult (if not impossible) to discern interests that could be clearly considered mutual or national in scope (short of those pertaining to national existence *per se*)." *Ibid.,* 869 (citing William S. Livingston, "A Note on the Nature of Federalism: Federalism as a Juridical Concept," 67 POL. SCI. Q. 81 [1952]). *See generally* Renaud Dehousse, Fédéralisme et relations internationales 96–100 (Bruylant, Bruxelles, 1991) (an innovative discussion). Viktor Knapp, "Central and Eastern European Federations: Communist Theory and Practice" in Karen Knop et al., Rethinking Federalism: Citizens, Markets, and Governments in a Changing World 316 (UBC Press, Vancouver, 1995). In the Czech and Slovak literature, the concept "asymmetric" has a specific meaning. It refers to the fact that certain Slovak institutions did not have counterparts in the Czech Republic, for example, the first autonomous Slovak organ under the 1948 Constitution, also the Slovak Academy of Sciences (there existed only the Czechoslovak Academy of Sciences in Prague), and—most important under the old regime—the "asymmetric organization" of the Communist Party.

19. Charles D. Tarlton, *ibid.,* 870; Dankwart A. Rustow, *supra* note 17, 350. There were 74 "federal, federacy/associated state and home rule arrangements" before the dissolution of the Soviet Union and Yugoslavia. Only four "confederal arrangements" were noted at the time: The Association of South East Asian Nations, Benelux, the Carribean Community, the European Communities, and the Nordic Council. Daniel J. Elazar (ed.), Federal Systems of the World: A Handbook of Federal, Confederal, and Autonomy Arrangements V–VII (Longman Group U.K. Limited, Harlow, Essex, U.K., 1991).

states would be located on the continuum "somewhere between the complete harmony of the symmetrical model and complete conflict potential of the asymmetric model."[20] The United States, the Federal Republic of Germany (particularly before unification), Austria, and Australia may be viewed as relatively symmetrical systems as contrasted with the strongly asymmetrical former Soviet Union and Yugoslavia, in the process of dissolution by secession.

After secession, a new state, if it comprises strong disparate groups, may itself be a victim of its high level of asymmetry (Russian Federation, Bosnia-Herzegovina). An affinity with, or outright intervention by, a foreign state, or activities of emigré groups, may contribute to the corrosive effects of the asymmetry (Canada, Belgium,[21] Yugoslavia, in some measure emigrés from Czechoslovakia).

Although the United States, Austria, and Australia are multiethnic, their component states are not organized on an ethnic-linguistic basis as are those of Canada and Belgium.[22] The position of these two on the continuum of symmetry and asymmetry is still in question. Two-unit states organized territorially on the basis of ethnicity or religion (such as Lebanon, the former Norway-Sweden Union,[23] and Czecho-Slovakia, and, in reality, Belgium and potentially Cyprus) pose a special problem due to pressures for absolute parity in representation and voting power, with the consequent danger of blockage. The problem is accentuated in a situation of a significant disparity in the size of the territory and population of the two components (the former Czecho-Slovakia). Moreover, secession from a two-unit state has unique consequences: the end of the composite state with implications in international relations and law.

---

20. Charles D. Tarlton, *ibid.*, 871 (1965).

21. The minister-president of the Walloon region of Belgium insisted in Paris on "privileged links" and "special relation" of his region with France at the economic and social levels along the lines of those existing between France and Quebec Province. EUROPE no. 5896 (n.s.), Jan. 13, 1993, p. 6.

22. Vladimír V. Kusín, "The Confederal Search," RES. REP. ON E. EUR., July 5, 1991, 36. Kusín considers Switzerland as essentially territorially rather than ethnically or nationality based. Spain constitutes "a blend of ethnic and administrative devolution." *Ibid.,* 37. On multiethnic states and nationalism, *see* Uri Ràanan, "The Nation-State Fallacy," in Joseph V. Montville (ed.), Conflict and Peacemaking in Multi-ethnic Societies 8–9 and *passim* (Lexington Books, Lexington, Mass., Toronto, 1990).

23. Under the Lebanese Constitution and the National Pact of 1943, as amended by the Taif Agreement of 1989, the president is a Maronite Christian, the prime minister a Sunni Muslim, and the speaker of the Chamber of Deputies a Shi'a Muslim. *See generally* Lebanon: A Country Study 144 (Federal Research Division, Library of Congress) (Thomas Collelo ed., 3rd ed., 1st prtg., 1989); U.S. Dept. of State, Country Reports on Human Rights Practices for 1991, at 1485 (1992). The Norway-Sweden Union lasted from 1814 to 1905. On Cyprus, *see* Report of the UN Secretary General of May 30, 1994 (S/1994/629) and UN Security Council Resolution (S/RES/939 [1994]) of July 29, 1994, envisaging a bicommunal and bizonal federation.

Asymmetry implies diversity. In an atmosphere of tolerance, diversity enriches and energizes the society. Intolerant nationalism, often abetted and exploited by ambitious leaders, brings conflict within and among the component units. Interests—or perceptions of interests—may change over time. A rising degree of asymmetry creates pressure for increased powers of the component units as against the center. The center may attempt to resist and suppress that pressure, in the extreme by armed force. In the alternative, the center may respond affirmatively in two ways. One is to allow the component units to share in central decision making ("consociation"); the other is to increase the scope of their independent action within their own sphere (devolution). The two responses may be combined.[24] Belgium, for instance, has been fairly successful at taming Flemish nationalism by successive rounds of devolution, but this "method of containing communal conflict may reach its limits when the remaining central powers cannot be devolved without hurting one side or the other."[25] In 1993, Belgium became a federal state with an institutional framework of a baffling complexity held together, it is often said, by its membership in the European Union. Many Belgians believe that if it were not for the huge complications posed by the predominantly French-speaking Brussels "region" their country would have split long ago. If the European Union should move toward common foreign policy and monetary union there may not be a lot left for the federal government.[26] In Canada, after a decade of negotiations, a plan for a further reduction of federal authority, and for recognition of French-speaking Quebec Province as "a distinct society" and of the inherent right of the aboriginal people to self-government, was defeated in a national referendum. In the 1995 provincial referendum, the Quebecois rejected independence for their province by the slimmest of margins, leaving the future uncertain.[27]

---

24. On the relationship between the federal and consociational model, *see* Arend Lijphart, "Consociation and Federation: Conceptual and Empirical Links," 22 CAN. J. POL. SCI. 499 (1979) and citations to other important work of the same author.

25. "Devolve and Rule," THE ECONOMIST, Oct. 12, 1991, 50–51.

26. In addition to the central and provincial institutions, the Belgian Constitution establishes three linguistic communities (four linguistic regions) and three territorial regions, all with their own organs—a costly and complex system. Despite the radical decentralization, the normally marginal Vlaams Blok Party moved from two to 12 seats in the Parliament as a result of the legislative elections of November 24, 1991, after a racist campaign advocating an independent Flemish state. EUROPE, Brief Notes, end of Dec. 1991, 1–2. On the new federal Constitution of 1993, *see* Francis Delpérée (ed. and coauthor), LA CONSTITUTION FÉDÉRALE DU 5 MAY 1993 (Bruyant, Bruxelles, 1993) (the English translation of THE BELGIAN CONSTITUTION, Belgian Chamber of Representatives, Feb. 17, 1994). THE ECONOMIST, Mar. 16, 1996, p. 50.

27. David Milne, The Canadian Constitution: The Players and the Issues in the Process that Has Led from Patriation to Meech Lake to an Uncertain Future (3d ed.) (J. Lorimer and Co.,

The symmetric-asymmetric continuum may be described in traditional terminology: if devolution fails to satisfy the claims arising from asymmetry, the system may be restructured into a "confederation," a loose composite in which the central authority with limited core powers derives its powers and continued existence from a consensus of the component "sovereign" units, which retain the right of secession.[28] At a certain point, the status of a "confederation" as an international person may come into question in the traditional discourse based on "sovereignty." "Confederations" have proved inherently unstable: they have either disintegrated or turned into more or less centralized federations as was the case with the United States, Switzerland, and Germany.[29] Some "confederations" in this sense have emerged from the ruins of the Soviet empire. Thus, in addition to the Commonwealth of the Independent States of the former Soviet Union, the new federal state of the Croatians and Muslims in Bosnia-Herzegovina was to be linked with the Republic of Croatia in a confederational arrangement.[30]

Beyond the confederation format is a variety of more or less loose functional, global, and regional associations such as the European Union,[31] Benelux, the British Commonwealth, and the numerous intergovernmental international regimes.

Toronto, 1991); Douglas M. Brown, "Canadian Integration and the Federal Bargain," 1 NEW EUROPE L. REV. 321 (1993); Robert Howse and Karen Knop, "Federalism, Secession, and the Limits of Ethnical Accommodation: A Canadian Perspective," *ibid.,* 269; WALL STREET JOURNAL, Oct. 28, 1992, p. A15; Susan Lavergne, "The Future of Canadian Federation," 23 GA J. INT'L & COMP. L. 63 (1993); "The Quebec Question," 1995 FOREIGN POLICY 69–88. For the most recent developments, see *infra,* chap. XV, note 42.

28. Federal law is enforceable directly against the citizens while confederal governments can reach them through the component units only. In European legal terms, federal government has "the competence of competence" while in a confederation it is the component units that retain that competence. *See also* Walter Rudolf, "Federal States," in 10 ENCYCLOPEDIA OF PUBLIC INTERNATIONAL LAW 165 (North-Holland, Amsterdam, New York, Oxford, Tokyo, 1987); and Felix Ermacora, "Confederations and Other Unions of States," *ibid.,* 60.

29. *See generally* Preston King, Federalism and Federation 133–45 (Croom Helm, London, Canberra, 1982); Karen Knop et al., Rethinking Federalism: Citizens, Markets, and Governments in a Changing World (UBC Press, Vancouver, 1995); Murray Forsyth, Union of States: Theory and Practice of Confederation (Leicester U. Press, Holmes and Merk Publishers Inc., New York, 1981).

30. Patrick Moore, "The Croatian-Muslim Agreements," RFE/RL RES. REP. ON E. EUR., April 1994, 20.

31. The European Union today is a sui generis body marked by high-level economic, monetary, social, and legal integration and low-level, incipient political integration; it is a hybrid between a confederate and federal structure. Eric Stein, "External Relations of the European Community: Structure and Process," Collected Courses of the Academy of European Law, vol. 1, book 1, 115, 128–30 (Martinus Nijhoff Publishers, Dordrecht, Boston, London, 1991).

4. A Parenthesis: On a Good "Gestalt"

On a more abstract level, the symmetry-asymmetry paradigm parallels the gestalt theory. As explained by Professor Rudolf Arnheim, in a structure composed of discrete units the needs of the units appear as

> directed tensions, that is, as vectors in a system of forces. . . . Their most basic striving . . . moves toward a structure . . . which wants to arrive at an optimal equilibrium, in which all vectors hold one another in balance to obtain a stable overall situation . . . the ideal structure at the simplest level compatible with that structure. A good gestalt is precisely such an ideal state . . . in which aspirations of a particular unit are reconciled with the structure of a whole, "a configuration or pattern of entities operating at maximum efficiency . . ."

In terms of the symmetry-asymmetry model I have just discussed, such an ideal state would correspond to the ideal symmetric system and the "vectors" would approximate "the interests" within the system. In political practice, however, Arnheim warns, this ideal state "is never reached or even much thought about in earnest." He believes that Jean-Jacques Rousseau's social contract, based on the common will or popular sovereignty, is the closest equivalent to the abstract realization of a good gestalt.[32]

---

32. Rudolf Arnheim, "The Split and the Structure," 1992 MICH. Q. REV. 195, 196. "Whichever the organization, whether it be hierarchical or coordinative, it will be distinguished by its particular level of dynamics. The level may vary from a state of tranquility to a maximum of inner agitation. Just as in the arts this measure of arousal distinguishes a Beethoven from a Gluck or a Baroque building by Borromini from the Parthenon, so will social structures differ in the intensity level of their vectors. They may conform in an easy harmony or balance at the high-tension level of powerful antagonistic forces. At each of these tension levels, however, a fully successful organization can be achieved, resulting in flawless functioning. A folksong is as perfect a structure as a Bach fugue, a small tribe can be as perfectly organized as a Western society." *Ibid.*, 202. The "can" in the last sentence should read as a conditional "could" in order to reconcile Arnheim's skepticism about the chance of a "flawlessly functioning" social organization, which in theory could but in reality does not exist (anymore as a "flawlessly functioning," ideal, symmetric organization). *See generally* Max Wertheimer, "On the Concept of Democracy," in Mary Henle (ed.), Documents of Gestalt Psychology 43–51 (U. of California Press, Berkeley and Los Angeles, 1961).

II

The Asymmetry of the Czech and
Slovak State

The 1960 Constitution,[1] substantially amended in 1968, remained in force after the revolution although modified by a series of postcommunist constitutional laws.[2] The 1968 amendment introduced a federal scheme embracing two component units, the Czech Republic and the Slovak Republic. In reality, the federal aspect proved at best an administrative division, at worst a hollow sham, but it led to an increase of Slovaks in the bureaucracy. The task faced by the constitution makers was to conjure up a new document in the context of conditions that, in the aggregate, would respond to the interests of the two component Republics in relation to each other and to the common system as a whole.

1. Environmental Conditions: Geography, Demography, Ethnicity, Economy

Czecho-Slovakia, the size of the state of New York, was located in the center of the European continent and, according to conventional wisdom, formed a bridge between East and West. Jan Masaryk, the son of Czechoslovakia's first president, complained that, as with any bridge, everyone felt free to trample over it, and it could also be easily blown up.[3] The precarious geographic

---

1. Ústavní zákon č. 100/1960 Sb.-Ústava ČSSR [Constitutional Law no. 100/1960 Sb. The Constitution of the Czechoslovak Socialist Republic], *translated in* 10 Constitutions of the Countries of the World, Czechoslovakia, Historic Constitutions, Albert P. Blaustein and Gisbert H. Flanz eds. (Oceana Pub., Dobbs Ferry, New York, 1974).

2. Ústavní zákon o československé federaci [Constitutional Law on the Czechoslovak Federation], no. 143/1968 Sb., consolidated text in Ústavní zákon Federálního shromáždění č. 103/1991 Sb.-ústavní zákon o čs. federaci, úplné znění [Constitutional Law of the Federal Assembly, no. 103/1991 Sb.-Constitutional Law on Czsl. Federation-complete text], as amended through Jan. 9, 1991; the Constitution may be amended by a so-called constitutional law, which requires the same procedure as the adoption of a new constitution.

3. Viktor Fischl, Hovory s Janem Masarykem [conversations with Jan Masaryk] 40 (MFD, Praha, 1991); Henry Brandon, Special Relationships: A Foreign Correspondent's Memoirs from Roosevelt to Reagan 23 (Atheneum, New York, 1988).

position at the crossroads of major powers has had obvious security implications that had to be taken into account in the policies if not in the institutional
structures of the country.[4]

The total population of under 16 million was substantially less than that of
New York state. Approximately 10.5 million live in the Czech Republic. In
addition to the Czech-speaking majority, some three million Moravians and
Silesians, who speak a slightly different dialect, live in the East and Northeast
of the Republic.[5] Five and a half million people live in the Slovak Republic.

The Czechs and Slovaks belong to the Slavic group, although almost 14
centuries of diverse influences and the absorption of Celtic elements in the
Czech lands left their imprints.[6] There are in Slovakia some 600,000 Hungarians settled predominantly along the border with Hungary (including a
substantial number of Hungarian-speaking Roma [gypsies]), 70,000 Poles, and
some 60,000 Ukrainians and Ruthenians. There are in both Republics some
60,000 to 100,000 Germans (a remnant of the three million expelled at the end
of World War II); several hundred thousand Roma, mostly in urban areas and in
eastern Slovakia; some remaining Vietnamese (originally 40,000 in number),
and more recently some hundreds of refugees from Romania and the former
Yugoslavia.[7] The exact number of Roma, estimated as high as 800,000, is

---

4. Except for some isolated voices in Slovakia, the "bridge role" concept is generally
rejected. The latest version, invented by Soviet Foreign Minister Kozyrev, conjured up Central
Europe as a bridge for Russia to join the highly developed democratic states. In a 1993 symposium,
this position was rejected: Russia will never be integrated in the Western system because "Russia is
Russia." STŘEDOEVROPSKÉ NOVINY, May 1994, no. 3, p. 1, supp. of LN of May 25, 1994.

5. Jan Obrman, "Minorities Not a Major Issue Yet," RFE/RL RES. REP., Dec. 13, 1991, 9–
10.

6. Prof. P. Piťha.

7. These data are based substantially on The Statesman's Year-Book: Statistical and Historical Annual of the States of the World for the Year 1990–1991, 408–9 (John Paxton ed., 127th
ed., St. Martins Press, New York, 1990); and World Almanac and Book of Facts 1990, 703 (New
York World Telegraph, Pharos Books, New York, 1990). It is widely believed in the West that
official census data have significantly underestimated minority numbers. On a possible reason, see
Laurence Tribe, Draft Paper on Federalism Issues for Consideration by the Framers of the Czecho-
slovakian Constitution 40 (1990) (unpublished manuscript). It should be kept in mind that while
there was a Czechoslovak citizenship there was no "Czechoslovak nationality." In the Czechoslovak census, the citizens were asked to register as belonging to one of a number of nationalities. The
figures made public by the federal Bureau of Statistics on the basis of the 1991 census show that of
the 10,302,215 citizens in the Czech Republic, 8,363,768 chose Czech, 314,877 Slovak, 1,362,313
Moravian, 44,446 Silesian, and 19,932 Hungarian nationality. In Slovakia, 4,519, 328 indicated
Slovak, 567,296 Hungarian, 52,884 Czech, 17,197 Ruthenian, 13,281 Ukrainian, 6,037 Moravian,
5,414 German, and 2,659 Polish nationality. Only 108,705 chose the Roma nationality. Also, 3,523
chose Czechoslovak nationality, 3,464 in the Czech Republic, 59 in the Slovak Republic. There
were 307,004 mixed nationality marriages. LN, Oct. 27, 1992, p. 2. The Czech News Agency
reported that there were 850,000 Roma, 600,000 in Slovakia and 250,000 in the Czech Republic,
but many declared other nationalities (Czech, Slovak, Hungarian) in the 1991 census. ČTK, Apr. 6,

difficult to establish since a majority declared themselves as members of other nationalities. Although many are assimilated and represented in the legislatures, they account for a disproportionate part of the unemployed and of certain crimes committed in the context of a dramatic rise of criminality after the November 1989 revolution.[8] Some 3.5 to four million Czechs and Slovaks live outside their country of origin, almost 80 percent in the United States.[9] The emigré groups played an important part in the establishment of the First Czechoslovak Republic and have continued to influence political life to a variable degree, particularly in Slovakia. In summary, one-tenth of the Czech-Slovak population consisted of minorities, a "birth defect"[10]—it is said—of the post–World War I settlement, which was alleviated but not remedied by the mass expulsion of the Germans. Thus, the two-to-one Czech-Slovak demographic asymmetry was greatly complicated by the extant minority problem, which today still haunts the new Slovak state.

In 1918, the Czech lands (Bohemia, Moravia, Silesia) contained four-fifths of the entire industrial plant of the Austro-Hungarian empire, while Slovakia was much less developed.[11] A great deal was done, particularly in the last 20 years, to put the Slovak and Czech economies on an equal footing with the result that the living standards between the two Republics today do not differ greatly. Nevertheless, Slovakia remains the more rural area with less productive land. The major part of important industries are located in the Czech Republic.[12] Although Slovak industry is relatively young and less obsolete than its Czech counterpart, it is concentrated in several branches, including armament and large, industrial establishments, substantially more vulnerable in the process of transformation into the free market economy. The

---

1992. This series of reports in the English language was provided by the Czechoslovak News Agency, ČTK National News Wire, and was available on Lexis Nexis. The citation "ČTK" or "ČSTK" refers to this series unless otherwise specified.

8. In 1990, crimes rose by 78 percent in the Czech Republic and by 48 percent in the Slovak Republic as compared with 1989. *See* Jiří Pehe, "Crime Rises in Czechoslovakia," RFE/RL RES. REP., Apr. 3, 1992, at 55.

9. ČSTK, Oct. 18, 1991.

10. "The hardest struggles in a democracy are those against the birth defects of the political community." Dankwart A. Rustow, "Transition to Democracy: Toward a Dynamic Model," COMPARATIVE POLITICS 360 (Apr. 1970). The basis of the post–World War I settlement is the treaty between the Allied and Associated Powers and Czechoslovakia, Sept. 10, 1919, U.K.-Fr.-Italy-Japan-U.S.-Czech, 226 CONSOLIDATED TREATY SERIES 170–81.

11. Lubomír Brokl/Zdenka Mansfeldová, "Von der 'unpolitischen' zur 'professionellen' Politik," in Peter Gerlich et al. (eds.), Regimewechsel: Demokratisierung und politische Kultur in Ostmitteleuropa 163, 195 (Böhlau Verlag, Wien, Köln, Graz, 1992), citing Z.V. Tobolka. In the Austro-Hungarian empire, the Czech literacy rate (93.77 percent) was the highest, while the Slovak rate in 1910 was about 60 percent. *Ibid.*

12. Jan Obrman and Jiří Pehe, "Difficult Power-Sharing Talks," RFE/RL RES. REP., Dec. 7, 1990, 5.

asymmetry in economic development, although greatly reduced, persists. While the Communist regime wreaked unmitigated havoc on the Czech developed economy, a major phase of Slovak economic modernization occurred during the Communist rule with the result that the predominant attitude toward the "socialist heritage" has been less negative in Slovakia than among the Czechs. This has added another element to the asymmetry.

2. Social Conditions: History, Religion, Culture

The history of the two peoples differs greatly. Until the end of World War I, the Czechs, Moravians, and Silesians lived in the Austrian sphere of the Austro-Hungarian empire with a measure of political autonomy, which allowed for the development of a civil society, an authentic national culture, and political consciousness. For 1,000 years the Slovaks were under the rule of the Magyars (Hungarians), which became heavy handed in the nineteenth century and was marked by a systematic Magyarization. As a result, in 1918 the Slovak society lacked practically any upper or middle class, intelligentsia, or culture of its own. The agreements among the Czech and Slovak emigré groups concluded during World War I promised the Slovaks equal treatment and autonomy in the newly independent Republic.[13] The 1920 Constitution, however, established a unitary state, which was administered centrally from Prague. A movement for autonomy developed in Slovakia in the 1930s, but the majority of the Slovaks voted consistently for all-state Czechoslovak parties.[14]

In 1939, under pressure from Nazi Germany, the Slovaks broke away from the Czechoslovak Republic and established their own fascist state. The head of that state, a Catholic priest, was hanged after the close of World War II as a war criminal.[15] This was the only Slovak experience of statehood as

---

13. The Subcarpathian Russia included in the Czechoslovak territory was to enjoy an autonomy status pursuant to a treaty with Allied powers. At the end of World War I, leading Slovak personalities opposed Slovak autonomy because the people had "neither a national nor human consciousness" and they called for strong centralism: the autonomous movement evolved later from the conflict between the governing Slovak Protestants (some 10 percent of the Slovak population) supporting unity and the opposition Slovak Catholics, whom the "progressionist-socialists" kept from jobs, and also from economic discontent and the "nationalist" friction between the Czechs and Slovaks. Ferdinand Peroutka, Začátky česko-slovenského soužití [Beginnings of the Czecho-Slovak Coexistence] 33–34, 88–89 (Ed. Sokolova, Paris, 1953).

14. Eva Broklová's thoughtful study "ČSR Chybná konstrukce nebo pozoruhodná výjimka? [Erroneous Construction or a Notable Exception?]," LN, Oct. 27, 1993, Názory, p. 6.

15. In 1991, some Slovak nationalist groups memorialized him as a hero, outraging Czechs. Vladimír V. Kusín, "Czechs and Slovaks: The Road to the Current Debate," RFE/RL RES. REP., Oct. 5, 1990, p. 4, 9. On history, see generally A.H. Hermann, A History of the Czechs (Allen Lane, London, 1975); Jozef Lettrich, History of Modern Slovakia (Praeger, New York, 1955); Edward Táborský, Czechoslovak Democracy at Work (George Allen and Unwin, Ltd., London,

compared with the Czech lands, which had existed as an independent state for some seven centuries before being absorbed in the Hapsburg monarchy. Following a Slovak uprising against the German occupation in 1944,[16] the Slovak National Council affirmed a continuation of the Slovak state, albeit within the Czechoslovak framework, but the postwar constitution of 1948[17] again disappointed Slovak aspirations. It provided only for a Slovak "Council of Mandatories" as a collective executive and for a limited legislative competence of the Slovak National Council. No comparable structure existed in the Czech Republic. More importantly, the all-powerful Communist Party pursued the ethnic policy of a unitary socialist Czechoslovak nation abetted by an unconcealed "anti-Slovakism" in the highest ranks of the party bureaucracy.

Finally, the "socialist" constitution of 1960[18] eliminated even the "Council of Mandatories." The centralist Communist policies evoked nationalist opposition in Slovakia, which was a corollary of the 1968 "Prague spring," a movement of reform Communists and liberal intellectuals. The 1968 constitutional law was drafted in great haste. There was concern that the Soviet government would stop the decentralization effort.[19] The Czechs were interested in democratic liberalization while the Slovaks pressed for federalization. The law came into effect in January 1969, but after the Soviet-led invasion Brezhnev-

---

1945); Robert William Seton-Watson, A History of the Czechs and Slovaks (Hutchison and Co., Ltd., London, New York, Melbourne, 1943); Sergio Bartole, Viktor Knapp et al., La dissoluzione della Federazione Cecoslovacca (in English) 3–43, 121–29, 163–202 (La Rosa Ed., Torino, 1994); Samuel Harrison Thompson, Czechoslovakia in European History (Princeton U. Press, Princeton, 1953); Carol Skalnik Leff, National Conflict in Czechoslovakia: The Making and Remaking of a State, 1918–1987 (Princeton U. Press, Princeton, 1988); Dějiny státu a práva [History of the State and Law], vols. 1 and 2 (Slovak Academy of Sciences, Bratislava, 1973); Frédéric Wehrlé, Le divorce tchéco-slovaque: vie et mort de la Tchécoslovaquie, 1918–1992 (Ed. ĽHarmattan, Paris, 1994); and Václav Bělohradský, Pierre Kende, and Jacques Rupnick (eds.), Democrazie da inventare: culture politiche e stato in Ungheria e Cecoslovacchia (Edizioni della Fondazione Giovanni Agnelli, Torino, 1991). The last two publications became available to me only after I had completed the manuscript for this book.

16. The two months' fighting in Slovakia cost 14,000 lives. 3,000 fell in Prague during the four days of attacks on the withdrawing Germans. LN, May 5, 1994, p. 12. According to MfD (May 5, 1995, p. 7), 1,700 Czechs and 900 Germans were killed at that time.

17. Ústavní zákon č. 150/1948 Sb.-Ústava 9. května [Constitutional Law no. 150/1948 Sb.-Constitution of May 9].

18. Const. Law 100/1960 Sb.

19. Const. Law 143/1968 Sb., *translated in* Constitutions of the Countries of the World, V Historic Constitutions 34; Zdeněk Jičínský, Vznik České národní rady v době Pražského jara a její působení do podzimu 1969 [The Establishment of the Czech National Council at the Time of the Prague Spring and its Functioning until the Autumn 1969] (Svoboda, Prague, 1990). *See also,* by the same author, Problémy československé politiky [Problems of Czechoslovak Politics] (NADAS-AFGH s.r.o., Praha, 1993).

style bureaucratic centralism was reimposed.[20] Thus, the federation so ardently desired by the Slovaks turned into a caricature of that form of government.

Two wings emerged in the Communist Party in about the mid-1980s: the "moderates," who succeeded in pushing through certain economic reforms; and the hard-liners, who in November 1989 attempted to use the police against harmless demonstrators, triggering the wave of massive protests. When Moscow made it clear that it was not prepared to intervene, it was the moderates who made the concessions that led to the roundtable talks between L. Adamec, a moderate, and Václav Havel and to the nonviolent end of the regime.[21]

History plays a role that is perhaps even more vital in Central than in Western Europe. Despite seven decades of a common political system (interrupted only in 1939–45 by the defection of the Slovak state), the asymmetry in historical memory has continued to stalk private and public life. "[A] shared forgetfulness is at least as important as common memories of a shared past for the emergence of a nation."[22] To this a Hungarian writer would reply that "the only wealth that people have in our part of Europe is history and memory."[23]

---

20. Milan Šimečka, The Restoration of Order: The Normalization of Czechoslovakia 1969–1976 (trans. by A.G. Brain) (Verso Ed., London, 1984); Stanislav J. Kirschbaum, "Federalism in Slovak Communist Politics," 19 CANADIAN SLAVONIC PAPERS 444 (1977); Jan Rychlík, "Unitární stát: jedna česká iluze [Unitarist State: One Czech Illusion]," 1/1992 PŘÍTOMNOST, p. 6. "Zpráva poslance akademika Viktora Knappa k zákonu o čs. federaci [Report of Deputy Academician Viktor Knapp on the Law on the Cz. Federation]," 1/1969 PRÁVNÍK 66, illustrates the situation in the 1968 Assembly.

21. The events of November 17, 1989, and the roundtable talks between the Communist government and the opposition have been the subject of a growing number of studies. See, for example, Timothy Garton Ash, The Magic Lantern: The Revolution of '89 Witnessed in Warsaw, Budapest, Berlin, and Prague (Random House, New York, 1990); Tony R. Judt, "Metamorphosis: The Democratic Revolution in Czechoslovakia," in Ivo Banac (ed.), Eastern Europe in Revolution 96–116 (Cornell Univ. Press, Ithaca and London, 1992); Jon Elster, Transition, Constitution-Making, and Separation in Czechoslovakia (unpublished manuscript, 1994); Oskar Krejčí, Proč to prasklo aneb Hovory o demokracii a "sametové revoluci" [Why Did It Crack or Talks about Democracy and "Velvet Revolution"], (Trio, Praha, 1991); William Echikson, Lighting the Night: Revolution in Eastern Europe (William Morrow and Co., Inc., New York, 1990); Viktor Osiatynski, "Revolutions in Eastern Europe," Review Essay, 58 U. OF CHI. L. REV. 823 (1991); William H. Luers, "Czechoslovakia: Road to Revolution," 69 FOREIGN AFFAIRS 77 (1990); Tim D. Whipple (ed.), After the Velvet Revolution: Václav Havel and the New Leaders of Czechoslovakia Speak Out, Focus on Issues, no. 14 (Freedom House, New York, 1991); and Theodore Draper, "A New History of the Velvet Revolution," N.Y. REV. OF BOOKS 14 (Jan. 14, 1993).

22. Giandomenico Majone, "Preservation of Cultural Diversity in a Federal System: The Role of the Regions," in Mark Tushnet (ed.), Comparative Constitutional Federalism: Europe and America 67, 69 (Greenwood Press, New York, Westport, Conn., London, 1990), paraphrasing Ernest Renan, Qu'c'est-qu'une Nation? (1882).

23. György Konrad in 9 CROSS CURRENTS 75, 92 (1990).

In the past, considerable divergence existed in religious attitude as well, although a substantial majority of both Czechs and Slovaks are Catholic. For the Czechs the Catholic Church was a bastion of Hapsburg power. While the Slovak (and Moravian) church wielded considerable influence in the Polish-conservative mode, Czech Catholicism was of a more liberal hue, suspected by the Slovaks of secularity and humanism. Protestant minorities exist in both Republics. Urbanization, industrialization, the Communist atheistic policy, and the cooperation of a part of the clergy with the Nazis or Communists took their toll on the influence of religion and reduced the antinomy between the two peoples. Nevertheless, while almost 40 percent in the Czech lands consider themselves without a religion, in Slovakia the number is less than 10 percent.[24] In general, the Slovak society is more traditional, marked by a fear of change, respect for authority, and intense longing for national identity.

A distinct language is generally viewed as a dominant characteristic of a nation. The Czech written language harks back to the Middle Ages while written Slovak emerged in the mid–nineteenth century only. Yet today the difference between them is hardly more noticeable than "between two Bavarian dialects."[25] Broadcasts alternated in Czech and Slovak and, with my Czech background, I am able to read and understand Slovak.

"What is the Slovak nation?" asked a Czech academic with a twinkle in his eyes. "They have no distinct language, no hero, no myth, no literature, not even a saint."[26] His statement was clearly intended as a bon mot and a hyperbole. In reality, the Slovaks had already under the Communist regime a complete education system, an entrepreneurial class, a press, and a layer of intelligentsia and artists, although greatly influenced by, and much thinner than, the Czech counterpart. In Slovakia, there were "even the nuclei of civic society— all from virtually nothing."[27] Nevertheless, the private remark illustrates the attitude prevailing among the Czechs of all classes. It is a heritage of the early,

---

24. Jan Rychlík in 11/1991 Přítomnost p. 5; Nedělní LN, May 30, 1992, p. 16. According to an opinion poll taken in the summer of 1993, in the Czech Republic only 20 percent were believers and only 13 percent were under 30 years of age. LN, Aug. 7, 1993, p. 3. While in 1991 40 percent of Czechs considered themselves Catholics, in a 1994 opinion poll this number dropped to less than 20 percent. Respect 16/18–23 April, 1995, p. 9. *See generally* Dennis J. Dunn (ed.), Religion and Nationalism in Eastern Europe and the Soviet Union 11–12 (Lynne Rienner Pub., Boulder, London, 1987); and Nils H. Wessell (ed.), "Revolution in East-West Relations," 38(1), Proceedings of the Academy of Political Science 120–22 (New York, 1991).

25. Jiří Sláma, "O dnešní situaci v Československu [On Today's Situation in Czechoslovakia]," 22 Listy 41, 45 (1992, no. 1). In 1992, a letter to the editor complained that the purity of the Czech language was being contaminated by many Slovakisms due to the media. LN, Oct. 13, 1992, p. 11.

26. Private conversation on Jan. 23, 1991.

27. Martin Bútora and Zora Bútorová, "Slovakia: The Identity Challenges of the Newly Born State," 60 Social Research 705, 735 (1993).

almost colonial relationship and actual or perceived discrimination as it evolved after 1918 when Czech teachers, officials, and entrepreneurs moved to Slovakia to help establish an indigenous system of education, economy, and administration.

It has been said that President Masaryk's idea of a single *political* (not cultural) nation in the image of modern West European states, essential as it was in 1918, became erroneously interpreted to apply in a cultural and ethnic sense as well.[28] During the First Republic (1918–38), the Czechs saw themselves as a governing nation in relation not only to the Slovaks but to the large German and Hungarian minorities as well. Although the government's minority policy was not without mistakes, there was a gradual improvement in Czech-German relations. German activists were part of the governing coalition from 1926 until 1938 when the rise of Nazism made any understanding impossible.[29] The benign view of the relationship between the Czech and Slovak peoples taken by the respected Slovak scholar Milan Šimečka is that the Slovaks have no hate for the Czechs but a permanent sense of being number two—a "younger and poorer brother";[30] the Czechs, in the depth of their hearts, feel this is true.[31] This psychological factor played upon by nationalist leadership fed the Slovak aspiration for recognition of their national identity that became the dominant Slovak goal in the negotiations for a new constitutional compact, overshadowing all other considerations.

3. An Interlude: A "Contempt" Theory

An American political scientist has designed a theory of contempt, drawing on the eighteenth-century English elite's attitudes toward working people,

28. Elena Várossová and Petr Piťha, "Vědomí národní, vědomí státu, [National Consciousness and State Consciousness]," LITERÁRNÍ NOVINY, Sept. 6, 1990, p. 3 (supp. of LN). Prof. Petr Piťha, a Catholic priest secretly ordained in the Netherlands during the Communist regime and a distinguished medievalist and linguist at the Charles University, was a member of a commission appointed by President Havel and ultimately served as Minister of Education in the newly independent Czech Republic.

29. *See* J.P. Stern, The Heart of Europe 260, summarizing Wolfgang Bruegel (Blackwell, Oxford, U.K., Cambridge, U.S., 1992). During my Czechoslovak army service in 1938, three or four Hungarians served in my Prague-based platoon. They kept to themselves in a more or less voluntary isolation from the Czechs and Slovaks, and shortly after the Munich "agreement" they vanished.

30. Letter from Viktor Knapp. See also "Naše podivná epocha, Rozhovor Adama Michnika s Václavem Havlem [Our Strange Epoch: A Conversation of Adam Michnik with Václav Havel]," 22 LISTY 37, 47 (no. 3, 1992).

31. Opinion polls in the spring of 1991 showed that only 9 percent of all Slovaks favored independence. 21 percent were for a "confederation," and 43 percent for a federation, but the polls did not indicate how much devolution to the Republics the Slovaks would insist on. Jiří Pehe, "Growing Slovak Demands Seen as Threat to Federation," RFE/RL RES. REP., Mar. 22, 1991, 1, 2.

women, Jews, and blacks. He found contempt based not only within the relationship of subordination (such as that perceived by the Slovaks toward the Czechs) but also in "the politics of identity": "To be a self is to be another's other," and "suppose that you and I can affirm one another as valuable selves by sharing contempt for some third self."[32] In Sigmund Freud's words, "it is a convenient and relatively harmless satisfaction of the inclination to aggression, by means of which cohesion between members of the community is made easier."[33]

This insight is confirmed by a personal episode drawn from the time before World War II when I was growing up in what is now the Czech Republic. A single Slovak boy attended the high school class in the provincial town of Hradec Králové where I started my secondary schooling. He was short, swarthy, powerfully built, with dark, fiery eyes and chips on both shoulders. It was a common diversion for most of the Czech boys at class recess to tease him and, when he defiantly responded, to beat him up not hatefully or viciously but as a light-hearted amusement—to affirm the "self" of the group as against a "third self." For me, as I recall, it was tempting to participate, to seal my belonging—but I did not, perhaps because I saw myself intuitively in the position of the Slovak: I was the only Jew in the class. I felt at the time more or less safe as part of the "self" of the majority group, and in fact I was never attacked as a Jew. In the small town where I started elementary school I was set upon by several classmates not necessarily because I was Jewish but because my parents spoke German and I was "rich"—and they were working-class poor Czechs—a curious admixture of class enmity, nationalism, and envy-based response to imagined contempt.

A snippet of an Anglo-Irish upper-middle-class conversation during World War I encapsulated an English-Irish "contempt" variant:

". . . England and Ireland are really one country."

"So the English soldiers evidently think when they sing 'It's a long way to Tipperary.' But it's always easy for the top dog to extend his sense of identity over his inferiors. It's a different matter for the inferiors to accept the identification."

---

32. Donald L. Herzog, "A Comparative Theory of Contempt," unpublished manuscript, 1994, p. 57.

33. Sigmund Freud, Civilization and Its Discontents (*transl. by* James Strachy) 61 (W.W. Norton and Co., New York, 1962). Freud's text immediately preceding this quotation reads as follows: "It is always possible to bind together a considerable number of people in love, so long as there are other people left over to receive the manifestation of aggressiveness. I once discussed the phenomenon that it is precisely communities with adjoining territories, and related to each other in other ways as well, who are engaged in constant feuds and ridiculing each other—like the Spaniards and Portuguese, the English and Scotch, and so on. . . . I gave this phenomenon the name of 'narcissism of minor differences,' a name which does not do much to explain it." *Ibid.*

"I can't understand this talk about inferiority. No one regards the Irish as inferior. . . . And I can't stand this jumped up Irish patriotism, it's so artificial. English patriotism is another thing. We have Shakespeare and the Magna Charta and the Armada and so on. But Ireland hasn't really had any history to speak of."[34]

I am confident that similar conversations, mutatis mutandis, can be overheard today among the "Anglos" in the bars of Montreal and among the "Francophones" in the brasseries of Brussels. These episodes illustrate one aspect of "cultural difference" that, in Donald L. Horowitz's sense, underlies ethnic conflicts, a more potent factor for "asymmetry" perhaps than the differences in language, religion, or economic interests and so readily subject to demagogic exploitation.

4. Political Conditions

For Czechs and Slovaks of the 1990s, except for the very old ones, the democratic experience in the First Republic of the 1920s and 1930s is a distant, if not subliminal, memory. The long-term impact of Nazi occupation and Stalinist modernization is still not fully revealed. The democratic institutions of the 1920 Constitution, based on a tripartite division of powers, respect for individual rights, rule of law, pluralism, and a market economy, were destroyed. They were replaced with "democratic centralism," a hierarchy of public power organs with the people's assembly at the summit, all subject to the "leading role" of the Communist Party. The division-of-powers idea was viewed as a bourgeois indulgence, and "social legality" replaced the rule of law. The federal framework, which was introduced as a dialectic reconciliation of the opposites of unity and diversity,[35] did not alleviate centralized policy making and party control on all levels of government.[36] A formidable security establishment guarded the regime against any opposition; it is estimated that one out of ten people cooperated in one role or another.

The 1960–68 Constitution made no distinction between the public and private spheres, leaving no aspect of the society immune from public power. To

---

34. Iris Murdoch, The Red and the Green 33 (Viking Press, New York, 1965).

35. For a socialist perspective, see Viktor Knapp, "Socialist Federation—A Legal Means to the Solution of the Nationality Problem: A Comparative Study," 82 MICH. L. REV. 1213, 1215–16 (1984); and Viktor Knapp, "Le fédéralisme et le développement de l'ordre juridique en Tchécoslovaquie," in Le fédéralisme et le développement des ordres juridiques, Travaux du Colloque de Moscou," Sept. 1970, 127–43 (Ed. Bruylant, Bruxelles, 1971).

36. Referring to the Soviet Union, Kusín speaks of "a unitary federalism of the party-state type, that is administrative regionalism with all policy making functions reserved for the center" and upheld by the political ubiquity of the party. Vladimír V. Kusín, "The Confederate Search," RFE/RL RES. REP., July 5, 1991, 35, 38.

maximize the monopoly of the party, the regime did all it could to atomize the society—"to destroy the institutions and bonds of solidarity and loyalty that hold society together as a society" and "to prevent the types of social, political and economic interactions that could promote individual and group autonomy."[37]

Socialization of property, or, in Václav Havel's terms, its anonymization,[38] was pressed in Czechoslovakia further than elsewhere in Eastern Europe. The end effect was the drowning of individual responsibility and initiative in a labyrinth of bureaucracy and indifference or hostility to the state and its property, combined with the expectation that the state would guarantee jobs and housing, what the Chinese call the "iron rice bowl." Pervasive negative egalitarianism frowned on individual success, and there was no tradition of risk taking. "From what new Protestantism should spring a 'market mentality' of the Czechs and Slovaks?" cried the Czech philosopher Václav Bělohradský.[39]

The political system of the First Republic (1918–38) was in the image of the Western European democracies. It was dominated by the interaction of five principal parties, ranging from the moderately nationalist right to the social democratic left, with a well-entrenched Communist Party in opposition. The president, although limited in terms of legal authority, exerted considerable influence. This party system, already undermined during the German occupation, was distorted in 1945 with the creation of the sham "National Front" within which the parties were reduced to discredited shells after the Communist takeover in 1948.

The political forces emerging from the 1989 revolution in both the Czech and Slovak Republics were quite different and did not divide along the political spectrum of the First Republic parties.[40] The Civic Forum in the Czech Republic and its Slovak counterpart, Public against Violence, were conglomerate political movements embracing a variety of different, even contradictory currents, held together by the rejection of the Communist regime and generally nonmaterial considerations. Together they were the controlling force in the first Federal Assembly, but by their very nature they were destined to fragmentation.[41]

---

37. George Schöpflin, "Post-Communism: Constructing New Democracies in Central Europe," 67 INT'L AFF., 235, 237–41 (Apr. 1991).

38. "Znovu vybudovat stát [To Reconstruct the State Anew]," LN, June 29, 1990, p. 1, 2: "everything is owned by all, in reality by no one."

39. Václav Bělohradský, Kapitalismus a občanské ctnosti [Capitalism and Civic Virtues] 28 (Český spisovatel, Praha, 1992).

40. *See infra,* chap. V. *See generally* Schöpflin, *supra* note 37, 237.

41. J.M.C. Rollo et al., The New Eastern Europe: Western Responses 28–31 (Royal Institute of International Affairs, Pinter Pub., London, 1990); Jiří Pehe, "Czecho-Slovak Conflict Threatens State Unity," RFE/RL RES. REP., Jan. 3, 1992, 83.

The 1989 "negotiated revolution" was a "devil's pact" with the Communist authorities, and it left a significant heritage. Although almost half of the deputies of the Federal Assembly were promptly replaced in accordance with an earlier precedent,[42] many felt that the cleansing of the institutions (styled "lustration," a curious latinism) did not go far enough, and the issue of how much to forgive and forget continued to haunt public life. Again, the process of negotiation itself and the adherence to rules established by the old regime created a strong presumption in favor of legal continuity, which, as we shall see, had palpable repercussions on subsequent constitutional developments.

This was the political setting in which the Federal Assembly and the National Councils (parliaments) of the two Republics appointed the bodies charged with the revision of their respective constitutions.[43]

---

42. Const. Law 183/1989 Sb. and 14/1990 Sb.
43. *See infra,* chap. III, 8.

III

The Threshold Issues

1. The Scope and Flexibility of Constitutions

A constitution being the highest in the hierarchy of norms, a crucial question facing a constitution maker is how much of the country's law should be given constitutional status and, as a corollary, what should be the modality of modifying it.[1] Dahrendorf illustrates the dilemma: "Whatever is raised to [the constitutional] plane is thereby removed from day-to-day struggle of normal politics . . . the line is drawn between rules and principles which must be binding on all, and differences of view which can be fought out within these rules."[2] President Havel told the Federal Assembly that in his opinion "our future constitutions should be utterly clear, simple and basic to the extent that our successors would not have to modify them each year by ever new constitutional laws and additions."[3]

---

1. For a detailed list of issues arising in post-Communist constitution making, *see* Steven Holmes, "Introducing the Center," 1 EAST EUR. CONST. REV. 13, 14 (1992). I touch upon most of these issues in this book. *See also* the useful study by Jon Elster, "Constitution-Making in Eastern Europe: Rebuilding the Boat in the Open Sea," 71 PUBLIC ADMINISTRATION 169–217 (1993), with a bibliography. *See also* Dušan Hendrych, "Constitutional Transition and Preparation of New Constitution in Czechoslovakia after 1989," in Joachim Jens Hesse and Neville Johnson (eds.), Constitutional Policy and Change in Europe 278 (Oxford U. Press, Oxford, New York, 1995) in process of publication. On general constitution making, *see* the 15 "rules of constitutional prudence for contemporary constitution makers," said to be based on Abbè Sieyès's experience with drafting four constitutional charters during the French Revolution, in Edward McWhinney, Constitution-Making: Principles, Process, Practice 133–36 (U. of Toronto Press, Toronto, Buffalo, London, 1981). *See generally* Rett R. Ludwikowski, "Searching for a New Constitutional Model for East-Central Europe," 17 SYRACUSE J. INT'L L. AND COM. 155 (1991); Peter Häberle, "Perspektiven einer kulturwissenschaftlichen Transformationsforschung etc.," in Herta Däubler-Gmelin et al. (eds.), Gegenrede, Festschrift für Ernst Gottfried Mahrenholz 133 (Nomos Verl., Baden-Baden, 1994); and Peter Häberle, "Constitutional Developments in Eastern Europe from the Point of View of Jurisprudence and Constitutional Theory," 46 LAW AND STATE 64 (Institut für Wissenschaftliche Zusammenarbeit, Tübingen, 1992).

2. Ralf Dahrendorf, Reflections on the Revolution in Europe 36–37 (Random House, New York, 1990). *See* Bruce Ackerman, The Future of Liberal Revolution (Yale U. Press, New Haven, London, 1992).

3. LN, June 30, 1990, p. 3.

In the series of meetings of the international advisory group with the Czechs and Slovaks in Salzburg and Prague, American participants recounted the Founding Fathers' experience with the sparse federal Constitution and its difficult amending procedure,[4] which accords the states an important voice along with Congress: a possibility of frequent amendments, James Madison argued, would promote factionalism and provide no firm basis for republican self-government.[5] In support of the proposition that more than approval by the federal legislature is necessary, the Americans quoted Madison:

> [T]he Constitution is to be founded on the assent and ratification of the people of America . . . this assent and ratification is to be given by the people, not as individuals composing one entire nation, but as composing the distinct and independent states to which they respectively belong. It is to be the assent and ratification of the several states, derived from the supreme authority in each state—the authority of the people themselves. The act, therefore, establishing the Constitution, will not be a national but a federal act.[6]

Although the Belgian and Netherlands' constitutions may be amended by no more than a special procedure in the legislature, in most unitary European democracies a constitutional amendment, after approval by the legislature or constitutional convention, is submitted either automatically or on request of a minority in the legislature to ratification by a vote of all the people. This practice prevails, for instance, in France, Italy, Spain, and Sweden.[7]

As for federal states, only in Germany may an amendment be adopted by a two-thirds majority of both houses of the federal legislature. In other divided-power states, a referendum is either optional (Austria) or obligatory (Switzerland) or the approval of a specified majority of legislatures of the component

---

4. U.S. Const. art V. Amending procedures require two-thirds of both Houses of Congress or two-thirds of state legislatures calling a convention. Ratification in three-fourths of the states is necessary. There have been 27 amendments to the Constitution.

5. Cass R. Sunstein, "Constitutionalism and Secession," 58 U. CHI. L. REV. 633, 636 n. 12, citing letter from James Madison to Thomas Jefferson (Feb. 14, 1790). One American in our group, a seasoned constitutional law scholar, was inclined to support a more flexible amending procedure but did not articulate his view. He may have been influenced by Jefferson, who thought that the Constitution should be amended by each generation in order to ensure that the dead past would not constrain the living present. *Ibid.,* 636.

6. The Federalist No. 39 (James Madison in The Federalist Papers 243, New American Library, New York, 1961).

7. La Constitution art. 89 (1958) (Fr.); Costituzione arts. 138–39 (1947) (Italy), *translated in* VIII Constitutions of the Countries 47, 83 (1987); Constitución arts. 166–69 (1978) (Spain), *translated in* XVI Constitutions of the Countries 43, 83 (1991); Regieringsformen [Form of Government] chap. 8, art. 15 (1975) (Swed.), *translated in* XVII Constitutions of the Countries 82, 99 (1985). See also Jon Elster, "Constitution-Making in Eastern Europe," *supra* note 1, 175–76.

units is necessary, following action by the federal legislature (Austria, Brazil, Canada and India in most matters, Mexico, the United States).[8]

Former Canadian prime minister Pierre Trudeau, a member of the international group, advocated a simple, short document with special, demanding requirements for any amendment. He cited the 15 regimes or constitutions in the past 200 years of French history as a model to be avoided. Some of the European members of the group were reticent on this subject. Yet it soon became clear that for the Czechs and Slovaks the answers lay elsewhere.

The first Czechoslovak Constitution of 1920, fashioned after the charter of the French Third Republic, had no less than 134 articles;[9] the 1960–68 Constitution[10] had 151; the early Civic Forum draft of a federal constitution, 160; President Havel's original draft, 180; and the Czech Republic government working draft, 195.[11] As regards the amending procedure, the 1960–68 Constitution required—in addition to an absolute three-fifths majority in the lower chamber—a three-fifths majority of the Czech and Slovak national groups in the upper chamber of the Federal Assembly.[12]

It became quite clear to us that, with respect to the scope of the Constitution, the Czechs and Slovaks would follow their own tradition, which they shared with most other states and which mirrored the turbulent history of the European continent, marked by frequent violent changes. For one thing, although basic decisions are made by politicians, constitution making is "the hour of the lawyers"[13] and the lawyers' way is paved with tradition and precedents. More importantly, the lack of trust on the part of the Slovaks fueled the tendency to spell out in detail the laboriously achieved consensus, far in excess of the minimum scaffolding of basic rights and institutions deemed necessary for a system based on constitutionalism and democracy. Moreover,

---

8. Grundgesetz [Basic Law] [GG] art. 79, 146 (F.R.G.), *translated in* VI Constitutions of the Countries 79, 116, and 161 (1991); Bundesverfassungsgezetz [Constitution] [B–VG] art. 44 (1929) (Aus.), *translated in* I Constitutions of the Countries 27, 60 (1985); Bundesverfassung [Constitution] [BV] arts. 118–23 (Switz.); Can. Const. (Constitution Act of 1867) arts. 38–49; U.S. Const., *supra* note 4; Const. of India part XXI, art. 368; Constitución Politica de los Estados Unidos Mexicanos [Const.] art. 135, *translated in* X Constitutions of the Countries (1988); Constituição Federal [C.F.] art. 60 (Braz.), *translated in* II Constitutions of the Countries (1990); Austl. Const. art. 128.

9. Ústava československé republiky [Constitution of the Czechoslovak Republic], 121/1920 Sb., *translated in* International Conciliation No. 179, Oct. 1922, 35–73.

10. 143/1968 Sb.; *see* chap. II, note 2.

11. The Basic Law of the Federal Republic of Germany has 146 articles, the Spanish Constitution has 186, French 92, Canadian 61, New York 20, California 21, and Michigan 12.

12. Ústavní zákon ČSFR [Federal Constitutional Law] 103/1991 Sb. (retaining art. 41 of the 1960–68 Constitution) (hereafter 103/1991 Sb.). To similar effect, *see* Ústava české a Slovenské Federativí Republiky, pracovní návrh, srpen 1991 (hereinafter Second Federal Draft), chap. 4, art. 12(3) (Aug. 1991, in my file).

13. Dahrendorf, *supra* note 2, at 86.

in the given circumstances, individual constitution makers were in no better position than anyone else to foresee the future role that they and their constituents would be able to play in the still unformed political system. This uncertainty was an added motive for including matters that would normally be left to the political process. Finally, unlike that of the United States, the Czechoslovak tradition follows the continental pattern in that it does not rely on the judicial interpretation of constitutional documents as the principal method of adapting them to changed requirements of the society.[14]

As one Czech expressed it, the U.S. Constitution could not serve as a model because the general conditions at the time of its drafting "were much simpler"; in view of the need to accommodate the power claims of the two Republics, the new constitution must be more detailed and, consequently, more easily amendable. "You vaunt the brevity of your federal Constitution," Dr. Čič, a prominent Slovak jurist told me, "but in reality it comprises thousands of Supreme Court decisions."[15] As for the call for Havel's "utter clarity," it is endemic to contentious negotiations such as those between the Czechs and Slovaks that a consensus is often reached only at the price of ambiguity.[16]

Evidently, with respect to both the content of the constitution and its flexibility, environmental factors such as demographic asymmetry, legal tradition, and history, as well as political conditions, including individual and group attitudes and interests and the political system, would prevail over both President Havel's voice and foreign advice.

It appeared equally probable at the time of our early meetings that the precedent of an amendment procedure without separate ratification by the two Republic National Councils (parliaments) would likewise be continued, regardless of what appeared to be the trend in modern federal constitutions. In short order, however, this expectation proved unwarranted, and the issue became one of the most contentious items in the constitutional negotiations.

2. On Modifying Constitutions

In the early spring of 1990, as we were driving from the meeting through the gray streets of Prague in a steady, slow drizzle—a "female rain" in Navajo

---

14. While revising a constitution through the amending procedure may be occasionally necessary, "the nation should not be made dependent on this process, because constantly reopening constitutional debate is fractious and politically destabilizing." Larry Kramer, "Federalism American Style," manuscript.

15. We shall encounter the adaptable Prof. JUDr. Milan Čič in various capacities: he was a member of the Communist government of the Slovak Republic before 1989, prime minister after 1989, and ultimately the first chair of the Constitutional Court of the independent Slovak Republic.

16. See, for example, Ústavní zákon Federálního schromážděni ČSFR č. 23/1991 Sb., kterým se uvozuje Listina základních práv a svobod [Constitutional Law 23/1991 Sb., which introduces the Charter of Fundamental Rights and Freedoms] translated in XI Constitutions of the Countries (1992), art. 6: "Human life deserves to be protected already before birth."

parlance—we passed demonstrators calling for a prompt prohibition of the Communist Party. The advocates of the prohibition wanted to turn a notorious section of the Communist Criminal Code against its progenitor, the Communist Party itself.[17] How can we do this, asked Dr. Rychetský, when we just negotiated the revolution with "them" and a party member was made federal prime minister as a part of the deal? The Communist Party, along with other major political forces, was represented in the federal government for the first five months of 1990. The discussion of the proposed bill of basic rights, which would include a right to free association, was in an early stage at the time.

I thought of the problems of constitutional crises and amendments. The ominous American constitutional crisis in the 1930s' depression was due, in large part, to the glaringly obsolete interpretation of the allocation of powers between the federation and the states in the federal Constitution. Applying "the outdated Constitution," the Supreme Court struck down vital social and economic federal legislation designed to alleviate the critical economic and social situation. Why did the president choose the controversial—and ultimately disastrous—attempt at "packing the court" rather than the natural course of invoking the amending procedure? Although assured of the necessary support for an amendment in Congress, was he concerned that the effort to obtain approval in three-fourths of the state legislatures was too aleatory or, perhaps more likely, too time consuming to meet the demands of the day, which, he felt, required "action"? Moreover, to seek an amendment implied the admission of a flaw in the Constitution that could not be remedied except through the cumbersome amendment procedure! In the end, the Court, particularly after its membership had changed through normal attrition, upheld the broadest federal power by an interpretation of the "Commerce Clause," which, in the minds of Continental jurists, amounted to "une expansion démesurée," "susceptible of englobing any aspect whatever of state activity."[18] In fact, eventually even federal civil rights legislation was ruled constitutional on the basis of the commerce clause.[19]

---

17. §260 of the Communist Criminal Code imposed imprisonment up to eight years on "whoever supports or propagates fascism or other similar movements"; §261 made it punishable by imprisonment from six months to three years for "any person who manifests sympathies toward fascism or other similar movements listed in §260." In 1991, the Federal Assembly amended the criminal code to punish any person supporting a movement directed at suppression of human rights or who "declares national, racial, class, or religious hatred (as—for example—fascism, communism)." The amendment did not outlaw the Communist Party. 557/1991 Sb., §257a. The bracketed portion was subsequently held unconstitutional by the Federal Constitutional Court.

18. Renaud Dehousse, Fédéralisme et relations internationales 23 (Bruylant, Bruxelles, 1991).

19. Katzenbach v. McClung, 379 U.S. 294 (1964). The applicable Federal Civil Rights Act cited both the Commerce Clause and sec. 5 of the Fourteenth Amendment, but the Supreme Court relied only on the Commerce Clause as the basis for federal power.

Bruce Ackerman advocates new constitutions over constitutional amendments, which in the Czecho-Slovak context were effected traditionally by "constitutional laws." After 1989, a new constitution was clearly called for as a "clean break" and a new commitment. Considering the ultimately insurmountable difficulties of reaching consensus in the regular organs of the federation, should the Czechs and Slovaks have followed an extraconstitutional course pioneered by the American "constitutional convention"? I shall return to this question in due course.[20]

3. On Supremacy of Federal Law

In the first series of our meetings in 1990—with the problem of jurisdictional conflicts in mind—we urged the adoption of a supremacy clause in the new constitution that would assure priority, within the allocated power, of federal over Republic legislation: modern constitutions have adopted the supremacy doctrine either in an express constitutional provision[21] or by implication and practice.[22] No such clause was contained in the 1968 Constitutional Law on the theory that federal and Republic competences, as delimited in the Constitution, were of equal hierarchic standing. "We cannot include a supremacy clause in our constitution," said Professor Boguszak at our Bratislava conference in 1991, "because unlike Germany, we have no concurrent [or shared] jurisdiction." But even in the absence of such a jurisdictional category, demurred the

---

20. Bruce Ackerman, The Future of Liberal Revolution 51 (Yale U. Press, New Haven, London, 1992). See *infra,* particularly chap. XV, vii.

21. Constitución Argentina art. 31, *translated in* I Constitutions of the Countries 3, 7 (1983); Austl. Const. chap. V, art. 109 (1986); GG, *supra* note 8, art. 31; Constitución Politica de los Estados Unidos Mexicanos *ibid.,* art. 133; U.S. Const. art. VI, cl. 2; Fed. Const. Of Malaysia art. 75, *translated in* X Constitutions of the Countries 7, 75 (1988); Constitution of the Federal Republic of Nigeria chap. I, pt. II, §4(5), *ibid.,* 18 (1989); Constitution of the Islamic Republic of Pakistan art. 143, *ibid.,* 50–51 (1990).

22. Belgium: so-called primauté, Rusen Ergec, Introduction au Droit Public 21 (Edition de l' Université de Bruxelles, Bruylant, Bruxelles, 1990); Brazil: conclusion from C.F. art. 24(4), *supra* note 8; Sabid Maluf, Direito Constitutional, 117 (3d ed., Sugestões Literarias, São Paulo, 1974); Canada: so-called paramountcy, decisions of the Privy Council, Hodge v. The Queen, [1883] 9 App. Cas. 117 (P.C.) (appeal taken from C.A.), Attorney-General of Ontario v. Attorney-General for Canada, [1894] App. Cas. 189 (P.C.) (appeal taken from C.A.); Peter W. Hogg, Constitutional Law of Canada, chap. 16 (2d ed., Carswell, Toronto, 1985); India: Tika Ramji v. State of U.P., 1956 A.I.R. 698–99 (S.C.); Switzerland: conclusion from art. 3 and art. 2 of the transitory provisions of the BV, *supra* note 8, Max Imboden, Bundesrecht bricht kantonales Recht, Diss. (H. R. Sauerlander and Co., Aarau, 1940), Ulrich Häfelin and Walter Haller, Schweizerisches Bundesstaatsrecht Rz. 369 (2d ed., Schulthess, Zurich, 1988); art. VI of the U.S. Constitution. For the situation in Austria, *see* Robert Walter and Heinz Mayer, Grundriss des Österreichischen Bundesverfassungsrechts, part II, 4, IV, 8, and part V, 1IIB (6th ed., Manzsche Verlags und Universitätsbuchandlung, Wien, 1988); and Robert Walter, "Der Stufenbau nach der derogatorischen Kraft im österreichischen Recht," 20 ÖJZ 168, 171 (1965).

University of Virginia professor Dick Howard, "one can never create air-tight compartments of jurisdiction, and there will be conflicts that will need to be dealt with." The matter of overstepping jurisdictions will be settled by the Constitutional Court, Professor Boguszak retorted, and it will be the only matter on which the Court will be able to rule in advance of an actual case.[23] It became clear at an early stage that such a clause would not be acceptable, because—apart from the doctrinal objection—it would be viewed by the Slovak side as a further strengthening of the central power. It was in fact on that ground that the Slovak spokesman, Vladimír Mečiar, rejected the clause in subsequent negotiations.

4. The Constitution as a Symbol

The differences in the perception of a constitution extend to its function in the society as well. In the United States, the Americans pointed out, people freely criticize the president, Congress, and the Supreme Court; while they may even burn the flag, not since the end of the Civil War have they burned the Constitution, which remains a unifying symbol of the country. Even the economic interpretation of the Constitution, which is advanced by those historians who view it as an artifact designed to maximize the interests of the property-holding class, has not diminished the broad attachment to that document. Most Americans remain convinced, along with Prime Minister William Gladstone, that the Constitution is "the most wonderful work ever struck off at a given time by the brain and purpose of man."[24] One may say that, in contrast with most "nation-states," the country is held together not by common ethnic ties and memories but by the Constitution and a related structure of beliefs. Similarly, the German Federal Basic Law of 1948 has been the foundation of "constitutional patriotism," which, over the last four decades, has superseded—one would hope—the mischievous features of a nationalist ideology.

The Czechoslovak liberal, pluralist tradition had its origin in the Constitution of 1920.[25] That charter, however, was turned into a scrap of paper after only 19 years when the president, acting under duress and in flagrant disregard of the Constitution, surrendered the country to Hitler's Germany. The brief effort after World War II to restore the constitutional tradition ended in 1948 with a Communist takeover and the president's resignation due to his refusal to

---

23. Proceedings of the Conference on Constitutional Preconditions for Economic Reform and Market Structure, June 22–24, 1991, Bratislava, pp. 18–19 (prepared by David Franklin). *See* annex I.

24. Page Smith, *The Shaping of America: A People's History of the Young Republic* 94 (McGraw-Hill, New York, 1980).

25. 1920 Constitution, *supra* note 9.

sign the Communist-influenced 1948 Constitution.[26] That Constitution, in fact, was not applied. The 1960–68 Constitution, a Communist creation in the Soviet image, became again, in most respects, a scrap of paper. History has not allowed the Czechs and Slovaks to develop a lasting sense of loyalty to, and identification with, the fundamental document. The problem was, a Slovak judge sighed, how to make the new constitution a document people would view "as their own."

The hope was, in this instance, that past would not be prologue and a new constitution—if and when it saw the light of day—would endure where its predecessors had failed. Of all the environmental factors, the fact that the country is located between the Western and Eastern empires has been the determinant condition of its constitutional history. Yet after 1989 there was a rare and magic moment in their history when the Czechs and Slovaks were in a position to determine their common destiny free of foreign dictates.

5. On Secession and Referendum

The third threshold issue of existential weight—it so appeared, at any rate, in the early stage of constitution writing—was whether the new constitution should specifically recognize the right of the two component Republics to secede from the common state.

To the amazement of the entire international group, the Civic Forum draft, and for that matter all the subsequent proposals that have come to our attention, contained a text affirming, in one form or another, the right of secession.[27] They disregarded President Havel's statement to the Parliament that he saw no purpose in grounding the right to secede in the new constitution.[28] For the Americans, a secession clause signified the very opposite of the "perpetual union" contemplated by Madison and affirmed by Lincoln, who declared that "[n]o government proper ever had a provision in its organic law for its own termination."[29]

---

26. Ústava Československé republiky [Constitution] 150/1948 Sb., *translated in* Constitutions of Nations 689 (Amos J. Peaslee ed., M. Nijhoff, the Hague, 1956).

27. Občanské forum-první návrh ústavy [Civic Forum—First Proposal for a Constitution (hereinafter Civic Forum Draft)] sec. 5(2) (Feb. 1, 1990); Federal Draft of 1990, art. 3(3); Second Federal Draft of Aug. 1991, art. 3/4; Slovak Rep. working draft chap. 5, art. 2(2) (1990).

28. Zdeněk Jičínský, "Problémy dvoučlenné federace [Problems of a Two-Member Federation]," LN, Oct. 25, 1990, p. 9.

29. Abraham Lincoln, First Inaugural Address (Mar. 4, 1861), *reprinted in* Selected Writings and Speeches of Abraham Lincoln 117 (T. Harry Williams ed., Packard and Co., Chicago, 1943). The Supreme Court has made it clear that a state of the Union has no right to secede since the Union "was something more than a compact" and was indissoluble. Texas v. White, 74 U.S. 700 (6 Wall.) 724–26 (1868). But Alexis de Tocqueville conceived of the Union as "formed by the

In the first series of joint meetings, the international group argued emphatically against a secession clause. They pointed out that there was no such clause in the body of the 1960–68 Constitution and no existing federal constitution contained any such provision.[30] Even subfederal, functional entities such as the United Nations and the European Union do not sanction withdrawal.

The reaction to our arguments on the Slovak side was one of surprise: Since the preamble of the 1960–68 Constitution guaranteed "the inalienable right of self-determination even to the point of separation," this was a nonissue, a closed matter beyond debate.[31] Five minor Slovak parties issued a statement describing President Havel's opposition to the constitutional right to secession as incomprehensible and contrary to the United Nations Charter and international law.[32] The Czech members responded with an air of resignation: that course was the only way—"a calvary," "a route through Balkanization"—toward a new—and one would hope lasting—relationship. The Czechs, it was said, wanted marriage, the Slovaks a contract. Some of us felt that the idea of providing for dissolution in order to avoid it was a paradox worthy of Hašek,[33] Kafka, and Václav Havel, the playwright of the absurd. Yet, as the reality unfolded, it became apparent that this issue was indeed foreclosed.

Instead—an omen of the things to come—the debate turned on the conditions under which the constitutional right of secession could be invoked and the complex problem of "fair compensation" in the case of a secession. Federal states have assets and liabilities, including transportation and communications systems, cash and bank deposits, foreign exchange reserves, armed forces, physical facilities of all kinds, domestic and foreign debts, rights and obliga-

---

voluntary agreement of states" with the consequent right of a component state to withdraw. See his *Democracy in America* 427 (Oxford U. Press, Oxford, 1946). One American writer, while grossly overstating the risks of including the right to secede in a founding document, in the same breath admits that "under certain conditions" (Yugoslavia, the Soviet Union, and—prophetically—Czechoslovakia) the inclusion may serve as an incentive to join in the first place, may have "few deterious effects," and "may prevent serious harms." Cass R. Sunstein, "Constitutionalism and Secession," 58 U. CHI. L. REV. 633, 634–35, 654 (1991).

30. The Constitution of the USSR referred to the 1922 treaty concluded by the component Republics in which the right to secede was recognized. The inclusion was intended by Lenin as an inducement, particularly for the Asian Republics, to join the Union. Ben Bagwell, "Yugoslavian Constitutional Questions: Self-Determination and Secession of Member Republics," 21 GA. J. INT'L & COMP. L. 489, 508–14 (1991) on the efforts to read a right of secession into the Federal Constitution of former Yugoslavia.

31. The preambular provision was, according to Václav Žák, the reason why the Slovak National Party was not excluded from the first Federal Assembly despite the fact that it had in its program the establishment of a Slovak independent state.

32. ČTK, Oct. 2, 1990.

33. Hašek is the creator of the immortal good soldier Švejk, the bane of the Austro-Hungarian imperial bureaucracy and army.

tions under domestic contracts, and international agreements and memberships in regional and global organizations, which would have to be apportioned.[34] With one exception, to which I shall return, the various drafts relegated this particular thicket to later constitutional laws or a popular vote.[35]

The character of the Czech-Slovak state as a two-member federation posed an additional complication: unlike in a multimember entity, a secession would mean the end of the federal state with direct consequences in international law and relations. Curiously, authors writing on the general subject of secession have taken little or no notice of this factor.

In the end, urged on by President Havel, the Federal Assembly, in July 1991, adopted a constitutional law,[36] which made possible a referendum on basic constitutional issues and, specifically, on any proposal for secession advanced by one or the other Republic. At that point in time, the Slovaks supported the law, which they saw as a potential means of pressure on the Czech side in the constitutional negotiations. The subsequent federal draft proposed to expand the scope of the referendum and to move a step further in regulating the modalities of a potential separation.[37] If a provision for secession was nearly unprecedented in a national constitution, clothing its consequences with a constitutional mantle was even more extraordinary. Yet, once an opportunity for separation was offered, there was a strong incentive to seek agreement in advance on the modalities as well—and in view of the absence of trust—to entrench the agreement in the Constitution.

The federal draft I have just described was never adopted. Nevertheless, a secession would have been constitutional if accomplished in conformity with the 1991 law on referendum. For that reason, the question of whether or not to invoke the constitutional right of secession became one of policy and morality. The secession alternative was treated prominently in public debate along with a potential referendum, and it appeared sporadically as a ploy in the subsequent negotiations. Yet—ironically—it was never pressed (or even seriously contemplated) by the responsible actors on either the Czech or the Slovak side.

---

34. Lloyd N. Cutler, "The Dilemma of Secession," WASH. POST, July 21, 1991, at C7.

35. Civic Forum Draft, *supra* note 27; Slovak Rep. Working Draft, chap. 1, art. 7(2); *But see* Second Federal Draft of August 1991 (limited exception).

36. Const. Law 327/1991 Sb.

37. The draft would require a division of federally owned realty according to its location, and it would allocate currency reserves and other movables to the Republics according to their respective populations. In the event of an all-state vote to terminate the Federation, both Republics would become fully sovereign states, but nothing was said about the succession with regard to treaties and other international obligations assumed by the Federation. If only one of the Republics voted to secede, the international personality of the federal state and its membership in international organizations would pass to the other Republic. Second Federal Draft of Aug 1991, art. 8. *See* chap. XIII, 2, 3, *infra,* for the actual legislation for division of property on separation, and so on.

Thus, on the face of it, the complex general questions regarding the normative and moral bases for a secession that dominate the academic discourse were ultimately bypassed by the consensual separation: "[S]imple unwillingness to stay together was deemed justified enough to consummate the uncoupling." "None of the usual talk of right versus wrong marked the occasion, and whatever differences of opinion may yet arise will revolve around the logistics of starting up two new households and how the bill for doing so will be footed rather than the morality or lawfulness of cutting the bonds of wedlock."[38] Nevertheless, since the Slovak insistence on "self-determination" was, to say the least, a major force leading to the separation, the case has certain implications for the current efforts to reconcile claims to self-determination with the principle of state integrity. I shall return to this aspect in the concluding chapter.

6. The Constitution and Society

The underlying theme of the discussion in our meetings was the issue of the essential principles of the new society and state. The question was posed to the Czechs and Slovaks: now that you have eliminated one ideology, what will you put in its place?

President Havel offered an answer in his address to the Federal Parliament:

> Our federative state should not be based on any official ideology or political doctrine even if it were a thousand times superior to the ideology of the system we have overthrown. The foundations of the state and its entire policy should be inspired by a single basic idea. That is the idea of respect of the unique human being, recognition of human rights in the broadest sense, including social and economic rights, and respect for the environmental, material and cultural legacy of our forebears. . . . To build a modern democratic state means to balance correctly the tasks and mutual relations of the legislative, executive and judicial powers . . . and a new balance between local autonomy and state administrations . . . changing totalitarian centralized anti-economy to normally functioning market economy . . .[39]

The "single basic idea" that Havel offered as a replacement for the hateful ideology is in effect a rich and complicated ideology. He clearly identifies with

---

38. Secession: The Morality of Political Divorce from Fort Sumter to Lithuania and Quebec, by Allen Buchanan, "Review by George Ginsburg," 19 REV. OF CENTRAL AND EAST EUR. LAW 771, 775 (1993).

39. LN, June 30, 1990, p. 3.

Karl Popper's critical rationalism of an "open society" and his ancestor, John Locke. Yet, I asked myself, can the new state of Havel's image be sustained by a society left in the wake of the old regime? Earlier in this book I speculated on the continuing impact of the totalitarian regime, "which succeeded in a mere forty years to disrupt the fragile gossamer of . . . relationships that had been formed by experiences of entire generations."[40]

Only gradually, and with mounting dismay, have I apprehended the "giant discrepancy between the institutions of the wished-for political democracy and the state of the civil society," which was forced into "an oriental mode."[41] Democracy, still according to Havel, is

> more than a mere compound of systemic arrangements, formal rules of the game or mere organizational tricks. . . . [It is] an outward expression of something very internal that no generation of computers or political science discoveries is able to fashion. Democracy is an artifact of a human being who has internalized his or her inalienable human rights and human responsibility and who respects human rights and believes in human responsibility of others.[42]

Democracy also demands self-limitation, bargaining, and compromise, which the post-Communist societies could not be expected to acquire overnight, for these attitudes can only result from years of practice.[43]

Havel felt that the germs of basic freedoms and pluralism had latently persisted in the society[44] and that they quickly surfaced during the first free election campaign. When I returned to Prague in 1991, I had the feeling that— on the surface at any rate—such freedoms had already become a matter of course to be taken for granted, even though the brief postrevolutionary identification of the people with the new government had again reverted to the "we and they" attitude toward "politicians."[45]

---

40. *Id.*

41. Kálmán Kulcsár, "Právní kultura, právní stát a rule of law," 3/1991 PRÁVNÍK 193, 203 (citing Tóth). *See also* Lubomír Brokl/Zdenka Mansfeldová, "Von der 'unpolitischen' zur 'professionellen' Politik," in Peter Gerlich et al. (eds.), Regimewechsel: Demokratisierung und politische Kultur in Ostmitteleuropa 163–64 (Böhlau Verlag, Wien, Köln, Gratz, 1992).

42. Havel in LN, June 30, 1990, p. 1.

43. Schöpflin, "Post-Communism: Constructing New Democracies in Central Europe," 67 INT'L AFF. 236 (Apr. 1991).

44. Some elements of the free society survived under communism: the managers, for instance, often behaved as owners.

45. I return to the problems of the civil society in the closing chapter. *See generally* Daniel N. Nelson, "Europe's Unstable East," 1991 FOREIGN POLICY 137, 141 (no. 82, 1991); Ethan Klingsberg, "The State Rebuilding Society: Constitutionalism and the Post-Communist Paradox," 13 MICH. J'L OF INT'L L. 865 (1992).

The transformation of the economy's basic structure with the consequent serious hardships of a transition posed an unprecedented challenge to the political process generally and, of course, to the constitution makers. They were faced with the task of writing a basic document for a society greatly different from Havel's vision and to do so at a time when the new society was at best only dimly discernible. Already, at an early stage, the negotiations for a new constitution, difficult as they turned out to be owing largely to the asymmetries discussed earlier, became complicated by disagreements over the economic reform process. In this respect, the task of the Czechs and Slovaks proved more demanding than that undertaken by the Founding Fathers of the United States. Even Germany and Japan after World War II and the postauthoritarian regimes in Latin America did not have "to reinvent capitalism . . . from scratch."[46]

7. What Federation?

The transformation of the 1968 federation into a federative structure that would fit the new democracy posed an exacting task for the constitution makers. Unlike the Founding Fathers of the American Republic, who had to "invent" modern federalism, their Czech and Slovak counterparts had been able to draw on extensive theory and practice as it has evolved since the eighteenth century.

At one of our early meetings in the spring of 1990, Pierre Trudeau addressed the Czechs and Slovaks with a threshold proposition, which on its face was quite obvious, and with a question, which was to turn out to be of fundamental importance. The proposition was that the international group saw itself in a position of advisor and expected the client to pose the issues; and the question, which in retrospect seems naive, was: "Do you want a state composed of one nation or two?" The Swiss member recalled his country's concept of one nation with four "nationalities" reminiscent of T.G. Masaryk's idea of one political and two cultural nations.

Yet both the proposition and the question received short shrift at that juncture because the entire international group, with the Americans at the forefront, unanimously pleaded for a strong federation—a posture taken previously in the papers prepared for the meeting: only a federation with sufficient power at the center would be able to accomplish the unprecedented restructuring of the economy internally and to integrate the country into the European

---

46. Robert Kuttner, "The Dustbin of Economics," NEW REPUBLIC, Feb. 25, 1991, 24. "During the twelve years rule of National Socialism, although private property was deprived of its all-economic functions, the property order as such and its related institutions remained preserved." Ernst-Joachim Mestmäcker, "Die Wiederkehr der bürgerlichen Gesellschaft und ihres Rechts," in MAX PLANCK-GESELLSCHAFT JAHRBUCH 1991, 24, 30 (Max-Planck-Ges., München, Verlag Vanderhoeck and Ruprecht, Göttingen, 1991). See also *infra,* chap. XV, 3b.

and international political and economic systems externally. Internally, if a federation was to be viable, it must have a mechanism for avoiding and dissolving blockages in the political process. In the international arena, it must speak with a single voice. If the two Republics were to play a role in foreign affairs, they must do so in full conformity with the federally set foreign policy, as is the case in Austria, Germany, and Switzerland. Additionally, the scope of their authority concerning federal control and international responsibility must be clearly defined for the benefit of the foreign partners.[47] In a later meeting in Bratislava, which I describe in some detail in annex I, a leading staff member of the Commission of the European Community joined us to reinforce our view.[48]

We were taken aback by the intensity of the negative response to this plea not only on the part of the Slovaks (we should have expected that) but by some on the Czech side as well. The prime target of Czech Professor Jiří Boguszak was the Communist-controlled federal bureaucracy, "seventeen ministries with some 2,000 staff each," the embodiment of mischievous centralization. The Slovaks, as they perceived their history, have always been ruled "from elsewhere," be it Vienna, Budapest, Prague, or Moscow. Prague was dominant not only because it was "Czech," and thus by definition in conflict with Slovak national aspirations, but also because it was the center of Communist power.[49] (The fact that some of the most powerful actors at the center were Slovak Communists was mentioned in private conversations only.)

The drafters of the Articles of Confederation of the United States reacted similarly against "the overbearing monarch and his minions" in America when they reached the fatal decision to dispense altogether with any central executive power, an error remedied in the federal Constitution. Constitutions, it seems, are written with an eye on—and against—the past that is known rather than on the future that is a mystery.

As the Czech and Slovak negotiations unfolded, it became clear that the Slovaks interpreted the international group's unquestioned support for a strong central authority as taking the side of, and giving comfort to, the Czech faction, insisting on a highly centralized state.[50] To my knowledge, only a single member, the American Lloyd Cutler, intuitively sensed as early as 1991 that—regardless of the critical need for central power—only a loose institutional structure, such as perhaps the Belgian model, would be compatible with the

---

47. Eric Stein, "Zahraniční věci v moderní ústavě [Foreign Matters in a Modern Constitution]," 1/1991 Právník 33 and 576. This paper was prepared for the meetings with the Czech and Slovak authorities.

48. *Infra*, annex I.

49. Vladimír V. Kusín, "Czechs and Slovaks: The Road to the Current Debate," RFE/RL Res. Rep., Oct. 5, 1990, 4, 11.

50. *See also infra*, annex I.

Slovak aspirations and could save the federation. Most of us, including the Belgian member, recoiled with horror at this idea, pointing to the complexity, expense, and—presumably—the ultimate unworkability of the Belgian constitutional conceit.

8. The Arena

a. The Principal Institutions

The ultimate power over constitutional issues in the Czech and Slovak Federative Republic was vested in the Federal Assembly. That body consisted of the Chamber of the People, with 150 deputies elected throughout the entire country (the lower chamber), and the Chamber of Nations (the upper chamber), with 150 deputies, half of whom were elected directly from the Czech Republic and half from the Slovak Republic.[51] Both chambers had equal functions. Although there were twice as many Czechs as Slovaks, the equal representation in the Chamber of Nations was one of the instrumentalities designed to protect Slovaks against the Czech majority. Another—and, if anything, even farther reaching—device serving that purpose was the so-called prohibition of majorization, according to which legislation concerning certain important matters such as citizenship, budget, taxes, votes of confidence, and domestic and foreign economic matters required an *absolute* majority of both the Czech and the Slovak components in the Chamber of Nations. Moreover, a new constitution or a constitutional amendment in the form of a so-called constitutional law required approval by a three-fifths majority of *all* deputies in the Chamber of the People as well as the consent of three-fifths of *all* deputies in both halves of the Chamber of Nations.[52] This meant that 31 Slovaks or Czechs (one-tenth of the Assembly membership) could defeat a constitutional amendment and other major acts requiring a three-fifths majority and 38 deputies could block any major legislation and vote the federal government out of office. This formula, although a harmless artifact under the old regime when the party made all the major decisions, was bound to cause serious problems in the new democratic order unless it was invoked with great discretion.[53] Yet it became apparent at

---

51. Const. law 103/1991 Sb., arts. 29–31. *See* David M. Olson, Jana Reschová, and Jindřiška Syllová, "První volební období demokratického parlamentu v ČSFR etc. [First Election Term of the Democratic Parliament in ČSFR, etc.]," 2/1993 PRÁVNÍK 125, 127. Both chambers consisted originally of 200 deputies each, but these numbers were reduced to 150 each. This was the only change in the Assembly structure on which an agreement could be reached.

52. 103/1991 Sb., art. 41.

53. *See generally* Lloyd Cutler and Herman Schwartz, "Constitutional Reform in Czechoslovakia: E Duobus Unum?" 58 CHI. L. REV. 511, 519, 544 (1991); Katarina Mathernová, "Czecho? Slovakia: Constitutional Disappointments" 7 AM. U. J'L OF INT'L L. & POLICY 471,

the very outset that the Slovak side, regardless of party orientation, viewed the bicameral Parliament with the "prohibition of majorization" as a "historic gain which it was unwilling to surrender."[54]

I thought of another, quite different, novel conundrum designed, however, to serve a similar purpose: the "override" or "opt-out" rule in the Canadian Charter of Rights and Freedoms, which allows the federal Parliament or the legislatures of the component provinces to exempt a statute from compliance with specified provisions of the Charter for a limited (but renewable) period of time.[55]

As in other parliamentary systems, executive power was divided between the federal government and the president (the "dual executive" system). The federal government, led by the prime minister, held most of the executive power of the Federation. The president's legal powers were limited, but, following the tradition of strong personalities in the First Republic, his political influence after the 1989 revolution was considerable.[56] Until the Republics adopted their own constitutions (which they did not do until late 1992), their powers and institutions were set forth in the federal Constitution.[57] The Republics had their own directly elected parliaments, "the National Councils," as well as governments headed by prime ministers but no presidents.[58] The "presidia" of the Federal Assembly and of the two National Councils were entrusted with significant functions.[59]

The responsibility for carrying forward the constitution-making process

---

482–84 (1992); and Katarina Mathernová in A.E. Dick Howard (ed.), Constitution Making in Eastern Europe 57, 64–65 (W. Wilson Center Press, Washington, D.C., 1993). If the two chambers disagreed, a conciliation committee (as a rule of 20 deputies) would take over. *See generally,* Helmut Slapnicka, "Das tschechoslowakische Verfassungsprovisorium," 37 Osteuropa Recht 257 (1991).

54. Zdeněk Jičínský, Československý parlament v polistopadovém vývoji [The Czechoslovak Parliament in the post-November Development] 27 (NADAS-AFGH s.r.o., Praha, 1993); Zdeněk Jičínský, Vznik České národní rady v době Pražského jara 1968 etc. [The Origin of the Czech National Council at the Time of the Prague Spring, etc.] (Svoboda, Praha, 1990).

55. Dale Gibson, The Law of the Charter: General Principles 124–31 (Carswell, Toronto, 1986).

56. 103/1991 Sb., art. 61, on the president's powers. The president's powers included foreign affairs, serving as commander in chief of the armed forces and appointing and recalling the prime minister and other members of the government. He did not have a legislative veto, and he could not dissolve the Federal Assembly and call for a legislative election unless the Assembly was unable to agree on a budget. Nor could he call for a referendum of the people in case of a constitutional crisis. See arts. 66–85 on the federal government.

57. Art. 142, Const. Law 142/1968 Sb., as amended by Const. Law 556/1990 Sb.

58. *Id.,* arts. 102–39a.

59. *Id.,* arts. 32(3), 33(2), 45(3), 49(3), 51, 52, 54, 56–59, on the federal presidium; *Id.,* arts. 104(2)–(3), 111(3), 116(3), 119–22 on the presidia of the two National Councils.

was in the hands of the leading political personalities: the president, the chairs and vice-chairs of the three parliaments, members of the three governments, and the leaders of the political parties represented in the three governments. The roles of the individuals and of the institutions, however, varied greatly in the successive phases of the negotiations.

b. The Early Process

Surprisingly, in the extensive federal apparatus in Prague there was no federal Ministry of Justice that could prepare or coordinate the preparation of legal texts. To fill the gap, Dr. Rychetský, the deputy prime minister in charge of legislation, organized a Legislative Council and several working groups consisting of personnel from various ministries and outside experts to assist not only in constitution writing but also in drafting extensive revisions of the codes and new federal legislation. Only in 1991 was a special institution for legislation established within the office of the prime minister.

The original idea, closest to the Czech perception, was for the federal constitution to be drafted first, with the Republic constitutions to follow. A "Commission of Deputies for the Preparation of a Proposal for a New Constitution" (hereafter the Commission of Deputies) was organized in the fall of 1990. It was composed of 14 members of the Federal Assembly (seven Czechs, seven Slovaks) and ten deputies each from the two Republic National Councils, reflecting the entire political spectrum. The chairs and other members of the presidia of the three legislatures were included. The chairs of the three legislatures alternated in presiding over the sessions.[60]

Although the allocation of powers emerged as the central issue, the Commission of Deputies did not concentrate on it, expecting the Republic National Councils to produce a common stand. It was said that chair Dubček did not provide effective leadership and that the Commission of Deputies served mainly as a sounding board "for monologues of the different political factions."

To assist the Commission of Deputies, the Presidium of the Federal Assembly appointed a Commission of Experts—again on a Czech-Slovak parity basis—composed of 18 members selected because of their special knowledge

---

60. The political agreement on the establishment of the commission was reached in a meeting at Svratka in Moravia on September 25–26, 1990, between the chairs of the presidia of the two National Councils and the delegates of the Presidium of the Federal Assembly (V. Žák). At the time of the creation of the Commission of Deputies, the chair of the Federal Assembly was Alexander Dubček, the chair of the Czech National Council was Dagmar Burešová, and the chair of the Slovak National Council was František Mikloško.

or experience. A majority was drawn from university law faculties, but federal and Republic deputies and officials were also included.[61]

In the course of 1991, for example, when—as I explain later—the quintessential issues of federalism were under negotiation, the plenary Commission of Experts met not less than 11 times in one-day sessions and twice for an entire week. During the same year, the plenary Commission of Deputies met only five times, always with the participation of the chair or deputy chair of the Commission of Experts; as a rule, a representative of the president's Chancery was also in attendance. The deputies discussed the materials submitted by the experts but generally failed to give adequate policy guidance to them.

In November 1991, a part of the Commission of Deputies working with some experts produced a formal proposal for the revision of the federal executive and legislative institutions, which was subsequently submitted by 14 deputies to the Federal Assembly;[62] it met again twice in January 1992 to consider a modified text worked out by a group drawn from the Commission of Experts.[63] The explanatory report attached to the original proposal was replete with references to constitutions of Western European states, indicating that the experts, in drafting specific provisions, took into account not only the existing and prior Czechoslovak constitutional texts but also the most recent constitutions of Greece, Spain, and Portugal, as well as the German, Italian, Dutch, Austrian, French, and, marginally, United States' constitutions.

Like the Federal Assembly, each of the Republic National Councils had its own constitutional commissions. A draft of a Slovak Republic Constitution was prepared under the leadership of Professor Karol Plank, chair of the Slovak Supreme Court, with some 40 collaborators in—it is said—a month's time. The Czech National Council Commission delayed the drafting due to internal disagreements, but a Czech proposal, allegedly kept secret, surfaced,

---

61. The original chair, Prof. Dr. Marián Posluch, formerly a member of the Federal Assembly from Slovakia, head of Constitutional Law Department at the Comenius University in Bratislava, and Slovak minister of justice, was appointed to the Federal Constitutional Court on January 31, 1992. The deputy chair was Prof. Dr. Jiří Boguszak.

As a rule, working drafts, texts of foreign constitutions, literature, and specialized studies were circulated in advance of the expert commission meetings. The proceedings centered usually on a chapter of the constitution, and the discussion resulted in a draft containing several variants and subvariants. This text was submitted with an explanatory report to the Commission of Deputies, which returned it with its comments and suggestions for modification and additions. Special questions were dealt with by groups of more limited membership drawn from the Commission of Experts, some delegated to elaborate a concrete variant.

For a detailed description of the working of the two commissions, see Vladimír Sládeček, "K legislativní činnosti Federálního shromáždění po listopadu 1989 [On the Legislative Activity of the Federal Assembly after November 1989]," 9/1992 PRÁVNÍK 761, 772–73.

62. F.A. PRINT FS 1071.

63. F.A. PRINT FS 1071/A.

albeit in an incomplete form. In fact, until the summer of 1992, constitution making at the Republic level was overshadowed by the effort to agree on a federal basic instrument.

Although the membership of the Federal and Republic commissions overlapped to a certain extent, there were no meetings or formal contacts between these bodies on a tripartite basis. President Havel deplored the inadequate cooperation and, with a view toward assuring coherence among the three constitutional charters, asked the three legislatures to establish "a small group of the best Czech and Slovak brains" to prepare a draft federal text in close cooperation with the drafters of the Republic constitutions.[64] In the changing political atmosphere, the president's call was ignored. Despairing of the ineffectiveness of the federal commission, Havel ultimately submitted his own draft of a constitution.

---

64. LN, June 30, 1990, p. 3.

First Act

IV

The Negotiations for Devolution (1990)

1. "The Hyphen War": A Revelation
(January–April 1990)

Amid the avalanche of transformation measures facing the Federal Assembly, the change in the name of the state would have seemed to pose the least of the problems.[1] Yet—with the benefit of hindsight—the episode becomes significant: first, as the herald of unexpected things to come; second, as an insight into Václav Havel's early presidency; third, as a testimony to the role of symbols; and last, but not least, as an example of "ignorance"[2] contributing to an ethnic conflict and posing a psychological barrier to an understanding.

In his first address to the Federal Assembly on January 23, 1990, the president, invoking his right of legislative initiative, proposed changes in the state emblems, in the name of the army, and in the name of the state (dropping the adjective "socialist" from "the Czechoslovak Socialist Republic").[3] According to the account by Professor Jičínský, who as a deputy chair of the Assembly played a leading role in the episode, Havel assumed and expected that all three proposals would be adopted promptly in the same Assembly meeting in which they were unveiled. There was no prior consultation and the deputies had not seen the proposals before. When the president was told that the two Republics must first agree on their own emblems and, at any rate, the proposals must follow the normal Assembly procedure, he was visibly disappointed. He wrote later that had the Assembly "ever so gently infringed the parliamentary usages" and dropped the word *socialist* from the name of the Republic it would have avoided the "hyphen war."[4]

---

1. On this section, *see generally,* Jan Obrman and Jiří Pehe, "Difficult Power-Sharing Talks," RFE/RL. RES. REP., Dec. 7, 1995; Peter Martin, "Relations between the Czechs and the Slovaks," RFE/RL. RES. REP., Sept. 7, 1990, 1–6.

2. Donald L. Horowitz, *supra,* A Framework, note 3.

3. Fed. Ass. Report of the 22d joint session of the Chamber of the People and the Chamber of Nations, Jan. 23, 1990.

4. Deputy J. Bartončík criticized the Assembly position as questioning the authority of the president, but Jičínský viewed his posture as a demagogic effort to curry the president's favor. The president wanted the Assembly to act on all his proposals simultaneously, and no deputy

With parliamentary action delayed, the country's new name turned quite unexpectedly into the popular subject of an emotional debate in the press that linked it with the general problem of Czech-Slovak relations. The president, this time after communicating with the Assembly leaders, proposed a new variant, "the Czecho-Slovak Republic,"[5] while a group of both Czech and Slovak deputies presented still another alternative, "the Czechoslovak Federative Republic," which the president also mentioned approvingly.[6]

The president's idea of the hyphen raised a storm of protest in a major part of both the Czech public and the deputies, but it was welcomed with an enthusiasm of corresponding intensity on the Slovak side. According to Assembly chair Alexander Dubček, the entire Slovak parliamentary representation accepted the president's new proposal, but the name offered by the group of deputies might have been supported as a second choice compromise.[7]

In an emotional debate, some Czech deputies rose in defense of the "maligned Czechoslovakism" and attacked the "hyphen" as "an insult to a significant part of the Czech nation."[8] Others warned of a return of "romantic nationalism";[9] "our roof leaks, our foundations are rotten, but we polish the sign of the firm"[10] and in any event the issue should be left for the first elected Assembly to decide; united "Czechoslovakia" was a world-renowned concept, a mark of good quality that should not be tampered with.[11] Yet a number of Czech deputies appealed to friendship and commonality with the Slovaks and indicated that they would accept the alternative "Czechoslovak Federative Republic."

The Slovak deputies embraced the "hyphen" version as a symbol of rejection of the despised Czechoslovakism: the Treaty of Versailles, the Pittsburgh agreement of May 1918, the initial postal stamps of the First Republic,

---

dared, according the Jičínský, to cross the influential president by suggesting a separate action on the change of the Republic's name. Report of the 22d joint session of the Chamber of the People and the Chamber of Nations, Jan. 23, 1990, p. 45, cited in Zdeněk Jičínský, Československý parlament v polistopadovém vývoji [The Czechoslovak Parliament in Post-November Development] 106–11 (NADAS-AFGH s.r.o., 1993); Václav Havel, Letní přemítání [Summer Meditation] 12–13 (Odeon, Praha, 1991).

5. F.A. PRINT 305.

6. F.A. PRINT 348.

7. Federální shromáždění Československé socialistické republiky, 26. společná schůze SL a SN 29.3. 1990 [Federal Assembly of the Czechoslovak Socialist Republic, 26th joint session of the Chamber of the People and the Chamber of Nations, Mar. 29, 1990] p. 310.

8. Ibid., 289, 295.

9. Ibid., 294, also 280.

10. Deputy J. Šašek, ibid., 285.

11. Ibid., 302. The hyphenated "Czecho-Slovakia" was briefly used in 1918–19, then during the German occupation, and before the establishment of the secessionist Slovak state in 1939, and thus it evokes a bitter memory for the Czechs.

all used the hyphenated "Czecho-Slovakia," which was lost only in the preamble to the 1920 Constitution.[12] The Slovak deputies praised the president's proposal as a brilliant move of a grand master, heralding a "new era of brotherhood" and providing visibility for Slovakia, which was indispensable for its entry into the new Europe.[13]

There were mutual recriminations and conflicting interpretations of recent history, but surprisingly both the Czechs and the Slovaks heaped unreserved encomia upon the president, ranking him with T.G. Masaryk.

When it came to voting,[14] the president's "hyphen" proposal was defeated by the Czech votes while the deputies' alternative text passed the lower chamber but was rejected in the Slovak section of the upper chamber by operation of the "prohibition of the majorization" rule. The Conciliation Committee, appointed to reconcile the positions of the two chambers, came up with an absurd compromise: since the hyphen had a somewhat different meaning in Slovak (the joining mark) than in Czech (the division mark) ("similarly the French use hyphens abundantly while it is almost existentially foreign to the English"), the name in Czech should read without, and in the Slovak with, the hyphen. This principle should be implemented by a special law.[15] The Slovaks, still according to Jičínský, saw in this recommendation another Czech gambit to trick them. Eventually, on April 19, 1990, after another contentious debate, the Assembly settled on the cumbersome "Czech and Slovak Federative Republic";[16] the *and,* it was said, had a conjunctive meaning in both languages and eschewed any hint of a division.

As the Assembly argued over the name of the state, several thousand Slovaks demonstrated in Bratislava for an independent Slovakia. The termination of the state surfaced as an actual option in a strident exchange between Czech and Slovak intellectuals, which appeared in two leading periodicals. The placing of a commemorative plaque for Jozef Tiso, president of the fascist Slovak Republic during World War II, upset the Czechs and sparked so many protests that it was removed.

"The insulted Czech pride made an appearance," wrote Václav Žák, a prominent member of the Civic Forum, "seeing the Slovaks as ungrateful, and unable to differentiate between the excesses of Slovak separatists and the

---

12. With three million Germans, the Czech nation without the Slovaks would have been a minority, hence the concept of a Czechoslovak nation. Deputy Chair J. Mičieta, *ibid.,* 269, 270. The presence of the Germans militated against autonomy for the Slovaks, since the Germans would presumably be claiming the same status.

13. *Ibid.* 294.

14. *Ibid.* 313–17.

15. *Ibid.,* 323.

16. Zdeněk Jičínský, Československý parlament, *supra* note 4, 115. Const. Law 101/1990 Sb. (change of the name); Const. Law 102/1990 Sb. (state symbols).

politicians with nationalist feeling."[17] In June 1990, a public opinion poll showed that only 39 percent of the respondents considered that relations between the Czechs and Slovaks were "friendly," 41 percent found them hostile, while 20 percent considered them neither hostile nor friendly.[18]

President Havel, at the height of his prestige but innocent of working with institutions, unintentionally and improvidently struck a spark to this first flare-up.

2. Negotiating a Power-Sharing Law (April–December 1990)

a. A Historic First: Lnáře

In early April 1990, the castle of Lnáře was the scene of the first encounter in the history of the Czechoslovak federation between the governments of the two Republics, agreed to by the Czech prime minister, Petr Pithart, at the urging of the Slovak side.[19] It was indicative of the status of the Czech Republic that Pithart brought upon himself the wrath of the then federal minister, Václav Klaus, who called his initiative "an unheard of ambush" because it was taken without any involvement of the federal authority.[20] The Slovaks first raised the budgetary problem pregnant with the controversy over "who subsidized whom." The Czechs were surprised and not ready for this issue. Under the second item, both sides agreed to work for a full Czech-Slovak parity representation in the federal government.[21] In a ringing communiqué issued after the meeting, the two governments asserted "the primacy, distinctiveness, and integrity of the national Republics" as against the remnants of "the centralist, dirigist, and bureaucratic system." New budgetary rules would end the problem of "who pays for whom," and the future federal constitution would be derived from the constitutions of the two Republics.[22] The earlier idea was for the federal constitution to be drafted first.

---

17. Václav Žák, "The Velvet Divorce: Institutional Foundations," in Jiří Musil (ed.), The End of Czechoslovakia 252 (Central European U. Press, Budapest, London, New York, 1995).

18. Peter Martin, "Relations between the Czechs and the Slovaks," RFE/RL RES. REP., Sept. 7, 1990, 1–6.

19. Conversation with M. Čalfa. The Slovak delegation was led by the then Slovak prime minister M. Čič.

20. Jana Klusáková—Petr Pithart, Nadoraz, 27 (Primus, Praha, 1992). The words in quotation marks are Pithart's. See also Pithart's self-criticism in NO, Aug. 10, 1992, p. 12: "I myself obviously could not stand up to the federal pressure, and in fact we began to include federal organs in our negotiations."

21. Conversation with M. Čič.

22. L'. Kubín et al., Dva roky politickej slobody [Two Years of Political Freedom] 81–82 (RaPaMaN, Bratislava, 1992), citing ČSTK April 11, 1990, 1816.

In early July, the newly appointed Slovak prime minister, Vladimír Mečiar, and Pithart met with their teams at the attractive spa of Luhačovice in what appeared close to a love feast: The Slovak prime minister stressed that their intentions were almost identical and their views were "determined not only by personal relationships but above all by objective circumstances forcing us to take common positions." In Pithart's words, "we shall start a tradition of direct, immediate, horizontal relations between both nations at every possible level"; federal regulatory power was a basic problem.[23] During the same month, in an atmosphere propitious for change, as a step toward decentralization and without much ado, a number of federal ministries were merged or abolished. Specified powers were transferred to the Republics.[24]

With the Federal Assembly expected to pass some 40 bills before the end of 1990, including the important privatization legislation, some in the federal and Czech governments thought that the transition to a market economy was the chief priority and wanted to leave the problem of Czech-Slovak relations until the federal and Republic constitutions would have been drafted by the new Assembly after the 1992 elections. The Slovaks, however, insisted that the power allocation issue be settled promptly by a separate constitutional law to be effective on January 1, 1991. That law would amend the prevailing division of powers[25] pending the adoption of the new constitution. The Slovak view prevailed.[26]

On the Czech side, it was Prime Minister Pithart who, responding to Slovak claims, signaled a reversal in the constitution-making process: The two Republic governments would now produce a list of those powers the Republics were willing to cede to the federation.[27] At the urging of federal Deputy Prime Minister Rychetský, a deadline was also set for the enactment of a new federal constitution and the Republic constitutions, one year and two years respectively from the date of the June 1990 elections, in any case prior to the 1992 elections.[28] Also at the insistence of Dr. Rychetský (and against the advice of his Civic Forum [CF] colleague, Professor Jičínský), a decision was taken to proceed by a special constitutional law with the formulation of a Charter of Rights and Freedoms.[29] It was clearly understood that the constitution making

---

23. L'. Kubín, *ibid.*, 83–84, citing ČSTK July 9, 1990.

24. Const. Law 295/1990 Sb.

25. Const. Law 143/1968 Sb. as amended.

26. The agreement on this point was reached at Trenčianske Teplice on August 8–9, 1990; *see infra,* chap. IV, 2.

27. Jan Obrman and Jiří Pehe, "Difficult Power-Sharing Talks," RFE/RL RES. REP., Dec. 7, 1990, 5, 6.

28. Peter Martin, "Relations between the Czechs and the Slovaks," RFE/RL. RES. REP., Sept. 7, 1990, 1, 5.

29. Const. Law 23/1991 Sb. Such separate treatment was suggested also in our meeting by Professor Charles Fried of the Harvard Law School.

was definitely to be completed within the two-year term of the first Assembly in order to take advantage of both the effective majority and the postrevolution momentum. The participants with whom I spoke seemed to believe that the deadlines were realistic, and the prevailing atmosphere seemed to justify the belief.

b. A Private Rendezvous (July 1990)

In July 1990, Prime Minister Mečiar met with President Havel, federal Prime Minister Čalfa, and Pithart in a small Prague restaurant. Mečiar was in a strong position since his party, the Public against Violence (PAV), had won the June election in Slovakia. The PAV leadership, composed mostly of liberal intellectuals, did not view the allocation of powers as the highest priority. Mečiar was in the process of giving the party a new direction. He appeared to belong to the group of Slovak politicians, most common at the time, who were not separatists but were intent on satisfying the national ambitions of Slovakia along with their own.[30]

In a convivial atmosphere, Mečiar proposed that the new arrangements should restore the allocation of powers between the federation and the Republics as it was originally defined under Slovak pressure in the 1968 Constitutional Law, before that law was substantially modified by a 1970 act bringing about a sharp recentralization to the prejudice of the Republics.[31] The reallocation of power was to be accomplished by a constitutional law in advance of the new constitution. This was Mečiar's first concrete claim, and the president promised to support it.

c. A Triad Quadrille (August–November 1990)

The three governments, joined from time to time by the president, leaders of the coalition parties, and experts, sought an agreement on a power-sharing law in a series of meetings in late summer and fall 1990. All encounters were held behind closed doors without the participation of opposition parties. They were not given careful advance preparation, and considerable scope was left to improvisation. The communiqués issued in some, but not in all, instances offered little information and often proved tendentiously optimistic. The participants' statements to the press were unsystematic and often contradictory. The pattern of "secret" confabs was set.

---

30. Václav Žák in Jiří Musil (ed.), *supra*, note 17, 254.
31. Const. Law 125/70 Sb. The changes appear vividly in the version set out in Vladimír Flegl, Dokumenty k vývoji československého ústavního práva [Documents on the Development of the Czechoslovak Constitutional Law] 201, 203–16 (Ústav státní správy, Praha, 1989). *See also* Zdeněk Jičínský, Československý parlament, *supra* note 4, 27–28.

The first such meeting took place in the Slovak spa Trenčianske Teplice on August 8–9 with the president absent on vacation. It was to deal exclusively with procedural problems such as setting up working groups, deadlines. Federal Prime Minister Čalfa originally did not plan to attend and sent his deputy Dr. Rychetský in his place, but when he arrived he found Pithart and Mečiar plunged deeply in a debate over the allocation of competences.[32] With the support of Pithart, Mečiar now proposed an extensive transfer of authority to the Republics, limiting the federation to defense, currency, foreign policy, and basic economic legislative powers, with the Republics taking over the rest, including a status in the international sphere.[33] Neither Pithart nor apparently Mečiar had a mandate from their governments to consider such a far-reaching proposal,[34] and the federal representatives refused any commitment. Nevertheless, a communiqué issued at the closing of the meeting heralded an agreement on "basic principles"[35] and reported that a decision had been made to establish ten commissions of experts with the task of transforming the basic principles into concrete proposals. That was in reality the only item on which a consensus was reached. The Czech press and parliamentary "right wing" were strongly critical, blaming particularly Pithart for "concessions" made to the Slovaks.

Shortly after the meeting in Trenčianske Teplice, the Slovak government announced the creation of its own Ministry of International Relations even though, according to the "agreed" principles, the federal government was to be responsible for foreign affairs. President Havel was not given advance notice, but the Slovak spokesman said that the new ministry would not interfere with the exclusive competence of the federation.[36]

Several subsequent meetings were devoted to the consideration of the product of the multiple commissions.[37] The hastily prepared reports proved to

---

32. Conversation with M. Čalfa.

33. Conversations with V. Žák and M. Čalfa.

34. Conversation with M. Čič. However, according to V. Žák, Mečiar acted in accordance with a declaration of his government and with the PAV election program.

35. The Federation would be competent for national defense, defense of state frontiers, legal codes, common currency, "emission activity," foreign affairs, regulation of the labor market, tax, price, and customs policies, some questions of environment, serious crimes, Interpol, aliens, and so on, with new power allocations to be made in transport and communications and the Republics taking over sectoral regulation when still necessary in the market economy. ČSTK, Aug. 9, 1990, 1726, cited in Ľ. Kubín et al., *supra,* note 22, 84–85.

36. Obrman and Pehe, Difficult Power-Sharing, *supra,* note 27, 6–7.

37. After a meeting in the Prague Castle on August 17, 1990, in which the commissions were exhorted to accelerate their work, the three governments met in *Piešťany* on September 10–11, 1990, and in Hrzánský Palace in Prague on November 5, 1990, to discuss the commissions' reports. The meeting in Kroměříž on September 27, 1990, was devoted primarily to the privatization problem. Ľ. Kubín, *supra,* note 22, 87, 88. *See generally* ČTK, Sept. 26, 1990.

be of variable quality and left a number of important gaps.[38] The effort by a special working group charged with consolidating the conclusions ended in failure.[39] The attempt to classify all the imaginable competences into categories of exclusive federal, exclusive Republic, and shared federal-Republic competence in much greater detail than specified in the 1968 Constitutional Law proved illusory. Thus, the negotiations returned promptly from the expert to the political level, but the federal government rejected a document prepared by the individual responsible ministers.[40] With issues coming into sharper focus, the negotiations proved increasingly more challenging even though the rhetoric of the communiqués resounded with affirmations of loyalty to the federation and warnings against intolerance, nationalism, and separatism.[41]

In a 45-minute address to the Federal Assembly on September 17, President Havel pleaded for "an authentic federation": "The popular catchword that strong Republics form a strong federation" applied only if the Republics "accept this Federative Union as their own." He then outlined his view of the allocation of powers, suggesting that time should not be lost by "discovering the discovered" and that firm and functioning federations such as the United States should be drawn upon as models. He considered it especially important that Czecho-Slovakia remain one indivisible political entity in international law as a condition for access to international institutions and an integrated Europe. At the same time, he said, it must be made clear "much more than to date" on the international scene "that this state is formed by two equal nations" and, with an obvious reference to the ongoing dispute in Slovakia over the

---

38. While the commissions reached an agreement on the division of powers in external economic relations, foreign policy, and single currency, views were still "wide apart" on finance, tax autonomy, a single bank of issue, transport, social policy, and institutions for antimonopoly measures. Agreement was also reached on communications, energy, fuel, and economic strategy, even though "preliminary agreement doesn't mean there are no more problems." Federal Minister for Strategic Planning Pavol Hoffmann in ČTK, Sept. 20, 1990. The disagreement was reported to continue the following month. ČTK, Oct. 1, 1990.

39. Zpráva svodné pracovní skupiny o výsledcích práce komisí, ustanovených na základě jednání představitelů vlád ČR, SR a ČSFR v Trenčianskych Teplicích ve dnech 8. a 9. srpna 1990, Příloha II, Rozhodnutí Hospodářské rady vlády ČSFR [Report of a summarizing working group on the results of the work of the commissions established according to the proceedings of the representatives of the governments of the Czech Republic, Slovak Republic, and ČSFR in Trenčianske Teplice on August 8 and 9, 1990, Annex II, Decision of the Economic Council of the Government of the ČSFR].

40. Conversation with V. Žák.

41. *See,* for example, the declaration on the 72d anniversary of the Czecho-Slovak Republic, issued at the meeting of the three prime ministers and the president at *Slavkov* on October 28, 1990. See also *infra,* note 48; and L'. Kubín et al., *supra,* note 22, 88–89.

language law, "that also the members of our national minorities are its equal citizens."[42]

Shortly thereafter the presidia of the two Republic National Councils, in a meeting with representatives of the Presidium of the Federal Assembly, established the Commission of Deputies for the preparation of the federal constitution I mentioned earlier, endorsed the concept of "authentic federation" (without, however, specifying its meaning), and pledged to ensure that the current federal Constitution would be respected during the reform process.[43]

Although some Czechs still did not take Vladimír Mečiar seriously, the initiative in the negotiations came from his side. In October, he brought his own draft of the proposed law to Prague, designed to accord the Republics full responsibility for economic and social development.[44] He noted earlier, with a touch of self-congratulation, that for Slovaks to take the initiative was unusual but it would be a permanent method until new institutions were adopted.[45] He said later that "we must not repeat the mistake made by Gorbachev—he began the reform with old structures"; failure to approve the legislation by the end of the year could "cause a serious political crisis."[46] This implied threat linked to a deadline resonated during the remainder of the negotiations.

In a speech to a committee of the Czech National Council, President Havel warned that the constitutional problems were the source of all doubts about Czecho-Slovakia abroad. He criticized the Matica Slovenská (an influential Slovak cultural institution founded in 1863) and the separatist Slovak National Party for misusing the debate over the Slovak language law by instigating demonstrations of tens of thousands of people. The Slovak Parliament

---

42. ČTK, Sept. 17, 1990. Havel listed defense, security, foreign policy, currency, and protection of borders as "indisputable" federal functions but also "decisive parts of legislation, rights and duties of citizens, strategic decisions on economy, ecology, power industry." See *infra,* note 47 on the language law.

43. Meeting, September 25–26, 1990, at *Svratka* in South Moravia. ČTK, Sept. 26, 1990. At the same time, after the initial objection of the federal and Czech Republic spokesmen, who insisted that the Charter of Rights be approved by the Federal Assembly exclusively, it was agreed that the document would come before the Federal Assembly in the form of a legislative initiative from the National Councils of the Republics. Conversation with V. Žák; L'. Kubín et al., *supra,* note 22, 88.

44. It was reported that the Slovak draft purported to change significantly the allocation of powers, with the Republics to assume full responsibility for their economic and social development and the Federation forming the strategy, basic legislation, the principles of the single market, and a single foreign policy but with limited authority for the Republics to enter into international contacts. If a minister was Czech, "a state secretary" would be a Slovak and vice versa. ČTK, Oct. 23, 1990.

45. ČTK, Sept. 30, 1990.

46. ČTK, Oct. 23, 1990.

was surrounded by demonstrators in what he described as "a serious situation." He appealed to all deputies to try to understand specific Slovak problems.[47]

After another meeting at Slavkov in Moravia,[48] the president embarked on a three-day visit to Slovakia with the intention of starting a tradition of presidential "officiating" at the Bratislava castle.[49]

The representatives of the three governments and the three legislative bodies, meeting at the Hrzánský Palace in Prague on November 5, approved the text of a power-sharing law to be submitted to the Federal Assembly by the two Republic Councils in the exercise of their legislative initiative. This was in recognition of the "from below" process, which the Czech "right wing" viewed with a jaundiced eye. With the powers of the Republics clarified, the focus was, Mečiar and Pithart said after the meeting, on defining the powers of the federation primarily in the economic and foreign policy areas. Pithart expected the negotiations on the draft law to be more complicated than they actually turned out to be, and Mečiar added that all three premiers probably were aware of the consequences of a failure.[50] Mečiar, under heavy stress, had to resort to medication.[51]

With the deadline set for the submission of the bill to the Federal Assembly approaching, the Slovak and Czech governments approved a draft of the bill on November 6 and 7, respectively. However, the federal government

---

47. ČTK, Oct. 25, 1990. After a months-long dispute, the Slovak National Council, on October 25, 1990, approved the coalition bill decreeing Slovak as the official language but allowing the ethnic minorities (primarily some 600,000 Hungarians) to use their languages in official contacts in areas where they formed at least 20 percent of the population. The Czech language could also be used in official communications. Slovak National Party deputies walked out of the session in protest. ČTK, Oct. 25, 1990. Some 80 people went on a hunger strike in protest against that law. ČTK, Oct. 28, 1990. For the text of the language law, *see* ČTK, Nov. 9, 1990. *See also* ČTK, Oct. 28, 1990.

48. At Slavkov, the three government heads meeting with the president, marking the 72d anniversary of Czecho-Slovakia, agreed, according to the president's spokesman, that they were willing and capable of arriving at a "unified conclusion" and there were no controversies or quarrels. ČTK, October 29, 1990. Prime Minister Čalfa said on Oct. 30, 1990, that transport, railways, the gas pipeline, and the banking system were the remaining problems. ČTK, Oct. 30, 1990. Federal Deputy Prime Minister Pavel Rychetský considered it "most important for the . . . Federation to preserve the principle of sovereignty in external relations." ČTK, Oct. 30, 1990.

49. ČTK, Oct. 31, 1990 (two reports).

50. ČTK, Nov. 5, 1990; Ľ. Kubín, *supra,* note 22, 90–91. Speaking in Belgium, Federal Assembly Chairman Dubček, while rejecting nationalist extremism, thought that nationalism and regionalism should not be viewed as specificities of Eastern Europe only, since it was much stronger in many other countries than in Czecho-Slovakia. Federal jurisdiction over foreign policy would not bar Slovak authorities from developing relations with such regions as Bavaria and Flanders. Speaking to the press in Bratislava on his return from Prague, Mečiar predicted that the federal government would lose its veto over the Republics' legislation so that the Slovak National Council would be free to draft legislation on its own status. ČTK, Nov. 6, 1990 (two reports).

51. Conversation with Dr. J. Čarnogurský.

insisted on additional provisions that would safeguard the functioning of federal agencies. Continuing his implied threat tactic, Mečiar warned again of an impending "deep crisis." Several meetings in the first part of November were inconclusive.[52]

With the approaching local elections, Mečiar was locked in a bitter rivalry with Dr. Ján Čarnogurský, the chair of the second largest movement in Slovakia, and he was also under pressure from the extreme nationalists led by the Slovak National Party. The polls indicated that the latter party would raise its support from the 14 percent received in the 1990 national elections to 24 percent—a prediction that proved dismally inaccurate.[53] Reports filtered from Slovak government circles of Mečiar's "isolation"[54] and unilateral decisions in connection with his dismissal of one of the ministers. Dr. Čarnogurský called Mečiar's behavior thoughtless and politically harmful. Although he—like Mečiar at the time—opposed sudden Slovak independence, he held "the national question" to be more important for Slovakia than were economic reform, foreign investment, and integration into international organizations. "We would rather enter a united Europe as independent Slovakia, not as [part of] a small federative Republic."[55] Thus, Čarnogurský's rhetoric sounded more "separatist" than Mečiar's, and as a result Mečiar was shown some sympathy in the Czech press at the time. A spokesman for the federal government commiserated that the whole process of negotiations was faulty because the points on which the commissions and the prime ministers could not agree should have been taken up at once by all three governments; many misunderstandings were due to the short time in which the complicated bill was drafted.[56]

On November 12, federal Prime Minister Čalfa set forth the stand of the federal government, introducing another meaningless concept of "a functional federation," which was enthusiastically embraced by the Czech side in subsequent negotiations. Mečiar promptly attacked "the very philosophy of the approach," "the worst I ever heard from him." The Slovak prime minister again anticipated a deep crisis and suggested that Čalfa resign.[57]

---

52. Luhačovice, November 9, 1990, Modra near Bratislava, November 10–11, and with the president joining in Prague on November 13, 1990. Jan Obrman and Jiří Pehe, "Difficult Power-Sharing Talks," *supra,* note 27, Dec. 7, 1990, 5, 7.

53. ČTK, Sept. 26, 1990. The party received only 3 percent in the local elections.

54. Slovak Interior Minister Anton Andráš was dismissed by Mečiar for "incompetence." ČTK, Oct. 22, 1990.

55. ČTK, Oct. 22, 1990, Dec. 11, 1990.

56. ČTK, Nov. 13, 1990.

57. Marián Leško, L'udia a l'udkovia z politickej elity [People and Little People from the Political Elite] 78 (Perex a.s., Bratislava?, 1993); L. Kubín et al., *supra,* note 22, 91–96.

A meeting in Prague on November 13, which included the chairs of the Republic legislatures, finally produced an agreed text but only at the price of an understanding that several matters on which consensus could not be reached would be dealt with in separate laws or in the new constitutions.[58] Mečiar's initial reaction was critical. According to Pithart, Mečiar called it "the greatest tragedy" but later denied having made the statement and appeared to accept the draft as the best possible result. Federal ministers Klaus and Dlouhý expressed "guarded optimism." Pithart, under continued criticism from the Czech side for being too "soft,"[59] saw no other possibility than to embark "on this risky path." He described the role of the Czech delegation as a moderator between the Slovaks and the federal government, taking care that the communications between them were not cut.[60]

d. The Power-Sharing Bill in the Parliaments— President's "Crisis" Proposals

The November 13 draft was quickly approved by the three governments and the Slovak National Council without any changes.[61] However, the constitutional committee of the Czech National Council, chaired by Deputy Chair Dr. Jan Kalvoda, was not in favor of the text, and the plenary Czech Council insisted on six changes, three of which were of major import.[62] The Slovaks, who assumed that the approval by the executive branches precluded any further modification, reacted angrily. According to Czech Prime Minister Pithart, the Slovak government delegation threatened to have the Slovak National Council declare supremacy of legislation passed by the Slovak National Council over any federal laws (shades of John C. Calhoun, who in the 1820s claimed the same right for his state of South Carolina against federal law under the

---

58. L'. Kubín et al., *supra*, note 22, 91–95; ČTK, Nov. 13, 1990. *See*, earlier, ČTK, Nov. 8, 1990, and Nov. 9, 1990. The issues excluded from the draft related to the power to declare an emergency and the division of state-run television and radio and the transportation system (especially the railroads). The three prime ministers met again on November 28 and agreed on rules governing the establishment of the three budgets. Obrman and Pehe, *supra*, note 27, 7.

59. ČTK, Sept. 20, 1990.

60. Obrman and Pehe, *supra*, note 27, 8.

61. Stenografická správa o schôdzi Slovenskej národnej rady, IX. volebné obdobie, 8.schôdza, II časť. [Stenographic Report of the Session of the Slovak National Council, 9th electoral term, 8th session, 2d part], p. 398 (Nov. 19–27, 1990).

62. The Council proposed that the Federation should be responsible for legislation on rights of nationalities and minorities, it opposed the provision on rotating governorship of the central bank (an issue that should be dealt with by internal procedure), and it proposed its own formula for the method of generating income for the Federation and the Republic. Jiří Pehe, "Power-Sharing Law Approved by the Assembly," RFE/RL. RES. REP., Dec. 21, 1990, 6–7.

doctrine of nullification).[63] Pithart disclosed the threat to the Czech National Council, which in response had a "catastrophic scenario" prepared to be applied in case of the sudden breakup of the country.[64] Mečiar and his colleagues later denied making the threatening statement, although Pithart insisted that he had "at least seven witnesses." The Slovak press highlighted the "scenario" as evidence of the Czech intention to dissolve the state. Mečiar implied that the Czech posture was due to a shift "to the right" in Czech politics, blaming Klaus and Dlouhý, as well as Čalfa, for not paying sufficient heed to Slovakia's economic needs.[65] He hinted at a secret Slovak plan that would be employed if the Federal Assembly should change the agreed text; if any crises occurred, "we are ready at any moment to conclude with the Czech Government an agreement on a state treaty and on remaining in a common state."[66] In Slovakia, Mečiar was blamed by the nationalists for having compromised the position achieved in Trenčianske Teplice, while the Czech press pictured him as a blackmailer who had succeeded in fooling the Czech side. A growing rift appeared between the two presumed allied groups, the Czech Civic Forum and the Slovak Public against Violence, since the latter had joined the other Slovak coalition parties in opposing the Czech amendments.

On December 9, President Havel reentered the scene by pointing out that Mečiar and others did not understand the separate roles of the legislative and executive branches: the fact that the three governments had reached an agreement did not mean that the federal legislature must approve it without changes. He warned that pressure on the Assembly might "break up the federation."[67]

The following day, hoping to resolve the deadlock, the president appeared before the joint session of the Federal Assembly with a somber, dramatic address. He saw the young democracy and the very existence of the state endangered by "our petty political culture, insufficient democratic awareness and mutual understanding . . . [and] lack of experience and our own bad qualities." He singled out the Slovak politicians, including specifically the Slovak prime minister, for threatening to impose Slovak legislative supremacy over federal law. He painted a dismal picture of the consequences of such unconstitutional action, envisaging a social and economic crisis, if not economic collapse, with grave international implications: "70 percent of Slovaks and 74 percent of Czechs agreed that efforts to divide the state are a high

---

63. Bernard Bailyn et al., The Great Republic 501–2 (4th ed., D.C. Heath and Co., Lexington, Mass., Toronto, 1992). *See also* Stephen Goode, The New Federalism: States Rights in American History 84–85 (Watts, New York, 1983) (describing the Virginia Resolution of 1798 and the Kentucky Resolutions of 1798 and 1799 on the federal Alien Sedition Act).

64. Václav Žák, *supra,* in Jiří Musil, note 17, 245, 256.

65. The two ministers reciprocated with charges of demagoguery. ČTK, Dec. 7, 1990.

66. *Ibid.*

67. Pehe, Power-Sharing, *supra,* note 62, 8.

political game and do not reflect the interests of ordinary people." Since there were practically no constitutional means available to deal with the threatening crisis, he offered several "very quick and radical measures" to cope with deadlock situations in the current provisional constitutional state. Apparently again without prior consultation with the deputies, he submitted two bills, one for the establishment of a constitutional court and the other on a referendum that would make it possible to determine the will of the citizens in the event of insoluble disputes between political organs. The referendum law "was meant to scare the Republics away from an attempt to gain independence. If one of the Republics decided to leave the federation, the recognition . . . of international law would transfer to the Republic that had not left the federation."[68] Finally, although he had thought in the past that the presidential powers should be limited, Havel now regretfully declared his intention to offer shortly a proposal for a temporary broadening of his powers. He called for an immediate consideration of the two bills even though this would mean "a brutal attack on the presently applicable rules and a rude violation of all established conventions governing legislative procedures." The Assembly, however, brushed aside Havel's request and decided to postpone the bills until after the passage of the power-sharing law even though he had hoped that his proposals would be adopted first so as to have the new mechanisms in place for use in case of the anticipated constitutional crisis.[69]

While all major political forces in the Czech Republic voiced support for the president's proposals, the Slovak leaders, including Fedor Gál, the PAV chair, and Vladimír Mečiar, favored the first two but opposed the idea of wider presidential powers as not necessary under the circumstances. Both Mečiar and František Mikloško, the chair of the Slovak National Council, were evidently surprised by the apocalyptic ring of the president's speech and wondered whether the situation was so bad. There were critics of the president's tone on the Czech side as well. Mečiar also made it clear that he considered Havel's statement addressed to Slovak leaders (and to himself) one-sided and unfair, since the federation was not jeopardized solely by Slovak nationalists; sentiments such as "it would be better without the Slovaks" existed in the Czech Republic as well. Havel, although evidently taken aback that the Assembly did not follow his call for immediate action, thought that his intervention had defused the crisis, and the following day, as the Assembly began its deliberation on the power-sharing bill, he left for a vacation in Spain.[70]

---

68. Václav Žák in Jiří Musil, *supra,* note 17, 261.

69. L'. Kubín et al., *supra,* note 22, 96–100.

70. ČTK, Dec. 11, 1990; Jiří Pehe, Power-Sharing, *supra,* note 62, 8. Mečiar observed that he would have liked best to leave political life and devote all his time to his hobbies.

More than 70 deputies participated in the Federal Assembly debate, proposing some 30 changes, most of which were voted down. Addressing the Assembly on behalf of the Czech National Council, its chair, Dr. Dagmar Burešová, stressed that the Czech National Council text was built on the original federalization law of 1968 but placed greater emphasis on macroeconomic regulation, with implementing powers left for the Republics and expanding the scope of their economic activity. It envisaged a "functional federation" respecting fully the Republics' sovereignty. She recognized that the bill under discussion constituted only a temporary adjustment, while definitive solutions were to be included in the new constitutions to be adopted before the June 1992 elections.[71]

Of the several modifications proposed by the Czech National Council, the Assembly accepted the one designed to retain federal legislative jurisdiction over nationality and minority issues, and it also decided to keep the responsibility over legislation on church affairs.[72] Responding to the appeal of its leaders to let reason prevail "over prestige-seeking, unitarism, and separation,"[73] the Assembly on December 12 adopted the bill by a vote of 237 to 24 with 17 abstentions.[74] The enactment of the bill was welcomed by most Assembly leaders as a significant achievement, avoiding a constitutional stalemate. Prime Minister Mečiar, supported the bill vigorously before the Slovak National Council as a completion of the first phase in the transfer of competences.[75] In this context, he remarked that, when negotiating with the Czechs, one must set the bar (over which to jump) much higher than the height at which one really aims.[76] It was this highly publicized statement that made Mečiar finally unacceptable to a majority of the Czech delegation involved in the negotiations. Yet Mečiar made this remark in defense of the power-sharing bill against accusations that it was less favorable to the Slovak cause than the

---

71. ČTK, Dec. 11, 1990.

72. The Assembly also voted to keep federal control over distribution of energy in the cases of emergencies and left the problem of the management of the pipeline for a separate agreement. It rejected the Czech National Council's proposal to change the rules on collecting revenues and on the alternating appointment of a Czech and Slovak for governor of the central bank. Jiří Pehe, Power-Sharing, *supra,* note 62, 8.

73. Chair of the Assembly Alexandr Dubček, *ibid.,* 9.

74. Const. Law 556/1990 Sb., amending Const. Law 143/1968 Sb., consolidated in Const. Law 103/1991 Sb. For a summary in English of the power-sharing law, see Karol Svoboda, "Legal and Political Events between 1989 and 1992," in Sergio Bartole et al., La dissoluzione della Federazione Cechoslovacca 66–67 (La Rosa Ed., Torino, 1994).

75. Stenografická správa o schôdzi Slovenskej národnej rady, 8.schôdza (II. časť), 19.–27. novembra 1990, 277, 291 [Stenographic Report of the Session of the Slovak National Council, 8th session, (2d. part), Nov. 19–27, 1990, 277, 291].

76. "So when we talk about retreat . . . the bar was set at 200, we revised it to 250, then we haggled about the 50 and we got 220." *Ibid.,* 364.

proposals in Trenčianske Teplice. His popularity among the Czechs at large, based on his original support of the federalist solution and opposition to extreme nationalism, waned rapidly.

The public reaction to the Assembly action was broadly favorable since it was seen as clearing the way for critical parliamentary business that had been slowed down by the festering constitutional controversy.

3. The New Power-Sharing Law (December 1990)

a. "From the Top" or "From Below?"

It makes at least a doctrinal and symbolic difference whether the power allocation is structured in the context of an extant common state by devolution from the central authority to component units (from the top—*shora* in the Czech parlance) or whether independent states create a new structure by accepting a common constitution (from below—*zdola*).[77] Those on the Czech side less sympathetic toward Slovak aspirations believed that the current process of constitution making could be nothing but a devolution, considering the inescapable fact of the existing Federation and its history. In their view, the only real question was the nature and extent of the powers conferred on the central authority that would determine the viability of the federal state. This was not the Slovak perspective. The Slovaks, although reaffirming in unmistakable terms their will to continue the common state, insisted on the "from below" method as "a new beginning" and the only way of asserting their national identity, particularly on the international scene. They also argued that federations built "from the top" have historically fared much worse (Yugoslavia, Belgium, Canada) than those built "from below" (the United States, Germany, Switzerland). The former Soviet Union, although built on a treaty preceding the constitution was, in reality, formed "from the top" and thus did not endure. As for the United States, in Chief Justice Marshall's words, the Constitution was made not by a compact among the states but by "the people" "assembled in their several states."[78]

---

77. Jan Rychlík, "Federace budovaná 'zdola' či 'shora'? [Federation Built "from Below" or "from the Top?]," *LN*, Jan. 14, 1992, p. 9; Jaroslav Krecht, "Federativní stát a jeho právní systém (Studie zaměřená k ústavní problematice) [Federative State and Its Legal System (A Study Aimed at the Constitutional Prolematic)]," 9–10/1991 Právník 721. Krecht's interesting study, strongly influenced by normative positivism, postulates a "treaty" between sovereign states as preceding the constitution in a "from below" building of a common state. There was no such treaty preceding the Confederation in the United States, only a Declaration of Independence.

78. In M'Culloch v. State of Maryland, 17 U.S. (4 Wheat.) 316, 402–3 (1819), Chief Justice Marshall declared: "In discussing this question, the counsel for the State of Maryland have deemed it of some importance, in the construction of the constitution, to consider that instrument

On its face, the new 1990 law employed the "from below" language. It incorporated (with minimal omissions of the ritualistic invocations of socialism and proletarian internationalism) the preamble and the "basic provisions" of the 1968 Constitutional Law: a ringing affirmation of the virtues of the common state and the single internal market was coupled with an equally eloquent assertion of the "inalienable right" of the two Republics to self-determination "up to separation" and no less than eight references to their sovereignty and right to self-determination.[79] It was the "Czech and the Slovak nations . . . represented by their deputies" in the Czech and Slovak National Councils "that have agreed on the creation of a Czechoslovak federation."[80] Yet the new law, although submitted by the two Republics, was adopted by the Federal Assembly in accordance with the prevailing procedure for a constitutional amendment, which did not require, as we have seen, either a ratification by the Republic National Councils or any other form of popular consent. In the

---

not as emanating from the people, but as the act of sovereign and independent States. The powers of the general government, it has been said, are delegated by the States, who alone are truly sovereign; and must be exercised in subordination to the States, who alone possess supreme dominion. It would be difficult to sustain this proposition. The Convention which framed the constitution was indeed elected by the State legislatures. But the instrument, when it came from their hands, was a mere proposal, without obligation, or pretensions to it. It was reported to the then existing Congress of the United States, with a request that it might 'be submitted to a Convention of Delegates, chosen in each State by the people thereof, under the recommendation of its Legislature, for their assent and ratification.' This mode of proceeding was adopted; and by the Convention, by Congress, and by the State Legislatures, the instrument was submitted to the people. They acted upon it in the only manner in which they can act safely, effectively, and wisely, on such a subject, by assembling in Convention. It is true, they assembled in their several States— and where else should they have assembled? . . . Of consequence, when they act, they act in their States. But the measures they adopt do not, on that account, cease to be the measures of the people themselves, or become the measures of the State governments."

There is even a question whether the 13 colonies were ever fully "independent states." Here are two samples of the views expressed by the U.S. Supreme Court on the subject: in United States v. Curtiss-Wright Export Corp., 299 U.S. 304, 316 (1936), Justice Sutherland stated that the 13 American colonies upon independence became a sovereign nation, the "external sovereignty" passing directly from the Crown "not to the colonies severally" but "in their collective and corporate capacity as the United States of America." Earlier, in Munn v. Illinois, 94 U.S. 113, 124 (1877), Chief Justice Waite stated that upon separation from Great Britain, the people of the United Colonies "retained . . . all the powers of the British Parliament . . . [which] they committed to their respective States. . . . Subsequently, when it was found necessary to establish national government . . . a part of the powers of the States and of the people of the States was granted to the United States and the people of the United States." *See generally,* Pavel Kalenský and Alois Wagner, "Sebeurčení národů a suverenita v diskusi o státoprávním uspořádání [Self-determination of Nations and Sovereignty in the Discussion on the Constitutional Order]," LD, Oct. 2, 1990, p. 6 (on the Czech-Slovak controversy).

79. Const. Law 143/1968 Sb., preamble. The sovereignty of the common state is also recognized, *ibid.,* art. 1(5).

80. *Ibid.,* last paragraph of preamble.

Slovak view, the law did not resolve the issue of the foundation of the common state and did not provide a mechanism for a potential dissolution. As I have mentioned, even before the Assembly debate, Prime Minister Mečiar hinted that "a new concept" of the Federation might be realized by a "state treaty" between the Republics, thus anticipating a new phase in the confrontation.

b. Allocative Patterns: A Comparative Aside

Federal constitutions generally enumerate the federal powers and leave non-enumerated powers to the component states. Apart from this common thread, however, the allocative patterns vary greatly from one constitution to another, evidently shaped by local, idiosyncratic influences. The German Basic Law, which employs exclusive and concurrent categories, presents, on its face, the most logical variant; however, it has been brought out of kilter by subsequent amendments and, above all, by a powerful drive toward centralization, comparable to the forces that have made the U.S. Congress almost all-powerful.[81] The patterns for power allocation in federal constitutions range from the sparse list in the U.S. Constitution to the wildly casuistic Swiss Constitution, which goes so far as to allocate the authority to issue gambling permits in *Kursälen* (salons in a spa).[82] Here is what Chief Justice Marshall had to say on this subject:

> A constitution, to contain an accurate detail of all the subdivisions of which its great powers will admit, and of all the means by which they may be carried into execution, would partake on the prolixity of a legal code, and could scarcely be embraced by the human mind. It would probably

---

81. Jiří Grospič, "Zákonodárná pravomoc a působnost v československé federaci a otázky jejího uplatňování [Legislative Competence and Activity in the Czechoslovak Federation and Questions of its Application], 15 STÁT A PRÁVO 5 (1973). The trichotomy of *exclusive* federal, *concurrent* federal-state, and *exclusive* state competences, with undelegated powers remaining in component states, prevailed in the Soviet constitutions and still applies in the German Basic Law (*supra*, chap. III, note 8, arts. 71–74) and in Canada (Can. Const., *ibid*). On the evolution of German federalism, *see* Peter Häberle, "Die Entwicklung des Föderalismus in Deutschland: Insbesondere in der Phase der Vereinigung," in Jutta Kramer (ed.), Föderalismus zwischen Integration und Sezession 201–43 (Nomos Verlagsges., Baden-Baden, 1993); for a perceptive comparative perspective, *see* Jochem Abr. Frowein, "Konkurriedende Zuständigkeit und Subsidiarität zur Kompetenzverteilung in bündnischen Systemen," in Peter Badura and Rupert Scholz (eds.), Wege und Verfahren des Verfassungslebens 401 (C.H. Beck's Verl., München, 1993).

82. Constitution Fédéral art. 35(2) (Switz.). The Canadian Constitution Act of 1867, as amended, retains the exclusive lists of provincial and federal legislative powers, and it was termed "the world's most complex system of federal distribution, which remains as an awe-inspiring example of what is to be avoided by modern draftsman allocating legislative powers." Geoffrey Marshall in Vernon Bogdanor (ed.), Constitutions in Democratic Politics 159–60 (Gower, Aldershot, U.K., Brookfield, Mass., Hong Kong, Singapore, Sidney, 1988).

never be understood by the public. Its nature, therefore, requires that only its great outlines should be marked, its important objects designated, and the minor ingredients which compose these objects be deduced from the nature of the objects themselves . . .[83]

American federalism has been cooperative from its beginning since most competences have been treated as shared by the federal, state, and local organs: "It is not a layer cake but a marble cake."[84] Tradition and politics of the day rather than any general principles have provided the context. The system is complex, costly, lacks transparency, and relies heavily on a subculture of lawyers. Yet it has proved flexible enough to serve a continent with an unprecedented continuity and an ever-widening base of popular participation.[85]

c. The Chosen Pattern

The basic scheme of the 1968 federal Constitutional Law was the starting point of the negotiations for the redistribution of powers.[86] Under that law, the Federation was allocated certain exclusive powers, with many competences shared between the Federation and the Republics, and the Republics were given exclusive authority in health, culture, and education policies. The new scheme reflected the pressure from the Slovak side toward broadening the Republic powers at the cost of the center. In contrast to the 1968 pattern, the new text omitted the listing of exclusive federal and shared competences. Instead, it:

(1) enumerated subjects falling generally in the competence of the Federation with no indication of any limits on the federal power (foreign affairs, war and peace, defense, currency, federal material resources, and protection of the federal Constitution),[87]

(2) singled out federal competences in enumerated subject areas limited in principle to legislative action, except where the Constitutional Law provided otherwise, and[88]

---

83. 17 U.S. (4 Wheat.) 316 (1819).

84. Daniel J. Elazar and Ilan Greilsammer, "Federal Democracy: The U.S.A. and Europe Compared—a Political Science Perspective" 97 (quoting M. Grodzins), in Capelletti et al. (eds.), Integration through Law, vol. 1, bk. 1 (Walter de Gruyter, Berlin, New York, 1986).

85. For a brief description of the system, see Terrance Sandalow, "Abstract Democracy: A Review of Ackerman's *We the People,*" *Constitutional Commentary* 309 (1992); Eric Stein, "Uniformity and Diversity in a Divided-Power System: The United States' Experience," 61 WASH. L. REV. 1081 (1986).

86. Const. Law 143/1968 Sb., arts. 7–9.

87. Const. Law 103/1991 Sb., art. 7(1). The list corresponds essentially to the enumeration of *exclusive* federal subjects in art. 7(1) of Const. Law 143/1968 Sb.

88. Const. Law 103/1991 Sb., art. 28b(2).

(3) left all unallocated competences to the Republics.[89]

In the second category of "singled out" competences, federal power was defined in often indeterminate terms, for example, "formation of strategy," "structural concepts with federal significance," or "common principles" (art. 10, 17), signaling the intention to limit federal action either to the German-type framework legislation (*Rahmengesetz*)[90] or to ordinary legislation.

Thus, federal power included basic legislation on general economic policy planning, transportation, environment, price and wage policy, labor relations, statistics, regulation of ownership and enterprises, protection of consumers, and basic rights. The power to implement and execute federal legislation, however, was, in principle, in the hands of the Republic institutions; exceptions were customs, sea, air and railroad transportation, and supervision of nuclear safety, in which the Federation was expressly given the entire panoply of power.[91] Although the Federation had the power to legislate on the protection of competition, it was specifically left to the Federal Assembly to determine the "division of execution" between the federation and the Republics.[92]

In other provisions, federal power was defined in such terms as "legal disposition," "legislative disposition," "determination of uniform rules," and "organization and direction," which promptly raised questions as to the reach of federal jurisdiction.[93]

Financial and budgetary policy was to be determined by agreement among the federal government and the governments of the two Republics; the Federal Assembly enacted principal tax legislation (value added and income taxes), but the Republics administered it. The Federal Assembly decided on the allocation of proceeds.[94] At the time, the three governments agreed on the budget based on a previous formula favoring the Slovaks, but there was no provision if an agreement proved impossible in the future.

Although the Slovak side first pressed for including in the Constitution a division between the Federation and the Republics of publicly owned resources and facilities, the idea was abandoned when it became clear that any effort for an all-inclusive enumeration would be incomplete—and the solution

---

89. *Ibid.,* art. 9.
90. GG, *supra,* chap. III, note 8, art. 75.
91. Const. Law 103/1991 Sb., arts. 13(2), 19d-e, 21b.
92. *Ibid.,* art. 24e.
93. *Infra,* this chap., 3,d; *see also* Const. Law 103/1991 Sb., art. 12(4), regarding administration of the tax laws. The legislative power of the Federal Assembly is expressly confirmed in art. 37(1).
94. *Ibid.,* arts. 11, 12.

was left with the political process.[95] The Federal Assembly, however, was given explicit authority to determine ownership of the vital oil and gas pipelines and certain electric networks.[96] The original Slovak idea of establishing three separate central banks was revised in favor of a single federal State Central Bank, an important concession by the Slovaks. As a compromise, "centers" of that bank were to be established for each of the Republics, but the role of the centers was not specified.[97] This issue became one of the central points of contention in subsequent negotiations.

Further federal legislative authority, limited, however, "to the extent required by the uniformity of the legal order," covered nationality, ethnic minorities, churches, health, lower education, copyright, and other matters.[98] This limitation on the federal legislative powers, carried over from the 1968 Constitutional Law, was, in a sense, a variant of the subsidiarity concept.[99] It was motivated, however, by an interest in legal coherence rather than preservation of Republic power.

History played a major role in shaping one important aspect of the power allocation. Typically, upon creation of a federation, a federal grid is superimposed on preexisting legal orders of states entering the federation: federal law is interstitial and supplementary. In 1918 Czechoslovakia, however, two different legal orders were embraced within a *unitary* state, one based on Austrian, the other on Hungarian, law. After World War II, in the still unitary state, the two legal orders were replaced with a uniform system of law; and it was in 1968 that the federal scheme was overlaid upon the uniform legal system. Preservation of uniformity was in potential conflict with the new lawmaking powers of the two Republics. The resulting compromise[100] kept the bulk of the uniform legal order—including the civil, commercial, and criminal codes—within the orbit of federal legislative power. However, where the

---

95. *Ibid.,* art. 4(3–7). For an example of a constitution that does specify the resources owned by a federation, *see* Constituição Federal art. 20 (Braz.), *translated in* II Constitutions of the Countries 1, 9 (1990).

96. Const. Law 103/1991 Sb., art. 4(4). Earlier constitutional law lists certain resources (mineral wealth, basic sources of energy, "basic forest fund," waters, etc.) as within "state ownership" without indicating Federal or Republic ownership. "Details" are left for determination by an ordinary law. Const. Law 100/1990 Sb. art. 10.

97. Zákon o Československé státní bance [The Law on the Czechoslovak State Bank], 22/1992 Sb., was modeled after the German Bundesbank legislation. It was passed along with general banking legislation. See Peter Martin, "Banking Reform in Czechoslovakia," RFE/RL Res. Rep., Apr. 10, 1992, 29.

98. Const. Law 103/1991 Sb. art. 37(3). *See also* Const. Law 103/1991 Sb. arts 5, 6 (addressing citizenship and equality of the Czech and Slovak languages).

99. For interesting definitions of subsidiarity, *see* GG art. 72(2) (F.R.G.); Treaty of European Union and Final Act [Maastricht Treaty], Feb. 7, 1992, Title II, art. G(5) (inserting a new art. 3b into the Treaty establishing the European Economic Community), 31 I.L.M. 247, 257–58.

100. Const. Law 103/1991 art. 37(2).

Federation did not preempt the entire field, the Republics could legislate. In any event, the "execution" of these codes and laws pertained to the Republics, and the Federal Assembly could "redelegate" its authority to the Republics.[101]

The already opaque lines between the federal and Republic competences of the 1968 text were blurred further in the 1990 law. A number of important issues that proved beyond the reach of a consensus were either omitted or left to the Federal Assembly. It was assumed that the actual scope of the intended devolution in domestic matters would be determined by practical application.

It is in the area of foreign affairs, which touched directly upon the "external sovereignty" and international personality of the Federation, that, on its face at any rate, the expansion of the Republic power was most evident. This reflected the increasing Slovak emphasis on "international visibility" as a crucial component in the drive for establishing a Slovak identity. The federal authorities were given the power to negotiate international treaties, legislate the basic lines and instrumentalities of foreign economic policy, and provide for representation of the Federation state abroad.[102] The Republics maintained their authority to participate in negotiations of international treaties and in the representation in international organizations on matters falling within the legislative competence of the Federation.[103] In addition, however, they acquired a measure of their own international personality. The Republics were empowered, "in harmony" with federal foreign policy, to conclude agreements with component parts of other composite states on a broad spectrum of subjects, ranging from economy and commerce to culture, health, and television. More importantly, they could conclude, when so authorized by the Federation, international agreements on matters within their legislative competence,[104] maintain their own representation abroad, and receive foreign representatives on the same matters.[105] The important question of the modalities of the federal authorization remained open and was to be regulated, presumably by a federal law.

d. The Emerging Jurisdictional Conflicts: The Constitutional Court Speaks

Even a cursory perusal of the text of the 1990 law revealed many ambiguities bound to result in conflicting claims of competence between the Federation and

---

101. *Ibid.*, arts. 37(2), 38(1–2), 28(b).

102. *Ibid.*, arts. 7(1)a, 16, 36(1)b, 36(3). For subsequent developments, *see infra*, chap. IX, 2a–b.

103. *Ibid.*, art. 25.

104. Art. 32(3) of the German GG was invoked as a model.

105. *Ibid.*, art. 7(2)c. The status of the representatives was to be determined by the receiving state. This section of the law follows closely the advice offered by the international group. *See infra*, chap. IX.

the Republics. This was already the situation under the 1968 text but—in the words of a Czechoslovak commentator—these differences were resolved at the time "during the elaboration of the legislation and other political decisions." "It is for this reason that during the . . . years of the functioning of the Czechoslovak federation [under the old regime] no conflict had arisen that would have had to be resolved by specific constitutional measures"—by the Constitutional Court that was provided for in the Constitution but never made operational.[106]

With the end of "the guiding role of the Communist Party" and "socialist legality," the need for authoritative dispute settlement of jurisdictional quarrels became imperative. Who, for instance, was to regulate forests when agricultural policy was federal but the Republics owned the forests?[107] Happily, the Constitutional Court, comprised of six Czechs and six Slovaks, was established in 1991 to deal with such controversies.[108] The first of several jurisdictional conflict cases involved important issues of communications policy, and the Court based its opinion on a strictly textual and contextual interpretation of the relevant, particularly obscure provisions in the 1990 law, with some consideration of prior legislative practice.[109]

---

106. Jaroslav Zacharias, "Rapport Tchécoslovaque," 17 REVUE BELGE DE DROIT INTERNA-
TIONAL 138 at 139–40 (1983).

107. In some cases, where federal legislative power was clear but the authority to adopt urgently needed implementing uniform regulations was disputed, such as with pensions, the federal government, to avoid controversy, proposed new legislation rather than issuing a regulation, which would be the normal course. This technique, while feasible in a few exceptional instances, obviously could not be employed as a general procedure. Anticipating a plethora of challenges to its power, the federal government proposed to clarify the ambiguity in a new proposal, which, however, was not acted upon. *See* Proposal for the Chapter of the Constitution Dealing with the Distribution of Competences between the Federation and Its Republics Elaborated According to the Position of the Government of the Czech and Slovak Federative Republic, Dec. 31, 1991, Prague, Č.j. 2956/91–PV.

108. Ústavní zákon o ústavním soudu České a Slovenské Federativní Republiky [Const. Law on the Constitutional Court of the ČSFR] 91/1991 Sb.; Zákon o organizaci ústavního soudu ČSFR a o řízení před ním [Law on the Organization of the Constitutional Court of the ČSFR and Proceedings before It] 491/1991 Sb. *See also* Herman Schwartz, "The New Constitutional Courts in Eastern Europe," 13 MICH. J. INT'L L. 741 (1992).

109. Judgment of April 9, 1992, Ústavní soud ČSFR [Const. Ct. of ČSFR], Č.j. Pl.ÚS 2/92; Ústavní soud ČSFR, Sbírka usnesení a nálezů [Constitutional Court ČSFR, Collection of Resolutions and Opinions], vol. 1992, no. 1, 1–9 (Brno, 1992). The federal Ministry of Communications asked the Court to resolve a dispute over the interpretation of the 1990 law with respect to jurisdiction over the communications network. The principal provision at issue appeared to distinguish between the three branches of the system: posts, radio communications, and telecommunications (Const. Law 103/1991 Sb., art. 20), and the Court was faced with the unenviable task to define and apply the puzzling textual variations: In the article in question (art. 20), the Federation was given the competence for issuing uniform traffic rules and tariffs for all three branches (par. b), providing "legislative disposition" on posts and telecommunications (par. a), organizing a

Unlike some other constitutional courts, such as the U.S. Supreme Court, the Court of Justice of the European Communities, and the German Constitutional Court, the Czecho-Slovak counterpart showed no ambition at this early stage to fashion fundamental constitutional principles or offer a grand doctrinal design for the "new" federation. Nor did it meditate over the consequences of its ruling, which affirmed as constitutionally mandated a schism between the modes of operation of the communications system, regardless of the problems

---

"uniform system of posts" (par. d), and organizing and directing a uniform system of telecommunications (par. e). (Art. 20c authorizes the Federation to issue stamps or other postal values.) Seizing upon the single word *directing,* which appeared only in connection with telecommunications, the Court ruled that in telecommunications the Federation possessed the entire gamut of powers ranging from legislation and generally binding implementing regulations to administration and individual decisions; regarding posts and radio communications, the Republics had the competence of administration, with the Federation confined to the issuance of uniform traffic rules. The Court, however, pointedly referred to the possibility of a "redelegation" of the execution of federal competences to the Republics by a law of the Federal Assembly (art. 38b[1]). (The competence to administer included, according to the ruling, the authority to organize state agencies or enterprises in the respective fields of communications. The Court did not seem to be impressed that in other instances, where the constitutional law allocated the power of administration to the Federation, it said so using the specific terms "state administration" or "execution," but neither of these terms was employed with regard to telecommunications. *See,* e.g., arts. 19d–e, 21b. "Execution" according to the Court, encompassed administration, organization, and direction.)

The Court found additional support for its conclusion in two general provisions: in the principle of "enumerated powers" (art. 9) and in the rule reserving "execution" of federal legislation to the Republics unless a constitutional law provided otherwise (art. 28b[2]). Presumably, the term *directing* is taken to provide the exception contemplated in this provision. Perhaps more importantly, the Court relied on the history of the constitutional development, which it read as indicating the intent of the constitution makers to change the regime of radio communications and posts in favor of the Republics while retaining federal administration of telecommunications as it had existed since 1971. The Court pointed out that the original text of Const. Law 143/1968 Sb., art. 20, entrusted the Federation with legislation, determination of uniform rules, and conception of development of the post and telecommunications systems; but it did not contain a provision analogous to the present text of art. 20e. The then current state of the law prevailed since Const. Law 125/1970 Sb. on communications had come into effect and Const. Law 556/1990 Sb. did not bring about any change in the federal competences to organize and direct the telecommunications system. In an interesting passage, the Court dealt with the arguments of the Republics based on administrative agreements between the federal and Republic ministries and minutes of sessions of the prime ministers. Although denying its own competence to pass upon the validity of such instruments, it considered them useful aids for interpretation to the extent that they were not in conflict with prevailing law. In the given situation, the Court disregarded them as contrary to its interpretation of the 1990 constitutional law. In the reasoning part of the opinion, the Court illuminated certain indeterminate concepts: "legislative disposition" meant power to enact legislation only, while "legal disposition" included the additional authority to issue "generally binding legal rules for implementation of legislation." The Court also offered an interpretation of the concept *soustava* (system) as used in art. 20d–e. Beyond that, however, the opinion focused scrupulously on the text of the specific clauses at issue. For another case involving a problem of competence, *see ibid.,* no. 10, 34–37.

this could entail for the economy of the common state.[110] Clearly, the Court was not willing to add to its burden—heavy as it was—of having to resolve ambiguities due more to a lack of political consensus than to drafting inadequacies. This reticence might have reflected also the prevailing concept of limited judicial function even at the highest level as well as the tension in the relations between the Czechs and Slovaks.[111] At any rate, the Court was not composed of personalities likely to strike out in an activist direction.

Surprisingly, in contrast with domestic matters, there was relatively little controversy in practice over the application of the foreign affairs powers in the new law. For one thing, since passage of the 1968 Constitutional Law, the federal Ministry of Foreign Affairs had assured Slovak participation in federal treaty-making proceedings, eventually including commercial treaties. The federal government was experimenting with the idea of federal framework treaties pursuant to which the Republics would conclude their own treaties on matters within their legislative competence. Even before the 1990 Constitutional Law, the Republics concluded several agreements with components of other states, including Bavaria, the Russian Socialist Federal Republic, and a Chinese province. The Republics maintained a variety of foreign contacts of their own in matters of their legislative competence, such as education, health, and culture, so that the two Republics' establishments were sufficiently occupied without crossing wires with the federal Ministry of Foreign Affairs.

Nevertheless, rumor had it that an ambassador of Slovak nationality had insisted on reporting to Bratislava rather than to Prague, and the Slovaks complained of insufficient Slovak representation in the federal diplomatic service. The first chief of the Slovak Ministry of International Relations, Milan Kňažko, an actor, filmmaker, and for a time Mečiar's close collaborator, pressed for an increase of the number of Slovak diplomats, sought to intensify the contacts with regional units in other states, and managed, to the displeasure of federal Minister of Foreign Affairs Dienstbier, to have Slovakia join the Association of European Regions.[112] After Prime Minister Mečiar's ouster in 1991, Kňažko was replaced by Pavol Demeš, a young scientist, reputedly with "a realistic conception" of his role within his ministry's limited budget. The

---

110. The post services bore heavy deficits, while telecommunications was profitable, a consideration that might have been at the origin of the case.

111. It has been suggested that the Republics would be viewed as "the losers" in the case. "Court Ruling May Threaten Telecommunications Monopoly," PRAGUE POST, Apr. 21–27, 1992, p. 4. Although the decision preserved the unity of the telecommunications branch of the system, "it heralds the eventual demonopolization of the network," since this was the policy of the federal minister. That policy, opponents claimed, would jeopardize current projects for massive foreign investments designed to modernize the system. *Id.*

112. Conversation with M. Kňažko.

Czech counterpart ministry was established in 1992 with only a minimal staff.[113]

At times, foreign missions in Prague were at a loss about their interlocutors on the Czech and Slovak sides. On treaties of general import, such as investment treaties, they negotiated with the federal government, but when it came to economic or technical assistance they dealt with Republic authorities as well. In some instances, foreign diplomats preferred not to seek guidance from federal authorities in order not to be precluded from dealing with the Republics.

In the foreign affairs field, at any rate, the new law combined with the existing practice seemed to provide a workable basis for Czech-Slovak coexistence. Yet there were rising voices in Slovakia complaining about the Prague "monopolization" of foreign relations, lack of Slovak foreign contacts needed for foreign investment, and inadequate information on offers of foreign aid.[114]

e. An Afterthought: Spotlight on the "Heroes"

During this period of a "window of opportunity in 1990," the role of President Havel, the "intervenor" in the negotiations, was obviously of great importance. A number of questions come to mind. Why was he not able to translate the prestige and respect, verging on adulation ("Havelmania"), into enough political influence to have the Federal Assembly suspend even the "technical" rules of procedure and deal promptly with his proposals? Why did he not heed the lesson of the "hyphen war," again submitting his far-reaching proposals without consultations with Assembly leaders, thus alienating the deputies? Was he not advised of the need to consult and negotiate with the Assembly leaders before formally submitting his important proposals? Did he "overdramatize" the situation, as claimed by the Slovaks, and greatly underestimate the chances for the passage of the power-sharing bill, which in the end was adopted by an overwhelming majority? Or did his intervention "diffuse" the crisis, as he claimed, and make its passage possible? Was it prudent at this stage to publicly castigate the Slovak prime minister, thus earning his enduring personal wrath, and to upbraid the citizens at large at a time of the most difficult social and economic transition when, one may argue, they needed a voice of comfort and reassurance? In a disarmingly frank and engaging appeal to his fellow citizens delivered in February of 1990 at the historic Old Town Square, Havel may have offered an answer to some of these questions: The president, he said,

> has a minimal experience with "presidenting" and he has nothing to latch
> on to since his predecessors did no "presidenting" but just went to party

---

113. In early 1992, the Slovak ministry had some 100 officials, the Czech less than a dozen. Oral information.

114. Václav Žák in Jiří Musil, *supra,* note 17, 248.

meetings. . . . I fly from place to place, keep a few excellent friends busy twenty-four hours a day, and despite this I do not achieve anything. I realize this and try to organize my office and working program in some sensible way to avoid an early collapse of us all at the Castle.

Referring to a report describing him as "gentle, romantic, and a naive dreamer rather than a real statesman," Havel agreed that he never considered himself a "real statesman."[115]

Even at this early stage, Havel was the target of scattered, muted criticism because of his broad amnesty, which allegedly contributed to the rising criminality, because of his refusal to confirm death penalty sentences (before that penalty was banned by the legislature), because of his and Foreign Minister Dienstbier's decision to prohibit export of heavy weapons, because he "apologized" to the Germans for the post–World War II expulsions as a manifestation of an immoral principle of collective guilt,[116] because, after his election, he visited Munich and Berlin before going to Bratislava, and even because he replaced the drab Castle guard uniform with a colorful garb reminiscent of the parade apparel of American Marines.

A few personal observations on the leading actors during this phase of negotiations are in order. The prime minister of the Czech Republic, Petr Pithart, is short in stature, inclining to obesity, with ample, curly, grayish hair, round face, and a rich goatee, which adds to the impression of a character from a Chekhov play. His father, an attorney and a Communist since 1938, was Czechoslovakia's ambassador to France; in 1968, he called on President DeGaulle to protest the Soviet occupation and that marked the end of his career. Petr Pithart joined the party at the age of 20, resigned six years later, taught theory of law and political science at Charles University, and joined Havel and others in dissent. He was briefly jailed and held a series of the usual jobs, ranging from night watchman to gardener. After Havel's election to the federal presidency in December 1989, he took over the chairmanship of the chaotic Civic Forum before being appointed Czech premier. Like Havel and others, he had a difficult time learning to govern on the job. The demands of public service ruined his private life. An intellectual and a prolific writer with more than the usual Central European dose of pessimism, he was an exception on the Czech side because of his knowledge of Slovak history and a professed wish to understand and respond to Slovak aspirations. He himself speculates volubly about his tribulations and failures in the negotiations.[117]

---

115. Václav Havel, Projevy [Pronouncements] 71, 73 (Vyšehrad, Praha, 1990).
116. Statement at the occasion of a visit by President Richard von Weizsäcker, Prague, March 15, 1990, *ibid.,* 81.
117. "People wanted me to be 'like Mečiar,' they reproached me that I kept retreating. . . . I

Marián Čalfa, the paragon of a civil servant, rose through the Communist regime bureaucracy from a legal staff position to become minister in charge of legislation. The "knights" of the 1989 Round Table chose this adroit lawyer to be federal prime minister because he was Slovak (a Czech was to be president) and still a party member. It was not easy to find an acceptable Communist since, as the story went, the prevailing noise in Prague at the time was the rustle of turning (party) coats. Čalfa remained in the party until January 1990. Although born in Slovakia, he was married to a Czech, spoke Czech, was trained and spent most of his professional life in Prague. The Slovaks generally did not consider him one of their own, he had his critics on the Czech side as well, and the anti-Communist reaction weakened his position.[118] Powerfully built, with sandy hair and smiling eyes, he played his passing role with skill and professionalism. He had President Havel's full confidence and for a time was acceptable to almost everyone.

Prime Minister Vladimír Mečiar emerged as the leader of the Slovak side. Of massive stature, with the physique of a one-time boxer, he was schooled in Moscow and Bratislava, was expelled from the Communist Party in 1970 for criticizing the invasion by Warsaw Pact forces (though allowed to complete his law studies), and in November 1989 served as a staff lawyer with a provincial enterprise in Slovakia. During the heady, chaotic days following the revolution, he joined the Public against Violence movement and with Alexander Dubček's support applied for the position of minister of the interior in the Slovak government. He won the "competition" for the job because he appeared to be "three classes above" the other two applicants. He impressed Fedor Gál, the leader of the powerful PAV, as "an assertive [*razantný*, an adjective that became his standard epithet], decisive, quick-witted, and hard chap . . . sympathetic."[119] In June 1990, having acquired a reputation for strong energy, prodigious industry, and the ability to communicate, he was promoted to the office of Slovak prime minister. This appointment, it is widely believed, has had disastrous consequences.[120] Yet at the time, in the constitutional negotiations,

---

explained all that but perhaps not enough and badly or both, on top of it I was almost alone: I had almost no one who would want to listen to me." See Jana Klusáková—Petr Pithart, Nadoraz 27 (Primus, Prague, 1992).

118. The Civic Forum weekly *Forum* called Čalfa "inexpressive and rather problematic" and criticized President Havel because after the 1990 elections he kept him in the office contrary to the rule in a parliamentary democracy according to which the head of the party victorious in the elections (that is the Civic Forum) should have been called to that office. ČTK, Sept. 20, 1990. Yet Čalfa at the time was a member of the Public against Violence, which was "victorious" in Slovakia.

119. Jana Klusáková—Fedor Gál, Nadoraz 8 (Primus, Praha, 1992). For a collection of Mečiar's statements, see František Javorský et al. (eds.), Dialógy Vladimíra Mečiara [Dialogues of Vladimír Mečiar] (HOS, Bratislava, 1992).

120. Conversation with Jozef Moravčík, Mečiar's former collaborator and briefly prime minister of the independent Slovak Republic.

Mečiar and his team, pressing for change, faced an alliance of the Czech and federal authorities. Many in Slovakia explained Mečiar's overstated demands, his exorbitant statements with contradictory denials, and his threats and warnings as a reaction to his difficult negotiating position. On the Czech side, however, his tactics made him lose credibility, it fostered an anti-Slovak reaction, and it weakened the position of moderates.

V

The June 1990 Elections and the Changing Scene

1. The Elections

The first free national elections held under the system of proportional representation[1] in June 1990, proved to be in effect a "plebiscite" sanctioning the
rejection of the Communist regime. The two movements that carried the revolution were the victors. In the Czech Republic, the Civic Forum obtained the
majority of all votes (53.2 percent) followed by the Communist Party (13.5
percent), the Christian Democratic Union (8.7 percent), and the Moravia-
Silesia Movement (7.9 percent). The outcome in Slovakia was similar, but the
Public against Violence, although first with 32.5 percent, did not do as well as
its Czech counterpart, the Civic Forum. Ján Čarnogurský's Christian Democratic Movement was in second place (19 percent), the Communists were third
(13.8 percent), the separatist Slovak National Party fourth (11.0 percent), and
the alliance of Hungarian parties was fifth (with 8.6 percent of votes). No other
parties received the minimum number of votes required for representation in
the Federal Assembly.[2]

---

1. "Czechoslovak Elections—Now, Govern," THE ECONOMIST, June 16, 1990, p. 53–54.
The elections were held under the system of proportional representation following essentially the
system employed in the First Republic, Law 47/1990. This occurred after a "passionate dispute"
with President Havel considering but ultimately rejecting the English-American model of majority
voting. See Jon Elster, "Rebuilding the Boat in the Open Sea," manuscript; and Peter Kresák,
Porovnávacie štátne právo [Comparative Public Law] 119–21 (Vydavatelské oddelenie právnickej
fakulty UK, Bratislava, 1993).
2. Jiří Sláma in NEDĚLNÍ LIDOVÉ NOVINY, May 30, 1992, p. 16. The minimum number of
votes was 5 percent in the Czech Republic and 3 percent in Slovakia. See Miroslav Pekník, "K
formovaniu a postojom politických strán a hnutí na Slovensku pred volbami roku 1990 [On the
Formation and Attitudes of Political Parties and Movements in Slovakia before Elections in
1990]," in Aleš Gerloch (ed.), Aktuální problémy demokratizace postkomunistických států střední
Evropy [Actual Problems of Democratization of Post-Communist States in Central Europe] 45–59
(Čes. spol. pro pol. vědy, AVČR, Praha, 1995). On the electoral system (essentially based on
proportional representation principle) and the distribution of seats in the Federal Assembly and in
the Republic legislatures, see Judy Blatt, East Central Europe from Reform to Transformation,
125–29 (Printer Publishers, London, 1991). See also Arend Lijphart, "Democratization and Con-

The constitutional discourse after the elections was influenced primarily by several factors: rising national sentiment in Slovakia and the Czech response, the impact of the economic transformation process, a radical fragmentation of political forces, and the emergence of new leadership.[3] These variables influenced each other and interacted in a variety of patterns both inside the two Republics and between the Czech and Slovak elites. An attempt to measure the respective roles of these factors in the constitution-making process would make little sense—as is the case with most multicause, complex developments. I believe, however, that a brief account of the political evolution between the end of 1990 and the 1992 elections is essential to make the subsequent constitutional developments understandable. The cardinal phenomenon proved to be the fragile legitimacy of the postrevolutionary political movements, their fragmentation and transformation into political parties, and the difficulties of arranging the political spectrum according to the traditional left-right scheme.

2. Political Differentiation in Context

a. In the Czech Republic: A Cleavage

President Havel refused to classify himself as left or right, but "most of all I am loath to describe myself as a man of the center. It seems absurd to define oneself in a topographical sense, the more so because the position of the imaginary center is entirely dependent on the angle from which it is viewed." Yet he noted such a stance was not popular:

> After decades of artificial uniformity, our society needs to learn how to think of itself in political terms once more, to restructure itself politically. This leads people to try to situate themselves "topographically."[4]

The newspapers—he complained—talked every day about how a particular politician or party thought of itself as on the left or on the right, or right or left

stitutional Choices in Czechoslovakia, Hungary, and Poland," 4 J'L OF THEORETICAL POLITICS 207, 211 (no. 2, 1992).

    3. See generally Jiří Pehe and Jan Obrman, "The Civic Forum Shifts to the Right," RFE/RL RES. REP., Nov. 23, 1990, 14–18; Jiří Pehe, "The Instability of Transition," ibid., Jan. 4, 1991, 11–16; Jiří Pehe, "The First Weeks of 1991: Problems Solved, Difficulties Ahead," ibid., Mar. 8, 1991, 5–10; Jiří Pehe, "The Civic Forum Splits into Two Groups," ibid., Mar. 8, 1991, 11–14; Jiří Pehe, "Political Conflict in Slovakia," ibid., May 10, 1991, 1–6; Jiří Pehe, "Czech-Slovak Conflict Threatens State Unity," ibid., Jan. 3, 1992, 83; Jiří Pehe, "Czechoslovakia's Changing Political Spectrum," ibid., Jan. 31, 1992, 1–7; Jiří Pehe, "Slovak Nationalism Splits Christian Democratic Ranks," ibid., Mar. 27, 1992, 13–16; Theodor Draper, "The End of Czechoslovakia," N.Y. REV. OF BOOKS, Jan. 28, 1993, 20–26; and Petr Pavlovský, "Co sceluje Československo? [What Unites Czechoslovakia?]" Č D, Jan. 16, 1992, p. 3.

    4. Václav Havel, Summer Meditations 61 (A.A. Knopf, New York, 1992).

of center.[5] The public was thoroughly confused by the use of these terms. In a poll conducted by the Institute for Research of Public Opinion in October 1990, 25 percent did not know the meaning of "the right" and "the left" while the rest attributed to the terms widely different meanings. Thus, for example, 10 percent linked "the right" with capitalism, 8 percent with "chances for all," and 11 percent with social advantages of the higher income strata.[6] Yet the craving of the people for simplification and the perceived need of the political groupings to respond made topographic labeling unavoidable as early as the winter 1991 when the true orientation of the emerging forces was hardly discernible.

The Civic Forum and the Public against Violence together dominated the federal and Republic executive and legislative institutions. They were, as I recounted earlier, loose movements of widely differing interests, philosophies, and personalities, led mainly by former dissidents who were opposed to any attempts to introduce formal membership or the internal hierarchy and discipline characteristic of conventional parties. President Havel, a founder of the CF, shared this concept of the "movement" in preference to a political party. In fact, it was with the campaign slogan "parties belong to party members, the Civic Forum to all" that the Forum won the elections.[7]

Yet—an omen of the future—as early as in the fall of 1990 a faction of CF deputies in the federal and Czech parliaments established a group of the Democratic Right under the leadership of federal finance minister Václav Klaus, one of the chief architects of the "radical" economic transformation program. Presumably in response to this move, some two months later, in December 1990, Dr. Rychetský and others established the Liberal Club, "a centrist grouping" of some 90 deputies, which Klaus regarded as a counter-weight to his own club.[8] In a contested election for the chairmanship of the CF, Klaus defeated the Liberal Club candidate, who was supported by the president. A struggle ensued over the structure as well as the political orientation of the movement in a series of "congresses." Klaus, while insisting he was doing his best to prevent a split, nevertheless viewed the differences as "infinitely deep . . . it would be absolutely false if we hid our heads in the sand."[9] After a bruising fight in which an effort was made to expel some members, a clear majority of the CF central congress, disregarding the president's strong warning, supported Klaus's call to turn the movement into a political party.[10]

---

5. *Ibid.*, 61.

6. ČTK, Jan. 8, 1991, 69th Rep.

7. ČTK, Jan. 6, 1991, 46th Rep., quoting Dr. P. Rychetský.

8. ČTK, Dec. 14, 1990. On the problems of participation in the federal government of "the left" along with "the right," see Petr Pavlovský, Choďte vpravo [Walk to the right] 19–20 (H and H, Praha, 1992).

9. ČTK, Jan. 5, 1991.

10. The vote was 175 to 126. ČTK, Jan. 12, 1991. In his message to the congress, President

In an effort at a compromise, President Havel—obviously concerned as a founder of the CF—rather than keeping aloof, called a meeting of the warring factions at which an agreement was reached that the CF would divide into two parts, one organized along party lines, the other with a looser structure, the two to form a firm coalition until the 1992 elections.[11] Yet a few weeks later Chairman Klaus told the CF special congress that a "standard political system based on the existence of clear-cut defined political parties" was the only solution; the CF, lacking any explicit program and political initiative, had started to endanger the solution of fundamental political problems and the implementation of economic reform.[12]

In the end, three different political groupings emerged: first, the Civic Democratic Party (CDP), led by Klaus, with an overriding priority on the rapid creation of a free market and insistent on nothing less than a "functional federation";[13] and second, "the center left" Civic Movement (CM), based on the Liberal Club and including most of the former dissidents such as Chairman Jiří Dienstbier, federal Minister of Foreign Affairs Dr. Rychetský, and Czech Prime Minister Pithart.[14] Some of the adherents of the Civic Movement were thought of as still believing in "the third way" (whatever this might connote), and some, including Professor Jičínský and the economist-rival of Klaus, Valtr Komárek, eventually left to join the ascending Czechoslovak Social Democracy Party.[15] It was no secret that the president inclined in the direction of the Civic Movement.[16]

Havel warned that a split of the CF into two or more parties would be a "thoroughly irresponsible decision," "tragic for all," "a betrayal of the voters." He called for new dynamization, a firmer leadership, and greater discipline in the CF, which at the same time should preserve its relatively pluralistic internal composition stemming from the broad antitotalitarian movement. ČTK, Jan. 12, 1991.

11. ČTK, Feb. 23, 1991, quoting Dr. Rychetský. Neither group would have the right to the original name of Civic Forum, which would be left to "a supracoalitional umbrella grouping expressing itself culturally rather than politically." Opponents of the transformation decision formed an "Initiative for the Preservation of the CF as a Movement," which had little impact on subsequent developments. ČTK, Feb. 21, 1991.

12. ČTK, Feb. 23, 1991.

13. The first CDP program called for transformation into a modern European state based on civil society, observance of political rights and private ownership "so long as its setup functions and will not hinder the transformation," resolute parting with state ownership, and support in Slovakia of forces that seek functional federation and radical economic reform. ČTK, Apr. 21, 1991.

14. ČTK, Apr. 26, 1991; on the first program of the CM, see ČTK, Apr. 27, 1991.

15. In April 1991, six CF deputies, including Valtr Komárek, a prominent figure of the 1989 revolution and a principal opponent of Klaus's radical reform, joined the Social Democrat Party, and four more deputies were expected to do so. ČTK, Apr. 2, 1991.

16. He wrote that his "heart may be left of center," although he had always known that the only economic system that works is a market economy as reflecting "the nature of life itself."

The third offshoot was the Civic Democratic Alliance (CDA) with an economic orientation basically identical to that of the CDP but with a libertarian and nationalist accent. When asked about the difference between his and the Klaus party, the CDA chair, Dr. Jan Kalvoda, said: "Compare the mottos of our election programs—'Road to Prosperity' [Klaus's CDP]—and 'Road to Freedom' [CDA]. . . . CDA conceives the transformation of the society in more complex terms—not just economic. . . . Establishment of a normal political scene is for us equally as important as the timely execution of an economic reform."[17] Slovak Prime Minister Mečiar described the CDA as based "on the principle of few personalities, as unitaristic, and from the beginning openly hostile to [Mečiar's] movement."[18]

To complete the picture of the political landscape in the Czech lands during the period of party differentiation, I must add that the Social Democrats, along with the Communists (the second largest party) and a small coalition, the Liberal and Social Union, evolved into the groupings on the left. After the dissolution of the Czech and Slovak Christian Democratic Party, its Czech component became part of the "right" of the spectrum. At the extreme right was the ultranationalist, xenophobic Republican Party, headed by the notorious Dr. Sládek.

b. In Slovakia: A Split, Mečiar Dismissed (April 1991)

In contrast to the disintegration of its sister movement in the Czech lands, the Public against Violence, the strongest grouping in the Slovak Republic, would remain a political movement, Chairman Fedor Gál vowed, "even though this need not be forever." By reason of its position on economic reform, its social program, and its political working method, he told a PAV congress in late February 1991 that his movement was a liberal one with a normally functioning market as its ultimate goal.[19] Prime Minister Mečiar did not rule out the appearance "of new streams and initiatives" and anticipated the emergence of several political parties from the movement after the 1992 elections. He ranked himself in the political center.[20] He accused the Gál leadership of having

---

Václav Havel, *Summer Meditations, supra,* note 4, 62. It is said that already during the "round-table" negotiations after the revolution Havel did not favor placing Klaus in a top position.

17. Roman Krasnický and Karel Kříž, "Filosofie dějin je luxus [Philosophy of History Is a Luxury]," LN, Feb. 4, 1992, pp. 1, 3 (interview with J. Kalvoda).

18. "Chtějí mluvit s ODS [They Want to Talk With CDP]," TELEGRAF, Jan. 16, 1992 at 2.

19. ČTK, Feb. 23, 1991. A prominent PAV member, Marián Čalfa, the federal prime minister, spoke of PAV as "as sort of center . . . left oriented as to its comprehension of the economic reform." ČTK, Mar. 6, 1991.

20. ČTK, Feb. 24, 1991.

turned away from its original program and of not considering Slovakia's specific conditions in pursuing economic reform.[21]

The simmering rivalry between Gál, supported by a majority of key PAV governing groups, and Mečiar, aided by Minister of International Relations Milan Kňažko, broke into the open when Mečiar accused the PAV leadership of an attempt to censure his upcoming television talk. The PAV board responded with a vehement denial and a series of public countercharges.[22] A committee established by the Slovak National Council heard accusations that Mečiar in his earlier position as minister of the interior had tampered with secret police files and misused them to intimidate some members of the government, that he had engaged in secret talks with Soviet generals concerning arms sales, and that he had made public statements that he was not accountable to the Parliament but only to the people.[23] The charges were widely publicized in the Czech press. The daily *Lidové noviny,* for instance, wrote: "Mečiar may be suspected of opposing the screenings [the 'lustration' legislation designed to remove former Communists from leading positions] so that he can use his information to protect some secret police agents, while blackmailing others."[24] "A campaign was launched against the Slovak premier," responded Milan Kňažko, "the slandering of Mečiar in the Prague press has become commonplace and the most active are, unfortunately, periodicals close to the Castle and Civic Forum. . . . [T]he public is to be gradually prepared for the removal of Vladimír Mečiar from the post of premier."[25]

After an investigation, the committee of the Slovak National Council submitted its report, but the deputies voted to keep it secret.[26] The Presidium of the Slovak National Council passed a resolution saying that some statements made by the prime minister had been impulsive, put in question democratic principles, and misinformed people.[27] It did not, however, take any position on the charges regarding the improper use of police files.

---

21. According to Mečiar, the PAV leadership with Gál would have never dared to attack him without "the blessing of some functionaries in Prague." ČTK, Mar. 6, 1991.

22. ČTK, Mar. 3, 1991 (two reports); ČTK, Mar. 4, 1991.

23. In some Czech quarters Mečiar's activities were linked with former Czechoslovak security officials who were given political asylum in Switzerland. ČTK, Apr. 16, 1991, Apr. 19, 1991; Jiří Pehe, "Political Conflict in Slovakia," RFE/RL RES. REP., May 10, 1991, 1, 2–3.

24. Cited in Jiří Pehe, "Growing Slovak Demands as a Threat to Federation," RFE/RL RES. REP., Mar. 22, 1991, 1, 4.

25. ČTK, Mar. 3, 1991.

26. Part of the report was obtained and published by a Czech weekly, RESPEKT, Nov. 11–17, 1991, pp. 5–6.

27. ČTK, Apr. 19, 1991. As an example, the resolution cited Mečiar's public statement that he had secret talks with Soviet generals regarding Slovak armaments production, which he denied but then admitted as "ironical remarks." Mečiar charged that the Czech press misrepresented what were legitimate talks exclusively on an economic level; he was made the object of a campaign of disinformation organized by central bodies in Prague in response to Slovakia's effort to follow its own path of democratization, including economic life in its territory, part of which was contacts

Mečiar and Kňažko in effect ceased to take part in the PAV organs. The avowed Mečiar-Kňažko alliance, I may add parenthetically, ended in a bitter confrontation after less than two years when Kňažko and several of his colleagues were expelled from Mečiar's movement. In March 1991, Mečiar with his supporters left PAV to organize a new Movement for a Democratic Slovakia (MDS), which rose quickly in popularity, primarily at the expense of PAV.[28] President Havel called the situation in Slovakia "very alarming" after the "dramatic split" of the most significant Slovak political force.[29] The PAV chairman, Fedor Gál, a sociologist by profession, complaining that he and his family were being subjected to harassment,[30] accepted an invitation from the University of London and withdrew from Slovak politics. Mečiar repeatedly called the federal economic program unsuitable for Slovakia and was believed widely by the Slovaks to be best qualified to press Slovak national aspirations and deal with the increasingly unpopular federal reforms.[31]

In the end, on April 23, 1991, the Presidium of the National Council, employing its Soviet-style power under the 1960–68 Constitution, dismissed Mečiar and several ministers, including Kňažko, from their positions on the ground that the government had become unable to function because of political conflicts.[32] In Slovakia, Mečiar became the most popular politician, "a victim of a plot centered in Prague." His dismissal led to widespread protests, threats of strikes, and demonstrations—some 50,000 just in Bratislava.[33] In Prague, on the contrary, his replacement in the office of prime minister, Dr. Ján Čarnogurský, was acclaimed as offering "a promising change"[34] and an improvement in the prospects of "fruitful" constitutional talks.[35] President Havel called the change "constitutional" and "a triumph of parliamentary democracy."[36]

Dr. Čarnogurský's Christian Democratic Movement for a brief period supplanted the PAV as the strongest political force in the Slovak Parliament,

---

with foreign countries. ČTK, Apr. 1, 1991.

28. ČTK, Apr. 1, 1991; Apr. 8, 1991.

29. ČTK, March 10, 1991.

30. ČTK, Apr. 8, 1991; Apr. 28, 1991.

31. In an opinion poll of Apr. 19, 1991, 81 percent of Slovaks considered him the most popular politician; only 25 percent of Czechs but 91 percent of Slovaks viewed him as "a guarantor of a free and democratic development in Slovakia." Pehe, "Political Conflict . . . ," *supra,* note 3, 1, 2. *See also* ČTK, Apr. 9, 1991, on another poll in Slovakia with a similar result.

32. ČTK, Apr. 23, 1991.

33. ČTK, Apr. 24, 1991.

34. Czech Prime Minister Pithart, ČTK, Apr. 23, 1991.

35. Dr. D. Burešová, chair of the Czech Parliament, ČTK, Apr. 23, 1991.

36. ČTK, Apr. 28, 1991. The dismissal was criticized by the Confederation of Slovak Trade Unions, the chair of the Slovak Party of the Democratic Left (former Communist Party) Peter Weiss, and the Czech Communist Party leader Jiří Svoboda, as well as by Alexander Dubček, the chair of the Federal Assembly, who called Mečiar "a resolute advocate of Czechoslovak federative arrangements." ČTK, Apr. 25, 1991; Pehe, "Political Conflict," *supra,* note 3, 4.

but it suffered heavy defections to Mečiar's new movement.[37] Primarily under
the impact of nationalist pressures, it, too, split into two factions.[38] One was
headed by Ján Čarnogurský, and the other supported outright independence.
The fracture among the Christian Democrats proved fatal for the final phase of
constitutional negotiations in early 1992. Čarnogurský himself clung to the
idea, which was particularly vexing to the Czechs, that the two Republics
would remain together only temporarily until they would join the European
Community as independent states ("with their own little stars"); until then, he
spoke of confederation or loose federation or a combination of both based on a
treaty, and he pointed to the Belgian model.[39] To the Czechs at large, this
meant preparing Slovakia for independence with Czech money.

The Slovak National Party, advocating independence, made a moderate
showing in the 1990 elections, but its support plummeted in the 1991 local
elections. Still in line with the drive toward differentiation, the Czech, predominantly "hard-line," "conservative" Communists divided from the Slovak
Communists, who renamed themselves the Party of the Democratic Left (PDL)
and adopted essentially a social democratic platform. Concerned with the
social impact of the economic reform and responding to the "Slovak first"
trend, they assumed a friendly stand toward Mečiar's party with which they
formed the core of the opposition in the Slovak parliament.

At the regional level, the Hungarian Independent Initiative in Slovakia
and two associations for Moravia and Silesia with ethnic or regional agendas
were represented in the Federal Assembly. I shall deal in more detail with the
rising voices for autonomy in Moravia and Silesia, which complicated further
the negotiations for a federal constitution. No significant federationwide political organization emerged, a factor symptomatic of different political cultures
that proved of great significance in later developments. The number of political
parties in the Federal Assembly rose from the original six to 16, and the
number of registered parties reached 70.[40] The political regrouping brought
extensive changes in all the three fledgling legislative bodies and made the
communications between the leadership—and the search for consensus—
inordinately complex.[41]

---

37. In forming the Slovak government, Čarnogurský refused to enter into coalition with
Mečiar's party and instead joined forces with what remained of the PAV and the tiny Slovak
Democratic Party. Jiří Pehe, "Czech and Slovak Conflict Threatens State Unity," *supra,* note 3, 83
at 84.

38. ČTK, Mar. 6, 1991.

39. ČSTK, Oct. 3, 1991; on the Belgian model, *see* ČTK, June 21, 1991.

40. ČTK, June 10, 1991. On the regrouping caused by the split in PAV, see ČTK, May 3,
1991 (two reports).

41. See the tables in Jiří Pehe, "Czechoslovakia: Parties Register for Elections," RFE/RL
RES. REP., May 1, 1992, 20, 21; see also Pehe, "Czech and Slovak Conflict Threatens State Unity,"
supra, note 3, 84–85.

As I was penning the lines on the transformation of movements into parties in the winter of 1993, I was struck by a paradox. At the same time, the historic socialist parties in the countries of Western Europe were engaged in a search for new identities to stem the decline of voter appeal. In France, former Socialist prime minister Michel Rocard caused an upheaval among those on the left by proposing that the Socialist Party—expected to lose the upcoming elections—should dissolve itself into a "grand, open, extrovert movement," which would comprise the entire political spectrum ranging from conservatives to liberal communists: the party must break away from its past, which it was no longer able to serve. Even in Spain, where the socialists appeared still firmly entrenched, the party chairman and Prime Minister Felipe Gonzales spoke of a movement that would include a number of groups rather than the original model of a unitary, disciplined party.[42] These musings promptly evaporated. Only in Italy did a new "movement" appear to take shape, Berlusconi's "Forza Italia," whose final destiny is still in abeyance.

3. An Afterthought: More on "the Heroes"

According to Petr Pithart, an understanding on the constitutional issues was several times within the grasp of the negotiators but Mečiar's dismissal caused a turn in a "different direction." It triggered Mečiar's vengefulness, his "basic quality"; he remembers any "wrong or betrayal," and he took the entire affair personally. Pithart believes that a drive for satisfaction against his "enemies" became the motivating source of all his subsequent actions.[43] In fact, Ján Čarnogurský, the principal villain, and "the Castle," an accomplice, became the enemies as a result of the dismissal. Sociologists would speak of conduct driven by "the social norm of revenge."[44]

Several informed Slovaks and Czechs told me that a drive for power has been the dynamic of Mečiar's mercurial, charismatic personality. When he achieves power, how does he wield it? A person in closest proximity to the Slovak prime minister described to me the situation prevailing during the fall months of 1990. Fedor Gál, who picked Mečiar for prime minister,[45] expected governmental decisions to be made as before by the PAV leadership. Mečiar's way, however, was quite different. He did not communicate with anyone.

---

42. *See,* for example, John Lloyd, "Nečekaná pomoc z nečekané strany [Unexpected Help from Unexpected Side]," LN, Feb. 23, 1993, p. 5.

43. Jana Klusáková–Petr Pithart 71 (Primus, Praha, 1992).

44. Jon Elster, The Cement of Society: A Study of Social Order 129 (Cambridge U. Press, New York, Dorchester, Melbourne, Sydney, 1989).

45. It was Dubček, the chair of the Federal Assembly, who brought Mečiar to Gál's attention. There were three other candidates for the office of prime minister: Čič, Stračár, and Gál. The latter two refused the job. Conversation with V. Žák. J. Moravčík believes the third candidate was Prof. M. Kusý, not Gál.

When his ministers wanted to get advance information on the next meeting of the government, they had to ask the cook. Following the system of the predecessor Communist government, a half-year work plan incorporated the items offered by the individual ministers. In preparation for a meeting, an assistant would lift a number of files from the top of a large pile, regardless of their importance or priority. In the night before a meeting, the prime minister would study these materials until the early morning hours. Endowed with boundless energy and prodigious memory and master of the subject matter, he would gleefully expose the ministers' ignorance of the details they had missed. He would announce a change in the government policy on television, and when his deputy Ján Čarnogurský suggested that the coalition partners should have been consulted he became enraged and screamed that he alone decided what to say on television. Čarnogurský turned red in the face but was too intimidated to react. Mečiar lost any contact with the PAV leadership and the coalition parties. At the time, he was discovering his own skills as a mass communicator. Yet he was "immensely alone."

In a conversation with Dr. Čarnogurský in 1993, I asked him why the Slovak National Council Presidium (which was under his strong influence) did not pursue the charges against Mečiar based on his activity as minister of the interior. There was, he replied, only one witness available in addition to circumstantial evidence, and considering Mečiar's growing popularity any condemnation after a lengthy investigation would be ignored by the electorate.

Václav Klaus, the federal finance minister and prime author and promoter of economic reform, was "a strong man" in the federal government. Although his political clout had grown significantly with his election as chair of the Civic Forum, he displayed a marked detachment with respect to the constitutional negotiations, leaving the ungrateful task to others. "I would prefer first to settle the economic relationships," he said in the fall of 1990, "after that, I believe, things will become clearer in the political area as well."[46] Obviously, his Slovak colleagues did not agree. As a young economist trained in Prague, Klaus joined the Economic Institute of the Czechoslovak Academy of Sciences, studied non-Marxist theories in Italy and the United States, and after 1969 was forced to leave the institute because of his writings. While in a minor banking job, and ultimately on the staff of the Forecasting Institute, he organized seminars and publications with a group of economists of similar orientation who became the core group forming the post-Communist economic policies. He never joined the party and kept contact with the dissidents, but, like many of his fellow citizens, he avoided an open conflict with the regime.[47] An

---

46. LN, November 2, 1990, p. 9.
47. Marián Leško, L'udia a l'udkovia z politickej elity [People and Little People of the Political Elite] 33, 37–38 (PEREX a.s., Bratislava?, 1993).

avid tennis player and cross country skier, Klaus is intelligent, quick to grasp new problems, a prodigious worker, self-confident bordering on arrogant, single-minded to a point of nearsightedness, and possessed of a political instinct unparalleled among his peers. In meetings, he is always well prepared and ready to listen, "sometimes even to modify his views."[48]

Another Czech political figure, Dr. Jan Kalvoda, is, like Petr Pithart, a son of a Communist diplomat, but he never became a party member. Barred from law practice in Prague, he worked as an attorney in the small town of Rokycany.[49] He was co-opted in the Czech National Council in February 1990, became a member and then chair of its constitutional committee, and ultimately became first vice-chair of the Czech National Council.[50] Dashing, fastidiously dressed, sporting a powerful black mustache, he evokes a figure of a Hungarian hussar. His photogenic face adorned the election posters of his party. In his elegant offices, two ladies, equally fastidiously dressed, serve coffee and sugar. Self-confident and articulate, he is given to interesting, expansive statements, some of which, on a closer look, prove illusive.

4. An Interlude: The Federal Assembly, a Success Story?

Viewed with the benefit of hindsight, the legislative achievements of the first freely elected Federal Assembly were nothing short of remarkable. For one thing, quick action was called for in view of the various time constraints, but there was no institutional memory of democratic lawmaking or experienced leadership among the predominantly youngish deputies. The relation between the hard-working government and the parliamentary party factions ("clubs") was not satisfactory. The Damoclesian sword of the "prohibition of majorization"[51] along with the three-fifths majority requirement for most important decisions, made the deliberations more than arduous. As a result of the fragmentation of the victorious movements and the emergence of new parties, the number of the clubs continued to rise (to reach 18) and their membership to

---

48. Conversation with P. Pitha. In a meeting of an influential New York organization, I heard Klaus dress down mercilessly the kindly chairman, who, to be helpful to Klaus, had expounded on Czech economic difficulties. Klaus denied emphatically any such problems and with great glee offered to send his financial experts to Washington to solve the federal budget deficit. The audience was not amused.

49. Conversation with Docent Vojtěch Cepl. After the breakup, Cepl became professor at the Charles University Law Faculty and judge of the Constitutional Court of the Czech Republic.

50. LN, February 4, 1992, p. 1. After the breakup, he became deputy prime minister in the Czech Republic.

51. Vojtěch Cepl, "Usilujeme o nefunkční stát, [We Are Struggling for a Nonfunctional State]," LN, June 11, 1992, p. 6.

change, making for a loose party discipline.[52] Last, but not least, from the very outset the Assembly was seriously distracted by the continuing debate over the shape of the federal constitution. That controversy, which baffled and alienated the public and contributed to the drop in confidence in the government, also slowed down the legislative process. Finally, the criticism of the Assembly proceedings by the press, which was taking full advantage of its newly found freedom but was unaccustomed to the inherently laborious lawmaking in any democracy, was not always objective or helpful.

Despite all these obstacles, some 200 pieces of legislation were logged (63 laws and 13 constitutional laws in the first five months of 1990 alone) before the impact of the political transformation had slowed down the process, and only 29 government bills were rejected on final vote, mostly by the negative vote of the Slovak component.[53]

The Assembly managed, as it was bound to do, to purge the 1960–68 Constitution of its most objectionable features, even though the president called the process of "gluing amendments and addenda to the Communist constitution" an "absurd business" dragging out the revolutionary phase.[54] Perhaps the most significant achievement in the political sphere was the adoption by large majorities of the constitutional laws on the Charter of Basic Rights and Freedoms and on the federal Constitutional Court.[55] The Assembly legislation created a framework for a multiparty democratic society and re-

52. David M. Olson, Jana Reschová, and Jindřiška Syllová, "První volební období demokratického parlamentu v ČSFR: Federální shromáždění 1990–1992 (komparační pohled) [The First Election Term of the Democratic Parliament in ČSFR: Federal Assembly 1990–1992 (Comparative View)]," 2/1993 PRÁVNÍK 125, 128.

53. František Formánek, "Dva roky federálního parlamentu—Uklidňující fakta, [Two years of the Federal Parliament-Calming Facts]," LN, June 4, 1992, p. 6; Viktor Knapp, "The Legislative Challenge for Former Socialist States in Europe," 1992 STATUTE LAW REVIEW (Oxford) 97–103. According to Lidové noviny, during the first two years of its work the Federal Assembly adopted 167 new laws. LN, May 1, 1992 p. 1. *See generally,* Kronika demokratického parlamentu [Chronicle of the Democratic Parliament] 1989–1992 (Cesty, Praha, 1992).

54. Havel, Summer Meditations, *supra,* note 5 at 23.

55. Const. Law, 23/1991 Sb., and 91/1991 Sb. I was tempted to deal both with the interesting international consultations and the Assembly debate on these two laws. However, the subject appeared to me to lie outside the main focus of my book. Space limitations were a contributing factor. Of course, an agreement by the Czech and Slovak elites of the day on a text purporting to define the basic societal values may be viewed as an indication that the cultural differences between the two peoples were not as extensive as may have been assumed. I touch upon some of the issues pertaining to human rights in chapter XIV as well as in chapter XV. The two laws have been analyzed competently elsewhere. *See* Lloyd Cutler and Herman Schwartz, "Constitutional Reform in Czechoslovakia: E duobus unum?" 58 CHI. L. R. 511, 531–44; Josef Blahož, "Human Rights, Their Guarantees, and the Constitutional Judiciary in the ČSFR," 1992 AUSTRIAN JOURNAL OF PUBLIC AND INTERNATIONAL LAW 31–71 (with English translations of the two laws); and Herman Schwartz, "Economic and Social Rights," 8 AM. U. J'L OF INT'L L. & POLICY, 551–65 (1992–93).

formed the army, the judiciary, police, private and public law, and local admin-istration; it abolished the Communist "Economic Code" and the arbitration courts for economic disputes, and it took the first steps to provide a legal framework for a modern market economy. As part of the transformation pro-gram, it adopted restitution laws for restoring property confiscated by the Communist regime and two far-reaching privatization laws.[56]

Understandably, the quality of the legislation was adversely affected by the quantity, urgency, and continuing reorganization of the administration and—last but not least—by the critical shortage of trained lawyers. In a situation of unprecedented, rapid change, a law, even if conceived by master drafters, would become obsolete before coming into force. A legislative in-stitute attached to the office of the federal government worked hard, and a number of specialized legislative commissions with the participation of law faculties labored "practically for nothing," only for the honor of helping the new government; they accomplished a great deal even though the possibilities were deplorably limited.[57] Federal legislation was rid of most of the "sedi-ments of the past." According to a member of the Charles University Law Faculty, broad, "generally binding legal norms" were replaced with simple "legal norms," "legal persons" was substituted for "organizations," and an effort was made to eradicate socialist declaratory pronunciamentos devoid of any normative content and paragraphs on "the purpose of the law"; federal legislation reached a higher legal culture than that of the Republics.[58]

The early impact of the federal legislative program on the national econ-omy was severe, but it proved more damaging in Slovakia where inflation and prices rose somewhat higher than in the Czech lands. Similarly, the drop in industrial production and exports in Slovakia exceeded that in the Czech Re-public and—most importantly—Slovak unemployment was twice, and ulti-

---

56. For a useful survey in English of the basic reform legislation, see Karol Svoboda, "Legal and Political Events between 1989 and 1992," 45, 53–65, in Viktor Knapp and Sergio Bartole (eds.), La Dissoluzione della Federazione Cecoslovacca (La Rosa Ed., Torino, 1994). For a collection of the 1990 economic laws, *see* Jaroslava Svobodová, Slavoj Vaněk, Alois Forejt, Nové ekonomické zákony [New Economic Laws] (Trizonia, Praha, 1990). *See,* for example, Zákon o zmírnění následků některých majetkových křivd [Law on reduction of consequences of some property injustices] 403/1990 Sb.; and Zákon o mimosoudní rehabilitaci [Law on Extrajudicial Rehabilitation] 87/1991 Sb.; the "small privatization law" 427/1990 Sb.; Zákon o podmínkách převodu majetku státu na jiné osoby [Law on Conditions for Transferring State Property to Other Persons—the large-scale privatization law] 92/91 Sb. See also Karel Dyba, Tomáš Ježek, and Daniel Arbes, "The Second Czech Revolution," FINANCIAL TIMES, Oct. 18, 1990, p. 48. See also Pavel Rychetský, "Vývoj právního řádu po 17. listopadu 1989 a výhled dalších systémových změn právního řádu [The Evolution of the Legal Order After the 17th November 1989 and a Prospect of Further Systemic Changes of the Legal Order]," 3–4/1992 PRÁVNÍK, 185–92.

57. Docent Irena Pelikánová, "Návrat právního nihilismu [The Return of Legal Nihilism]," LN, Feb. 9, 1993, p. 9.

58. *Ibid.*

mately three to four times, higher.[59] The bulk of foreign investment went to the Czech Republic with only a fraction (some 8 percent) to Slovakia, another ground for Slovak complaint against "Prago-centrism."[60] The differential in the economic and social dislocation was due—it was said—to the structure of the Slovak economy (heavy arms industry, some giant companies, less productive land) rather than the level of living standards or industrialization.[61] However, it was pointed out that "[e]ach [adverse] social impact in this transitional period has an antifederal effect in Slovakia, each such impact can be explained by the assertion that 'this was thought up in Prague.'"[62]

In the Czech Republic, some felt that a continuation of the federal state would place an undue burden on Czech resources. Even among the Czechs, the timing and the extent of the economic reform was controversial.[63] Pointing to the "alarming statistics," Federal Deputy Prime Minister Rychetský felt that

---

59. ČTK, May 7, 1991. "In the Slovak Republic, consumer prices in March were 67.9% higher than in the same period the previous year. The prices of industrial goods and food were 13% and 4% higher than in the Czech Republic. In the first three months of 1991, industrial output in Slovakia was 14.3% lower than in the same period in 1990. In all Czechoslovakia, the drop in industrial products during the same period averaged 11.9%." Peter Martin, "Economic Reform and Slovakia," RFE/RL RES. REP., July 5, 1991, 6, 9. *See also* Ivan Svítek, "The Assessment: Czechoslovak Economic Reform in 1991," *ibid.*, May 22, 1992, 45–49.

60. Why does the bulk of foreign investment go to the Czech lands? The following reasons have been suggested by different sources:

1. Application of the economic reform program was more consistent and the perception that economic outlook was less problematic in the Czech lands;
2. Different structure of industry (see above);
3. Geography: closeness to Western Europe, the major investor;
4. Lesser dependency on Eastern markets;
5. Competition for resources with Slovakia;
6. Conflict of interest in the federal bureaucracy favoring investments in the Czech Republic; and
7. Lack of information of a positive nature about Slovakia available in the West.

61. Gross domestic product for a worker in 1991 was $3,589 in the Czech Republic and $3,312 in Slovakia. Stephen Engelberg, "Breaking Up Is Not So Hard To Do, Etc.," N.Y. TIMES, Jan. 3, 1993, sec. 4, p. E5. Martin suggests the following causes of the differential: Slovakia's energy-intensive primary production, depending on raw materials from the Soviet Union, and its exports oriented primarily toward the East. The conversion of the largely heavy arms industry (65 percent of the arms production of the Federation) posed particular difficulties with the threat of a layoff of up to 80,000 workers. Foreign capital inflow was lower and the need for imports for its energy-intensive industries higher, causing higher production costs. Peter Martin, *supra,* note 59, 10.

62. Federal Deputy Prime Minister Rychetský, ČTK, Apr. 5, 1991. He felt that the Slovak fear of the consequences of the economic reform could be overcome only by the preservation of the federative state.

63. In an opinion poll published in October 1991, 70 percent of Slovaks wanted the radical economic reforms changed or stopped, but more than 50 percent of Czechs thought the reforms were going well. Weekly Record of Events, RFE/RL. RES. REP., Oct. 4, 1991, 39.

"reform is not feasible under such conditions"; the spokesman for the Civic Forum, Vladimír Železný, warned of "text book formulas in the style of the late Chairman Mao-Tse-Tung."[64] In the end, however, the "radical" program authored primarily by Finance Minister Klaus prevailed: lifting of most price (not wage) controls; rapid privatization, including a novel method of coupons made available to each individual citizen; freeing foreign trade; and devaluation and internal convertibility of currency. The dispute over the economic program injected a new and highly volatile variable into the already charged negotiations over the federal constitution. It added fuel to the internal tensions and rivalries within the Czech delegation and to the radicalization on the Slovak side.

---

64. AP, April 19, 1991, cited by Martin, *supra,* note 59, 9.

Second Act

VI

Negotiations on a "Treaty" (Winter–Spring 1991)

1. The Proposal for a "State Treaty," "a Bombshell?" (February 1991)

Early in February 1991, Alexander Dubček, chair of the Federal Assembly, had in his hands six drafts of a federal constitution submitted by different political parties.[1] This presumably did not count the proposals offered by President Havel (which embodied the power-sharing law of December 1990 and the Charter of Fundamental Rights and Freedoms of January 1991) or the several chapters approved by the Assembly's own Constitutional Committee. The committee's text, however, did not contain the crucial power-sharing section. That subject, which the Czechs had hoped was "settled" by the adoption of the 1990 law, was reopened a few weeks later, in February 1991, by Dr. Ján Čarnogurský, the chair of the Slovak Christian Democrats. His proposal envisaged a "state treaty" to be concluded between the two Republics in advance of the adoption of the federal constitution.[2] The parentage of the proposal is disputed but some "insiders" credit Mečiar with the original idea.[3] Such a treaty would not only redefine the allocation of powers between the center and the Republics but would also stipulate a new basis for the common state. Secretary General Gorbachev's treaty for the restructuring of the Soviet Union was obviously a model. The proposal and the Czech response opened up a Pandora's box of new constitutional issues, which assumed a dominant role in the negotiations.

2. Comments by the International Group

It was at this point in time—in the early spring of 1991—that senior Federal Deputy Prime Minister Dr. Rychetský asked the international group for com-

---

1. Jiří Pehe, "The First Weeks of 1991: Problems Solved, Difficulties Ahead," RFE/RL RES. REP., Mar. 8, 1991, 5, 8.
2. Jiří Pehe, "The State Treaty between the Czech and Slovak Republics," RFE/RL RES. REP., June 7, 1991, 11–12.
3. Conversations with Marián Čalfa and Jozef Moravčík, who worked with Prime Minister Mečiar at the time.

ments on the Slovak proposal. This request was followed by an invitation from Dr. Čarnogurský, at that time still federal deputy prime minister, to a meeting in Bratislava on which I touched earlier and to which I return in annex I.

In our written observations, we all raised the obvious question of the competence of the two Republics, as component units of a federation, to conclude what was intended as a treaty under international law. "As the Republics are not sovereign states under the present constitution"—concluded Swiss Professor Jean-François Aubert—"they could only be turned into such states either through a procedure provided for in the existing Constitution or through a 'revolutionary' one."[4] In the absence of a specific provision in the Constitution, the procedure would entail a constitutional law adopted by the Federal Assembly that would dissolve the federation.[5]

Apart from the constitutional concerns, the wisdom of resorting to an international treaty that, among others, would retain a right of unilateral withdrawal was questioned by the Americans in the advisors' group.

Professor Laurence H. Tribe sought to draw a lesson from American history. He noted that the 1787 Constitution

> owes its endurance in significant part to its quite explicit rejection of the treaty model as a basis for federation. . . . [C]onsistent with this basic theory of union, the indivisibility of the United States of America was reaffirmed through a bloody civil war. . . . Had the United States Constitution incorporated a right of unilateral withdrawal we would not today be a constitutional republic. . . . It is an illusion to suppose that a meaningful constitutional union can rest on a mere alliance or treaty of convenience. Whatever international law might say in addressing such an alliance, I know of no constitutional philosophy or precedent that could reconcile it with a constitutional order that is a coherent whole as viewed from within . . .
>
> I do not want to be understood as suggesting that it is utterly impossible for a treaty-based constitutional contraption to muddle through and perhaps even endure. All things are possible. But the odds are not favorable, and the American experience would certainly counsel against any such approach . . .[6]

"The Czechoslovak State exists since 1918"—argued French State Counselor Roger Errera—and

---

4. J.-F. Aubert, Note, Apr. 20, 1991. This and the other materials prepared by the advisers are in my files.

5. *See* on this, Alexander Dubček in Bratislava, ČTK, April 1, 1991.

6. Tribe, Memorandum, Apr. 5, 1991, 2, 3, 7.

[t]o introduce now the idea of such a treaty amounts to pretending that nothing exists at all, except the two Republics, that the future Federation will come into existence as a product of the treaty and that the Republics do indeed have jurisdiction (primary or derived) to sign such an instrument.[7]

Reviewing possible historical analogies from the Confederation of the Rhine to the 1871 German Reich, the Austro-Hungarian compromise of 1867, and the "personal" and "real" unions, Errera characterized the proposed treaty as "a legal and political time-bomb."[8]

Aubert, evidently reflecting a somewhat different historical experience, took a more charitable view of the general concept of a treaty-based structure:

Provided there are two independent states the signature of a treaty is a normal way of evolving toward a federation. Further it can either lose its contractual features if amendments are subject to a majority rule or keep it, if unanimity is required, as will always be the case when there are only two parties . . .

but he stressed the difficulty of a two-unit structure with a provision for secession.[9]

We all criticized a number of specific features of the draft treaty such as what we felt was "the unheard of" authority[10] of the Republic parliaments to stop the discussion of a bill in the Federal Assembly, the priority of Republic law if adopted earlier than federal law, absence of any provision for a conclusive determination of constitutional conflicts, and the extended "prohibition of majorization."[11] The treaty was to come into full effect when approved by the two Republic parliaments.

It was Professor Aubert who articulated the ultimate thought shared by at least some, if not all, of us:

[O]ne could wonder whether total independence for each of the Republics would not be better than such a system that cripples both the Federal Republic and each of the single [Republics] in exercising their competences.[12]

---

7. Errera, Note, undated, at 2.

8. *Ibid.,* 5.

9. Aubert, Note, Apr. 20, 1991, 2.

10. Errera, Note, at 5.

11. Professor Herman Schwartz, Memorandum, Apr. 12, 1991; letter, Etienne Gutt, President Emeritus, Cour d'Arbitrage, Professor Emeritus, Université Libre de Bruxelles, May 2, 1991; R. Errera and J.-F. Aubert, *supra,* note 4; in my Memorandum of May 4, 1991, I raised inter alia certain foreign affairs problems.

12. Aubert, Note, *supra,* note 4, 2.

Echoing this idea, President Havel said in one of his radio fireside chats that it would be "better to have two separate republics than a non-functional federation," thus bringing the separation alternative within the parameters of public discourse.[13] The position of the international group was articulated strictly in terms of existing constitutional and international law, but it necessarily discouraged any "revolutionary" route toward constitutional change. The distinct "antifederalist" nature of the draft treaty raised the question of the credibility of the Slovak proponents and obviously contributed to the negative attitude of the international group. It came as no surprise that the unmitigated criticism voiced in unison by the foreign advisors was used by the Czech side in support of its opposition to the treaty idea, and it very likely had some impact on the substantial modification of the Slovak proposal in subsequent negotiations.

3. The President's Legislative Initiative (March 1991)

Reacting to the difficulties in the constitutional negotiations, in early 1991 President Havel proposed a series of measures designed to avoid and, if necessary, to resolve a potential constitutional crisis. These included proposals for strengthening the president's emergency powers in case of an internal threat or legislative deadlock, for changing the structure of the federal legislature, and for a popular referendum. Dissatisfied with the work of the Assembly's Constitutional Commission, he also submitted a draft of a new federal constitution prepared at his direction. We shall see that, with a single exception, none of these proposals, although amply amended, fell on receptive ears in the Federal Assembly.[14]

The international group was consulted after the emergency powers bill was submitted to the Assembly.[15] However, the Slovak National Council rejected the bill on January 23, 1991, after the argument by Mečiar (then still Slovak prime minister) that it was open to much too broad an interpretation and

---

13. THE ECONOMIST, March 18, 1991, p. 44. President Havel's press secretary used the same words on Mar. 14, 1991, according to Jiří Pehe, "Growing Slovak Demands Seen as Threat to Federation," RFE/RL RES. REP., Mar. 22, 1991, 1, 8.

14. For a description of these proposals, see Lloyd Cutler and Herman Schwartz, "Constitutional Reform in Czechoslovakia: E Duobus Unum," 58 U. CHI. L.R. 511, 545–46, 548–50 (1991). I shall return to these proposals, which were submitted in heavily amended form and were debated in the Federal Assembly in the winter of 1992. For the text of the president's proposal of a federal constitution, see NO, Mar. 14, 1991, Documents, p. 7–10, and HN, Mar. 14, 1991, pp. 5–9.

15. Roger Errera of France, Etienne Gutt of Belgium, Marc Lalonde of Canada, Helmut Steinberger of the German Federal Republic, and Herman Schwartz and Laurence H. Tribe of the United States wrote memoranda on crisis legislation and practice in their respective national systems with comments on the bill.

left too much power in the federal government.[16] That was the end of this important presidential initiative.

Some of the drafts offered by the president were criticized for inadequate formulation and ineffective presentation due in part to the absence of professional experts in the president's Chancery. The single lawyer on the president's permanent staff resigned and was not replaced. The president relied on a consultant, Vladimír Klokočka, a Czech emigré professor of constitutional law in Munich. Whether by design or for lack of political sophistication on the part of the staff, some of these proposals arrived at the desks of the surprised deputies without any prior communication or exploration of the chances of adoption. As seen by the Slovaks, they all were directed toward reducing Slovak power.

4. "From Castles to Manors": Presidential Talks (Winter–Spring 1991)

a. Prelude to Kroměříž: "The Plank Compromise"

The Christian Democrat proposal for a treaty was at the center of a series of four meetings called by President Havel in the spring of 1991, bringing the total number of presidential talks on constitutional matters to 12.[17] The first meeting with Slovak political leaders took place on April 17, the second with leading Czech politicians on April 24, and the third, with leading Czech and Slovak federal and Republic personalities, on May 10.[18] Very little is known about these informal confabulations of politicians who peregrinated under the patronage of the president from one government-owned establishment to another. The countryside is dotted with more or less grand estates formerly owned by Austrian nobility. With its characteristic penchant for irony, the Czech press dubbed these meetings "from castles to manors."

The Christian Democrat draft treaty received the support of the Slovak Public against Violence, itself subject to the pressures of its nationalist wing.[19] But it faced unanimous opposition on the Czech side. According to President Havel, "the Czechs were utterly shocked" by the idea of an international treaty between two independent states. "[W]hat else was it but a demonstration of the independence of both republics, and an attempt to establish their coexistence

---

16. Jiří Pehe, "The First Weeks of 1991: Problems Solved, Difficulties Ahead," RFE/RL RES. REP., Mar. 8, 1991, 5, 7.

17. For a detailed description, see Jiří Pehe, "The State Treaty between the Czech and Slovak Republics," RFE/RL RES. REP., June 7, 1991, 11–15.

18. ČTK, Apr. 30, 1991.

19. Jiří Pehe, "The State Treaty between the Czech and Slovak Republic," *supra,* note 17, 11, 12.

on the basis of a mere treaty, not on a federative basis?"[20] The Czech representatives were trying to understand the reasons and motives behind the Slovak request and were trying to meet it in accordance with the way in which they saw the whole problem.[21]

As an alternative to a treaty, the Czech side first suggested that the adoption of the constitution be preceded by a political declaration that would have no legal impact.[22] But the only matter on which the principal political groups were able to agree in the earlier round was that Czechoslovakia would be a federal state composed of two sovereign and equal republics. Federal Prime Minister Marián Čalfa, while rejecting "any kind of state treaty because there are no states that could conclude it," insisted that a way must be found to fulfill the Slovak will to live in a common state—through an agreement to be an equal partner in the creation of a federative state.[23]

---

20. Václav Havel, Summer Meditations 43 (A.A. Knopf, New York, 1992).

21. *Ibid.,* 44.

22. After the third round of presidential meetings ending on March 4, the official press agency reported that the representatives of the Civic Forum and PAV agreed to recommend the following principles for the elaboration of the federal constitution:

1. Czechoslovakia will be a federal state made up of two sovereign and equal Republics linked voluntarily and of the free will of their citizens.

2. The free will of the citizens of the two Republics will be expressed in a joint declaration on coexistence which will be adopted and declared parallel by the two national councils (Republics' parliaments). The federal constitution will be the fundamental document of the federal state.

3. Powers which the constitution will not delegate to the Federation will be given to the Republics or directly to citizens. The constitution will fix firmly the right of the Republics to decide in a constitutional way about their remaining in the Federation.

4. Both national councils would parallel adopt a declaration on coexistence on the eve of the adoption of the three new constitutions.

5. All three constitutions would be adopted parallelly.

6. A timetable of coordinated creation and discussions about all three constitutions and the declaration on coexistence must be worked out, and culminate by a ceremonial adoption of the documents in the autumn.

7. —[omitted]

8. Representatives of the Christian Democratic Movement agree with the principle expressed in item no. 1. As regards other items the Movement insists on its proposal for concluding a state treaty between the two Republics, stressing that this treaty would be a legal document and not only a political declaration.

9. Participants in the meeting were informed that the issue of Moravia and Silesia is being solved by the Czech National Council as a problem of regional and administrative setup of the Czech Republic.

10. The next meeting, which will deal with legislative, executive and judicial powers and principles of a democratic society in new constitutions will be held on March 26. (ČTK, Mar. 5, 1991) (English text)

23. ČTK, Apr. 30, 1991. Federal Finance Minister Klaus considered the treaty "absolutely unacceptable to the Czech side." ČTK, Apr. 24, 1991.

Czech Prime Minister Petr Pithart suggested that a formula might be found to meet the Slovak demand. "A more detailed study of the constitutions of other states shows that the term *state treaty* is used also in other, less clear-cut senses."[24] Pithart may have had in mind the "compacts" among states of the United States authorized by the federal Constitution or comparable agreements of German *Länder*. This was the alternative I stressed in my contacts with the Czech and Slovak spokesmen.[25]

Finally, on May 2, 1991, Karol Plank, chair of the Constitutional Commission of the Slovak National Council, announced in a press conference, attended by representatives of the Slovak government and all political parties, that a "consensus" had been reached on a compromise: the relationship between the two Republics must be founded on a Czech and Slovak treaty, which, however, would not be based on international law. Though not subjects of international law, the two Republics are nevertheless subjects of "state law": "No one on the Slovak side is demanding an international treaty but rather a contractual basis for relations between the two Republics." Such a treaty would not nullify the current federation, which was "a reality." The aim of a treaty was not to establish a new federation but to redistribute the division of powers. The proposal would limit the powers of the federal president and Parliament and would change conditions for joining or seceding from the federation. No further details were provided, but President Havel sent an invitation for a meeting at his country residence at Lány for May 10,[26] presumably to explore the Slovak compromise offer.

In his reflections, written several months later, Havel observed that the idea of an "internal" treaty, designed to serve as a basis for a federal constitution, was slowly gaining the support of the political forces in Slovakia "and even was no longer shocking to the Czechs," as they began to understand the Slovak reasons.

Several times in the past, the coexistence of the Czechs and Slovaks was based on certain written or at least oral understandings—[which] were always broken or not upheld, by the Czech side. The Czechs paid little attention to this; the agreements were forgotten and today only a handful of Czech historians are aware of them. In Slovakia, on the other hand, this history of unkept agreements is still vividly remembered, and it was one source of the calls for a new treaty. This time, the Slovaks wanted an

---

24. ČTK, Apr. 1, 1991. But the chair of the Czech Parliament, Dr. Burešová, is quoted as opposed. ČTK, Apr. 4, 1991.

25. U.S. Constitution, art. 1, sec. 10(3). *See also infra,* chap. IX, 2b.

26. ČTK, May 2, 1991.

112   Czecho/Slovakia

agreement that would be truly binding, one that would be a properly executed, legal act.[27]

At the May 10 meeting with the president in Lány, reacting to the Czech objections of unconstitutionality, Slovak leaders first demanded that the Federal Assembly pass a special constitutional amendment enabling the Republic legislatures to adopt the treaty, which would be binding on the Federal Assembly. The Czechs objected that such an amendment would jeopardize the authority not only of the Federal Assembly but of the federation as a whole. For most of the Czechs, the very idea of a treaty was difficult to contemplate because it would inject a corrosive "confederate element" into the structure. Eventually, however, in what was viewed on the Czech side as a major concession, it was agreed to recommend the adoption of the Plank compromise: legal experts should immediately start working on the text of the Czech and Slovak agreement, which would affirm the will of the citizens of both Republics to live in a common federal state and contain the basic principles of both the constitutional structure and the division of powers.[28] Shortly thereafter, the chair of the Czech National Council, Dr. Dagmar Burešová of the Civic Movement, submitted a draft treaty based on these principles.[29]

b. Who Stands Where for What?

Among Slovak parties, the Plank compromise was supported without reservation at first only by the Public against Violence (whatever was left of it after Mečiar's defection). No spokesman for Mečiar's growing Movement for Democratic Slovakia was present at Lány, and shortly after that meeting the former Slovak international relations minister and deputy chairman of that movement, Milan Kňažko, insisted on a treaty as an international legal document.[30] Mečiar himself, a few weeks after his dismissal from the office of prime minister charged the Czech government with using ultimatums in support of a "rigid" federation. Yet he staunchly defended the 1990 power-allocation law, which Kňažko termed a "cosmetic adjustment."[31] If the Czechs were dismayed at the proposed reopening of the crucial power-allocation issue,

---

27. Václav Havel, Summer Meditations, 43–44. (Alfred A. Knopf, N.Y., 1992)

28. Jiří Pehe, "The State Treaty between the Czech and the Slovak Republics," *supra,* note 2, 11, 13.

29. ČTK, May 17, 1991.

30. ČTK, May 22, 1991. Another MDS representative confirmed in June that the basis of the Federal Constitution must be an international treaty. ČTK, June 12, 1991. The chair of the Slovak National Party Jozef Prokeš, agreed that a "state treaty" must respect Slovakia as an "international legal subject." ČTK, May 3, 1991.

31. ČTK, May 15, 1991; Kňažko, quoted by Czech Prime Minister Pithart, ČTK, Apr. 2, 1991.

many Slovak politicians were visibly angered by the Czech pretense that the 1990 law—in their eyes a hurriedly patched up artifact—should be viewed as the last word on the subject.

In an ambiguous statement, Dr. Čarnogurský, the new Slovak prime minister, spoke of a state treaty to precede a federal constitution, which would express the will of both nations to live in a common *federation* and define the powers delegated by the Republics to the federation.[32] He deplored the Slovak Republic's "weak global standing;" this will be remedied when it joins the European Community where it will be able "to speak for itself."[33] Čarnogurský obviously wanted to distinguish his position from Mečiar's and to support the Lány consensus without alienating the nationalist wing of his party.

The Czech reaction to the Lány understanding, although tentatively positive in some quarters (particularly the president and the "moderate" Civic Forum members), was negative in others. In a public exchange, characteristic of the spirit of the times, Federal Minister of Finance Václav Klaus, then already chair of the rising Civic Democratic Party, told the press that the Czechs were growing impatient with Slovak demands in the current wrangling over the future of the state structure and were fed up with the pretense of preserving the federation.[34] Josef Zieleniec, member of the Klaus party and future Czech minister of foreign affairs, declared at the same press conference that his party would introduce a bill in the Czech Parliament on holding a referendum in the Czech Republic; a referendum would be the only way to decide whether the Czech side should accept a state treaty with Slovakia. He said his party was worried about the direction the talks on the constitution had taken: they turned into roundtables of dozens of politicians, usurping the role of the Parliament. He also criticized the lack of information made available to the public about the talks.[35]

In response—confirming the deep division on the Czech side—a spokesman of the Civic Movement, the "center" of the former Civic Forum, charged that the Civic Democratic Party had apparently started its preelection campaign. He labeled Klaus's statements "irresponsible, hysterical and populistic"; at the present time, he continued, factual attitudes and willingness to compromise were necessary and "not attempts to break what unites us."[36]

---

32. ČTK, May 26, 1991.

33. ČTK, May 31, 1991.

34. "If we are going to draw the line anywhere," Klaus is quoted—"it has to be at this point so that no Slovak politician will be able to get away with such behavior any longer." He rejected as "completely unacceptable" Slovak Prime Minister Čarnogurský's stand that Slovakia intended to remain in the Federation only until such time as Czechoslovakia became part of a united Europe. ČTK, June 12, 1991.

35. Lubor Kynšt in ČTK, June 12, 1991.

36. ČTK, June 14, 1991. Peter Weiss, chair of the Slovak Party of the Democratic Left, is

An added challenge faced in the talks was the sketchy nature of the Plank compromise. The proposal left unanswered some fundamental questions regarding the parties of the proposed internal agreement (the Slovaks continued to speak of a "treaty") and its status under the prevailing federal law, including the controversial demands pressed by the Slovak side at Lány for a constitutional amendment and the ratification of the future federal constitution by the Republic parliaments.

It is important to keep in mind that by that time the dramatic shift in the public support of political groupings was already in full swing. According to an authoritative opinion poll, Václav Klaus's Civic Democratic Party already enjoyed the strongest popular backing in the Czech Republic (17 percent) with the center Civic Movement holding only 7 percent.[37] In Slovakia, Mečiar's opposition Movement for Democratic Slovakia emerged as the dominant force with 38 percent, while the formerly ruling Public against Violence was reduced to a mere 3 percent.[38] The Slovak coalition led by the Christian Democrats, still the strongest force in the Slovak government but in effect a minority in terms of popular support, drifted into increasing conflict with the Slovak National Council.[39] With the political disarray in both Republics and the shift of public and party support away from the victors of the 1990 elections, it was not at all clear who should negotiate with whom for a meaningful agreement.

c. Kroměříž: The President Bows Out (June 1991)

The next meeting in this series was viewed by the president as "of decisive importance for the future of Czechoslovakia."[40] He, too, was concerned that

---

quoted as declaring that time had been wasted by discussing pseudoproblems on the form rather than content of the constitutions. Referring to the impending talks at Kroměříž, he said there were political forces in the Czech Republic that consider it possible to quickly integrate with Germany's economic potential, regardless of possible endangerment of the Czech and Slovak identity. Forces in Slovakia underestimated justified demands for self-determination as well as the consequences of a quick and emotional separation of the two Republics. ČTK, June 11, 1991.

37. The CDA showed no support. The Communist and Christian Democrats appeared stable at 10 percent each, 5 percent for the Movement for Self-Governing Democracy/Society for Moravia and Silesia, and about 5 percent for the Republican (neofascist) party. Prague-based Institute for Public Opinion, in ČTK, June 5, 1991.

38. Slovak Prime Minister Čarnogurský's CDM dropped from 21 to 8 percent, and PDL and the SNP would receive about 15 percent each. Thus, the Slovak government coalition would obtain only 15 percent.

39. For a speculation as to the possible impact of the defection of the PAV deputies to Mečiar's MDS on the Federal Assembly activities, see MFD, summarized in ČTK, May 3, 1991. On alignment of forces in the Federal Assembly, see also ČTK, May 3, 1991.

40. President Havel called still another meeting in the last days of May 1991, at Budmerice near Bratislava in which, according to Dr. Čarnogurský, for the first time representatives of the

the ability of both sides involved to reach an agreement was decreasing and stressed the importance of elaborating the constitution before the June 1992 elections.[41] The talks were held on June 17, 1991, in the historic town of Kroměříž. This time—for the first time—representatives of a broad spectrum of opposition parties were included. The locale was an ominous portent since it was to this Moravian backwater that the hapless Austrian "constitutional" Parliament was relegated during the 1848 revolution: the constitution drafted by that Parliament was never applied.

At the outset of the meeting, the president distributed a questionnaire in which the participants were to mark each of the 19 questions with a yes or no and sign at the end.[42] The document was prepared with some sophistication by professor Vladimír Klokočka, consultant to the president. It was designed to elicit the views on the major open issues relating to both the status of the projected treaty and to the power allocation. Although the experts present did their best to explain the document, most participants, particularly on the Slovak side, with little background in constitutional and international law, were baffled by the complexity of the options and by the unfamiliar concepts.

The tally of the answers offered little comfort to the president. In the first place, representatives of some major political groupings, such as Mečiar's Movement for a Democratic Slovakia, the Slovak Party of the Democratic Left (PDL), and the rising Czech Civic Democratic Party of Václav Klaus, failed to respond to a number of questions. Thus, while a majority voted against a "looser, for instance, confederate" tie between the two Republics, the members of the two dominant movements in Slovakia, the Christian Democrats (CDM) and Mečiar's MDS, along with the Slovak Greens (a minuscule party represented in the National Council), were in favor. Although only the Slovak National Party (SNP) "orally" supported a dissolution, the PDL failed to take a stand even on this issue or the question of terminating "the international continuity" of the existing state.

For better or for worse, one outcome of the exercise was the first articulation, in the form of questions, of the issues regarding the status and implementation of the treaty, which were left wide open by the Plank compromise:

1. Should the two National Councils be the parties to conclude the treaty and present it to the Federal Assembly in the form of a "legislative

---

parliamentary opposition were to take part, a condition he thought was necessary. ČTK, May 29, 1991. Spokesmen for the opposition SNP, who apparently also participated, noted thereafter an increasing effort to solve the problem of Slovakia's future regardless of the stance of the majority of Slovaks and criticized the government for preventing the opposition's role. ČTK, May 31, 1991.

41. ČTK, June 16, 1991.

42. Slovak text of the questionnaire in L. Kubín *et al.*, *Dva roky politickej slobody* [Two Years of Political Freedom] 105–7 (RaPaMaN, Bratislava, 1992). The text of the questions and answers was made available to me.

initiative" (as proposed by the Czech side) or should the parties to a "state treaty" be the two existing Republics? What, if any, would be the status of the Republics in international law?

2. Would the treaty bind the Federal Assembly, if not under international law then under internal public law (as demanded by the Slovak Christian Democrats but opposed by a number of participants on the Czech side)?

3. Would such a treaty be normatively superior to the federal constitution? With the Czechs opposed or abstaining, the Slovak Christian Democrats were in favor.

4. Was it necessary for the Federal Assembly first to adopt a constitutional law empowering the two councils to negotiate such a treaty, which would bind the Assembly itself when writing the federal constitution? The Czech side was concerned that this would undermine the constitutional position of the Federal Assembly.

5. Must the federal constitution contain a clause providing that before the treaty came into effect it must be ratified by the two National Councils? Here the division was almost entirely along national lines, the Slovaks voting in the affirmative while the Czechs were against or abstained. Later on, the Slovak side expanded the demand for ratification by the National Councils to cover not only the constitution itself but any subsequent amendments as well.

These complex issues, in addition to assuming more than a casual acquaintance with the underlying law, called for a liberal, goal-oriented interpretation of the constitutional texts and for a modern approach to such concepts as "sovereignty" and "international personality" lest the negotiations become drowned in a quagmire of abstruse legal argumentation, susceptible to abuse for political aims.

No written record was made of this important round of talks, and not much information became available at the time. The federal and Republic governments' participants made a concerted effort to take a positive view of the outcome. President Havel said in his regular Sunday broadcast that the talks were long and complicated but did yield a result.[43] What was the result?

First, with the exception of the Slovak National Party the participants agreed that the "common state" should continue.[44] This term insinuated itself into the political rhetoric of the day only to obfuscate further the already murky constitutional discourse in which the terms *actual federation, functional federation,* and *confederation* had been bandied about as empty labels. Accord-

---

43. ČTK, June 23, 1991. To similar effect, *see,* Federal Deputy Prime Minister Rychetský, deputy chair of the Civic Movement, ČTK, June 21, 1991.

44. Dr. Rychetský, *ibid.*

ing to Czech Prime Minister Pithart, only the spokesman for the Slovak National Party openly opposed the idea of a federation, but the Slovak Greens expressed serious reservations and Mečiar's movement "had fewer reservations."[45] Yet a few days after the talks Mečiar spoke of a confederation or a "union,"[46] Ján Čarnogurský's Slovak Christian Democratic Movement envisaged a federation (albeit with some confederation elements),[47] and the Public against Violence saw a consensus on a federation and was opposed to a confederation as leading to a breakup.[48]

Second, substantial disagreements continued on the allocation of powers problem.[49]

Third, according to Michael Žantovský, the president's spokesman, agreement was reached on the president's proposal for a Federal Council, a new constitutional organ designed to replace the upper chamber and appointed by the Republic parliaments, and only the Christian Democratic groups opposed the president's proposal for a referendum as the only way of deciding about a possible breakup of the state.[50]

Fourth, it was agreed that there should be a treaty (*not* based on international law) the nature of which remained to be clarified, but the Slovak idea for a special constitutional law to empower the Republics to conclude it was dropped.

Fifth, despite the negative posture in the questionnaire, most of the Czech spokesmen accepted the Slovak claim for a ratification of the new federal constitution by the National Councils.[51]

Finally, and here the consensus proved real, the method and forum of the constitutional negotiations were to change. Instead of the behind-closed-doors

---

45. ČTK, June 24, 1991.

46. ČTK, June 22, 1991; ČTK, June 26, 1991. Commenting on the meeting in general, Czech Prime Minister Pithart observed "a certain inconsistency and fickleness of views" from the Slovak side, citing as one example the responses to questions concerning the Federation, which made any talks harder. ČTK, June 25, 1991. Mečiar, in another skirmish with Pithart, rejected the latter's view that his MDS was not well prepared for the meeting: in fact the Movement was the only participant to submit an alternative scheme worked out on the basis of European principles and standards. The Slovak premier Dr. Čarnogurský also complained that Mečiar's Movement was "an unreliable discussion partner" because it constantly changed its views: it will be the task of the Slovak Parliament to formulate a united stand of the Slovak side. ČTK, June 21, 1991.

47. ČTK, June 20, 1991.

48. ČTK, June 19, 1991; ČTK, June 27, 1991.

49. Dr. Rychetský reported that railways, roads, communications as well as energy and finances remained in dispute. ČTK, June 21, 1991. Similarly, Prime Minister Čalfa blamed some participants for taking extreme positions. ČTK, June 21, 1991.

50. ČTK, June 18, 1991. The two Republic parliaments were to appoint commissions to draft a treaty, and the three constitutions were to be completed before the June 1992 elections. *Ibid.*

51. The information in the fourth and fifth points is based on the record of the meeting at Hrádeček, *infra,* chap. VII, 3c, note 48, SL 9 (Dubček), 15 (Pithart), 22, 25, 28 (Havel).

talks of political leaders umpired by the president, the two Republic parliaments should reach an agreement on a treaty that would serve as a new foundation for the constitution of "the common state."[52] Although he was at the time a prominent member of the federal government, Finance Minister Václav Klaus took a different view of the proper forum for the negotiations: the "roundtable" form was useful as an exception, but now the time had come to return the negotiations to the parliamentary forum of the Federal Assembly because the voters might fear with some justification that the legitimately elected Parliament was being bypassed; the optimistic communiqués concealed serious conflicts and the public should be told the truth; and thus far only procedural matters—"no serious questions"—were involved and not a word was said about the type of taxes, the disaggregation of pipelines—"and this was right because these real matters of competence should be solved by experts."[53]

d. On Negotiation Forums and Tactics

Several interesting questions bearing upon the methodology of negotiations may be identified. The decision to change the forum by shifting the responsibility to the Republics was hailed at the time as a step in the right direction. Yet two years later several prominent participants told me that they considered it "catastrophic" because it entailed bringing in the opposition parties represented in the legislative bodies. However, with the rapidly changing political constellation and the Slovak government coalition losing support, I wonder whether negotiating without the opposition would have held out any promise. I may add, in anticipation of the further course of events, that, contrary to what presumably was to be a two-party process, the members of the federal government continued their involvement, almost invariably in support of the Czech side.

Again, one might ask about the utility of the questionnaire technique in a multi-issue, essentially two-party negotiation with multiple, diverse representation on both sides. In theory, at any rate, this may appear a simple, useful device for assessing the range of views and interests involved and—as a minimum—for framing the issues and educating the less knowledgeable. Yet in practice the players are likely to be less inclined to take a position in writing without being aware of the other side's stance; and even if they do so they are less likely to make concessions than in an oral bargaining context.[54] One factor

---

52. ČTK, June 20, 1991.

53. MFD, June 17, 1991, p. 3.

54. Meeting in Bratislava on June 19, 1991, the Slovak National Council took notice of its chair's report on the Kroměříž discussions, and it viewed its conclusions as a starting point for a further course. These conclusions were: the two National Councils representing the two Republics

hindering the course of the negotiations was the failure of regular communication at the staff level in between the confabulations of the "principals." The staff of each delegation did the preparatory work, but they did not exchange information and views in advance of the meetings of the politicians, "who wanted to do all the negotiating by themselves."[55]

Finally, the legal expert did what experts are expected to do: he accepted as his political premise the Plank compromise and unfolded the options open to the decision makers. But this approach overestimated the level of sophistication of his audience and complicated the subsequent negotiations immensely.

When I passed through Prague shortly after the Kroměříž meeting, I was given to understand that one purpose of this last of the series of talks (on the Czech "federal" side at any rate) was to extricate the president from what appeared to be an increasingly disheartening enterprise and pass the direct responsibility for the constitutional negotiations to others.[56]

5. A Side Issue: Moravia-Silesia

The constitutional negotiations were complicated further by the rising calls for more autonomy in Moravia and Silesia. As I mentioned earlier, although the Czech and Moravian-Silesian regions have the same language and practically the same culture and religious traditions (the Catholic Church is somewhat stronger in Moravia), they nevertheless have a historical identity of their own and their autonomous status was abolished only by the Communist government in 1949.[57] Of the several proposals advanced, the most radical one would have Moravia and Silesia form a third component republic in the federal state; other alternatives were to turn them into one or two autonomous lands on an equal footing with the Czech land and possibly also the city of Prague, or, finally, to organize the Czech Republic generally into a number of autonomous districts.

The most radical "federal" solution was advocated by the Movement for Self-Governing Democracy/Society for Moravia and Silesia (MSD-SMS)

---

will adopt a treaty that the Federal Assembly will accept as the foundation for creating the federal constitution; and the federal constitution shall become effective upon ratification by the two National Councils and provision for such ratification will be secured by a federal constitutional law. The Council also noted the proposal for a Slovak constitution prepared by the commission appointed by its Presidium and the Slovak government; it discharged the commission and established a new Commission for the preparation of a common proposal for a Slovak constitution. The National Council also took notice of the proposed Declaration of Slovak Sovereignty. L. Kubín et al., *supra,* note 42, 107–9.

55. Conversation with V. Žák.

56. Conversation with P. Rychetský.

57. Jiří Pehe, "The First Weeks of 1991: Problems Solved, Difficulties Arise," RFE/RL Res. Rep., Mar. 8, 1991, 5 at 9; *see generally,* Jan Obrman, "The Issue of Autonomy for Moravia and Silesia," RFE/RL Res. Rep., Apr. 12, 1991, 13–22.

which was represented in both the Federal Assembly and the Czech National Council; it was joined by other regional groups and claimed (without any basis in reality) to represent the overwhelming majority of the people in the area.[58]

The Czech National Council, where the various proposals were debated, postponed the topic indefinitely. As a result, the MSD-SMS Party pulled out of the Czech government and on February 19, 1991, its deputies walked out of the National Council not to return until late that month. Demonstrations in major Moravian towns—50,000 reported in Brno—protested "discrimination" and demanded a "fair" portion of the budget and a tripartite federation.[59] The deputy chair of the Czech National Council, Kalvoda, called such demands irrational—"a step back, against the trend towards integration of Europe."[60]

A federation composed of three republics of approximately the same size ("Czechia," Moravia-Silesia, and Slovakia) would obviate the particular handicaps inherent in a two-component system. However, as confirmed by Federal Prime Minister Marián Čalfa, it would run into objections in Slovakia. "Slovaks would probably consider that by elevating Moravia and Silesia to a republic, their own status as a nation had been degraded," since the people in the two regions could not be considered by any rational criteria a separate nation or nations.[61]

President Havel changed his mind several times.[62] In February 1991, both he and Czech Prime Minister Pithart expressed tentative support for the tripartite structure, but they abandoned the idea in the face of the Slovak opposition. The Czech Christian Democratic leaders favored the tripartite federal solution, but most other politicians reacted cautiously.[63] The dominant Civic Forum advocated regional autonomy and blocked any vote in the Czech National Council.

One can readily understand why the majority in the Czech National Council was unwilling to continue the debate on this issue despite the clamorous voices from Moravia and Silesia: any proposal for a change in the federal structure would inject a new controversy into the already conflicting relationship with the Slovaks, and at any rate it would fall within the competence of the Federal Assembly rather than the Czech National Council. Yet the ghost of this

---

58. ČTK, Feb. 3, 1991; ČTK, Apr. 8, 1991.

59. ČTK, Mar. 2, 1991.

60. ČTK, Feb. 3, 1991.

61. Ján Čarnogurský thought that a tripartite federation might be acceptable only if Czechoslovakia were transformed into a confederation in which the possibility of two Republics outvoting the third did not exist. Jan Obrman, "The Issue of Autonomy for Moravia and Silesia," *supra*, note 57, 18.

62. LN, Mar. 15, 1993, p. 8.

63. ČTK, Feb. 6, 7, 28, 1991; ČTK, Apr. 22, 23, 1991.

controversy would return less than two years later to haunt the freshly born Czech state.

6. An Interlude: Bratislava and Prague in Spring 1991

The joint meeting in Bratislava that I describe in annex I was my first visit to the Slovak capital. Although Bratislava was the capital of Hungary from 1541 to 1784, my impression was of a cozy, provincial city with an Eastern flavor. I noticed few signs of a transformation and hardly any tourists. At the center, I passed a number of handsome baroque or neoclassic town houses and palaces, but a part of the old town had been destroyed by the former regime's bridge construction.

The international group was housed in the Bôrik Hotel, an ungainly structure situated in an ideal location high on a hill overlooking the Danube. It was built in "Moscow-style" luxury for the party nomenclature and its guests, such as Secretary Brezhnev. My suite with large glass panels opened on a wide view across the river deep into the pleasing Austrian landscape. Later on, Bôrik was to be the scene of some crucial phases in the Czech-Slovak negotiations.

The international meetings kept me occupied at the hotel except for one brief excursion. I was driven a few miles out of the city to the dramatic ruin of the castle Devín, built on a high cliff precipitating into the Danube. It originated in the first century B.C., was rebuilt in the thirteenth century, and was destroyed by Napoleon's soldiers in 1809. A memory from early school days evoked the tale of the legendary prince Svatopluk, the lord of the Great Moravian Realm, which included parts of the Czech lands. The prince, so went the story, on his deathbed warned his sons against disunity, a warning that, alas, they disregarded with fatal consequences for the "common state."

At a reception offered by the newly appointed Slovak minister of international relations, whom I mentioned earlier, several members of the Hungarian minority, all with strong federalist views, were concerned about the drift of the constitutional negotiations. I was struck by the intensity of their concern about "being left alone with the Slovaks."

On my way home, I stopped briefly in Prague. I had a long talk with the chief of the section on treaties and international law at the Federal Foreign Affairs Ministry in the cavernous Černín Palace. There I was shown the window from which Jan Masaryk, the last chief diplomat of the democratic Republic, fell to his death in the wake of the 1948 Communist takeover. In the quiet courtyard submerged in afternoon sun, I recalled that during my days with the U.S. Department of State I had interviewed Masaryk's personal physician, his novelist friend Marsha Davenport, and others in an unsuccessful effort to learn more about the mystery of his death.

With the first round of privatization in progress, the city bristled with new shops next to vacant premises. The first waves of tourists, young and old, crowded the streets, about to turn into a veritable flood. Some of the stately, nineteenth-century bourgeois houses along the wide, sparkling Vltava River had already been tastefully restored, while many were still badly run-down. A massive Lenin statue had vanished, and in a frenzy of removing reminders of the old regime Lenin Street had become Europe Avenue. The attractive modern structure on the river where we used to meet as students in the popular coffee house Mánes was in a wretched state of neglect. But the nearby newly spruced up National Theater was in full operation with an ambitious international program. The theaters still played to full houses, but tourists supplied a major part of the audience. The "locals," occupied by daily worries and watching their budgets warily, found diversion in the new political life and on television.

The euphoria of a year ago was rapidly dissipating in the face of rising prices and economic uncertainty. With political freedom now taken for granted, concern for the future was the prevalent state of mind.

In the higher governmental circles, I sensed a growing skepticism regarding a possible understanding with the Slovaks.

VII

Slouching toward Bethlehem[1]
(Summer–Fall 1991)

1. The Darkening Sky

A series of extraneous events impinged upon the attitude of the negotiators although the impact could not be gauged with any degree of precision.

— The initial opposition of the European and U.S. governments to a fragmentation in former Yugoslavia and the outbreak of violence there strengthened the supporters of the common state.[2] The reversal of the stance of the international community and the prompt recognition of the new states carved out of Yugoslav territory was invoked by the Slovaks, including Dr. Čarnogurský and Vladimír Mečiar, as a precedent in support of the Slovak claims.[3]

— In May 1991, the Czech National Council in a closed session debated the so-called catastrophic scenario, a program to be applied in case of a dissolution of the federation. This evoked expressions of surprise in Slovakia where, it was asserted, no such alternative had ever been discussed.[4]

— Federal politicians were infuriated by a proposal for the establishment of a Slovak Home Defense, which was tentatively favored by Prime

---

1. With a bow to W.B. Yeats, "The Second Coming."
2. The poll by the weekly *Reflex* reported a drop in the percentage of those opposed to a federation when the fighting in Yugoslavia began, ČTK, July 8, 1991. PAV Council Chair Kučerák spoke of the situation in Yugoslavia as a "grave warning." ČTK, July 8, 1991.
3. ČTK, July 3, 1991 (Mečiar); NO, July 29, 1991, p. 13, in FBIS-EEU–91–147, July 31, 1991, p. 17 (Mečiar); RFE/RL RES. REP., 27 July 5, 1991, 51 (Čarnogurský). But *see* Jan Obrman, "Yugoslav Crisis Has Little Impact on Czechoslovak Politics," RFE/RL RES. REP., Aug. 9, 1991, p. 29.
4. ČTK, May 23, 1991; May 24, 199. Vladimír Mečiar thought the debate "seems to be the continuation of the policy of reluctance to partnership with Slovakia" and called for "adequate reaction." ČTK, May 24, 1991. *See,* on the origin of the "scenario," *supra,* chap. IV, 2d.

Minister Čarnogurský. The proposal failed in the Slovak National Council.[5]

— When Alexander Dubček of "Prague spring" fame, who was viewed as a significant moderating influence in Slovakia, resigned from the Public against Violence, a number of Czech party leaders, including Dr. Kalvoda of the CDA, called for his resignation from the post of chair of the Federal Assembly—and this caused bitterness across political lines in his native Slovakia, where he enjoyed wide popularity. Dubček, although he was elected on the PAV list, refused to resign his post. A few months later, he became a victim of a fatal automobile accident.[6]

— When President Havel came to Bratislava to take part in a rally in celebration of the anniversary of the founding of Czechoslovakia in 1918, he was prevented from speaking by a group shouting for an independent Slovakia. After about a minute, Havel left the tribune without a word. The Slovak leaders uniformly condemned the behavior. There was evidence, however, that the incident hardened the attitude of some of the influential presidential advisors whom the Slovaks accused—probably with some justification—of harboring anti-Slovak sentiments.[7]

— It is difficult to estimate the influence of the emigré organizations in Slovak politics, but the World Slovak Congress was reported to be close to the Movement for Democratic Slovakia, and in August 1991 it appealed to Slovaks not to miss the historic opportunity for freedom and "state sovereignty."[8]

— There were statements to the press, domestic and foreign, and "counterstatements adding to the deteriorating atmosphere."[9] When Pres-

---

5. ČTK, July 24, 1991. But *see* Ján Čarnogurský's ambiguous position in ČTK, July 25, 1991. *See* Jiří Pehe, "Controversy Over the Referendum on the Future of Czechoslovakia," RFE/RL RES. REP., Aug. 30, 1991, 27, 28.

6. For example, calling for Dubček's resignation, František Houska, chairman of the Czech CDP's deputies club in the Federal Assembly. ČTK, July 24, 1991. Similarly, the CDA. In opposition to resignation, CM, the Czech Communist Party, the Czech Christian parties, the Social Democrats, and the Movement for Self-governing Democracy—Society for Moravia and Silesia. ČTK, July 24, 1991.

7. ČTK, Oct. 28, 1991.

8. *See,* for example, ČTK, June 12, 1991; and ČTK, Aug. 29, 1991.

9. Dr. Čarnogurský in the French daily *Liberation* sees an independent Slovak state as inevitable around 2000, although "my attitude is more progressive and more European. I am not an ally of the Slovak nationalists." ČTK, July 22, 1991. Federal Prime Minister Čalfa saw "Czechoslovakia's future entirely different," warning that a "state entity such as the Slovak Republic or the Czech Republic has no chance of survival . . . with the neighbors it has . . ." ČTK, July 23, 1991. Another Slovak, MDS Deputy Chair Michal Kováč, agreed with Čarnogurský's aim, but "if it is to be realized the two Republics must become the subjects of international law already now." ČTK, July 24, 1991. If Čarnogurský's view prevails, said František Houska, chair of the CDP's club of

ident Havel's spokesman referred to the danger of a "revival of the ideas of National Socialism" in Slovakia, the *Economist* observed that "even sensible people are finding it hard to keep a sense of proportion."[10] The Czech and Slovak press gave all these skirmishes the fullest coverage, often with comments fanning the more or less hidden resentments on both sides.

— Slovak nationalists gained control of the most important cultural association, Matica, which joined the Slovak National Party in calling for "the adoption of the Declaration of Sovereignty and a new Slovak constitution" of a "sovereign state"—a subject of international law.[11] In September 1991, 30,000 people demonstrated in Bratislava for Slovak "sovereignty" while 3,000 to 5,000 met in response to a call for a common state.[12]

— Another controversy flared up when Prime Minister Čarnogurský and František Mikloško, the chair of the Slovak Parliament, objected to the reference in the pending federal treaty with Germany to "a legal continuity" of the Czechoslovak state since 1918. They claimed that the Slovak Nazi puppet state was created in 1939 in accordance with the Czechoslovak Constitution, thus breaking the "continuity." This claim, denied by the Institute of State and Law of the Czechoslovak Academy of Sciences, revived old wounds and caused a furor on the Czech side.[13]

— There was little airing of the potentially adverse consequences, particularly any economic damage from a dissolution of the federation. Ján Čarnogurský, at the time Slovak prime minister, questioned the assertion of the federal foreign trade minister, Jozef Bakšay, that an independent Slovakia would need thousands of millions of crowns to pay for its defense, customs, and diplomatic services, and he observed that money was not an issue in the establishment of an independent state.[14]

— In a September 1991 public opinion poll in Slovakia, more than half

---

Federal Assembly deputies, "the only thing we can recommend is a quick separation." ČTK, July 24, 1991. In an attack on the Slovak government, Mečiar said that "if the [Slovak] government is changed we are capable of obtaining German credits of up to 9,000 million deutsche marks, a sum almost equal to the Slovak budget." ČTK, Aug. 7, 1991. This statement was generally ridiculed by the Czechs. Dr. Pavel Rychetský, deputy chair of the federal government, told the press that "a fundamental break occurred in Czech-Slovak relations in the past five months. In the Czech public, this break was apparently caused by the expressions of Slovak separatism and nationalism." ČTK, June 7, 1991.

10. THE ECONOMIST, Mar. 18, 1991, p. 45.
11. ČTK, June 8, 1991.
12. ČTK, Sept. 19, 1991.
13. ČTK, Sept. 20, 1991.
14. ČTK, Sept. 23 and Sept. 27, 1991.

of the respondents supported "a federation" (without any specification), 18 percent were for independence, 11 percent for a unitary common state, 8 percent preferred the *current* form of federation, and the same percentage supported "a confederation." A full third backed Vladimír Mečiar's Movement for Democratic Slovakia, with Prime Minister Čarnogurský's Christian Democrats claiming a mere 9 percent, the PAV suffering a sharp drop from 13 percent in May to just 4 percent, the Slovak National Party 10 percent, and the Party of the Democratic Left 12 percent.[15]

— In an October 1991 poll, 40 percent of Slovaks wanted radical economic reforms changed or stopped and more than 50 percent of the Czech Republic inhabitants thought the reforms were going well.[16]

— In the summer of 1991, 60 percent of Slovaks were said to believe that the Czechs "received preferential treatment" in the federation while 48 percent of Czechs and 34 percent of Moravians thought that the Slovaks were preferred.[17]

Whatever reservations one might harbor toward opinion polls, in this case they signaled confusion among the Slovaks over the preferred form of the common state, a strong disagreement with the Czechs over vital economic policy, and a decline in the perceived value of coexistence.

2. The Referendum Law Adopted

In one instance, the federal legislators did respond to the president's urgent appeal and—in July 1991—adopted a law on referendum that he had urged as an ultimate means for resolving fundamental constitutional issues, including the question of continuation of the common state.[18] According to the new law, the president was to call a referendum if one was proposed by the Federal Assembly or by one or both of the National Councils. If more than 50 percent of the voters in either of the two Republics voted to secede, the federal Republic would cease to exist within a year.

Unhappily and contrary to the expectations of its proponents, the law— rather than opening an opportunity for a way out of the deadlock—added still one more cause of discord. As soon as the law was adopted, support for an

---

15. ČTK, Sept. 18, 1991.

16. Weekly Record of Events, RFE/RL RES. REP., Oct. 4, 1991, p. 39.

17. ČTK, July 30, 1991.

18. Const. Law on Referendum of 18 July 1991, 327/1991 Sb.; Jiří Pehe, "Controversy over the Referendum on the Future of Czechoslovakia," RFE/RL RES. REP., Aug. 30, 1991, 27–30; Jindřiška Syllová, "Celostátní referendum—instrumentální institut [All-state Referendum—an Instrumental Institution]," 2/1992 PRÁVNÍK 105.

early referendum was voiced across the entire political spectrum in the Czech Republic; in Slovakia, on the contrary, only the dwindling profederalist Public against Violence and the minuscule Social Democratic Party joined early in the support.[19] The reason why the Slovak nationalists were opposed was quite obvious: even the chair of the Slovak National Party, Jozef Prokeš, while advocating independence, admitted at a press conference that a referendum would show the majority in favor of a federation.[20] Also opposed—for quite a different reason—was Alexander Dubček, who shortly before had resigned from the PAV. He pointed out that no Slovak party, with the single exception of the Slovak National Party, had independence in its program. Christian Democratic leader Dr. Čarnogurský did not favor a referendum because not all possibilities of talks had been exhausted.[21] In contrast with the Slovak stance, the Czech Civic Movement announced that it would initiate the process for holding a referendum in the next session of the Parliament.[22] The federal foreign affairs minister, Jiří Dienstbier, chair of the Czech Civic Movement, thought that if the will for a continued existence of a common state were shown in a referendum, "any speculations on gaining political capital from the power-sharing disputes will be ruled out."[23]

By the end of October 1991, more than half a million Czechs and Slovaks signed an "appeal from citizens" for an early referendum, which was initiated by Pavel Tigrid, a close friend and advisor to the president.[24] President Havel himself called for prompt adoption of the legislation implementing the law on referendum, and he repeatedly urged an early call for it.[25] In a nationwide poll, 78 percent in the Czech Republic and 66 percent in Slovakia supported such a call, and ultimately the number of signatures on the appeal for a referendum reached more than two million.[26] Yet—as we shall see—only a few weeks later the drive for a referendum foundered on the rocks of the Federal Assembly's indecision.

---

19. ČTK, Aug. 16, 1991 (chair of the Slovak Social Democrats, Boris Zala).

20. ČTK, Aug. 14, 1991.

21. ČTK, Sept. 22, 1991; ČTK, Aug. 11, 1991.

22. ČTK, Aug. 10, 1991.

23. ČTK, Aug. 9, 1991. On the position of the MDS, *see* ČTK, Aug. 14, 1991. MDS Deputy Roman Zelenay said it would be incorrect raising the referendum issue in the Parliament "without prior public discussion."

24. Jiří Pehe, "Bid for Slovak Sovereignty Causes Political Upheaval," RFE/RL RES. REP., Oct. 11, 1991, 10, 12.

25. The Federal Assembly adopted the law on the procedure for carrying out a referendum, 490/1991 Sb. of November 6, 1991. The president proposed a referendum in the Federal Assembly on September 24, 1991. ČSTK, Nov. 25, 1991.

26. ČSTK, Nov. 15, 1991; ČSTK, Dec. 5, 1991.

3. The Republic Legislatures Take Over: New Bottles—
Old Wine (September–November 1991)

a. In Bratislava: Some Progress?

After the summer holidays, as agreed in Kroměříž, the presidia of the two
Republic National Councils assumed the responsibility for the negotiations.
There were four principal meetings, the first in Bratislava, on September 5
and 6.[27] Ivan Čarnogurský, brother of Ján and deputy chair of the Slovak
National Council, opened with a *tour-d'horizon* of the problem areas ranged
in ten points,[28] whereupon all participants were invited to state the basic
views of their respective political parties or movements. On the Slovak side,
only the Slovak National Party advocated separation "by constitutional process," but a deep division appeared between the PAV and some small parties advocating a federation and Mečiar's MDS supporting a confederation.
Even the spokesman of the coalition Christian Democratic Movement would
place "economic instruments in the hands of the Republic governments" and
suggested the European Community as a model. Doc. Fogaš of the Democratic
Left suggested the adoption of a constitutional law on a new constitutional
system.[29]

On the Czech side, all party spokesmen, ranging from Kalvoda's CDA to
the Communist Party, echoed in more or less specific terms the Civic Forum
position articulated by Dr. Burešová in support of a federation and in opposition to any confederate form, which—the lady warned—would cause succession problems internationally and difficulties in property allocation internally.
The order of the adoption of the Czech-Slovak treaty and the three new constitutions was discussed inconclusively, and a referendum was mentioned as an
ultimate solution, with a warning that time was running out if the constitutional
issue was to be kept out of the next election campaign.

The decision was made to divide the participants into two groups, economic and constitutional. At the center of the debate in the "constitutional"
group was the issue left open at Kroměříž regarding the legal nature of the
proposed treaty, the Slovaks insisting again that it must legally bind the Federal
Assembly and the Czechs claiming that the Republics could do nothing more
than to offer the treaty as a legislative initiative to the Assembly.[30] The two

27. Original corrected record (untitled) in the Library of the Czech Parliament.
28. *Ibid.*, 6–11.
29. *Ibid.*, 18.
30. This section is based on "Stenograficky záznam rokovania skupiny predsednictiev ČNR
a SNR pre ústavnoprávne otázky dňa 5. septembra 1991 v Bratislave, Příloha II [Stenographic
Record of the Deliberations of the Group of the Presidia of the CNC and SNC for Constitutional

experts in attendance advised—in line with the prevalent formalistic approach to constitutional interpretation—that the Slovak demand would raise constitutional objections. The Czech expert agreed that the current Constitution would have to be changed by a constitutional law, which Dr. Burešová felt had no chance of adoption in the Federal Parliament.[31] A confused debate followed regarding the limits of the powers of component states in a federation.[32] In a revealing contre-temps, Ivan Čarnogurský challenged Dr. Kalvoda's suggestion made earlier that, in view of the deadlock, the state should be dissolved and thereafter the two Republics might explore appropriate new ties. The breakup, according to Čarnogurský, although not "a terrible thing," would be inappropriate for psychological, economic, and cultural reasons.[33]

In a joint communiqué[34] issued after the Bratislava meeting, the two presidia agreed "on the continuity of the Czech and Slovak Federative Republic" and on adhering to the "constitutional processes." Yet the statement only hinted at the diametrical difference in the interpretation of these concepts. The Slovak side "does not consider the present federation . . . as final," and in the preparation of the constitution "it will pursue the principle of sovereignty of the Slovak Republic." The Czech side viewed the negotiations "as a continuation of the Kroměříž agreements" and "considers as most fundamental an agreement on the preservation of the continuity of the ČSFR and of the constitutional processes." The presidia exchanged their positions on the division of competences. Both sides agreed on the need for "a common economic space" to be further specified and on the creation of expert commissions on the allocation of competencies in various sectors, which would take into account also "the international contexts." A treaty should contain a common proposal for a constitution, which was to be ratified by the National Councils (a reaffir-

Questions of September 5, 1991, in Bratislava, Annex II]" in the Library of the Czech Republic Parliament.

31. Prof. Dušan Hendrych, *ibid.,* II/62, II/28. The Slovak expert, Professor K. Plank, suggested that under the prevailing Constitution only a "law" but not "a treaty" could be made the subject of a legislative initiative from the Republics. *Ibid.,* II/34.

32. It was this time Dr. Burešová, chair of the Czech National Council, who attempted to redirect the debate toward the concrete issues of allocation of powers.

33. It would bring out "certain passions" of antipathy between the two nations and impair long-term cultural and economic ties (II/1–5). During the debate on allocation of competences, the Czech side was said to have pressed for federal powers over pricing, social, and wage policies. ČTK, Sept. 5, 1991. No record appears available of the proceedings in the economic group.

34. For the text of the communiqué, see the stenographic record of the working committee of the presidia of the Czech and Slovak National Councils for the elaboration of the closing communiqué, Bratislava, Sept. 6, 1991, 32–33, in the Library of the Czech Republic Parliament. After a difficult discussion the text was approved for the Slovak Presidium by a vote of 12 for, four against, and three abstentions, while for the Czech Presidium the vote was 21 for, one against, and one abstention. The text is in the Library of the Czech Parliament. *See also* ČTK, Sept. 5, 1991; Sept. 6, 1991.

mation of the Czech concession in Kroměříž), and the current Constitution was to be amended to make this possible. All the basic instruments were to be completed by the end of the year.[35] President Havel, who had just returned from "a working visit" to Slovakia, hailed the results achieved at Bratislava.

The Bratislava encounter brought into relief the changing political scene, particularly the growing rift within both the PAV and the Christian Democratic Movement, the principal groups that had endorsed the Bratislava "conclusions." Important factions of both movements were turning toward ex-premier Mečiar's party, the MDS, which in a public opinion poll was supported by a full third of the Slovaks.[36] Mečiar, once the enthusiastic federalist, now shifted his position toward "a confederation." He skillfully capitalized on the disarray

---

35. Ľ. Kubín et al., Dva roky politickej slobody [Two Years of Political Freedom] 111 (RaPaMaN, Bratislava, 1992). Federal Premier Marián Čalfa did not agree with the Czech view on timing: "There is no deadline limiting our negotiations . . . we must talk until absolutely every possibility is exhausted." ČSTK, Nov. 3, 1991. This is a rather rare instance of disagreement between the spokesmen of the Czech Republic and the Federation. On the fall negotiations generally, see Jan Obrman, "Further Discussions on the Future of the Federation," RFE/RL RES. REP., Sept. 20, 1991, 6, 8–10; and Jiří Pehe, "Czech and Slovak Leaders Deadlocked over Country's Future," RFE/RL RES. REP., 1 Nov. 28, 1991, 7–9, 11–13. At the conclusion of the conference, Chair Mikloško, a leading member of the PAV, declared that only Mečiar's MDS did not favor a federation, insisting on a confederation, while the SNP called for independence. Mikloško, a deeply religious Catholic, "during his audience with the Pope allegedly obtained a papal blessing for his idea for the Slovak nation to become a bridge to the Russian Orthodox Church." ČTK, Sept. 11, 1991, quoting ZM of Sept. 11, 1991. On the basic constitutional problems, see Mikloško and Jičínský in NO, Sept. 23, 1991, p. 3.

36. In an opinion poll, contrary to the increased popularity of the MDS, the PAV suffered a sharp drop from 13 to just 4 percent, the Christian Democrats to 9 percent, 12 percent for the PDL and 10 percent for the SNP. ČTK, Sept. 18, 1991. Ivan Čarnogurský predicted that a bill for Slovak independence would go through the Slovak National Council in October. Ibid. Two other parties in the Slovak government, the Democratic Party and the Hungarian Independent Initiative, supported the Federation. ČSTK, Oct. 4, 1991. The leading Christian Democratic Party was said to be splitting into three factions: the first, led by Prime Minister Čarnogurský; the second represented by Ján Klepáč, deputy chair of the Slovak National Council; and the third "steered from a distance by some high-ranking leaders of the Catholic Church." The second and third factions criticized the Čarnogurský's faction for "excessively soft attitudes" toward Prague and wanted Slovak independence. These groups were close to Mečiar's movement and like it "are linked by a similar geopolitical orientation—toward the East. . . . The Christian Democrat Movement . . . is based on moral and spiritual and anti-Western values, while the orientation of the MDS is based on the Slovak (armaments) industry lobby, which would like to return to the bottomless Soviet market . . ." Mečiar would like to detach the Čarnogurský brothers from the CDM and "create a grand coalition with them." The Czech farmers' daily ZN, Sept. 11, 1991, summarized in ČTK, Sept. 11, 1991. At the time, formally, in the 150 member Slovak National Council, the CDM held 31 seats, the PAV 24, and the MDS 19. Ibid.

Alexander Dubček, Jiří Dienstbier, and Pavel Rychetský spoke in support of the Bratislava result. ČTK, Sept. 13, 1991. Rychetský supported referendum and warned of economic trouble from reform. ČTK, Sept. 14, 1991.

in his Slovak "enemies'" camp, and in the Czech Republic he sought to exploit the controversy about Moravia.[37]

In October, looking forward to the next session of the two Republic presidia, President Havel, returning to the fray, called two meetings of the heads of the three governments and the chairs of their legislatures, the first in Prague and the second in the well-known spa of Karlovy Vary. In the latter gathering, Federal Prime Minister Čalfa suggested a new approach: a comparative examination of world federal systems with a view toward distilling the commonality of interests of the component units. Prime Minister Čarnogurský was intrigued,[38] but the proceedings quickly returned to the "old" agenda: the allocation of competences and the nature of the common state. Agreement was reportedly reached that foreign affairs, defense, currency, customs, and criminal police should remain federal.[39]

At the same time, in Slovakia, representatives of ten Slovak parties and legal experts met to examine the drafts of the proposed treaty and the new Slovak constitution. In the end, the texts contained a number of alternative provisions, with Mečiar's MDS and the SNP dissenting.[40]

After the presidia meetings, both Chair Mikloško of the Slovak National Council and Prime Minister Čalfa thought that progress had been made, although Mikloško, who referred to the president's "great authority," was concerned that the results might not be acceptable to Slovak party leaders.[41]

---

37. Taking note of the debate among the Czechs on the status of Moravia, a part of the Czech Republic, Mečiar suggested that if the two Republics failed to agree on a treaty, "we have promised the Moravians that we are ready to make a separate agreement with them if our relations with the Czechs collapse. . . . The rest of the Czech Republic may then join us." In retaliation, the CDA claimed that Mečiar's statements may have exceeded the bounds of constitutionality by being aimed at disruption of the constitutional status of the Czech Republic and requested that he be stripped of his parliamentary immunity as a deputy in the Federal Assembly and be made the subject of an investigation. ČSTK, Oct. 30, 1991; ČSTK, Nov. 1, 1991.

38. M. Čalfa.

39. ČSTK, Oct. 29, 1991. In the Prague talk of October 5, 1991, the bill on referendum procedures was also discussed. ČSTK, Oct. 5, 1991. On October 17, 1991 in Karlovy Vary, the discussion centered on competences in the areas of wage and social policy, treaty making, budget formation, tax schemes, execution of customs laws, federal material reserves, and the environment, which were to remain federal. L'. Kubín et al., *supra,* note 35, 112. This, according to the official press agency, was the eighth meeting of this composition since February 1991 when the demand for a treaty was first raised. ČTK, Oct. 17, 1991. The federal "lustration law" adopted on October 4, 1991, was also discussed. ČSTK, Oct. 17, 1991.

In mid-October, 73 percent of the population of the country rated Havel as their favorite politician, 82 percent in the Czech Republic, but only 56 percent in Slovakia, where he came fourth on the list of most popular politicians. ČSTK, Oct. 17, 1991.

40. L'. Kubín et al., *supra,* note 35, 112. The two-day meeting took place at Častá-Papierníčka. ČSTK, Oct. 18, 1991.

41. ČSTK, Oct. 18, 1991; ČSTK, Nov. 3, 1991. Before the president's intervention, Fran-

b. In the Baroque Štiřín

The presidia of the two National Councils assembled again on October 22–23, 1991, this time at the baroque castle of Štiřín near Prague.[42] As was the case in Bratislava, the president was not present; obviously chastened by past experience, he was said to be prepared to resume negotiations with the country's leaders only if he had the assurance that the talks would lead to clear, public results, binding the participants who would have to sign a joint communiqué.[43]

On the table was a text prepared by the experts summarizing the outcome of the previous encounter in Karlovy Vary and two drafts submitted by the two sides. Most of the time was devoted to the definition of the powers of the central government. An understanding was reached on a number of items while those on which consensus proved impossible were pushed forward in a "bulldozer" fashion and referred to experts. Their role in this context proved constructive: they offered alternative formulations, answered questions for clarification, and asked for political guidance. In the crucial foreign affairs field, when the Slovak side insisted that the Republics should have the power to conclude treaties within the sphere of their competences, not only with components of other states but with such states themselves, an abstruse debate on international responsibility for violation of such treaties, particularly in the commercial area, led to a dead end and a request for advice from international law specialists.[44] Disagreement persisted in other areas, including currency, emission institutions, environment protection, citizenship, and energy. Although the Republics were to have general powers of implementation and enforcement, a debate centered on exceptions in such areas as customs administration and protection of the frontiers where arguments were advanced for shared powers.

---

tišek Mikloško, the chair of the Slovak National Council, gave his view of the state of the negotiation: "We have reached no agreement on fundamental issues concerning the setup of the state. All federal bodies are Prague based, their bureaucratic apparatus is made up mainly of Czechs. . . . If there is . . . a Slovak minister in the cabinet, decisions will still be taken by the Czech political scene. . . . A state created by two nations cannot be unitary"; if Slovakia separates, it must be done in accord with law, but "[d]ue to its economic structure the Republic is practically unable to exist on its own. . . . As many powers as possible must be transferred from the federation to enable Slovakia to function as a sovereign economic organization." Interview with Warsaw daily *Zycie Warszawy,* summarized in ČSTK, Oct. 16, 1991.

42. See "Stenografický zápis z jednání předsednictev České národní rady a Slovenské národní rady, konaného ve dnech 22. a 23. října 1991 ve Štiříně u Prahy [Stenographic Record of the Negotiations of the Presidia of the Czech National Council and the Slovak National Council Held on Oct. 22 and 23, 1991 in Štiřín Near Prague]" in the Library of the Czech Parliament.

43. President's spokesman Michael Žantovský in ČSTK, Nov. 3, 1991.

44. Chair Dr. Burešová again insisted on the "single subject of international law" concept challenged in an artless way by Ivan Čarnogurský. *Supra,* note 42, 48/3–4.

Little time was left for the second subject on the agenda, the status of the Czech-Slovak treaty. The debate in which Chair Mikloško pleaded for "no polemics" was a replay of the earlier confrontations, with Ivan Čarnogurský insisting on "reconstruction" of the state and the legal validity of the treaty, Dr. Kalvoda again denying the competence of the Republics to be parties to the treaty, and Pithart harping on "federation and nothing else" and undivided "international personality."[45] In a conciliatory vein, Czech Deputy Žák thought to dispel the Slovak suspicion that the Czechs considered the federation as their own and that its preservation was the starting point of the Czech thought: he pleaded for a "trustworthy, functioning state, where the Republics flourish and do not harm each other."[46] A cryptic joint communiqué spoke of an agreement on a number of competences with those not agreed upon left for discussions by groups of experts and government ministers, an obvious attempt to camouflage the lack of real progress.[47] One positive aspect of the meeting was to help the deputies to grasp the consequences of their attitudes.

c. In the President's Mountain "Hut" at Hrádeček: A Major Czech Concession?

In the face of the Štiřín experience, President Havel resumed his initiative by calling another of the leadership meetings for November 3, 1991,[48] at his cottage near the Krkonoše Mountains in the Northeast of the Czech Republic.[49] It was nearby that, under the old regime, State Security had established a special unit for permanent surveillance of Havel's "subversive" activities such as writing his essays on human rights, seeing other dissidents, and hosting concerts by underground rock bands.

The informal get-together started pleasantly enough with a rare brand of *slivovice*[50] in the afternoon at five and a plan for a dinner break with Havel's own special goulash at seven-thirty. But shortly before midnight the exasper-

---

45. *Ibid.,* 70/4–72/3: "Functional," not just "functioning" federation (Pithart repeating Kalvoda).

46. *Ibid.,* 73/2.

47. Ľ. Kubín, *supra, note* 35, 113.

48. This section is based on a complete transcript of the stenographic record, which was obtained by the SLOVENSKÉ LISTY, a monthly published in Prague for the Slovaks living in the Czech Republic, and it was published in 93 pages, by installments, in numbers 1 to 9, 1994 (hereafter cited as SL).

49. Present were Alexander Dubček, Dagmar Burešová, Jan Kalvoda, Michael Žantovský, František Mikloško, Marián Čalfa, Ján Čarnogurský, Petr Pithart, Federal Deputy Prime Minister Pavol Hoffman, Slovak National Council Deputy Chair Ivan Čarnogurský, Slovak Deputy Prime Minister Anton Vavro, Czech Deputy Prime Minister Jan Stráský, Prof. M. Kusý, J. Křižan.

50. A prune-based, clear, strong liqueur. Havel's neighbors in a community that made him an honorary citizen buried the bottle in an orchard in 1968 to keep it from Soviet soldiers, dug it out in 1989, and made a gift of it to him. SL, *supra,* note 48, 3.

ated president declared that unless a communiqué was agreed upon within half an hour "I shall get in my car and drive to Hell," announce the breakdown of the talks, and after some two days of thinking, figure out "some emergency solution."[51]

At the outset the president circulated a five-part proposal for the structure of the Czech-Slovak treaty with specific steps and deadlines (May 1, 1992, to be the final date) and a referendum in December of that year.[52] To fill the gap left at Štiřín, the president suggested a crucial concession of highest priority to the Slovaks: the treaty to be concluded by the two National Councils "on behalf of the Republics" would have the status of a legal instrument binding under internal law.[53] Moreover, he tentatively wondered—in view of the Kroměříž consensus that the new federal constitution would require a ratification by the National Councils—whether future changes of the constitution might also be subject to such ratification.[54]

The chair of the Slovak National Council, Mikloško, called the president's suggestion "a giant shift,"[55] and he was echoed by the other Slovaks. Yet it was Dr. Kalvoda, the deputy chair of the Czech National Council, who, seconded in part by Czech Premier Pithart and Dr. Burešová, the chair of the Czech Parliament, effectively blocked a consensus. In a running duel with the Slovak premier, Dr. Čarnogurský, Kalvoda insisted that under the prevailing federal Constitution the Republic parliaments were incapable of concluding a legally binding agreement ("a source of law"), only a political document that would be offered to the Federal Assembly in the form of a legislative initiative.[56] This strictest of strict constructions elicited an emotional response from the Slovaks: it meant a denial of their status as an equal "contractual partner" and it made impossible the building of "an entirely new federation."[57] Kalvoda remained impervious to the pleas of the president, Federal Premier Čalfa, and others that the minimal deviation (if it was one) from the letter of the Constitution was unlikely to have any practical impact and meant the least price to pay for avoiding the destruction of the state.[58] Although Kalvoda claimed that his

---

51. *Ibid.*, 76.

52. *Ibid.*, 4–6. Also in SMENA, Nov. 5, 1991, p. 6.

53. The treaty was to be effective simultaneously with the coming into force of the three constitutions, with the idea that the constitutions originated in it and that it would have its permanent legal validity as some "public law" document parallel to the constitution. SL, *supra*, note 48, 5. The federal Constitutional Court would see to the avoidance of a conflict, suggested Čalfa. *Ibid.*, 27.

54. *Ibid.*, 25.

55. *Ibid.*, 7.

56. Kalvoda: a political treaty permanently valid but not a source of law. *Ibid.*, 42.

57. Čarnogurský. *Ibid.*, 32, 52.

58. Havel, *ibid.*, 63, 64, 70. At one point the despairing president sketched "a catastrophic

hands were tied by a resolution of the Czech Parliament, he apparently believed in the rationality of his position. Yet it was suggested to me that, considering his subsequent public posture, he found it politically helpful to appear as a shining knight riding against the ungrateful Slovaks in defense of the federation—and of Czech interests.

As for the Slovak demand for ratification of the federal constitution by the Republic legislatures, Premier Pithart and Dr. Burešová would accept the "first" ratification but not the subsequent ratification of constitutional changes; they viewed the requirement as "a purely confederate element" and a "revolutionary principle."[59] In the end, the seemingly endless debate was drowned in a morass of legal and pseudolegal argumentation about "sovereignty," "international subjectivity," and so on, revealing for the most part a lack of understanding of a living federalism and a sensible constitutional interpretation. At one point, Premier Čalfa delicately touched upon the possibility of the dissolution of the Federal Assembly and an election of a Constituent Assembly, but he beat a hasty retreat: "The [current] parliaments would not give up their powers."[60] The lineup was clear: the federal and Slovak Republic spokesmen led by the president against those holding the highest offices in the Czech Republic. The final communiqué, if read with some care, gives a true picture of the fundamental discord.[61]

The same principal participants met five days later in Prague but apparently without any progress.[62] In fact, the proposal advanced shortly before in

---

scenario": if we don't agree, Slovakia will declare independence, Mečiar will be prime minister and—addressing the Slovaks—"you will immigrate one after the other to the Czech lands. We all will weep over the outcome. . . . We have a true crisis situation . . . by Christmas the state might wildly break up, a state of double law might occur . . ." The only alternative is to make a treaty that both National Councils will accept. *Ibid.*, 70.

59. *Ibid.* 32, 69. Burešová cites the U.S. Constitution but ignores that any "subsequent" amendment to that constitution is also subject to "ratification" by the states. *Ibid.* 14. The Slovak basic argumentation, in my judgment, made a great deal of sense if one accepted their premise of a new basis for the federation. It took a formalistic, positivist interpreter to deny the "sovereign" Republics the right to conclude with each other legally effective agreements just because the prevailing federal constitution lacked an express authorization to that effect. If one followed the same restrictive interpretation, it was plausible to argue that an attempt to bind the Federal Assembly by such an inter-Republic treaty would be unconstitutional since it would impair the status of the Assembly as the central constitutional organ. But even those unwilling to go beyond the strictly defined confines of the constitution should have been willing to seek an appropriate constitutional amendment.

60. *Ibid.,* 69.

61. Text in ČSTK, Nov. 3, 1991. Slovak version in SMENA, Nov. 5, 1991, p. 4. For some, mostly Slovak, comments on the Hrádeček meeting, see NO, Nov. 5, 1991, p. 1, 6; p. 3.

62. In Prague, the parties agreed only that the treaty "will be embodied directly in the constitution" and the sovereignty of both Republics was to be explicitly stated in the preamble. Also, the future state was to be in a decisive measure more federal than confederal. Ľ. Kubín et al.,

the Slovak National Council by a dissident Christian Democrat deputy for a "Declaration of Sovereignty" of Slovakia was viewed by the Czech side as another attempt at political pressure—and an unfavorable signal from the Slovak side. It was supported by Mečiar. Dagmar Burešová indicated that such a step would be unconstitutional and would force the Czech National Council to take certain steps for ensuring its own existence.[63]

Czech Prime Minister Pithart, true to his position at Hrádeček, in his weekly radio address, rejected the president's proposed concessions to the Slovak position on the ground that the Slovak conception of the treaty would "humiliate" the Federal Assembly, override the Republic constitutions, and create a "confederate setup."[64] Yet only four days later, on November 9, he made a major conciliatory television speech, deploring the history of Czech disparagement of Slovakia, "Czech paternalism," and "the conceit of an older brother," and he proposed a discussion of "a type of coexistence . . . looser than the present state," a *dvojdomek,* (a "double house").[65] The Czech media saw in the statement a call for further concessions to the Slovaks, and, in fact, Slovak Premier Dr. Čarnogurský applauded Pithart's "comprehension" of Slovak demands for a looser coexistence but regretted that the Czech side failed to accept the president's suggestions.[66] Whatever Pithart's intention, the statement branded him as a hopeless "pro-Slovak."

d. In Častá-Papiernička: Facing the Core Issue

The fourth meeting of the presidia representatives took place in the Slovak Častá-Papiernička on November 11 and 12, 1991. On the table was the text of the proposed treaty consolidated by the experts on the basis of the comments received from both sides.[67] This time the president joined the parliamentarians to press his Hrádeček concessions to the Slovaks; he urged the participants to concentrate on the question of the legal status of the treaty, which should have

---

supra, note 35, 114–15. ČSTK, Nov. 10, 1991.

63. ČSTK, Nov. 8, 1991.

64. ČSTK, Nov. 5, 1991.

65. For the text of Pithart's speech, see L'. Kubín et al., *supra,* note 35, 115–17. A tension appeared within the federal government coalition as well. ČSTK, Nov. 1, 1991. Czech Republic Minister of Education Vopěnka declared that Pithart took over the Communist explanation of the First Republic "along with some inventions of Slovak primitive nationalists." Marián Leško, L'udia a l'udkovia z politickej elity [People and Little People from the Political Elite] 55 (Perex a.s., 1993).

66. ČSTK, Nov. 10, 1991. Dr. Čarnogurský said that if no agreement were reached that would respect the sovereignty of the two Republics his movement would assert a looser union than a federation, maybe a confederation or some other type of state—and if the Czechs did not agree then the CDM would not be opposed to a referendum. He opposed the Declaration of Slovak Sovereignty. ČSTK, Nov. 10, 1991.

67. Ivan Čarnogurský in SMENA, Feb. 3, 1992, p. 3, reviewing the state of the negotiations.

the highest possible legal status, not as a mere legislative initiative insisted on by the Czech side, and it should remain valid after the adoption of the three constitutions "into which it would be projected," implying that any subsequent constitutional change would require Republic ratification. The president pointed out (somewhat optimistically) that in other respects the text of the treaty was ready, although the two sides still differed on certain variants of allocation of powers. He warned of the increasing impatience of the people with the protracted talks.[68]

The first day was devoted to the Štiřín agenda and the president's proposals. By that time, however, the president had little, if any, influence on the deputies of the CDP and CDA. Once more, written questions were circulated on the controversial issues, but, according to Pithart, "either we may have formulated the questions badly or the Slovak side is unwilling or incapable of clearly defining its attitude toward the common state."[69]

In an evening encounter of the deputy chairs of the two National Councils, Ivan Čarnogurský made it fairly clear that Slovakia would be independent in the near future. CDA's Kalvoda and CDP's Vlach decided that night to disclose this private conversation to the newspapers and on television. As a result, the next day was taken up with a discussion of their indiscretion and there was no time for substantive talks.[70] The closing communiqué is a testimony to the failure to achieve a major breakthrough. Of the 88 provisions in the draft treaty, the Slovak side had reservations on 15, the Czechs on five, and both sides on two. The character of the treaty remained "the most complex problem," which the Slovak side proposed to resolve by a modification of the current Constitution.[71]

e. In the Federal Assembly: The End of the Referendum Route?

On November 13, a day after the conclusion of the meeting in Častá-Papiernička, the scene shifted back to the Federal Assembly. After seven hours of confused debate, none of the proposed wordings of questions for a referendum on the future of the federation won enough votes, even though both the chair of the Assembly, Alexander Dubček and Slovak Prime Minister Čar-

---

68. ČSTK, Nov. 11, 1991.
69. ČSTK, Nov. 13, 1991.
70. V. Žák.
71. Communiqué of Nov. 12, 1991, Library of the Czech Republic Parliament and in L'. Kubín et al., *supra,* note 35, 118. As I reported earlier, the Czech side rejected the proposed Slovak solution as not feasible.

nogurský, dropped their earlier opposition to a referendum.[72] "The majority of Slovaks and virtually all Communist deputies banded together to defeat the six draft texts."[73]

On a brighter side, on the day of the "referendum massacre" in the Assembly, the Slovak National Council decided to drop the controversial draft Declaration of Slovak Sovereignty from its agenda—a step welcomed by Dr. Čarnogurský and other leaders of the Slovak coalition government,[74] and two days later, on November 15, the same council adopted a resolution envisaging further negotiations on the treaty.[75]

The federal government, noting the absence of progress and the damaging effects of the impasse, announced its decision to reenter the negotiation process with its own proposals and to use all its powers to halt the destruction of the legal and institutional foundations of the Federation; if the representatives of the Republics failed to agree, the state would not cease to exist and the federal government would ensure its effective functioning.[76]

72. ČSTK, Nov. 13, 1991; Nov. 10, 1991 (Dubček); Nov. 12, 1991 (Čarnogurský). Petr Brodský, "V Tatrách bez občanských práv—Nač se ptát v referendu [In the Tatry without Civil Rights—What Questions in the Referendum]," RESPEKT, no. 45, Nov. 11–17, 1991, p. 8; Jan Kavan, "When is a Crisis Not a Crisis" PRAGUE POST, Dec. 17–23, 1991, p. 10.

73. Jiří Pehe, "Czech-Slovak Conflict Threatens State Unity," RFE/RL RES. REP., Jan. 3, 1992, 83, 84.

74. Of the 150 deputies of the National Council, 63 backed the proposal. All MDS and SNP deputies, some deputies of the CDM, some Greens, and some PDLs signed the draft. Chair Mikloško said if an agreement continued to elude them both sides were inclined to preserve the current Federation until after the next elections. ČSTK, Nov. 13, 1991.

75. The resolution, envisaging further negotiations on a treaty, noted that consensus was reached on the majority of legislative and executive powers of the common state, insisted on the "legal and permanently binding" character of the treaty to be made possible by an appropriate modification of the existing constitution, expressed dissatisfaction with the approach of its own Presidium with regard to the preparation of the negotiations with the Presidium of the Czech National Council and required a series of preparatory documents. Ľ Kubín et al., *supra,* note 35, 120–21.

76. Text as read by Prime Minister Čalfa in NO, Nov. 15, 1991, p. 1, 2; and in Ľ. Kubín et al., *supra,* note 35, 119.

VIII

The President's Call to Arms
(Fall 1991–Winter 1992)

1. An Appeal to Citizens

Like the federal government, President Havel viewed the deadlock as a crisis situation requiring his intervention. He was presumably encouraged by the success of the campaign "for a common state," which had obtained more than two million signatures, most of them, however, in the Czech lands. So this time he decided to launch a direct appeal to the people, urging them to support his initiative with their deputies. Speaking on November 17, 1991, he recalled that as early as January of that year he had published his own proposal for a federal constitution, "betting on a dialogue and a political will to an understanding." But he had exhausted the possibilities of this effort: "The politicians are interested more in the instructions from their party boards than in my proposals, and the negotiations that I organized over such a long period begin to turn in an errant circle and are the object of revulsion, even of ridicule, of the citizens and the media." He announced a series of new legislative proposals that he would send to the Federal Assembly within the next few days.[1] He ended in a conclusion, which revealed Havel the playwright behind the president, signaling his legislative initiative:

> Dear cocitizens, I said some time ago at one of the great manifestations that truth and love must win over lie and hate. Today I should like to add that reason, humility, and responsibility must win over shortsightedness, pride, and license (*svévole*). In a certain sense, more is at stake today than there was two years ago. At that time, the question was whether we shall tolerate for some more time the disintegrating totalitarian system or whether we say to it a clear "no." The question today is whether we shall become a civilized European democracy or a contemptible sphere of continuing conflicts and confusions. I am convinced daily that you are for the first of the two alternatives. I ask you to express your will clearly.[2]

1. Projev k občanům ČSFR, Praha, 17.11.1991 [Address to the Citizens of the ČSFR]," in Václav Havel, Vážení občané—Projevy, červenec 1990—červenec 1992 [Esteemed Citizens—Addresses, July 1990–July 1997) 118–20 (LN, Praha, 1992).
2. *Ibid.,* 120.

Thousands of Prague high school and 10,000 university students demonstrated in response to Havel's appeal, as did some 10,000 gathered on the historic Wenceslas Square.[3]

On November 21, the president addressed a crowd of some 40,000 assembled in Wenceslas Square. A rally of some 1,500 of the president's supporters was held simultaneously in Bratislava.[4] A few days earlier, on the Czechoslovak national day, Havel was prevented from speaking in the main square of Bratislava by an egg-throwing, jeering crowd of separatists. On his visit to eastern Slovakia, the president was met by warm but small crowds, with most people showing little interest, confirming local leaders' views of voters' passivity and the president's declining popularity.[5]

In his Prague speech, Havel thanked the participants for their support, which came in the form of a "great upheaval of public will" and had brought the first fruit in the form of the Federal Assembly decision to speed up the consideration of his initiatives. He added, however, that "it was not necessary to conduct daily demonstrations."[6] It was indicative of the tension between the president's advisors and the Slovak political quarters that Alexander Dubček, chair of the Federal Assembly, found it proper to complain in a press interview that the organizers of the Prague rally did not allow him to address the people.[7]

A few days earlier, in a broadcast to Slovakia, the president had criticized the Czech "let them [Slovaks] go" attitude, which revealed "a particular Czech historic inclination; whenever someone complicates our lives—we say let him go. In this way we got rid of three million of our fellow [German] citizens after World War II."[8] The citizens' response to the president's "call to arms," con-

3. ČSTK, Nov. 19, 1991 (two reports).

4. ČSTK, Nov. 21, 1991.

5. Henry Kamm, "As Slovak Separation Gains, Havel Faces the Unthinkable," N.Y. TIMES, Nov. 20, 1991, pp. A1, A7. According to a late November 1991 opinion poll, Havel's approval was at 81 percent in the Czech Republic but at 49 percent in Slovakia (a loss of 7 percent since early November). While rated as most popular among the Czechs, he was in the fifth place in Slovakia after Mečiar (68 percent), Dubček, Valtr Komárek (a Czech economist known to oppose radical economic reform), and Peter Weiss (chair of the PDL). ČSTK, Nov. 26, 1991; Nov. 28, 1991.

6. Havel, Vážení občané, *supra*, note 1, 121–22.

7. ČSTK, Nov. 23, 1991. Deputy Chair of the Federal Assembly Jičínský regretted the unfortunate beginning of the campaign in the Czech lands when Havel's adviser P. Tigrid, its principal initiator, turned sharply against Slovak nationalists "without distinguishing the legitimate demands for Slovak emancipation from nationalist separatism." In Slovakia, the campaign was conceived as a "further manipulation of retaining Czech hegemony . . ." Zdeněk Jičínský, "K ztroskotání československého federalismu, [On Foundering of Czechoslovak Federalism]," in Rüdiger Kipke, and Karel Vodička (eds.), Rozloučení s Československem [Parting with Czechoslovakia] 67, 77 (Český Spisovatel, Praha, 1993).

8. The president referred to the forcible expulsion of more than three million Sudeten Germans in 1945. ČSTK, Nov. 17, 1991.

fined as it was primarily to the Czech capital, did not come close to approaching the massive outpouring of support for the "velvet" revolution two years earlier—and there was little reaction in Slovakia.

In a formal address delivered before the Federal Assembly on December 3, the president again spoke of a deep constitutional crisis.[9] Obviously reacting to the sporadic criticism in the press and by some politicians, he continued, after reviewing his efforts:

> Certainly, I cannot be blamed for inactivity, lack of patience, or determination to form a space for a quiet dialogue of representatives of the people,

yet the negotiations of the National Councils for a treaty "ended at a dead point," the Federal Assembly failed to agree on a question for a referendum, and the Slovak National Council had to cope already several times with the temptation to deal with the declaration of Slovakia as an international subject.

> The week all this took place, I spent in Slovakia and there I was faced daily with the foreboding sense of danger. It seemed to me that this sense in Slovakia is much stronger than in the Czech lands.

He realized that his direct appeal to the people was resented by the deputies as "an attack on your legitimacy," but he felt it was the only possible step to take.

> I do not know whether Czechoslovakia is doomed to a collapse into a legal chaos, to permanent constitutional crisis, to a breakdown of the public administration, to a wild breakup, and to becoming a domain of political adventurers. . . . I am glad . . . that after the initial shock from my public appeal you understood the ethos and comprehensive meaning of my initiative and that you took a welcoming stance toward it.[10]

2. The Five Legislative Proposals

The president then proceeded to describe the individual proposals as aiming first at a breakthrough in the constitutional negotiations and, second, as providing "a system of emergency fuses" in case the negotiations failed.

The first of the five measures would constitute a requirement of ratification of the new federal constitution by the National Councils—a novel princi-

---

9. For the text of the address, see Havel, *Vážení občané, supra,* note 1, "Projev ve Federálním shromáždění, Praha, 3.12.1991 [Address in the Federal Assembly, March 12, 1991]," 123.

10. *Ibid.,* 125, 126.

ple, which, however, was not in conflict with the idea of a federal system, was recognized in other federations, and conformed to the efforts at changing the common state into a federation based on the true equality of both Republics. It was unrealistic to imagine, he suggested, that the Federal Assembly could adopt by a qualified majority a constitution that would not reflect the will of the Republics, particularly since the constitution would have to be based on a treaty between the National Councils. "It would be a '*single-instance*' ratification"; subsequent eventual change in the constitution "would be subject to a different mode of control by the Republics, grounded directly in the new constitution."[11] Clearly, the president, offering his Hrádeček ideas, intended to meet a crucial point of the Slovak demand with a new compromise on the issue of subsequent ratifications, which the Czechs continued to oppose.

The second proposal called for a modification of the flawed referendum law by introducing the possibility for half a million Czech voters and a quarter million Slovaks to demand a referendum, including one on the question of leaving the federation. A proviso to this effect was in Havel's original draft of the referendum law, but it was eliminated in the Federal Assembly, thus reducing greatly the effectiveness of the law. Under the circumstances, the recourse to "civic initiative" appeared to be the only way to a popular vote since the move in the Federal Assembly had failed. Under the prevailing law, the National Councils could call for a referendum, but there was no majority for it in the Slovak Council[12] and a referendum in the Czech Republic alone would be of little avail except in the most unlikely event that the majority of the Czechs would vote for a secession, leaving the Slovaks in the position of claiming the status of successor state.

The third and fourth drafts restated in substance the earlier, abortive proposals for the structure of the legislative, executive, and judiciary branches offered by the president, which were the subject (in the version of the Federal Constitutional Commission) of the consultations by the international group in Bratislava that I describe in annex I. The president's newest text of the "three heads" of the constitution would—he explained—clarify and expand the president's power to dissolve the Parliament in specified instances of deadlock and would authorize him to enact interim presidential decrees, a provision that Havel expected to encounter "massive repulsion" on the part of the deputies.[13] Furthermore, the existing Federal Assembly would be replaced with a single-chamber Parliament with a Federal Council composed of deputies elected by the National Councils. The Federal Council, sitting in Bratislava, would have

---

11. *Ibid.,* 126.

12. Fifty-two percent of Slovaks backed the Federation according to an opinion poll in November 1991. ČSTK, Nov. 10, 1991.

13. Havel, Vážení občané, *supra,* note 1, 128–29.

the power of a suspensive legislative veto, and its procedure would retain the prohibition of majorization. The Federal Assembly took up the proposals for "the three heads" of the constitution only two months later—and I shall return to them in that context.

The fifth, and final measure proposed by the president was a new electoral law based on a modified majority principle, introducing an alternative to the federal government's own draft.

3. The Politicians Respond

The reaction to the president's initiative among the Czech politicians was mixed. Of the Czech parties, only the center Civic Movement spokesmen voiced unreserved support, albeit with a varied degree of pessimism; in Slovakia, only the Public against Violence and the small Democratic Party took a positive view. The rest of the responses consisted of various shades of skepticism.[14] Federal Deputy Prime Minister and Finance Minister Klaus said that his party (the CDP) had mixed reactions.[15] According to Dr. Čarnogurský, the president "overdramatized the situation" with his proposals, which were "not thought out clearly enough" and will not achieve their goal.[16] The chair of the Slovak Party of the Democratic Left, Peter Weiss, characterized the president's appeal to the people of November 17 as "a dramatic diverting of attention from the real causes of the problems," caused by the strong centralistic and unitarian tendencies on the Czech side,[17] but he welcomed the president's initiative for resolving the political deadlock as evidence that the head of state recognized his share of responsibility for the lack of progress in the Czech and Slovak negotiations.[18]

4. The Federal Assembly Response

a. The Debate on the President's Proposals

The Federal Assembly, meeting in a joint session of the two chambers, opened its constitutional debate in January of 1992. It rejected decisively that part of Havel's proposals that would give the president the power to dissolve the Parliament in specified circumstances of a constitutional deadlock. The draft received only half the votes needed for its approval in both chambers.[19] The

---

14. ČSTK, Nov. 17, 1991; Nov. 18, 1991; Nov. 19, 1991.
15. ČSTK, Nov. 19, 1991.
16. ČSTK, Nov. 21, 1991.
17. ČSTK, Nov. 23, 1991.
18. ČSTK, Nov. 20, 1991.
19. ČSTK, Jan. 28, 1992.

same fate befell Havel's amendment to the electoral law, which would have combined proportional representation and majority voting systems; voters would cast their ballots for individual candidates rather than for a party ticket.[20] The Assembly voted for a law retaining the proportional representation method subject to the requirement that a party must receive at least 5 percent and alliances of parties at least 7 to 10 percent.[21] It also refused to approve Havel's proposals for the ratification of the new federal constitution by the National Councils and for the modification of the referendum law.[22]

The deputies had before them not only the president's text containing the third and fourth proposals (the "three heads" on the institutional structure)[23] but also an alternative bill offered by a group of deputies that corresponded to the version of the Federal Constitutional Commission. That variant, which was the subject of the consultation with the international group, substantially modified the president's ideas. It was now reworked still further in Assembly committees and party factions ("clubs").[24] The bill was to become the heart of the new constitution.

It was a mark of the difficulty of the consensus-building process that the Federal Assembly received the views of the federal government and the two National Councils on these important bills as late as the day of the opening of the debate.[25] Early in the proceedings the president withdrew his institutional proposals[26] since his idea of a single parliament with a Federal Council had met with almost unanimous opposition by the deputies of all political orientations, who preferred a two-chamber legislature in the tradition of the first Czechoslovak Republic and the "new European democratic constitutions."[27] The second chamber, the Senate, was to be seated in Bratislava. The debate

---

20. Fed. Ass. Proposal by the President, 1991, 6th sess., no. 372; no. 1079 (to amend law no. 490/1991, etc.). Address of the President in the Fed. Ass. on Dec. 3, 1991, in Václav Havel, Vážení občané, *supra,* note 1, 123. Jiří Pehe, "Federal Assembly Adopts Electoral Law," RFE/RL RES. REP., Feb. 14, 1992, 27–30. For an analysis of Havel's proposal, *see* Petr Pavlovský in LN, Jan. 7, 1992, p. 7; and LN, Jan. 14, 1992, p. 9 (Jan Rychlík).

21. ČSTK, Jan. 29, 1992.

22. *Ibid;* Zdeněk Jičínský, "K ztroskotání československého federalismu," *supra,* note 7, 67, 77.

23. Print no. 1077, withdrawn by the president.

24. Prints no. 1071, with some further variants no. 1071A, and a proposed text of a resolution of the two chambers, no. 1212. See annex I.

25. Deputy Chair Jičínský described the process of elaboration of the proposals in "Zpráva o 20. společné schůzi Sněmovny lidu a Sněmovny národů, VI. volební období, 22. a 23. ledna 1992, 2. část [Fed. Ass. Report on the 20th joint session of the Chamber of the People and the Chamber of the Nations, 6th elect. period, Jan. 22 and 23, 1992, 2d part]," 197–200 (hereafter cited as Fed. Ass. Rep., Jan. 22 and 23, 1992).

26. *Ibid.,* 217.

27. Christian Democratic Movement Deputy I. Šimko. *Ibid.,* 168.

took place for the most part before "a half-empty hall,"[28] an inauspicious portent for the outcome.

The record suggests three sets of widely differing attitudes of the participants but with one common element: awareness of the approaching elections, which made the search for a consensus substantially more difficult. Moreover, almost all speakers suggested some reservation or modification, and this resulted in a massive number of amendments.

i. Yes in Principle
Subject to two important exceptions, dealt with subsequently, the coalition of parties represented in the federal government supported the deputies' bill more or less warmly: this included the center-oriented Civic Democratic Union, its Slovak ally the Public against Violence, and the Christian Democrat groups. The parliamentary faction of the Hungarian Coexistence also took a generally favorable view of the bill.[29]

An affirmative posture was registered by the opposition Social Democrats and the Czech Communists. The Christian Democratic Union, the larger of the two Christian Democratic groups, while supporting the bill, had some reservations with respect to the powers of the president, which, however, were capable of resolution. It also objected to the introduction of the institution of secretary of state (*státní tajemník*), conceived as an alter ego of each minister with full membership in the cabinet: if a Czech was minister, a Slovak would be the secretary, and this could mean expanding the cabinet to 30 members. Like the Hungarian party, it questioned the proposed location of the Senate in Bratislava on the ground that the physical separation from the first chamber in Prague would impair the functionality of the legislative process.[30] The last two provisions were opposed by other deputies as well. Mention was made in this context of another proposed extension of the Czech-Slovak parity principle envisaged in the bill: even the quorum required in the Chamber of Deputies would be determined by the nationality of the deputies.[31]

ii. Yes But (Really No?)
Two parties of the federal government coalition voiced serious, if not fatal, objections to the bill. The Civic Democratic Party of Václav Klaus rejected the

---

28. Deputy M. Tahy. *Ibid.,* 218; I. Fišera, *ibid.,* 224.

29. However, for organizational and financial reasons it preferred seating both chambers in the same location (in fact, in Prague, an interesting position for a Slovakia-centered party), and it opposed the ratification of the constitution by the Republics out of concern that a failure of approval by one Republic Council, while retaining the current Constitution, would create a "situation that would politically be hardly tenable." *Ibid.,* 320–22 (Deputy I. Bajnok).

30. *Ibid.,* 250, 251 (Deputy J. Lux).

31. *Ibid.,* 294 (Deputy J. Mečl).

provision for ratification of the new federal constitution by the National Councils demanded by the Slovaks. This feature of the president's proposals was rejected earlier in the Assembly—allegedly because of a misunderstanding on the part of the deputies—but it was now reintroduced as part of the deputies' bill and, as we shall see, a few weeks later it was apparently accepted by the CDP.

The opponents of subsequent ratification cited Professor Weyr, a leading Czech scholar, claimed by some to have "invented" the normative theory before Hans Kelsen,[32] whose paternity is generally recognized. Yet in a federal context it makes little sense to invoke the normative theory concept that a single legislative body (in this case the Federal Assembly) must have the sole ultimate say over all legislative competences.

The most fatal objection, however, was advanced by Kalvoda's Civic Democratic Alliance and articulated in a formal amendment: it would remove the prohibition of majorization that under the deputies' bill would remain in the second chamber, the Senate, although it would not apply in the first chamber. The CDA position was opposed by all Slovak parties and by most Czechs as well, who had accepted the inevitability of this "dual principle" device in a two-member federation.[33]

iii. No

I would place in the third category those party representatives and individual speakers who opposed the very foundation of the bill either on principle or because of improper timing. The Slovak National Party, the persistent, and the only open, advocate of Slovak independence, considered it inappropriate to adopt extensive constitutional reform before the enactment of the Republic

---

32. "If, however, the normative unity of the legal order (and thereby of the state as well) is to be maintained, it is inevitable that one of the legislative bodies be given the so-called competence of the competence, in other words, the competence supremacy, that is, the ability accorded by the legal order to regulate its own competence as well as the competence of the second (or further) level legislative bodies." The CDP also objected to the secretaries of state and, obviously noting its favorable standing in the opinion polls, insisted that the president be expressly required to offer the position of prime minister to the party victorious in the election. Finally, since more time, more discussion, and more understanding and will to unity is required for the assertion of certain ideas, it would not be a tragedy if the Federal Assembly failed to act. Fed. Ass. Rep., Jan. 22 and 23, 1992, *supra,* note 25, 209 (Deputy T. Kopřiva, also invoking the Kroměříž agreement).

33. The CDA would replace the prohibition of majorization in the Senate by a higher (three-fourths) majority, which would also be required for the same level of legislation in the first chamber. In an extensive series of amendments, the CDA also proposed changes regarding the election of the president (in the image of the German Basic Law) and the president's powers, the formation of the government, and so on. *Ibid.,* 262–69 (Deputy J. Skalický). Note Skalický's reference to "the famous Madison definition" of parliamentary democracy at 257.

constitutions, and, in any event, it would radically restructure the federal legislature to assure equality of the two nations.[34]

The objection of the Moravian-centered Movement for Self-Governing Democracy/Society for Moravia and Silesia went to the heart of the deputies' bill: it insisted on a three-member federation, including the Czech land (Bohemia), Slovakia, and the historic Moravia-Silesia land, a solution unacceptable to the Czechs and to Slovaks who refused to accept the Moravian claim of equality with the Slovak "sovereignty" status.[35]

It did not come as a surprise that the MDS of former Prime Minister Mečiar opposed the bill as a whole. Its spokesman viewed the proceedings in the Federal Assembly as a "second-front" attempt to reconstruct an obsolete federation "from the top": competences allocated from the top are easily recaptured by the center. Thus, Assembly action was incompatible with the negotiations between the two Republics. The speaker criticized the "undesirable dramatization" and "unreal deadlines."[36] He and others argued that the new Assembly, as it would emerge from the impending elections, should not be faced with "a fait accompli" and should be free to write the new basic document. Moreover, in the present Assembly many, if not a majority, of the deputies now belonged to parties other than those for which they were elected. The present Constitution, faulty as it was, sufficed for the remaining election term, and the current crisis could not be solved by the Assembly adoption of "a torso" of a proposed constitution. The counterarguments were to the effect that revamping the essential institutional framework would have a calming effect on the country and would facilitate the work of the newly elected Assembly.[37] Clearly, Mečiar, sensing electoral victory, was not prepared to accept any commitment in the current Assembly. The Slovak Party of the Democratic Left, prudent as ever and, like MDS, concerned about the integrity of the negotiations between the Republics, ultimately ended up, as we shall see, in the negative column.

The Assembly voted to adjourn in order to enable its constitutional committees to prepare a composite text of 26 amendments, some of which ran over several pages.[38] The Assembly took final action only after the ultimate attempt

---

34. *Ibid.*, 236 (Deputy J. Šedovič).

35. *Ibid.*, 246–49 (Deputy Matochová). *See* in this context an amendment that would make a change to the three-member arrangement possible, offered by CDP deputy S. Hanák, in Fed. Ass. Rep., 20th joint session, 6th elec. period, Feb. 17, 1992, 7th part, 1408.

36. *Ibid.*, joint sess., Jan. 22 and 23, 1992, *supra,* note 25, 211 (Deputy Ondrejkovič).

37. *Ibid.*, 211, 213, 283, 301, 311; *see also* session of Feb. 17, *supra,* note 35, 450–51, 1401, 1438.

38. Print no. 00170 of Feb. 18, 1992; *see also* Print no. 00024 of Feb. 21, 1992 (from CDA); and LN, Feb. 19, 1992, p. 1.

by the representatives of the two Republics to reach an agreement on a treaty. I shall return to the Assembly plenary at that time.

5. Some Thoughts and Afterthoughts

On both the Czech and Slovak sides, some participants in the debate pursued a positive outcome in good faith while others, looking over their shoulders, sought to tailor their own and their party's positions to fit the upcoming election campaign. Thus, at a considerable risk to his political future, one Czech deputy, referring to a commitment ("given by his colleagues in the Czech National Council") to the principle of "repeated ratification" of the most important constitutional changes, would extend this principle to cover all constitutional laws.[39] As an example of the opposite, a Slovak MDS deputy, clearly playing up to the nationalist gallery, would want to replace the Federal Assembly with a "composite parliamentary body" created by the two National Councils, a proposal that—he admitted—had very little chance of success.[40] In the same vein, it was not surprising that the CDP of Václav Klaus, sensing the scent of victory, would propose that the Constitution should restrict the president's discretion in choosing the prime minister by explicitly requiring him to call on the party victorious in the elections. Although followed in the practice of parliamentary democracies, this procedure is not commonly prescribed in constitutions.

Legal arguments are often employed in support of political preferences; in fact, political arguments are framed in pseudolegal terms. The legal argumentation advanced by the Czech CDP in the ratification controversy and based on an interpretation of the normative theory was incompatible with the essence of divided power systems. Yet the Slovaks, with their mushy " 'from above' and 'from below' mantra" did not succeed in offering an effective rebuttal based on modern doctrines of divisible sovereignty.

Apart from a sensible intervention by Deputy Prime Minister Rychetský, there was little visible evidence of a Federal Government role in the Assembly process. Federal Prime Minister Čalfa was listed as absent from two out of the three crucial meetings. As for the leadership of the Federal Assembly itself, Deputy Chair Professor Jičínský provided informed responses, while the likable but ineffective Chair Dubček, unwell at the outset of the debate, limited himself to an anodyne statement complaining of the time restraints imposed on the constitution making. The debate was laced with personal invective and

---

39. Deputy P. Kučera in Fed. Ass. Rep., 20th joint session, Feb. 17, 1992, 7th part, 1451.
40. Fed. Ass. Rep., 20th joint sess., Jan. 22 and 23, 1992, 2d. part, sess. of Jan. 22, 1992, 334–36 (Deputy R. Zelenay). That idea was advanced in, and rejected by, the Federal Constitutional Commission.

innuendo, including an allegedly physical attack in the Assembly dining facility.[41]

The difficulty of making an institutional structure, designed for the Soviet-style centrally controlled system, function in the democratic, pluralist context of a two-component federation was confirmed when a minuscule opposition to the vital institutional reform was able to thwart an overwhelming majority—a result unthinkable under the old regime. Vojtěch Cepl, vice-dean of the Prague Law Faculty and later a judge of the Czech Constitutional Court, argued that the first and most critical objective of the constitutional negotiations should have been the abolition of the prohibition of majorization, which had made this outcome possible.[42] Yet this principle was accepted by most Czech groups in view of the sine qua non insistence by a unified Slovak front that treasured it as the crowning achievement of the 1968 federation. It was significant, however, that of the Czech parties rising in influence, one, the CDA, opposed the prohibition of majorization as a "communist conceit," allegedly incompatible with membership in the European Community, while the other, the CDP of Václav Klaus, was apparently resigned to accepting it.

Organizational deficiencies added to the difficulties of consensus building. Deputy Assembly Chair Jičínský assumed, but evidently had some well-founded doubts, that Assembly deputies would coordinate their positions with the views of their factions in the respective National Councils,[43] and even the federal government had problems in providing a timely, agreed point of view on the constitutional legislation. The Slovak federal deputies (with the exception of Mečiar and Kňažko who stopped coming to the Assembly sessions) had even less influence on Slovak political parties than their Czech counterparts had on the Czech parties.

Foreign constitutional practice was referred to in a number of instances. Thus, while Zdeněk Jičínský advocated a lean, framework-type constitution, Václav Žák pointed to the modern, detailed, specific instruments of Greece, Spain, and Portugal as models in view of the lack of Czecho-Slovak constitutional conventions to fill the gaps and the distrust among the Czech and Slovak political forces. However, as one of the deputies observed, although the drafters of the bill in certain instances could have chosen between several institutions employed in other European constitutions, "their final decisions were strikingly influenced by the need for a political consensus" determined by the "contemporary division of forces in the parliament."[44]

---

41. Fed. Ass., sess. of Jan. 22 and 23, 1992, sess. of Jan. 23, 1992 *supra,* note 25, 345.
42. V. Cepl, LN, June 11, 1992, p. 6.
43. Fed. Ass., sess. of Jan. 22, 1992, *supra,* note 25, 199.
44. *Ibid.,* 181 (Deputy O. Világi, a joint reporter of the constitutional committees).

Views may differ on the potential of a referendum as a way of resolving the Czech-Slovak issue, and I return to this subject in the concluding chapter. Whatever one may think of its potential usefulness under the circumstances, the Assembly's refusal to provide the necessary legislative means for calling a referendum in the face of a demand by "at least three million citizens"[45] is surprising even if the large majority of signatures on the citizens' petitions came from the Czech lands.

Shortly after the defeat of the president's proposals in the Assembly, the "Citizens Appeal" initiative ceased its activity. Pavel Tigrid, the president's friend and principal organizer of the movement, felt that the Assembly would not go unpunished for ignoring a large part of the society and the citizens would "not forget and act accordingly in the June 1992 elections."[46] It is difficult to say, even with the benefit of hindsight, whether the Assembly's failure to act had any effect on the outcome of the elections. It may have confirmed the voters' low esteem for the legislative branch. According to a public opinion poll, the already low public support of the Assembly dipped a further 9 percent between November 1991 and February 1992, bottoming out at 26 percent.[47]

Perhaps most astonishing was the defeat of Havel's proposal for a constitutional amendment that would require the federal constitution to be endorsed by the Republic legislatures. The group of deputies of the Civic Movement considered it incredible that this provision, "which was unanimously accepted" in the Kroměříž talks,[48] was rejected, and it charged the Assembly with falsely assuming that it had unlimited powers (i.e., the power to reject completely the presidential bills) even if it "runs counter to the internationally acknowledged principle on the division of power."[49] If the opposition was based on a purported "principle" rather then on politically popular anti-Slovakism, it showed a glaring ignorance and misunderstanding of federalism.

Of particular interest was the rejection of the president's effort to modify the electoral system in the direction of increasing respect for citizens' preferences by introducing a partial majority voting system. Clearly, the tradition reaching back to the first Republic, in which parties were supreme, and the reluctance of the current parties to loosen their control over the political system made the Assembly retain the proportional representation method with the

---

45. Statement by the Civic Movement's parliamentary faction, ČSTK, Jan. 29, 1992.
46. ČSTK, Jan. 25, 1992.
47. ČSTK, Feb. 27, 1992.
48. There is some question about this. See *supra,* chap. VI, 4c.
49. ČSTK, Jan. 29, 1992.

minimum percentage limitation drawn from the German model.[50] Critics of the president's proposal for a majority system[51] saw in it a confirmation of his distrust of political parties and his preference for "personal" or "personality politics." An articulate politician viewed the contraposition of "party-personality" as a false dilemma: the problem was the inability of political parties to articulate positive programs, which was due to an insufficient crystallization of political parties and had as its consequence an exaggerated role of personalities. The president, so went the argument, wanting to preserve his position "above the political parties," refused to criticize individual parties for specific actions, with the result that he directed his criticism against parties as such.[52]

6. Coda: Behind the Budget Imbroglio

During the waning weeks of the year, the constitutional issues became intermingled with the traditional annual negotiations on the allocation of revenues and expenditures between the Federation and the Republics for the next year's budget. To the existential Czech-Slovak tension was added a disagreement between the federal and Czech Republic governments when Czech Prime Minister Pithart insisted on modifying the funds allocation pattern in favor of the Czech Republic.[53]

When the Slovaks proposed in the budgetary negotiations that each Republic should live off its own revenues, the Czechs were astounded by this cavalier attitude: the Slovaks appeared more interested in the highest degree of independence than in the actual funds-allocation rate. This posture was taken by Slovak legislators ignorant of the budgetary process, to the dismay of the Slovak ministers. After difficult negotiations in a meeting chaired by the president, Finance Minister Klaus, evidently concerned about the Slovak economy, put through, against the opposition within his own party ranks, a non-

---

50. The new Assembly adopted the "old type" of election law with "a moving consensus." Jan Sokol, deputy chair of the Chamber of Nations, in LN, Feb. 11, 1992, p. 1; and *ibid.*, Feb. 12, 1992, p. 1, 3.

51. The draft was prepared by Prof. Klokočka, a professor of Czech origin at the University of Munich, an outside consultant to the president and later judge of the Constitutional Court of the Czech Republic.

52. "Falešné dilema [False dilemma]," LN, Jan. 14, 1992, p. 9.

53. As early as in spring 1990, agreement was reached by the two Republic governments that *all* revenues would go first to the Republics and only then, as the Republics considered it necessary, would a portion be redistributed to the Federation. This was viewed by the Czechs as the end of a federal budget and of the current reallocation process to the Republic.

transparent budget.[54] According to the compromise, a more favorable distribution was assured for both Republics than in the preceding years at the cost of the federation. In addition, the federal government agreed to a one-time transfer of a sizable amount to both Republics' budgets to be allocated in proportion to their population. In effect, however, the current Slovak advantage was preserved.[55]

A leading Czech politician commented on the situation:

[The Slovaks] are not horrified by the idea of each [Republic] being on its own. Some believe that this is in fact already the case and others pay so little attention to it that the Czechs find it strange and even suspicious. The Czechs have the impression that no rational talk is possible with the Slovaks . . . [and] they [the Czechs] worry that without the redistribution processes in favor of Slovakia the Slovak living standard comparable to the Czech level cannot be maintained and both economies will begin automatically to deviate from each other. Hence they are incensed at the Slovaks wanting a "loosening" of the federation when they cannot afford it. The Czechs take it as an expression of ingratitude and point out that the Slovaks have better highways, a better housing fund, better. . . . For [the Czechs] the issue is the quickest return to the advanced lands of Europe, for the Slovaks, national self-affirmation. The Slovaks are ready to risk the loss of the advantages of a federation, and they contrive an unviable conception of a "negotiating confederation" in order to obtain this self-affirmation.

What was the source of this self-confidence? Possibly "the faith in the creative powers and quality of an awakened nation . . . [that will] overcome the existing economic differences . . . [and] the pitfalls of the permanent negotiations with

---

54. In a 1991 seminar for Czech deputies with the Czech government, Czech Republic Finance Minister Karel Špaček estimated that the Czech Republic contributed seven billion crowns beyond its share based on the size of the population. The minister did not comment on the press reports, vehemently contested by the Slovaks, that the Czech Republic contributed to the federal budget ten times more than did the Slovak Republic. Record of a seminar held on September 19, 1991, pp. 2/2, 9/2, in the Library of the Czech Parliament.

55. Minister Klaus succeeded in preserving the current model of budget structure, which was favorable to Slovakia. Due to the inadequacy of the tax system, it was impossible to measure directly the amount of the transfer of funds to Slovakia. Estimates ranged from 15 to 40 billion Kčs, that is, about 3 to 8 percent of the overall amount of the budget. However, the transfers were lower than in previous years, and this caused difficulties in Slovakia. Ivan Svitek, "The 1992 State Budget in Czechoslovakia," RFE/RL Res. Rep., Feb. 28, 1992, 34–35.

the Czechs if only they will be equal with equals and perhaps even save the common state."[56]

The budget issue stimulated a spirited personal attack by then Federal Finance Minister Klaus against Czech Prime Minister Pithart, now "the defender of Czech interests," who reacted in kind.[57]

---

56. Jan Stráský, "Rozpočet a federace [The Budget and a Federation]," Přítomnost 10/1991, 9. *See generally,* Peter Martin, "Slovakia: Calculating the Cost of Independence," RFE/RL Res. Rep., Mar. 20, 1992, 33–38.

57. RP, Jan. 15, 1992, p. 3; Telegraf, Jan. 16, 1992, p. 2. For Klaus charging that the Republics behaved "in a socialist way," *see* ČSTK, Jan. 8, 1992.

IX

Back to the Republics' Legislatures: The Last Hurrah (February 1992)

1. Prelude to Milovy

In January 1992, while the Federal Assembly was in the process of decimating the president's program of constitutional reform, preparations were made for the next phase of the negotiations between the National Councils' presidia.

The Slovak National Council approved a draft of the treaty, which according to a Slovak Christian Democrat spokesman was "the first time in the history of Czech and Slovak coexistence, excluding the years under Communism, that Slovak politicians had come to a unified position." Significantly, according to this text, it was the two Republics that were to be parties to the treaty.[1]

Plaudits were heard from "the Castle" in Prague since of the original 22 controversial issues "only three or four are yet to be settled."[2] Press reports, on the other hand, indicated that little was settled on the fundamental issue addressing the nature of the common state. Prime Minister Čalfa expressed his skepticism and Ivan Čarnogurský complained that the Czechs had reverted to their original dominant federation, while Vladimír Mečiar, speaking for the opposition MDS, called the approved text the "debacle of Ján Čarnogurský" (a handy campaign theme) and said that his party continued to support a confederate form "while not excluding other possibilities."[3]

A new suggestion originating within the Civic Movement would include in the treaty only the basic principles underlying the common state, leaving the institutional parts for action by the Federal Assembly. This trial balloon was

---

1. ČSTK, Jan. 9, 1992; first paragraph of the preamble and art. 1 of the proposal amended according to the outcome of the voting of the Presidium of the Slovak National Council, Jan. 7, 1992 (my file).

2. ČSTK, Jan. 17, 1992; SS, Jan. 14, 1992, pp. 1, 3.

3. LN, Jan. 20, 1992, p. 2 (Čalfa); and Jan. 16, 1992, p. 2 (Mečiar). Mečiar sees CDA as "based on the principle of a few personalities," "unitarian," and "from the beginning openly hostile to his MDS. He views CDP as a real political power and he would admit cooperation with it. LN, Jan. 16, 1992, p. 2; TELEGRAF, Jan. 16, 1992, p. 2. On Ivan Čarnogurský, *see* SMENA, Feb. 3, 1992, p. 3.

promptly shot down by others on the Czech side.[4] A split within the Czech Civic Movement itself and within the Civil Democratic Alliance broke into the open on the festering issue of " 'repeated' ratification."[5] Czech Prime Minister Pithart, harking back to "Kroměříž," repeated his view "that a permanent principle of ratification turns this state into a confederation and I have never considered confederation."[6]

Eventually, the representatives of the presidia of the two National Councils, meeting in Bratislava, agreed to set up a committee from among their members, which, together with the spokesmen for the three governments and the experts, was to prepare materials for the next talks on the treaty.[7] This "internal committee" was viewed "as a new element in the marathon of the Czech-Slovak negotiations," and, according to the chair of the Czech National Council, Dr. Burešová, the very fact of its establishment testified to the will for a common state on both sides.[8]

2. In Snowbound Milovy: An Agreement in Sight?

a. On the Status of the Treaty

The meeting of the committee selected by the presidia of the National Councils took place from February 3 to 8 (with interruptions for consultations in Prague and Bratislava) in the southern Moravian village of Milovy, covered with a heavy layer of snow. The icy road made access difficult. The federal ministers Klaus and Dlouhý arrived in a helicopter. With the exception of the minuscule groupings, each political party was represented, as were the three governments. A retinue of Czech and Slovak legal experts was also on hand. The president was absent.

Consensus was reached on most, if not on all, of the competences to be allocated between the Federation and the Republics, and I shall return to this topic. However, at the center of the discussion were again the elusive problems of the nature of the treaty and "international legal subjectivity." The last mentioned issue more recently had become a preeminent point pressed by the Slovak side.[9]

The experts, led by Pavol Holländer, a Slovak and member of the Bratislava Law Faculty (and after the division of the country a judge at the Czech

---

4. Deputy Chair of the Czech National Council Jan Kalvoda in TELEGRAF, Jan. 16, 1992, p. 3. The idea was supported by the Christian Democrat Movement's Ján Petrík in *ibid.*, p. 1.

5. CM spokesman L. Konvička and the CDA's Jan Kalvoda in *ibid.*, p. 3.

6. *Ibid.*, p. 1.

7. ČSTK, Feb. 2, 1992.

8. "Neformální optimimus [Informal Optimism]," LN, Feb. 5, 1992, p. 1.

9. In this section, I rely primarily on the transcribed shorthand record of the Milovy meeting available in my file and cited as "transcript." The page numbers refer to the transcript. A differently paged transcription is in the Library of the Czech Parliament.

Constitutional Court), offered a proposal for a compromise weaving together the issues of the parties to the treaty, its legal nature, the ratification of the new federal constitution by National Councils, and the hierarchy between the federal and Republic constitutions:

1. The two National Councils, using their right under the current federal Constitution would offer the agreed text of the treaty to the Federal Assembly as a joint legislative initiative. The treaty would be a political act, "a point of departure (*východisko*) and a foundation" for the new federal constitution.[10]
2. The Federal Assembly would incorporate the treaty in the constitution. The constitution itself would be the treaty, as is the case in the United States.
3. However, the constitution approved by the Federal Assembly would become effective only after ratification by the National Councils. Moreover, major subsequent changes of the constitution would require ratification by the National Councils. This provision was necessary (in the Slovak view) to avoid a potential situation in which—because of a different constellation of political forces in the Federal Assembly and the Republic legislatures—one Republic disagreed with a change approved by the Assembly. As a result of the ratification clause, a new constitutional order would be created by the two Republics, although the process would be grounded in the prevailing constitution and a legal continuity would be preserved.
4. The federal and Republic constitutions would conform to the treaty and would be in harmony with each other, but the federal constitution would be the measure of the harmony.[11]

The response came from Ivan Čarnogurský, deputy chair of the Slovak National Council:

I am afraid that in your thinking you all are way off the track. You all move perfectly in a constitutional solution and in some valid constitutional order. . . . But do not forget one thing—even the Constitutions of the United States, France, the new Commonwealth of Independent States,

---

10. Transcript, p. 53. The Czech position relied on art. 107 of the 1968 constitutional law, allowing the National Councils to pass upon matters of internal policy, and art. 45, authorizing them to propose legislation to the Federal Assembly. It was essentially the Kalvoda-Pithart position at Hrádeček. The Slovaks relied on art. 3, speaking of an association of two nations and the right to self-determination.

11. Transcript, 53, 54, 56. The summary of the compromise offer is my own. On this phase of the negotiations, *see* the interview with Dr. Burešová in LN, Feb. 7, 1992, p. 1, back page.

new Yugoslavia, these are all constitutions that emerged after a revolution, after an abnormal, great explosion (*třesk*), which had brought about a new situation. . . . With us . . . instead of an abnormal, great explosion there are noisy negotiations, that is our revolution. And thereby should begin a new constitutional order. . . . A discussion continues as if nothing had happened . . . and we can't move from the spot. That's why I say, this piece of paper [the treaty] materializes the revolution; it expresses new rules on the basis of which we want to create a constitutional order and express it in the constitution.[12]

In a similar vein, albeit in a less effusive tone, a deputy in the Slovak National Council, Jozef Moravčík of the MDS, invoked the historic experience of broken understandings with the Czechs and insisted on a "legal character of the treaty" and on "legal guarantees," even if the situation would not correspond entirely with the current legal status.[13]

Jan Kalvoda, deputy chair of the Czech National Council and leader of the CDA, asked just what alternative solution to that described by the experts would be acceptable. What guarantees did deputy Moravčík have in mind in case of a violation of the treaty and exactly what status for the treaty? Moravčík replied that "we are for a certain cooperative power as it is being construed in Europe . . . roughly the integration of nations in Europe, that means after Maastricht";[14] "in that respect, positions of the political representations in Slovakia are not entirely uniform."[15] The legal constitutional guarantees sought by Moravčík were to be found, docent Holländer explained, not in the treaty itself but in the institution of ratification, and this was the basis for the formation of the entire new system. To give the treaty directly a legal status, it would be necessary to pass an amendment to the current Constitution that would "anchor" the treaty and impose upon the Federal Assembly an obligation to respect it.[16] This idea, as I related earlier, was rejected as early as in Kroměříž.

---

12. Transcript, p. 54. Ivan Čarnogurský, who ended up supporting the Milovy draft, told the press some days later: "What we are doing is really a bloodier revolution because we want to start a new legal and constitutional state. If we succeed without a single shot, we would deserve a Nobel Prize." To this, Jan Kalvoda responded: "In that case, there should be introduced Nobel Prizes for demagogy." MFD, Feb. 10, 1992, p. 2.

13. Transcript, pp. 63–64. Moravčík was then a docent and dean on the Comenius Law Faculty in Bratislava.

14. *Ibid.*, 37.

15. *Ibid.*, 64.

16. This possible approach was noted in the resolution of the Slovak National Council of November 15, 1991, mentioned earlier. L'. Kubín et al., *Dva roky politickej slobody* [Two Years of Political Freedom] 120 (RaPaMaN, Bratislava, 1992).

A member of the PDL, Deputy Ftáčnik, envisaged a treaty concluded by the National Councils in the name of the Republics; the new constitution would state that in principle it originated in the treaty. The treaty would be offered as "a higher order" legislative initiative, but the federal constitution would be the highest law of the common state and would remain in the legal order of both Republics as an obligation of one Republic toward the other.[17]

On the Czech side, the only dissent from the expert exposé came in a rather strident tone from Dr. Jiří Payne, a scientist of American ancestry and chair of the Foreign Affairs Committee in the Czech National Council. Echoing Prime Minister Pithart, he declared: "One-shot ratification—and that's the end. We shall not negotiate on further matters."[18] He saw a systematic and conscious attack on the present federal state and "an utterly dishonest approach to negotiations."[19] "Repeated ratification means something else than a common state and we have no mandate for it; it would preclude our membership in integrated Europe."[20] Payne was also greatly concerned to see a treaty as a political obligation parallel with constitutional norms.[21] Yet, after an explanation by Dr. Rychetský, Payne appeared to join the consensus on the Czech side.

In an atmosphere of general fatigue following an extensive debate, the expert draft was referred to a small group including among others Ivan Čarnogurský and two experts. This group produced a draft that eliminated any reference to the Republics as parties to the treaty. Instead, the preamble, following the text of the 1968 Constitutional Law, spoke of "we, the people of the Czech and Slovak Republics represented by the two National Councils."[22] It included the clause that the new constitution, after ratification by the two councils, would form "the continuation of the common state on a new, contractual foundation." The constitution must "proceed from this treaty." However, the provision for a repeated ratification was marked as "not negotiated." Paralleling Docent Holländer's original recommendation and contrary to insistent Slovak demands, the formulation did not identify the Republics as parties to the treaty, nor did it say that the treaty was a legal document of a continuing binding character. Moravčík (MDS) viewed this attempt at an intentional ambiguity as "burying the idea of a state treaty" and a success of the Czech side.[23]

---

17. Transcript, p. 63.
18. *Ibid.,* pp. 35, 36.
19. *Ibid.,* pp. 12, 25.
20. *Ibid.,* p. 55.
21. *Ibid.,* p. 56.
22. It is reported that this suggestion came from the Czech expert Dr. Zoulík.
23. NO, Feb. 10, 1992, p. 3; Feb. 19, 1992, p. 3. According to Chair Mikloško of the Slovak National Council, the Civic Movement appeared ready to make concessions on this issue, but the "right wing parties" led by Dr. Kalvoda absolutely refused: the treaty as a legal document between the Republics would be a definite precursor of the breakup. In the back of the Czech position was

160   Czecho/Slovakia

Intentional ambiguity is quite common on constitutional issues and in a less conflicting setting it may have been a solution. But Moravčik was quite correct in saying that the ambiguity was heavily slanted toward the Czech position. It was in this form that the text was eventually sent to both presidia.

i. First Parenthesis: The Curse of "Sovereignty"
Before the meetings in Bratislava and Milovy, I received a call from the chair of the Czech National Council, Dr. Dagmar Burešová of the Civic Movement. On the question of the parties to the treaty, I raised the idea of the "people," since it was used not only in the U.S. Constitution[24] but also in the preamble of the 1957 treaty establishing the European Community and in the preamble of the 1960–68 Czechoslovak federal Constitution. I wondered, however, why the Czech side would not concede that the Republics themselves, recognized as "sovereign" in the same Constitution, should be the parties to the treaty. This seemed to be the very core of the Slovak position. The component states of the United States, Germany, and other federations have the power to enter into "compacts" with their sister states, and such agreements have legal status under internal law. While the 1960–68 Constitution did not expressly delegate this power, it did not forbid it, and it would not impair the supremacy of the federal constitution.[25] Why not deideologize the problem at very little practical cost to the Czech position? I also said that I saw no theoretical or practical objection to the principle of repeated ratification. There is no reason why—in a genuine federation—the component states should not be given the last word about the federal constitution. The proof of the pudding was in the allocation of competences and that was, I thought, where Czech attention should be centered and where a large measure of agreement had been achieved. Some 18 months later, I spoke to then Professor Pithart, who at the crucial time was Czech prime minister. He told me: "I wish we had followed your advice."

"Sovereignty" as a normative and political concept both within a divided power state and in international relations has changed over time. With modern international human rights law intruding into the most intimate ties between the state and its own citizens and a plethora of international bodies performing important functions, it is absurd to speak of an "indivisible sovereignty." The

the concern that the anticipated leftist victory in Slovakia might spill over to the Czech lands. NO, Feb. 14, 1992, p. 3.

24. Walter Berns, "The Writing of the Constitution of the United States," in Robert A. Goldwin and Art Kaufman (eds.), Constitution Makers on Constitution Making 146–47 (American Enterprise Institute, Washington, D.C., 1988).

25. JUDr. Gabriel Brenka, at the time director of the Department of International Law and Treaties in the Federal Ministry of Foreign Affairs, told at a seminar held on May 12, 1992, at the ministry that it was possible for component states of the Federation to conclude treaties among themselves that would be governed by constitutional law. He thought it might even be useful. (Text in my file.)

Czech side used federal "sovereignty" to protect the status quo while the Slovaks invoked Republic "sovereignty" as leverage for change.

b. On Foreign Affairs Powers and "International Subjectivity": Milovy Continued

According to Jozef Moravčík and Ivan Čarnogurský, the goal of the treaty in the foreign affairs area was to assure that, in contrast with the present situation, the common foreign policy would result from "the harmonization of both Republics' [policies]."[26] On the table was a version of a treaty text, which had been approved earlier by the three executive branches and the presidia of the two National Councils:[27]

1. Relations with other states and international governmental organizations are within the competence of the common state. This does not affect the rights of the Czech and Slovak Republic to maintain independent foreign relations in harmony with the foreign policy of the common state.
2. The Czech Republic and the Slovak Republic may, with the *consent* of the common state, in areas falling within their competence, conclude international treaties in their own name.[28]

Slovak Minister of International Relations Demeš pointed out that the only discrepancy between this and the Slovak version was the word *consent,* which the Slovaks wanted to replace with *understanding.* Deputy Docent Fogaš of the Slovak PDL suggested adding an enumeration of areas in which the Republics could act without even "an understanding" with the common state. Dr. Burešová objected strenuously: "With an understanding" is out of the question since it implies two equal subjects, whereas the Federation is the only subject of international law and only the Federation could and would be responsible to other states for treaty obligations; moreover, any action would be blocked if there were no understanding: "I ask again, do we want a common state with all indispensable attributes?"[29]

After a discussion in which alternative terms were considered ("upon authorization," "upon empowerment," etc.), the decision was made to insert a

---

26. Transcript, p. 3.
27. Letter from JUDr. Gabriel Brenka, director of the Department of International Law and Treaties, Federal Ministry of Foreign Affairs, Nov. 22, 1991, in my file. I. I. Lukashuk, "Legal Foundation of International and Foreign Economic Relations of Subjects of the Russian Federation," 21 REVIEW OF CENTRAL AND EAST EUROPEAN LAW 545 (no. 6, 1995).
28. Transcript, p. 4, emphasis added.
29. Transcript, p. 5. In view of certain Slovak statements, there was concern on the Czech side that the Slovak Republic might want to conclude arms agreements with "risk" countries, contrary to the federal policy.

sentence that would in effect defer the issue by providing that the mode of assuring harmony with the foreign policy of the common state would be determined by a law of the common state.[30]

As regards the specific aspects of foreign relations power, I deal with the discussion on the allocation of treaty-making authority in the next section. As for foreign representation—an important element of international "visibility"—the Czech side agreed that the Republics would be able, within the areas of their competence, to send their own representatives abroad and receive foreign representatives.

In the waning days of the Federation, a somewhat expanded version of the agreed text actually became a part of federal law.[31]

---

30. As eventually agreed, the text read as follows:

Art. 10

The legislative and executive power of the common state includes:

(a) foreign policy, conclusion of international treaties, representation of the common state in international relations, and decisions on questions of war and peace.

This does not affect the right of the Czech Republic and of the Slovak Republic to appear in their own name in international relations in harmony with the foreign policy of the common state. This right consists of:

(aa) the right of the Czech Republic and of the Slovak Republic to conclude international treaties in their own names on matters falling within their competence as defined in the constitution of the common state; a law of the common state will regulate the mode of assuring harmony of such treaties with the foreign policy of the common state,

(ab) to conclude agreements with component parts of federal states in areas within the competence of the national Republics,

(ac) to represent the Czech Republic or the Slovak Republic and to receive foreign representation in areas within their competence; the status of these representations is determined by the legal order valid in the territory of the receiving subject . . . (Art. 10, proposal of treaty version 2.4, Milovy, Feb. 8, 1992).

The remainder of the article enumerates the remaining powers of the common state, including defense and implementation of international obligations.

31. In October 1992, when it was clear that the federal state would come to an end, the Federal Assembly adopted the final devolution law, which followed the Milovy text with some modifications: the Republics' treaty-making authority was expressly limited to bilateral international "agreements" (*dohody*) on matters within their competence, and it had to be "in harmony" not only with the federal foreign policy but also with international treaties binding the Federation. Moreover, the areas within which the Republics were authorized to conclude "agreements" of cooperation with *components* of composite states were specifically enumerated to include commercial, economic, cultural, scientific, educational, health, environmental protection, civil defense, sports, press, broadcasting, and television. Finally, the Republics were empowered to establish their own representation at the "subjects" with which they concluded agreements and to

ii. Second Parenthesis: The Disputed Treaty-Making Power

The text of the "treaty power" article has a long history.[32] In the fall of 1991 and the winter of 1992, I was asked to comment on several versions and—apart from the observations I made on specific drafts—I took the view that the increased legislative power of the Republics may be reasonably accompanied by their increased capacity in the international forum, including the power to enter into international agreements, exercised in harmony with the common foreign policy and under some safeguards ensuring such harmony.[33]

I suggested that the common state would remain the principal "international person" in relation to the outside world, but the international capacity of the two Republics would be recognized within specific limits. The Austrian, Swiss, and other constitutions offered precedents to such arrangements. The foreign state-partner in the negotiations should be able to accept such a format, providing the competence of the Republics was made clear. I saw no merit in the Czech idea that a treaty negotiated by the Republic with a foreign state had to be "in the name of the common state."[34]

An agreement between the Republics and a component part of another state would not be classified as an international treaty in the classic sense. The status of this type of an agreement is not very clear, even though it has been used in practice by Austria, the Federal Republic of Germany, the United States, Canada, Mexico, and Switzerland. These agreements deal usually with local problems and amount typically to arrangements for mutual cooperation. Even if the scope were broadened as contemplated here, I would argue that

---

receive their representatives, all that, of course, in harmony with federal foreign policy and federal treaties. Const. Law 493/1992 Sb. of Oct. 8, 1992, art. I(4). The instruments of foreign commercial policy are established by the Federation organs "in cooperation" with the two Republics, art. I(10); and the federal president, "taking note of the positions" of the three governments, "entrusts the chiefs of diplomatic missions so as to ensure equal representation of Czech and Slovak citizens," art. I(26).

32. *Supra,* chap. IV, 3.

33. I paraphrase here my faxes sent to the Czech National Council from Florence, Italy, on October 26, 1991, in response to a series of questions and on Jan. 22, 1992, from Ann Arbor, Michigan.

34. This requirement would confuse the foreign partner by raising something akin to the agency concept, and it would obscure the question of international responsibility: if the other state breaches the treaty, who will be entitled to press an international claim: the common state (which is not a party to the treaty) acting alone or jointly with the Republic; or the Republic, which is a party, although the treaty is "in the name" of the common state? Even the protofederal system of the European Union does not allow this sort of an arrangement. It is possible for the Union as such to join the member states in making an international treaty with a nonmember state when such a treaty deals with subjects within the separate jurisdictions of the Community and of the members, but it is not possible for the member states to conclude a treaty "in the name" of the Union authorities.

only the Republic party to the agreement and not the common state would be bound and that the common state would not be responsible for compliance.[35]

The situation would be somewhat different in the case of agreements between a Republic and another state, a full international person. The international law character of such an agreement would be more pronounced. There would be a greater likelihood of a conflict with federal policies and a greater need for assuring harmony with such policies. If the agreement were generally of a procedural nature, setting forth modes of cooperation and eschewing substantive obligations, one could take the view that only the contracting Republic was bound and responsible, but there might be some doubt about this. In any case, there was the problem of assuring harmony with the federal policy, particularly in the commercial field where the common state had a specific treaty power.

As for the form of a guarantee of harmony with the common state foreign policy, I suggested consulting the Austrian Constitution as amended in 1988.[36] In view of the insistence by the Slovaks on increasing the "international visibility" of Slovakia, I suggested also that the Belgian arrangements, laborious, inefficient, and costly as they may be, ought nevertheless to be considered. According to the broadly amended Belgian Constitution, the subnational linguistic communities and regions wield exclusive treaty-making powers in matters within their internal competence; a complex conceit based on cooperation of the central and regional authorities is to assure the conformity of such treaties with the Belgian federal foreign policy and international obligations, and the modalities of the conclusion of these regional treaties are left for determination by a law to be adopted through procedures reminiscent of the prohibition of majorization in the Czech-Slovak federal Constitution.[37]

---

35. The negotiating foreign state could be charged with the knowledge of the particular constitutional provisions, but, better still, the partner state should be advised of it at the outset of the negotiations.

36. Constitution of the Republic of Austria, art. 16, *translated in* I Constitutions of the Countries 45 (1985). According to that constitution, the federal government must be notified before the component *"Land"* starts negotiations, the federal president empowers the *Land* to negotiate (and may refuse to do so), and the federal government must give its consent before the conclusion (if not given within eight weeks it is presumed as given). If the *Land* does not comply with its treaty so concluded, the federal government takes over the implementation, but the *Land* is free at any time to undertake compliance, in which case the federal authority ceases.

37. Robert Anderson, "Les Compétences," in Francis Delpérée (ed. and coauthor), La Constitution Fédérale du 5 May 1993, 125, 138–53 (Bruylant, Bruxelles, 1993), including references to the specific provisions. The system was criticized in Belgium as being "of an extreme complexity and making considerably more burdensome the decision-making process at a time when international relations and the conclusion of treaties are subject to development without precedent." *Ibid.,* 152. The most recent relevant amendments to the 1831 Constitution are in 163 Moniteur Belge, May 8, 1993, no. 91. *See supra,* chap. I, note 27.

Thinking back with the benefit of hindsight, it might have been wise to stress the Belgian pattern more vigorously, although in the end it may not have proved acceptable to the Czechs, nor would it have met the demands for full "international subjectivity" ultimately advanced by Mečiar and Kňažko.

c. Once More: The Allocation of Competences— "Sovereignty" Again: Milovy Continued

Docent Holländer explained at Milovy that the objective of the expert proposal was to eliminate the imprecise and unclear division of competences in the 1990 law,[38] which was replete with concepts lacking any legal content. The new, "simple" approach conjured up the enumeration of two sets of competences: first, the areas in which the Federation would have both legislative and implementing (sublegislative) powers; and, second, the areas in which it would have legislative power only. But the allocation of the implementing power would be left to ordinary legislation since a detailed division in a constitution was not workable. Deputy Moravčík objected that shifting the vital decision on implementing jurisdiction to an ordinary law meant that "all [constitutional] guarantees are lost."

As a remedy, Deputy Ftáčnik, supported by Deputy Tatár, suggested that any such ordinary law must be accepted "after an understanding" with the Republics. This, according to Docent Holländer, would mean "creating a new parliament," and Dr. Kalvoda termed it an unacceptable "transposition of federal principles into a disguised confederation."[39] "As you know," said Deputy Payne, "I cannot consider your objections, which you present as ignorance, but as a design [against a common state]."[40] After another exchange on the nature of a federation, Deputy Ftáčnik agreed to drop the "after an understanding" clause in favor of an alternative that would require that certain laws allocating the implementing jurisdiction (in matters of prices, wages, and environment) would be in the form of a constitutional law while all other such laws would be subject to the prohibition of majorization that would protect the Republics.

The allocation of jurisdiction for the protection of frontiers and customs legislation sparked another episode of a highly theoretical legal debate. Would Republic competence in this important field impair "the external sovereignty" or "the territorial sovereignty" of the Federation as the "sole international subject"? In arguing for the Republic jurisdiction, the Slovaks had some practi-

---

38. Transcript, *supra,* note 9, 21.
39. *Ibid.,* 21, 22.
40. *Ibid.,* 23.

cal concerns in the back of their minds.[41] Deputy Žák of the Civic Movement
attempted to inject some realism into the issue by pointing out that the Republics as well as the common state must have "sovereignty": the question was
what was "minimal sovereignty" for the common state. He noted that a series
of competences had been "returned" to the Republics, but among the existential competences that define a common state were customs and frontier protection.[42] When the discussion turned from abstract concepts to an analysis of the
existing arrangements "on the ground" for the protection of frontiers and
collection of customs, a compromise became possible.[43]

During the detailed discussion of competences in the economic area, the
leading role was assumed by the Czech ministers in the federal government,
particularly the widely respected Minister Dlouhý. Ivan Čarnogurský complained about the continuing effort to strengthen the common state on the
pretext of improving its functionality: what was needed in the first place was a
functioning single customs territory and single capital market *of the Republics*
and only then a harmony of the two sectors in the framework of the common
state.[44] On that, Federal Deputy Finance Minister Kočárník observed that the
Republics could function only within the framework of a single market: "we
want the market to function, nothing else."[45]

Deputy Moravčík claimed more taxing power for the Republics, pointing
to the great flexibility "even in federal states."[46] Minister Dlouhý preferred the
competence regarding wages to be dealt with together with prices rather than as
a part of the social package, but he did not persist. Ivan Čarnogurský urged
three central banks, but in the end the Slovak side accepted a single bank of
emission—a concession infused with symbolism.[47]

---

41. Chair Mikloško of the Slovak National Council told the press that the Slovaks were
nervous because "certain expected personnel changes" of people "who could not be controlled"
had not been made, and about "small mafias," and above all that complaints against Slovak
customs decisions must be decided via Prague. But he realized the need for a single control organ,
a customs council. NO, Feb. 10, 1992, p. 3.

42. Transcript, p. 11. Deputy Payne again complained that the Slovaks insisted on changes
in the present system by pressing proposals that "do not conform with a common state": "This
strikes me as an utterly dishonest approach to negotiations." PDL Deputy Docent Fogaš was
unhappy "about this tone" and thought the statement confirmed the Czech unwillingness to
negotiate except strictly on their own terms. *Ibid.*, p. 12.

43. Deputy Ivan Čarnogurský noted that a solution was found on the participation of the
common state to be determined by a law of the Federal Assembly, "which would prevent unilateral
solution" (p. 32). *See also* views of Kalvoda, Ivan Čarnogurský, and Dobrovský in "Neformální
optimismus," *supra,* note 8, p. 1, back page.

44. Transcript, p. 28.

45. *Ibid.,* 28.

46. *Ibid.,* 25.

47. Minister Dlouhý told the press: "We shall not retreat on the question of two central
banks." LN, Feb. 7, 1992, p. 1. For the eventual compromise text, see the final proposal in LN, Feb.
7, 1992, p. 1.

The Slovak side objected to the term "single market" and suggested "common market" instead. Federal Deputy Prime Minister Rychetský proposed that the government of the common state should be able, with the consent of the Republic governments, to appoint coordination institutions for unifying the processes of the executive organs in matters entrusted to the Republics.[48] The proposal was accepted.

The discussions, conducted partly in smaller groups with alternative drafts produced by the experts, suggested a substantial degree of consensus, which Chair Dr. Burešová wanted to be expressed in a vote. Dr. Kalvoda disagreed. The Slovak National Council chair, František Mikloško, confirmed that on the Slovak side, the government coalition accepted the allocation of competences but the opposition did not, a problem to be faced by the Slovak Presidium and the plenary National Council.[49]

d. The Institutions: "The Three Heads"

The Milovy deliberations on restructuring the institutions paralleled the Federal Assembly debate on "the three heads" and had the explicit blessing of the Assembly leadership as hopefully paving the way to an affirmative solution in the Assembly. Dr. Burešová told the press that—in view of the pending elections—a failure (in Milovy) to agree on the treaty would block the action on this subject in the Federal Assembly as presently constituted.[50]

The discussion at Milovy about the structure of the legislature was drowned in the controversy over the ratification of the new constitution by the National Councils and the principle of prohibition of majorization, which I described earlier.[51] A consensus crystallized, however, on the composition of the legislative Chamber of Deputies and a Senate "created on the principle of [Czech and Slovak] parity" and on the president as the head of the common state, elected by the legislature.

A dispute persisted over further devices that would meet Slovak claims for parity. The arguments for and against "state secretaries" in all ministries (a Slovak to a Czech minister and vice versa), which were heard in the Federal Assembly, resonated here, but the institution was generally rejected as a parity device. The deputies Moravčík and Ftáčnik supported a compromise, according to which the state secretaries would be appointed only in "key ministries." Federal Prime Minister Čalfa as well as Civic Movement Deputy Žák would

---

48. Transcript, p. 31.
49. *Ibid.,* p. 33.
50. "Neformální optimismus," *supra,* note 8, p. 1, back page.
51. *Supra,* chap. 3, 8a.

accept this solution, providing that the state secretaries would not be full-fledged members of government.

There was some support for a rule requiring Czech-Slovak parity in the composition of the federal government and for a rotation between the federal Czech president and a Slovak prime minister. However, the view appeared to prevail that a better approach, outlined by Dr. Rychetský and seconded by Dr. Kalvoda, was to rely on "political mechanisms" and avoid complicating the already difficult process of selecting a government.

Although Deputy Ftáčnik questioned the need for a common Supreme Court, it was agreed that it, as well as the Supreme Auditing Board, should be organized on a parity basis, as was already provided for the Constitutional Court.

An announcement was made that during the ensuing noon intermission the representatives of the National Councils' presidia would inform the media, but a sharp disagreement surfaced over the content of any public statement.[52]

---

52. *Chair of the Slovak National Council František Mikloško:* We can affirm that in the basic questions of competences and in the basic questions of the formation of the supreme organs . . . agreement was reached, which we shall submit to the presidia. With the addition, I can state that on the Slovak scene there are certain reservations, but the Slovak coalition parties achieved a consensus with the Czech side.

Deputy Chair of the Slovak National Council Ivan Čarnogurský: That is not a wise formulation. We prepared in our committee a proposal for a formulation of the problem. It is for the National Councils to vote definitely on this text. We should not say in advance who agrees with it and who does not. We succeeded in making a text that will be presented to the National Councils.

Deputy Moravčík: I raised a basic comment on the competences. It is up to you, Mr. Chairman, to decide whether you will present it. I will make it public . . .

Chair of the Slovak National Council František Mikloško: May I recall that as a result of the presence of the federal organs, the material was accepted on the part of the federal ministers?

Deputy Chair of the Government Pavel Rychetský: It would be good to say that the committee of the Presidia of the two National Councils invited representatives of the Republic governments and of the federal government for the solution of concrete problems in the area of executive competences. . . . We cannot say that the [federal] government completely agrees. I for myself believe that in terms of the principles of the defined competences the model is more functional than that we have today.

Chair of the Slovak National Council František Mikloško: There were reservations in principle against any changes in the executive power on the part of the Civic Democratic Party.

Deputy Chair of the Slovak National Council Ivan Čarnogurský: Although among us no absolute agreement was reached, full agreement was reached among experts representing the Czech, Slovak, and federal governments.

Deputy Oldřich Kužílek: I would plead that nothing should be concealed. . . . I turn to Madam Chair to communicate that there is a dispute on the Slovak side.

Deputy Karel Ledvinka: I consider it important to praise the understandings of all three

It is reported, however, that at the very end of the meeting, on February 8, although no document was signed, there was "an impression" of a consensus on the final text and champagne was offered to celebrate it. The parting was said to have been quite moving, with a feeling of a last chance saved and disaster avoided.

The same day, February 8, the two chairs of the National Councils, Dr. Burešová and František Mikloško, told journalists that the committee had reached an agreement as regards power sharing between the Federation and the Republics and on the fundamental structure of the common state.[53]

President Havel's spokesman viewed the result of the committee's talks as a "significant progress," though "any jubilation would be premature." It was important that the prevailing consensus on the wording of the agreement be maintained and endorsed as soon as possible by the Republic parliaments.[54]

e. Summing Up

Dr. Burešová described the "informal" committee as a "new element in the marathon of Czech-Slovak negotiations, a 'nonorthodox, operational,' sondage and feeling out of attitudes, which proved impossible at the official level."[55] However, on the face of it there appeared to be little difference between "the committee" and the preceding broader gatherings of the presidia representatives. The complexity of this two-party, multiissue negotiating mode was little short of astounding not just because of the ongoing regrouping of the political forces but because of the laborious process of consensus making both within the parties and between them. Involved were the top organs of the political parties, which were organized at the Republic level, the "clubs" (factious) of their deputies in the Federal Assembly (ten small clubs of the Czech parties' deputies) and in the two National Councils, the presidia of the Councils, and finally the plenary councils, which formulated the negotiation mandates for the presidia representatives. The federal and Republic ministers' input varied from topic to topic and from one personality to another. The profusion of actors (mostly lacking any relevant experience), interests, and interactions was daunting.

The two chairpersons of the National Councils, Dr. Burešová and Fran-

---

governments . . .

Deputy Tatár: It is possible to state that different political parties have a different view of the problem.

(Transcript, *supra,* note 9, 50–51).

53. ČSTK, Feb. 8, 1992.

54. ČSTK, Feb. 10, 1992. For a published brief summary of the draft, see ČSTK, Feb. 10, 1992.

55. LN, Feb. 5, 1992, p. 1.

tišek Mikloško, directed the proceedings, although in some parts other participants (Dr. Kalvoda and Ivan Čarnogurský) presided. President Havel was absent, and the presidency was the only organ that had no representation, a further indication of its diminished influence. The legal experts performed a useful function in sharpening issues and offering alternatives regarding the allocation of disputed competences.

The essentially two-party, multiissue discourse remained the rule, even when federal ministers—presumably "guests"—assumed the principal role, as on the issue of certain competences where their experience and knowledge of facts proved indispensable; the Czech Republic spokesmen retreated into the background, tacitly supporting the federal officials in the interest of a "functional federalism." This interplay was obviously noted by the Slovak side. Ivan Čarnogurský, deputy chair of the Slovak National Council, told the press:

> The intervention of the Federation complicates the entire negotiation to such an extent that at times we don't know whether it is about a treaty between the Republics or an improvement of some federal model.[56]

In the same vein, the opposition PDL spokesman Docent Fogaš told me later, the rephrasing of competences in the economic field made in response to the federal economic ministers was the reason why he ceased to favor the text.[57] Finally, according to Prime Minister Pithart:

> [T]he situation might not have ended the way it did if from the beginning the Czech and Slovak Republics had negotiated as partners, Czech government and Slovak government, . . . both parliaments . . . but as soon as we [the Czech Republic spokesmen] appeared together with the Federation, and in a majority of instances with almost identical views, we confirmed the Slovak delegation in their fixed idea that the Federation is merely a prolonged arm of the Czech Republic. This one attitude worsened the negotiations to such an extent that the Slovak representatives discovered "the state treaty" and began to insist on it.[58]

Others argued, however, that the cause of the ultimate failure was the decision to pass the responsibility from the executive branches to the legisla-

---

56. LN, Feb. 8, 1992, p. 1.
57. Conversation in June 1993.
58. Petr Pithart in PROSTOR, July 8, 1992, p. 12.

tures of the two Republics, which were not organized in a way to be capable of effective negotiations.

On the Czech side, Deputy Žák and up to a certain point Deputy Prime Minister Rychetský led the "moderates." Dr. Burešová, although emotionally anxious for a compromise, appeared more than others a prisoner of theoretical concepts hindering practical solutions, particularly on the issue of the parties to the treaty and "international subjectivity." As was the case before, doctrinal arguments were used by both sides in support of their political objectives. Czech Deputy Dr. Payne's emphatic interventions elicited corresponding lively reactions on the Slovak side, but in the end, after several late night telephone conversations with Dr. Burešová, he was reported to have acquiesced in the final text, as did Dr. Jan Kalvoda.

Kalvoda's statement made at the margin of the conference illuminates his basic tactical posture. On the face of it, he said, to take a responsible attitude would entail acting on the basis of the awareness that a breakup of the state would be a catastrophe. However, anyone coming to the negotiations burdened by this weight is at the mercy of the partner; "responsibility in my view is a readiness in this situation to accept the risk [of the breakup]."[59] He criticized the Czech representatives for not employing all available means in the negotiations, including the budget.[60] Yet in the final stance the Czech side appeared to have papered over its differences.

On the Slovak side, Chair Mikloško was the moderating influence, as was Prime Minister Čalfa, to the extent that he chose to intervene. The spokesmen for the opposition MDS, deputies Moravčík (MDS) and Ftáčnik (PDL), carried the message for "a change," invariably supported by the deputy chair of the Slovak National Council, Ivan Čarnogurský, even though his Christian Democratic Movement was the strongest member of the coalition in the Slovak government and as such was expected to take a more moderate line. The other opposition PDL deputy, Fogaš, carefully avoided any appearance of a conflict with the Moravčík-Ftáčnik duo.

The Milovy text was welcomed by the mainstream Czech media, by some even with enthusiasm, as "an unexpected victory of constitutionalism and law."[61] Surprisingly, considering his rhetoric at Milovy, it was endorsed strongly by Ivan Čarnogurský, who even agreed with Jan Kalvoda that the final text did not contemplate a treaty with the Republics as parties—since such an interpretation might contravene the current constitution. Chair Mikloško— clearly aware of the neuralgic point of the consensus—sought to belittle this "most problematic" issue; he termed the crucial preambular provision (refer-

59. LN, Feb. 4, 1992, pp. 1, 3.
60. *Ibid.*
61. MFD, Feb. 10, 1992, p. 2.

ring to "the people") "a mere festive introduction," and stressed the provisions in the body of the text which spoke of national states and their sovereignty.[62]

The text was approved also by the Christian Democrat leadership, including Ján Čarnogurský, because, although expressed in a "somewhat Solomon-like way," it envisaged a treaty between the Republics and devolved more powers from the center to the Republics, and by the chairman of the Hungarian Civil Party, Laszlo Nagy. It was opposed, however, by Vladimír Mečiar, SNP Chair Jozef Prokeš, and, last but not least, Peter Weiss, the chairman of the Party of the Democratic Left, who called the draft "a political failure of the Slovak government."[63] Both Weiss and Fogaš favored more powers for the Republics but—perhaps more importantly—they saw which way the nationalist wind was blowing in Slovakia. This meant that practically the entire opposition in the Slovak National Council did not favor the text.

3. The Milovy Text in the Presidia

On February 11, 1992, the Milovy draft treaty was approved by the Presidium of the Czech National Council "as a basic platform" for talks on the final version of an agreement. It was rejected by the Slovak Presidium a day later by a ten to ten vote, with 11 votes required for approval.[64]

The decisive negative votes were cast by four dissident members of Ján Čarnogurský's Christian Democratic Movement. These dissidents and some others had been defeated in the earlier party convention and left the party

---

62. In an interview, Deputy Ftáčnik stated that, during an intermission at Milovy, Ivan Čarnogurský and Kalvoda agreed that parties to the treaty would not be named: "In substance, we fogged in the whole thing. It is not possible to read from the formulation whether the Republics are the subjects of the treaty." By a reference to the prevailing legal situation "we attempted to conceal the things in a certain way." SMENA, Feb. 10, 1992, p. 2. *See also* Ivana Vajnerová, "ČNR-SNR: nekrvavá revoluce [Bloodless Revolution]," *ibid.;* ČSTK, Feb. 13, 1992. For the Slovak reaction, see NO, Feb. 11, 1992, p. 12.

63. ČSTK, Feb. 14, 1992. According to Mečiar, acceptance of the Milovy text would have been a tragedy since it denied the Slovak Republic the status of a subject as well as the principle of building the state from below, strengthened the central bureaucracy, and showed lack of tolerance and understanding on the Czech side and the "servility" of the Slovak representatives. Radio-žurnál, Feb. 11, 1992, in PRAVDA, Feb. 12, 1992, p. 3. On Čarnogurský, *see* NO, Feb. 12, 1992, p. 3; ČSTK, Feb. 18, 1992; and Karol Svoboda, "Legal and Political Events between 1989 and 1992," in Viktor Knapp and Sergio Bartole, La dissoluzione della Federazione cecoslovacca 45, 71 (La Rosa Ed., Torino, 1994).

64. On February 25, 1991, the plenary Slovak National Council took note of its Presidium's rejection of the Milovy text, recommended that the clubs of deputies pass on their observations to the Presidium, asked the Presidium of the Czech National Council to take a similar step with a view toward mutual exchange of information, and it recommended to its own Presidium to meet as soon as possible with the Czech Presidium in order to explore in common the possibility for concluding a treaty. Uznesenie Slovenskej národnej rady 253 z 25. februára 1992 [Resolution of the Slovak National Council of Feb. 25, 1992], 253.

shortly thereafter (on March 7) to form a new nationalist-oriented party called the Slovak Christian Democratic Movement.[65] The members of the governing board of the Christian Democratic Movement sitting in the Presidium did not have the time to consult before the crucial vote and thus voted their personal consciences. The party board itself was divided, inclining toward a negative view of the draft, primarily, Ján Čarnogurský said, because it failed to specify the Republics as the parties to the treaty.[66]

When asked to explain their negative vote, the leader of the dissenters, Ján Klepáč, deputy chair of the Slovak National Council, listed the following reasons: first, the elimination from the text of the "fundamental element" of the Slovak proposal, naming the Republics as the parties to the treaty; and, second, "significant shifts" in the allocation of competences in foreign affairs, internal security, protection of frontiers, customs, and a central bank, a single unit replacing "the Slovak proposed three." "We want a document that makes visible the two subjects."[67]

In the spring of 1993, I posed the same question to another member of the Slovak Presidium who cast a negative vote, Dr. Milan Zemko, who at the time of Milovy was deputy chair of the Slovak National Council and after the breakup was made responsible for internal policy in the office of the president of the new Slovak Republic. He voted "no" in protest against Mikloško and Čarnogurský's insistence on a yes or no vote, even though the Czech Presidium had approved the text "as a starting point" only, and also because he was convinced that the text would fail in the plenary National Council, causing a serious crisis. Furthermore, he cited the same two grounds invoked by Klepáč, adding that, since under the proposal the Federal Assembly was given too much power, there would be pressure for removing the principle of prohibition of majorization, ending eventually with a "unitarian legislature"; although most of the allocation of competences was acceptable, a danger of continuing conflicts was too great.[68] The lack of trust ran deep on the Slovak side.

---

65. ČSTK, Mar. 19, 1992.

66. ČSTK, Feb. 23, 1992. Forty-five members of the governing board were against the draft, 35 supported it, and 21 abstained. ČSTK, Feb. 25, 1992.

67. "Slovensko není vidět [One Cannot See Slovakia]," LN, Feb. 18, 1992, p. 3: since a federation based on the "civic principle" is unacceptable to the majority of Slovaks and a confederation to the majority of Czechs, and the independent states way means excessive risk for both, the solution is in the image of the 1867 Austrian-Hungarian duality.

68. A PDL member of the Presidium of the Slovak National Council explained the negative vote on the Milovy text: it did not make the treaty a legal and permanently valid document as demanded by Resolution 197 of the Slovak National Council, it transferred certain competences to the Federation, and in the Presidium the vote was forced without a possibility for offering modifications. Milan Ftáčnik, chair of the PDL club in the Slovak National Council in PRAVDA, Feb. 19, 1992, p. 7. Similarly, *see* PDL Fogaš in RP, Feb. 19, 1992, p. 3.

There was wide speculation as to whether the draft would or would not have passed the plenary of either council, with those opposed to it taking a negative view of the prospects. Contrary to pessimistic press predictions, Jan Kalvoda told me later that passage in the Czech Council, at any rate, would have been very likely.[69]

4. "The Three Heads" in the Federal Assembly: The Dead End

The Federal Assembly returned to the bill on the institutional structure of the federal constitution on February 18, 1992, shortly after the defeat of the Milovy draft treaty. The Slovak PDL deputies proposed amendments that would make it clear that the constitution was adopted "on the basis of a treaty concluded between the Czech Republic and the Slovak Republic" and that any changes in the constitution required the ratification by the Republic National Councils.[70] This was clearly an effort, supported by the Czech Communist Party, to salvage the two Slovak basic claims thought to have been abandoned in Milovy. The amendments were defeated. In fact, only four of the many proposed modifications obtained the necessary majority, including the Slovak proposal for expanding the Senate competence (and thereby the scope of the prohibition of majorization) to important areas of tax and the major legal codes.[71] When the bill as amended was put to a vote, it failed by three votes in the Slovak part of the Chamber of Nations.[72] Subsequent proceedings in the Assembly "conciliation committee"[73] ended without an agreement, and the final effort to revive the bill failed in the Chamber of Nations by four votes.[74]

---

69. A Czech daily predicted a defeat in the Czech Council plenary: the Christian Democrats, the CDP, CDA, and others opposed the "national principle" expressed in the clause "association of national states," and CDA wanted further negotiations on the inclusions of the "repeated ratification." CDP Jiří Payne expected more amendments and a "stormier discussion" (MFD, Feb. 12, 1992, p. 2); however, CDP nevertheless would vote for the text (LN, Feb. 12, 1992, p. 3). In Deputy Žák's, opinion, the text would have failed in the Czech National Council because of the "repeated ratification" clause; the plenary Slovak National Council would have rejected it because the Republics were not made parties to the treaty.

70. F.A. Rep. of 20th joint sess., 6th elect. term, 7th part, Feb. 17, 1992, p. 1446, amendment by PDL Deputy P. Kanis. Kanis explained the position of his party in a full-page interview in NO, Mar. 2, 1992, p. 9. PDL Milan Ftáčnik confirmed the fear that the acceptance of the "three heads" would end any interest in the reconstruction of the state and render the treaty between the Republics "an useless act." SMENA, Feb. 3, 1992, p. 3.

71. Fed. Ass. Rep., 20th joint session, 6th elec. term, 8th part, Feb. 18, 1992, pp. 1689, 1699–1701.

72. *Ibid.*, 1727; ČSTK, Feb. 18, 1992.

73. That committee is comparable to the U.S. House-Senate conference, which is called when there is a discrepancy between the versions of a bill as adopted by the two houses.

74. Zdeněk Jičínský, "Ke ztroskotání československého federalismu [On the Foundering of the Czechoslovak Federalism]," in Rüdiger Kipke and Karel Vodička (eds.), Rozloučení s

After the rejection of the Milovy draft in the Slovak Presidium, the two chairpersons of the National Councils, Dr. Burešová and Mikloško, attempted valiantly to restore the dialogue between the two parliaments in line with a resolution of the Slovak National Council. However, the Czech Presidium agreed with Dr. Kalvoda and a CDP spokesman that after the failure in its Slovak counterpart there was nothing to discuss until the Slovak side came up with new proposals.[75] Despite a lonely appeal by the Czech Prime Minister Pithart for more talks, it became increasingly clear that the task of writing a new constitution would have to be left for the newly elected Assembly.[76]

On March 11, Dr. Burešová and Chair Mikloško called on President Havel at the Hradčany Castle to inform him of the decision to suspend the talks, with the idea that they would be resumed after the elections. The president thought that representatives of the two Republics might review the achievements of the talks and identify the issues to be decided by the new Assembly.[77]

In a nostalgic mood, Dr. Burešová looked back at the four sessions of the presidia, the role of the federal Constitutional Commission, and the president's own initiatives at the "castles and manors"; the lack of success was due, in her opinion, mainly to the failure of the Slovak Presidium to accept the Milovy draft, a basis for "an authentic federation composed of two equal Republics." Chair Mikloško, on the other hand, opined that for the Czech politicians the theses of an authentic federation were mere words. This is why in 1990 then Prime Minister Mečiar initiated a change in the allocation of competences but the resulting 1990 law "was made quickly and not well under tremendous political pressure." After its enactment, the Czech side complicated the situation by considering the matter closed. Since the Czech side never came up with a new model for a federation, the Slovak representatives had the burden of always starting the negotiations and urging further reallocation of powers; this caused a split of the Slovak political scene, and certain forces in Slovakia drew political capital "from the struggle against the Czech Republic." The Milovy document failed in a number of areas, including the absence of the definition of the parties to the treaty. All ended in the unsuccessful vote in the Slovak Presidium. Mikloško praised President Havel's initiatives.[78]

Československem [Parting with Czechoslovakia] 67, 78 (Český spisovatel a.s., Prague, 1993); ČSTK, Feb. 20, 1992; ČSTK, Feb. 23, 1992.

75. Comment by Chair Mikloško in NO, Mar. 7, 1992, p. 3; ČSTK, Mar. 11, 1992; and ČSTK, Mar. 12, 1992 (Alexander Dubček's response to Kalvoda's statement that there is no longer anything to discuss). *See generally,* LN, Mar. 7, 1992, p. 8; and LN, Mar. 11, 1992, p. 1 and back page.

76. ČSTK, Feb. 25, 1992; ČSTK, Mar. 11, 1992.

77. Spokesman M. Žantovský in ČSTK, Mar. 11, 1992.

78. "Sbohem a volby [Fairwell and Elections]," LN, Mar. 12, 1992, p.1; ČSTK, Mar. 11, 1992. On Mikloško's final report to the Slovak National Council, *see* ČSTK, Apr. 1, 1992. In its

The first freely elected Parliament in 40 years, with a record of 167 new laws adopted in two years, concluded its last session with the Czechoslovak national anthem.[79] When saying their goodbyes, the deputies were unusually "kind and friendly," some leaving for good and others hoping to return after the elections.[80] Most of those hoping to return were in for a bitter disappointment.

final report on the activities of the Deputies' Commission for the Preparation of the Federal Constitution, its chair, Alexander Dubček, put the blame for the failure of the Assembly effort on the inability of the two National Councils to agree on the treaty.

79. LN, May 1, 1992, p. 1.
80. LN, May 4, 1992, p. 1.

X

Onward to the Elections (Spring 1992)

1. The Campaign

The 1990 elections were in effect a people's referendum on the rejection of the Communist regime with little doubt about the outcome and some 96 percent of the eligible voters taking part. In the 1992 elections, on the other hand, it was not "the people" but the individual voters who had to choose from 40 parties (13 more than in 1990) offering a confusing profusion of mostly similar platforms.[1] A commentator (with obviously elite tendencies) wrote that it was "almost a cruel joke that literally everyone has the right to decide on the fate of the nation, including those who do not understand and are manipulated, and the widest variety of nincompoops [imbeciles]."[2] This aspect of democracy dawned upon the people unaccustomed to making free choices at a time of diminishing optimism about the new state of affairs and increasing impatience with the "endless" and baffling constitutional negotiations.

A number of parties rushed into alliances designed to overcome the minimum votes requirement for admission of a party to a legislative body, but no party or alliance was effectively organized on an all-federal basis.[3] That fact did not bode well for the profederal forces.

Three principal issues dominated the campaign.

First, the ways and means and the pace of the economic reform were a major subject in both Republics. In the Czech Republic, the right-of-center groups advocated a radical and rapid reform program while the center-left and

---

1. Substantial literature deals with the elections in Central-Eastern Europe. Some of it is cited in David M. Olson, "Dissolution of the State Political Parties and the 1992 Elections in Czechoslovakia," 26 COMMUNIST AND POST-COMMUNIST STUDIES 301 (no. 3, 1993). *See generally* Jiří Pehe, "Czechoslovakia: Parties Register for Elections," RFE/RL RES. REP., May 1, 1992, 20–25; and Jan Obrman, "The Czechoslovak Elections: A Guide to the Parties," *ibid.,* May 29, 1992, 10–16.

2. Jiří Franěk in LN, June 5, 1992, p. 1.

3. The uniform requirement for a minimum of votes required for election in the Federal Assembly and the two Republic Councils was 5 percent, 7 percent for coalitions of two or three parties, and 10 percent for four or more. Pehe, "Czechoslovakia," *supra,* note 1, 1. The revised election law, 59/1992, while retaining the system of proportional representation, increased the weight of preferential votes for candidates on fixed party lists.

177

the leftist parties, stressing the social impact, urged a more measured pace and criticized some aspects of the government policies. In Slovakia, where unemployment was substantially higher, the reform issue was broadly used against the "Prague dictated" forms of privatization and in support of continuing state intervention.

Second, the form or existence of the common state played a more important role in Slovakia than in the Czech Republic. The Slovak parties advocated a more or less radical change in the structure of the common state; only the vanishing Public against Violence and the Hungarian minority parties stood firmly for a federal arrangement. The Slovak National Party was the only group with a platform openly calling for independence, although the breakaway Slovak Christian Democratic Movement came close to that position. The program of the Movement for Democratic Slovakia offered several options, with independence as only one of the variants.

Third, the federal law of October 1991 on screening government officials for links with the former secret police and top Communist hierarchy (the "lustration") also caused a division between "the right" and "the left." In the course of the campaign in the Czech Republic, some right-of-center parties advocated more radical measures than those imposed by the controversial federal law. The leftist parties, on the other hand, called the law an unconstitutional witch-hunt. The latter view prevailed in Slovakia where "the left" joined Vladimír Mečiar's MDS in opposition to the law, which in fact was never applied in that Republic.[4]

It is a testimony of the successful federal foreign policy as articulated by the president and Foreign Minister Dienstbier that the only problems in that area that became marginally entangled in the campaign were relations with Germany and the attitude toward German investment. Some voices on "the left" criticized a treaty recently concluded with Germany on the ground that it recognized the removal of the German Sudeten population in 1945 as an "expulsion," and they were concerned about a "sellout" of the Czech economy to German capital.[5]

Several other issues and events intruded into the campaign, which started officially only on May 13:

Certain scandals connected with allegedly improper profits from privatization of state property were stressed by the opposition parties.

A report of the Defense and Security Committee of the Slovak National Council offered evidence of former Premier Mečiar's link to the notorious State Security.[6] The report was given broad publicity in the Czech

4. Jiří Pehe, "Czechoslovakia," *supra,* note 1, 25.
5. LN, Apr. 23, 1992, p. 1.
6. See *supra,* chap. V, 2b.

media, but it was not surprising that the accused called the charges 100 percent wrong while Prime Minister Čarnogurský viewed them as 97 percent right.[7] The publication of the report had no impact on Mečiar's popularity in Slovakia. After the disastrous experience with accusations of Mečiar's abuse of secret personnel files in April 1991, the Slovak government was in no mood to press a formal proceeding against him and the issue quickly petered out.[8]

A sharp controversy was sparked by the publication, deemed illegal by the government, of a confidential document listing 262 Czech and 114 Slovak journalists suspected of collaboration with the State Security.[9] President Havel criticized the publication and wide circulation of the list. Some viewed this action as an effort to undermine the position of the leftist parties in the elections.

Several thousand Slovaks paraded with slogans against the federal state and for an independent Slovakia. A Czechoslovak flag was burned in the end. A demonstration celebrating the anniversary of the 1939–45 Slovak puppet state was disavowed by leading Slovak political leaders, including Alexander Dubček, but it was widely noted in the Czech press.[10]

In the Slovak National Council, the defections of deputies from the coalition parties for which they were elected reduced government support to not more than one-third. With the closing of the plenary session, the lawmaking powers of the Council passed to the Presidium on a temporary basis. In response to the political realignment, the Presidium decided to add to its membership several opposition deputies (including Jozef Moravčík of the MDS and L'ubomír Fogaš of the PDL) so as to assure, pending the elections, equal representation of the opposition with the coalition parties. This move, benefiting mostly the Party of the Democratic Left, was viewed by some as enabling the opposition to yield power without corresponding responsibility in the government.[11]

There were further unsuccessful efforts—led this time by the dissident Slovak Christian Democratic Movement—to have the National Council adopt

---

7. Federal Interior Minister Ján Langoš complained of unacceptable political pressure from Prime Minister Čarnogurský to put off the initiation of criminal proceedings against Mečiar until after the elections. ČSTK, May 20, 1992. After the publication of the report on Mečiar, he was favored by 47.44 percent (48 percent the previous month) in a poll held in Slovakia. ČSTK, Apr. 24, 1992.

8. See "Pozadí případu Doktor [The Background of the Case Doctor]," RESPEKT, Mar. 2–8, 1992, p. 4.

9. RFE/RL RES. REP., May 15, 1992, p. 63.

10. *Ibid.,* Mar. 27, 1992, p. 77; ČSTK, Mar. 14, 1992.

11. LN, Apr. 29, 1992, p. 3.

the controversial Declaration of Sovereignty for Slovakia. The declaration was termed "the height of political primitivism" and "a criminal daredevil game in the fate of the citizen" by Prime Minister Čarnogurský and as "causing a government and parliamentary crisis."[12] At the time, the National Council failed to act on the proposal, but the move and its potential impact was widely criticized in the Czech Republic.[13] Dr. Čarnogurský's opposition to the document, although consistent with his "gradualist" approach to independence, turned out to be a fatal political mistake, contributing to his party's rout in the upcoming elections.

In the course of his preelection talks with the leaders of political parties, the president received Vladimír Mečiar, whose party according to opinion polls led in Slovakia by a wide margin. With what was described as a surprising concreteness and clarity, Mečiar described his postelection plans: the adoption by the Slovak National Council of the Declaration of Sovereignty, which, however, would not end the common state; a referendum on Czech-Slovak coexistence; and the enactment of a new Slovak constitution, which would terminate in Slovakia the federal constitution but not the common state or "valid" federal legislation. The economic reform in its present form "didn't fit" Slovak needs, and the "lustration law" was a "legislated illegality."[14]

The answer to Mečiar's position came from the Legislative Council of the federal government. The Council's statement pointed out that the adoption of a Republic constitution in the form promised by Mečiar would constitute an unconstitutional secession and would not affect the continuing validity of the federal Constitution; under the federal Constitution, "sovereignty" could be acquired by a Republic only on the basis of a referendum.[15]

In his regular Sunday radio broadcast, the president related that he had queried Mečiar for two hours about his thoughts on future developments. The president said that he agreed with some of Mečiar's ideas but others he viewed as "very controversial, not thought out, contradictory, and dangerous."[16]

The majority of the Czech politicians at the time sought to avoid polemics with Mečiar since any Czech criticism could only add to his popularity in Slovakia. However, the rhetoric of both the CDA and CDP spokesmen turned

12. ČSTK, Apr. 2, 1992; LN, May 8, 1992, pp. 1, 8.

13. LN, May 8, 1992, p. 8.

14. LN, May 5, 1992, p. 3.

15. "Pouze referendum [Only Referendum]," LN, May 12, 1992, p. 3; "Demontáž na pokračování [Dismantling by Installments]," LN, May 15, 1992, p. 8.

16. "Hovory z Lán, [Talks from Lány]," LN, May 11, 1992, p. 8. For a comprehensive statement of the MDS program by R. Filkus, one of the targets of Mečiar's later purges, see LN, June 3, 1992, p. 3: improved conditions for foreign capital, not a paternalistic state but state help, common currency and monetary policy, coordination of foreign policies (*not* single foreign policy), harmonization of the tax systems (not a single tax system), *not* a confederation, agreement on concrete processes, not an independent state for Slovakia, not a secession, "I hope we shall agree."

noticeably more strident. CDA's Kalvoda warned that a victory of "nationalist policies" would mean the end of the Czech and Slovak federation. CDP Chair Klaus went as far as to oppose the "sacred" principle of prohibition of majorization; he reiterated the opposition to the nonfunctional "icon" of a common state and affirmed his readiness for a rapid separation.[17]

Two days before the elections, the president urged the citizens to support those willing to reach an agreement and not to vote for those "who promise that they will solve everything for you . . . those with inclinations toward dictatorship, those who change their views too often . . . offer unreasoned and irresponsible solutions . . . [and] for whom their own power is more important than the fate of the nation," concealing "vanity and pride." He stressed the European and worldwide implications of the elections: on one hand the danger of a renewed beginning of a division of Europe into East and West, and on the other hand the chance of being something different than a bridge for which "soldiers particularly like to fight . . . an example of understanding and quiet cooperation."[18]

The president made it clear that he was available for reelection upon the expiration of his two-year term in October 1992. He would stand for the office "not because I want to be president at any price and under all circumstances but because I want to contribute to the realization of certain values. . . . I talked here about my ideas of the future, among other reasons in order to make it possible for the political forces that will participate in the elections to form an opinion about where I stand, what can and cannot be expected from me, and whether I still fit the office."[19]

The Civic Movement, the CDP, CDA, the Christian Democrats, and the Hungarian spokesmen promptly endorsed his candidacy, but Mečiar took a negative view on the ground that the president had "clearly given his backing to right-wing parties, thus rejecting cooperation with MDS."[20] Even though the president did not name him or his party, Mečiar understandably read Havel's appeal to the voters as directed against him and his party; moreover, the old suspicions of the "Castle's" role in his dismissal from the office of Slovak prime minister in April 1991 obviously rankled in Mečiar's mind and fed his hostility toward the president.[21] He is said never to forget or forgive.

---

17. LN, May 6, 1992, p. 3; May 7, 1992, p. 3; May 11, 1992, p. 8; May 30, 1992, p. 3.

18. Václav Havel, Vážení občané, Projevy, červenec 1990–červenec 1992 [Esteemed Citizens, Addresses, July 1990–July 1992], Projev k občanům [Address to Citizens], June 3, 1992 185–86 (LN, Praha, 1992).

19. Address to the Federal Assembly, Apr. 14, 1992, *ibid.,* 168–69.

20. ČSTK, June 3, 1992; Zdeněk Jičínský told the press that 18 candidacies for the post of the president were received by the Federal Assembly by June 2, 1992. ČSTK, June 2, 1992.

21. ČSTK, June 10, 1992. See also *supra,* chap. V, 2b.

Before the start of the campaign, each political party was allocated a portion of the total 21 hours reserved for this purpose on the official television station. No election agitation was allowed in private broadcasting and no opinion polls were to be published seven days before elections.[22] The amounts spent on the campaign varied greatly. The parties relied heavily on meetings and the wide use of posters plastered all over the country. CDA, for instance, made a great deal of Chair Kalvoda's photogenic face. In Prague, there were "Hyde Park I and II" meetings with mass participation sponsored by news media in which politicians of different parties responded to questions. Klaus's CDP, the Communists, and Mečiar's MDS in Slovakia attracted the largest audiences—a testimony to an efficient organization—while the Civic Movement, to the extent that it campaigned at all outside Prague, made a limited showing. CDA held a huge musical entertainment party in the Prague Trade Fair Palace.[23] Slovak nationalists organized a "pilgrimage" through some 70 Slovak towns, singing patriotic songs and distributing publications about J. Tiso and his Slovak state of 1939–45.[24]

On the whole, it was a lackluster election campaign with surprisingly limited media coverage.[25] According to a late May public opinion poll, the extent of Slovak support for the Federation increased from one-fourth to one-third while the proportion of those supporting independent Slovakia fell from 19 to 11 percent.[26] One-third supported "a confederation," most likely without a clear notion of that term's meaning. On this basis one might say, simplifying the situation, that more than 40 percent of the Slovaks were dissatisfied with the prevailing constitutional system.[27]

---

22. "Ve znamení voleb [In the Sign of Elections]," LN, May 14, 1992, p. 1.

23. LN, June 2, 1992, p. 1, 16.

24. LN, May 14, 1992, back page.

25. Jan Obrman, "The Czechoslovak Elections," RFE/RL RES. REP., June 26, 1992, 12. The federal commission in charge of supervising the regularity of the elections received 151 complaints, mostly from MDS. To the general astonishment, the commission found that the television broadcasts violated the election law in five news reports and demanded that a criminal proceeding be initiated. Moreover, the commission suggested personnel changes in the administration of the station. LN, June 5, 1992, p. 3; June 6, 1992, p. 1. After the elections, the new government dismissed the director. The commission move was sharply criticized as an attempt at censorship. Jaroslav Veis, "Černá kaňka [A Black Spot]," LN, June 6, 1992, p. 1. President Havel declared that particularly the publicly controlled media did their best to perform their legitimate role in the campaign and defended them against the attacks. "Hovory z Lán [Talks from Lány]," LN, June 8, 1992, p. 8.

26. ČSTK, May 26, 1992.

27. In her analysis of public opinion in Slovakia, a member of the Bratislava Center for Social Analysis wrote:

The pre-election climate in Slovakia was in marked contrast to the euphoria of the November days. An almost universal distrust rooted itself among the population against the new power elite, represented primarily by the political parties, the Public Against Violence and

2. The June 1992 Elections: "The Center Cannot Hold"

No major irregularities occurred during the elections,[28] and the voting took place in a peaceful, democratic atmosphere.[29] The turnout—84.5 percent of eligible voters (84.2 percent in Slovakia)—was more than satisfactory and did not confirm the warnings of voter apathy. The outcome, however, was termed a "black Friday for the Federation."[30]

The most surprising element of the election results was the utter devastation of the parties of the political center and the ensuing polarization toward "the right" in the Czech Republic and toward "the left" national populism in Slovakia.

a. With the Czechs to the Right

The liberal Czech Civic Movement of the center was wiped out, with the result that most of the post-Communist elite, the protagonists in our earlier story, had to leave public office. As expected, the right-of-center Civic Democratic Party of Václav Klaus, running in alliance with the small Christian Democratic Party, was the victor: it received more than a third of the votes, although it failed to attract any appreciable support in Slovakia.[31]

The Czech Communist Party, in coalition with minor left-wing groups under the temporary title "the Left Block," came in second with 14 percent of the total vote, about the same as in the 1990 elections. The other right-of-center group, Dr. Kalvoda's Civic Democratic Alliance, narrowly made it to the Czech National Council, but it surprisingly failed by a fraction of 1 percent (3,000 votes) to win the 5 percent necessary for the Federal Assembly.

---

the Christian-Democratic Movement. It was fed by the disappointments with the work of the new parliaments and weariness from the lengthy and difficult-to-read talks on constitutional issues. An authoritarian nostalgia was gaining ground with widespread yearning for a strong hand policy and decisive action . . . general dissatisfaction . . . frustration over the threat of weakening social securities . . . more conciliatory attitudes to Communists; less frequent stress on personal accountability; more frequent state paternalistic orientations; more deeply embedded egalitarianism; distrust in entrepreneurs; privatization; and more frequent anti-Western attitudes. (Zora Bútorová, "A Deliberate 'yes' to the Dissolution of the ČSFR?" 1 CZECH SOCIOLOGICAL REVIEW 58, 59–60 [no. 1, 1993]

28. Section title quoted from William Butler Yeats. This section is based on tables printed in MfD, June 11, 1992, p. 1, 6, reprinted and analyzed in Jan Obrman, "The Czechoslovak Elections," RFE/RL RES. REP., June 26, 1992, 12–19. *See also* LN, June 8, 1992, p. 1. On the new composition of the Federal Assembly, see ČSTK, June 19, 1992.

29. ČSTK, June 7, 1992; Jan Obrman, "The Czechoslovak Elections," *supra,* note 25, 1.

30. LN, June 8, 1992, p. 2.

31. In Slovakia, the CDP ran in alliance with the small Democratic Party, an arrangement that was said to have further weakened the CDU-PAV.

The chauvinist, xenophobic, far-right Republican Party of Miroslav Sládek, the Social Democrats, the Christian Democratic Union–Czechoslovak People's Party, and the left-of-center Liberal and Social Union gained enough votes (between 5 and 7 percent) to be represented in both the Federal Assembly and the Czech National Council. The regional group for Moravia and Silesia gained access to the Czech National Council only.[32]

b. "The Earthquake" in Slovakia

The center did not hold in Slovakia either. The liberal Civic Democratic Union (successor to the Public against Violence), like its Czech ally at the center, was left with a meager 4 percent, and with it went such leading figures as Fedor Gál and František Mikloško. Alexander Dubček left the center movement before the elections to join the Slovak Social Democrats.

Prime Minister Čarnogurský's Christian Democrats lost more than half of their votes as compared with the 1990 elections but managed to retain a foothold in the Slovak National Council (with over 8 percent of the total vote). After the reconstitution of the Slovak government, the former prime minister himself was denied the preferred chairmanship of the International Affairs Committee of the Slovak Council—the grapes of Vladimír Mečiar's wrath. However, Dr. Čarnogurský should have found some consolation in the fact that the supernationalist Slovak Christian Democratic Movement, the breakaway from his party, failed miserably with a meager 3 percent. In a predominantly Catholic country, the poor showing of Christian parties told a tale of the diminishing influence of religion. A Christian Democrat deputy criticized the Catholic Church for getting involved in politics in an inappropriate way by "openly supporting nationalism despite the Catholic Church's universalism," a charge that was rejected by the Slovak metropolitan archbishop.[33]

Mečiar's Movement for a Democratic Slovakia did even better than was predicted by the opinion polls, gaining more than a third of the seats in the Federal Assembly and falling just two seats short of a majority in the Slovak National Council. The second strongest showing (more than 14 percent) was made by the Party of the Democratic Left (the restructured former Communist Party), which combined a socialist program with strong national accents. The left-of-center Social Democrats led by Alexander Dubček won only five seats in the Federal Assembly's Chamber of Nations and none in the Slovak National Council.

---

32. The distribution of seats in the Czech National Council was as follows: CDP-Christ. Dem. Party, 76; Left Bloc, 35; Lib. Soc. Union and Czech Soc. Dem., 16; Chris. Dem. Union–People's Party, 15; Movement for Self-Gov. Moravia and Silesia, Civ. Dem. Alliance, and the Republican Party, 14 each. ČSTK, June 10, 1992.

33. ČSTK, Aug. 3, 1992.

The proindependence, extremely nationalist Slovak National Party obtained over 7 percent for both the Assembly and the Slovak National Council, and the Hungarian coalition group Coexistence-Együtteles ended in a similar position with more than 7 percent. In contrast with the Czech neofascist Republicans, who received enough support to pass the 5 percent barrier, the corresponding extremist Slovak People's Party, which openly eulogized the Nazi-sponsored state of 1939–45, failed totally.[34]

3. Monday Morning After and Hindsight

The extent to which the political establishment was swept away by the elections was truly astounding. It exceeded by far the usual postelection change in the American Congress, and it was substantially more radical than the sweep resulting from the 1994 elections in scandal-ridden Italy, where two-thirds of the Parliament failed to return. Only slightly more than 17 percent of the deputies in the Federal Assembly were reelected.[35] Most of the presidia members in the Republic Councils and most of the federal and Republic ministers lost their jobs as well as their parliamentary mandates.

A poignant photograph in the press shows "the big four" of the Civic Movement, Dienstbier, Rychetský, Pithart, and Burešová, clearly and justifiably in a depressed mood.[36] While Dienstbier, who continued to score high in popularity polls, remained at the head of the Civic Movement and "in charge of its rehabilitation," the other three moved into more or less lucrative law practice, teaching, and political writing.[37] The departure of these and other officials from government service meant a loss of valuable experience—whatever one may think of their individual accomplishments. The "lustration" and the voluntary exodus into the greener pastures of the new free market had already taken their toll, particularly on the judiciary. The question was to what extent the

---

34. For a distribution of seats in the Slovak National Council, see ČSTK, June 11, 1992. A number of parties with radical leftist and nationalist agendas failed to gain any seats. A total of 6 to 7 percent of the voters scattered their votes for such splinter groups.

35. Thirty were reelected in the 150-seat House of the People and 28 in the 150-seat House of the Nations. ČSTK, June 10, 1992.

36. LN, June 8, 1992, p. 8.

37. Where are they now? In mid-1995, Čalfa headed a prosperous consultancy, Dienstbier continued as chair of the remnants of the Civic Movement (the Free Democrats) and as political commentator, Rychetský had been denied an appointment to the new Constitutional Court, was a partner in a successful law firm. Burešová retired from law practice and public life, while Pithart returned to his professorial calling. In the 1996 elections Pithart and Rychetský were elected to the Senate but Burešová failed in her candidacy for that body. Pithart became chair of the Senate and Rychetský chair of the influential Senate Constitutional Committee. Kalvoda resigned as minister of justice and head of his party and as a deputy when it became known that he had used the title doctor-of-law without having obtained that degree. Dienstbier gave up the chairmanship of his foundering party.

postelection sweep would reach lower levels of government, reducing the already limited ranks of experts and adding further strain on the infant political system. The problem loomed large particularly in Slovakia where the relatively thin elite was about to be further depleted by a number of Slovak experts deciding not to return from Prague to Slovakia.

The election results were interpreted by some as confirming the existence of "two different societies" based on different values. The Czech voters—it was said—were afraid of the return of socialism, which they saw as rising again in Slovakia. The post-totalitarian heritage played in favor of "strong men," particularly in Slovakia, where the political culture was less developed.[38] In another variant, the Czechs were seen as proreform and anti-Communist, while the Slovaks were nationalist and left leaning. Clearly the influential Slovak left was concerned about the predominance of the right in the Czech lands.

Whatever the depth of the societal differences, focusing on the actual conduct of the campaign may offer a less dramatic interpretation. Here is Václav Klaus speaking in April 1992:

I appeared in meetings on the average twice a week, and now, before the elections, let's say six times . . . for me also it would have been the simplest thing to play the role of a technocratic finance minister who only contemplates the nuances of tuning and returning economic instrumentalities of the reform. But I realized in time—hopefully in time—that I myself had to conquer political support. . . . In the last meetings in which I took part the halls were literally jammed and transmission had to be arranged into stairways and adjoining rooms . . .[39]

The simple and unabashedly repeated call for continuing economic reform as the only way out of the post-Communist misery and the "either-or" stand toward the Slovaks came across loudly and clearly in the CDP program. Yet some Czechs saw the self-confident Klaus, who had learned to use the media, including television, effectively, as brimming with intolerance, even arrogance.[40]

In stark contrast, Petr Pithart, assuming a share of responsibility for the defeat, rated his Civic Movement's campaign as "bad." With too many CM ministers in the government,

---

38. *See,* for example, Social Democrat Deputy P. Kučera in LN, June 8, 1992, p. 1; and Petr Pithart in PROSTOR, July 8, 1992, p. 12.

39. Václav Klaus, Rok-Málo či mnoho v dějinách země [A Year: Little or a Lot in the History of the Country] 9, 13 (Repro-Media, Praha, 1993).

40. Slavomír Ravik, Zahradní slavnost pro 15 milionů [Garden Celebration for Fifteen Million] 44–53 (Pražská Imaginace, Prague, 1993).

we devoted minimum time to CM. It may have been good generally for the country but for us it was not good. . . . Our people were immensely used up and didn't even see the urgency of devoting time to the Movement and elections. . . . More than by its center position, CM was hurt by the fact that it was a government party, and people simply rejected the government party.[41]

Others felt that the center message should have been simpler and more aggressive to combat the accusations of being pseudo-Communist and harboring most of the "sixty-eighters"; a great mistake was to concentrate on cities, ignoring the rural areas and relying on the visibility of its leaders.[42]

In Slovakia as well, Dr. Ján Čarnogurský opined that "moderate slogans proved to be less successful,"[43] the understatement of the day. Vladimír Mečiar, free of any governmental responsibility (he had ceased for all practical purposes to attend the Federal Assembly) and a master of handling crowds, crisscrossed the country with a simple, irresistible message combining a promise of economic relief with a vision of Slovak sovereignty within an undefined common state. His principal lieutenant, Milan Kňažko, who was to become the Slovak foreign minister before falling from Mečiar's grace, campaigned in the countryside with the idea of Slovak visibility. In Petr Pithart's perception, a major part of Slovak voters saw in Mečiar "a compensation of their own certain feelings of inferiority . . . [and] saw in his person the self-confidence that Slovakia lacks—and it is its own [Slovak] fault. . . . And it is precisely Mr. Mečiar's style that is so foreign to us [Czechs], his *razantnost* [assertiveness] . . . that is exactly what Slovakia wants to see and hear at this moment. . . . Only a smaller part of the voters voted for him because of some direct or indirect leftist inclinations or his separatist policy."[44]

Mečiar, and to some extent Klaus as well, took advantage of, and encouraged, the forces working against the unity of the two peoples. We face here again, as in the case of President Havel, the existential question of the relative roles of a Nietzschean hero imposing his will upon the structural factors, Hegel's zeitgeist.

The elections were held again under the proportional representation voting system. Had the alternative majority system prevailed, as advocated earlier by President Havel and others, the CDP and the MDS would have obtained majorities in the legislative bodies, resulting in a concentration of power in the

41. Petr Pithart in PROSTOR, July 8, 1992, p. 12.

42. *See generally,* "Discussing the Elections: The Czech Point of View—An Interview with Martin Palouš and Petr Janyška," RFE/RL RES. REP., June 26, 1992, 23–27.

43. Jan Obrman, "Outgoing Prime Minister on the Future of Slovakia," RFE/RL RES. REP., June 19, 1992, 32–34.

44. Petr Pithart in PROSTOR, July 8, 1992, p. 12.

two victorious parties with—some might have feared—unpredictable effects on the young democracy.

4. Prague in Spring 1992: The Last Interlude

a. A View from an Island

When I returned to Prague in late June of 1992, shortly after the elections, I was struck by the paradoxical situation: the defeated "establishment," understandably in a state of funky depression, the city vibrant and more appealing than ever, the people confused about the constitutional negotiations, some disillusioned and tired but others hard at work on "getting ahead."

This time, my wife and I rented a small apartment in the most romantic corner of Prague, the island of Na Kampě on the Small Town side of the Charles Bridge. The building was almost directly across the street from the original home of the two brothers Čapek, to which President Masaryk regularly descended from the Castle for his Friday get-togethers with the intellectual elite of the First Republic. In the view from the adjoining park across the river, the late afternoon sun brought out the pastel colors of the buildings on the other bank and called for a Monet palette. In the park, in disregard of the signs prohibiting entry on the grass, were young couples in varying states of repose. The world at large seemed to have made a rendezvous on the fourteenth-century Charles Bridge. A trio of teenagers from the music conservatory of the northern town of Teplice played Dvořák and Mozart. In front of them was a small suitcase filled almost to the brim with banknotes offered by the appreciative crowd. Stalls selling trinkets lined the bridge under the statuary of saints and heroes. A group of leather jacketed, absurd-looking punks passed, heckled by teenagers perching on the railing, dressed in the regulation T-shirts and jeans—an incident in the making except for the policemen walking on the heels of the punks, in flawless blue uniforms, nonchalantly swinging their wooden sticks, ostensibly their only weapon.

A Charles University professor saw the doings on the bridge in another light, as evidence of the "antispirit, a denial of Europeanism . . . . a victory of marketeering, greed, and lack of taste not only of those who sell but also of the flocks of tourists who are not at all interested in viewing the [important] statues. . . . The jewel of Christian architecture is entirely desecrated by merchants, grocers, hatters. . . . [On the street leading to the Castle] new currency exchange offices, restaurants."[45] This perception illustrates the ambiguity in which sections of the society, including a number of intellectuals, viewed their new world.

The Mánes building, which I recalled earlier with nostalgia, was still without a café, but was now the home of a bright, functional art gallery with an

---

45. LN, Nedělní noviny, Aug. 29, 1992, p. 2.

exhibition of impressive, contemporary Czech graphics. Yet the immediate surrounding area was still an ugly mess, and the ownership of the building was being contested in court. The high, wooded hill of Petřín overlooking the Small Town quarters was a brief walk from our apartment. From the top, one sees the roofs of Prague, with the "hundred" church towers (so goes the lore) dotting the panorama. Far away on the horizon were rows of gray, Communist-built, apartment high rises. Descending, I passed the "Hunger wall" built by the Holy Roman Emperor Charles IV, more as a public works project to help alleviate a period of famine than to add to the city fortifications. It struck me as a curious coincidence that this was the fourth famed wall that I had been able to see in the last few years. The others were the Great Wall of China near Beijing, a feat of a boundless imperial folly; the Jerusalem Wailing Wall, where old men in black caftans and pale boys with ungainly hair locks swayed back and forth in prayer; and the Berlin Wall, now a picturesque detritus along which former East Germans sold Russian army hats and insignia.

b. The Lady Has a Toothache

Our first call, on June 29, was at the seat of the Czech National Council, a beautifully reconstructed baroque palace. Just beyond the entry was a tall sandstone wall decorated with rows of squares containing the carved coat of arms of the Bohemian Kingdom and a large statue of the "Czech lion" in a somewhat expressionist style. On the white walls of the red carpeted corridors and in the hall, where the press congregates, are Czech paintings ranging from realist and impressionist to contemporary minimalist and neoexpressionist styles. The lighting varies from traditional crystal to modern concealed fixtures. The outgoing chair of the National Council, Dr. Dagmar Burešová, whom we have met as a leading player in the constitutional negotiations, received us in her large, high-ceilinged office. The beige walls were richly adorned with rococo stucco and contrasting dark wood. Handsome, lithe, with a lean face and gray hair, she was in the process of vacating her office. But the lady confessed to a severe toothache with no chance to see a dentist before the recess. With admirable self-restraint, she talked about a referendum that she supported and deplored the failure in the Slovak Presidium of the "good text of the treaty we had in Milovy" but thought that there were questions about it on the Czech side as well.

We watched the opening session of the new Parliament from the crowded visitors' gallery in the ornate main assembly hall, decorated in the shining white and gold of the empire style. Adding insult to injury, because the National Council had failed to agree on a new chair, Dr. Burešová was required to preside over the swearing in ceremony of the newly elected deputies. An elegant, erect figure, she stood on the floor, shaking the hands of each and every deputy, as he or she approached her, first on the left side of the hall, then moving to the right, responding to their bows with a courageous smile and no sign of the toothache. Not a single candidate of her badly defeated CM party was among the members, and her own political career was at an end.

c. Havel Not Reelected

A few days later, on July 3, the Federal Assembly was scheduled to elect a federal president, since Václav Havel's term was to expire in October. He was the only credible candidate. As we approached the building of the Assembly on the morning of that day, a crowd of some two dozen watched the arriving deputies, greeting with applause the dashing, sunburned Minister Macek clad in a pastel suit. The building is a "chrome and glass" functional structure with little appeal. With its later addition, it appears jarringly misplaced next to the neoclassic National Museum.[46]

The main hall gave the impression of heavy portentousness, its upper part ringed by a balustrade reminiscent of a prison gallery for guards. The ceiling was covered with a mass of brass strips suspended under concealed neon lights. The play of light and shade produced an interesting effect of a massive, swirling movement—a modern day abstract baroque apotheosis. The deputies' desks and chairs were of dark wood, adding to the feeling of heaviness. Tension pervaded the atmosphere as we watched the deputies on the floor huddled in groups before the house was called to order. This is when I saw Alexander Dubček for the last time before his untimely death. Numerous procedural points required repeated interruptions of the session.

At lunch in the deputies' dining room, Professor Jičínský, by then a member of the Social Democratic Party, and some of his Slovak colleagues thought that Václav Klaus did not want a common state for fear of an economic collapse in Slovakia. They considered Prime Minister Mečiar "autocratic" but reactive, easily appropriating arguments of others and offering them as his own. I indicated my doubts about the utility of the ongoing theoretical debate on sovereignty, international personality, and so on: why not discuss concrete arrangements? My hosts raised the latest Slovak demands for membership in international organizations. There were, I suggested, compromise solutions such as a joint representation in international institutions, possibly membership of both the common state and the component Republics in the European Community mode.

In both the first and the second round of voting, Havel's candidacy failed to receive the required majority in the Slovak part of the Chamber of Nations. A small, disappointed crowd watched the deputies as they were leaving the building and there was some altercation.

---

46. The building will serve as the new home for Radio Free Europe–Radio Liberty since the Czech Republic Parliament resolved to remain in its current quarters in the Small Town.

d. Up and Down with Law Students and Lawyers

I could not fail to revisit my first "alma mater," the Charles University, founded by Emperor Charles IV in 1348. The new dean of the Law Faculty, Docent Valentin Urfus, a Romanist, discussed the problems facing the school and the legal profession. The legal profession, he recounted, reached the lowest level of public esteem in the 1950s, as reflected in the propaganda slogan: "I am a miner, who is more? I am a lawyer, who is less?" (At that time, according to then Vice-Dean Docent Cepl, the entering class numbered a mere 90 of which 60 graduated.) After 1969, the "administrative absolutism" discovered the need for lawyers, and the progeny of elite families initiated the trend from medicine to law study. Since 1989, the popularity of law study has risen dramatically. Of the 7,000 applicants in 1992, 6,000 took the admission test and only 450 were accepted first, the number to be raised to 650 (and eventually to 800), a maximum dictated by the size of the lecture rooms. I recalled that my own class in 1934 had 5,000 nominal members. There are law faculties in Brno, Olomouc, Bratislava, Košice (in Eastern Slovakia), and a new one in Plzeň, but law is taught in other schools as well. Of the 130 teaching staff in Prague, Dean Urfus said, 30 left after 1989, causing important gaps, particularly in such areas as legal theory.[47] There were three types of teachers: specialized assistants (the largest group, mostly not Communist Party members), the docents, and the professors, appointed predominantly as a reward for loyal service to the party. The dean intended to press for promotions from the first group.

After 1989, libraries were in a deplorable state, with major sections of books not accessible. Students complained that "the old time lecturers have learned the new laws but teach on the old principles of 'just copy and learn by heart.' "[48] There were some 500 vacancies in the Czech judiciary alone, due partly to "lustration" but also to resignations because of low salaries and new, more lucrative opportunities in the expanding private sector. Later on I heard bitter complaints about the level of competence of judges as well as the bar and about the slowness of the restructuring of law faculties, with low salaries as one of the problems.

The principal themes of my conversations were again the referendum, the dire predictions for a Slovakia without "the billions of Czech subsidies" (a

---

47. Of 3,500 teachers at the entire Charles University, 500 were dismissed.
48. Marlise Simons, "Czechoslovakia's Colleges: Burden of Communist Past," N.Y. TIMES, Dec. 24, 1992, p. 1, A6. At the faculty of philosophy, a predominant part of teachers who were there over the preceding 20 years remain and consider those who returned after 20 years as intruders. "Fraška v naší jeskyni [Farce in Our Cave]," talk with Professor Karel Kusík, Nedělní L.N., Aug. 29, 1992, p. 2.

chaos—a division of the country between Hungary and the Ukraine), and, among lawyers, the problems of secession or division.

e. On Havel, Lincoln, and the King of Sweden

With the buzz of these motifs still in my ears, we left Prague for the United States to join, after a brief interruption, my wife's family's 116th consecutive reunion in her home state of Arkansas. Some 135 members assembled at the family's cemetery, founded in the mid–nineteenth century. The nearby site of a mill owned by the family ancestors was the scene of a Civil War battle on April 25, 1864, in which a large federal supply train was ambushed and destroyed by the Confederates.[49] The night before the reunion, two strong young men in blue cowboy hats roasted a large pig prostrated over an open fire pit in preparation for the common feast to the tune of a bluegrass band. As I watched the starlit southern sky, images of the Civil War blended in my mind with the Prague impressions. This was the day before Václav Havel resigned from his office as federal president, refusing to preside over the dissolution of the state. My thoughts veered to his and Abraham Lincoln's agony. Could Havel have done more—and could he still do more to sustain the "union?" Lincoln acted from a powerful political base established by his party's victory in the national elections of 1860. Havel's great influence was reduced by a series of failed initiatives and missteps in Slovakia, and it was gravely impaired by the last elections, which had swept most of his ardent supporters from the political scene. Lincoln seized on a compelling idea, the necessity to salvage the novel American experiment in governance, the federal republic, "the city on the hill" of the early tradition, beckoning the people longing for freedom everywhere. A lawyer and experienced politician, he employed this theme, buttressed subsequently by the call for the abolition of slavery, with consummate skill. Havel, with no experience in politics, had no program of comparable potency, no nationally based political party. Perhaps the more apt analogy was to the position held by King Oscar II at the time of the peaceful dissolution of the Swedish-Norwegian state in 1905.[50] Could one say that, like the aging monarch, President Havel did all that was within his power under adverse circumstances to hold the union together?

Breaking into this rumination was a query recurring in my mind with a rekindled intensity since my "returns" to Europe: is there more to "American exceptionalism" than the utopia of "the city on the hill?" "[T]he fact is," wrote

---

49. For the description of the battle of Marks Mill, *see* Shelby Foote, 3 The Civil War: A Narrative 72 (1974). One historical marker lists a supply train of 240 wagon loads of supplies as their booty, but another, some hundred feet away, raises it to 2,400!

50. On the dissolution of the Swedish-Norwegian Union, see *infra*, chap. XV, 2c, ii.

Gordon Wood, "that for better or worse nineteenth-century America became an even more attractive 'poor man's country' than it had been in the eighteenth century: by 1920 the arrival of over 35 million immigrants over the previous century testified to the reality of the 'utopian notion.'"[51]

---

51. Gordon S. Wood, "Letters," N.Y. REV. OF BOOKS, Dec. 1, 1994, p. 61.

Third Act

XI

The Lion v. the Unicorn: The Breakup (Summer 1992)

1. The Five Rounds (June–July 1992)

a. Round One: Testing

Shortly after the elections,[1] President Havel called on Václav Klaus as the head of the "victorious" party[2] to form a new federal government and formulate a governmental program. In pursuing this charge, Klaus met with Vladimír Mečiar, his Slovak counterpart "victor," in the first of the six fatal rounds of negotiations that in the end went far beyond the original mandate.[3]

The encounter took place on June 8 in the Moravian capital of Brno. The locale was a villa built in the early 1930s for a local industrialist after a design by Ludwig Mies van der Rohe, the last head of the famed Bauhaus. The house is considered a true jewel of the European functionalist style.[4] The secret rendezvous of the two leaders, accompanied by the principal functionaries of their respective parties, was promptly discovered by a flock of journalists who patiently waited in front of the villa from the early evening hours along with a handful of "Moravist" nationalists protesting the "suppression" of the rights of Moravia. At ten minutes before three in the morning, in a driving downpour, Mečiar emerged from the meeting and departed—uncharacteristically silent—while Milan Kňažko told the journalists that agreement in principle had been reached; however, when asked about the future of the Federation, he replied: "Excuse me, it is raining!"

Klaus, showing considerable fatigue, was more responsive the following day, when he gave his own account of the meeting at a press conference: "We

---

1. On this chapter, see generally Jiří Pehe, "Czechoslovakia: Stage Set for Disintegration," RFE/RL Res. Rep., July 10, 1992, 26–31.
2. Jan Obrman, "The Czechoslovak Elections," RFE/RL Res. Rep., June 26, 1992, 12. Klaus's CDP obtained 83 out of the 300 seats in the Federal Assembly while Mečiar's MDS won 57.
3. ČSTK, June 8, 1992; LN, June 8, 1992, p. 2.
4. LN, June 8, 1992, p. 2. In the early 1930s, Brno was a laboratory of new architecture: at the Technical Institute lectured Gropius, Corbusier, and the local native A. Loos. *Ibid. See also* LN, June 9, 1992, p. 1, 16.

are for a functional common state at the level of a reasonable federation, for a continuation of the economic reform, and we fully support V. Havel about whose candidacy [for federal president] we refuse to speculate." While these were the non-negotiable conditions, the Czech side was amenable to offer the Slovaks key positions in the new federal cabinet. On the Slovak side, according to Klaus, "the MDS does not envisage a common state but rather an economic-defense community and two states with a separate international legal subjectivity. These views," Klaus emphasized, "were not expressed casually but . . . were presented in a comprehensive formulation. We do not share the views of our partners about the reasonableness and stability of such a peculiar form [of a state]," Klaus continued, "we do not share the illusion of a possibility for a slow, easy passage to such a union of a directed, controlled divorce at no cost."[5] Klaus was described as surprised and angered by the Slovak proposal and unyielding posture, which he saw as an irreversible effort to end the Federation. Mečiar gave the impression to some Czech participants that he had heard of the union scheme in the particular form presented for the first time from the mouths of his party colleagues.[6]

According to subsequent reports, both parties favored limiting federal bureaucracies; the Slovak scheme contemplated a common army and "common" (not a single) currency,[7] with two banks of emission and the facility for Slovakia to adjust economic, tax, and financial policy to its own needs; as for international subjectivity, "some diplomatic missions abroad could be used jointly by both Republics" with the obvious implication that Slovakia would have some missions of its own. Deputy Chair of the CDP Macek called the Slovak model "Slovak independence with a Czech insurance policy,"[8] a phrase that gained popularity among the habitués of Czech beer pubs.

---

5. LN, June 10, 1992, pp. 1, 8. "If the CDP agreed with the MDS conception, it would sign a death sentence of the Czech economy." Klaus in SMENA, June 12, 1992, p. 2.

6. MFD, Sept. 22, 1992, p. 7.

7. As interpreted by a Czech expert, "common currency" in the MDS sense meant effectively two currencies issued by two central banks, tied together by a fixed rate of one to one and in free circulation in both states, as in Belgium and Luxemburg (Benelux). This, however, was not possible in Czechoslovakia because of different political-economic objectives of the two governments; if Slovakia wants common currency, it must drop its own emission bank and use the Czech currency, as does Lichtenstein, using the Swiss franc. Josef Kotrba, "Jaká koruna, [What Crown]," LN, June 11, 1992, p. 3.

8. Karel Vodička, "Koaliční ujednání etc. [Coalition Bargain, etc.]," in Rüdiger Kipke and Karel Vodička (eds.), Rozloučení a Československem [Parting with Czechoslovakia] 83, 90–91 (Český spisovatel a.s., Praha, 1993), relying on a wide spectrum of periodicals. The participants with Mečiar at the first meeting were A.M. Húska, M. Kňažko, and M. Kováč. R. Filkus, another prominent MDS member, told Lidové noviny earlier that he did not favor two emission banks while A.M. Húska did. M. Čič indicated some possibility of supporting Havel. Klaus consulted with the Social Democrat and LSU chairs J. Horák and F. Trnka. Mečiar spoke with P. Weiss of PDL and J. Prokeš of SNP. LN, June 10, 1992, p. 1, 8; ČSTK, June 8, 1992.

MDS public comments came from Mečiar's spokesman B. Géci, who accused the Klaus side of having violated a understanding on publicity and giving out incomplete information about the negotiations: CDP expressed its agreement with the "legitimacy" of the MDS attitude; Klaus came with a requirement of a unitary state, a model that would damage Slovakia; and Mečiar would not take part in the day's planned meeting with the president because he did not agree with the president's actions during the election campaign, after the elections, and during the constitutional negotiations, which he viewed as "not correct and unfortunate."[9]

A few days later, Mečiar said that "the CDP ambushed us. After 40 minutes, they told us that they are able to announce that the state is dissolved. In the end we had to tame them" and remind them that neither side had the mandate for such an act, which could be accomplished only by a referendum.[10]

b. Round Two: Facing Two Alternatives—Federation or "Confederation"

The second round of negotiations took place on June 11, from early afternoon to half past eleven at night, at the offices of the CDP Secretariat in Prague's picturesque Small Town.[11] As usual, the talks proceeded behind "hermetically closed doors."

This time, according to a Czech source, the Slovak side asked the Czechs to specify their constitutional ideas, a subject never reached during the first round. In the discussion about the common economic space, the core of the Czech concept, Michal Kováč, deputy chair of the MDS (later chair of the newly elected Federal Assembly and even later, the first president of independent Slovakia) insisted on a "common currency" with two emission banks, which Klaus termed an economic impossibility. Even Mečiar appeared to agree in part with this view. An endless debate turned on the meaning of the terms *federation, confederation, union, and independent state.*[12]

Klaus opened a press conference shortly before midnight: "We didn't make any progress. It would be entirely false to offer the public any different information." The MDS did not accept the CDP conception of a "looser federation." The "revealing point" in the negotiations was the attitude toward interna-

---

9. LN, June 11, 1992, p. 1.

10. NO, June 13, 1992, p. 1, 6.

11. ČSTK, June 11, 1992. Participants were, in addition to Mečiar and Klaus, CDP vice-chairmen J. Zieleniec, M. Macek, P. Čermák, and J. Kovář; on the Slovak side were M. Kňažko, M. Kováč, and A.M. Húska. PROSTOR, June 13, 1992, p. 1. No official record was kept at the first round. Subsequent rounds were all recorded with the understanding that the texts would be published in one year's time. To my knowledge no such publication had occurred by 1996. MFD, Sept. 22, 1992, p. 7; SLOBODNÝ PIATOK, July 17, 1992, p. 3.

12. MFD, Sept. 22, 1992, p. 7.

tional subjectivity. The Slovak side confirmed that it sought Slovakia's own membership "in international organizations of the UN type." The MDS did not change its negative position on Havel's reelection. There was no agreement on the composition of the federal government.[13]

Speaking for the Slovak side M. Kováč declared that the MDS program did not speak about a breakup of the state and it envisioned a free association between two independent states. The process should be (as outlined by Mečiar to the president), first, the adoption of the Declaration of Slovak Sovereignty, then the enactment of a Slovak constitution, and eventually the election of the Slovak president. The formation of the federal government would be tied to a referendum on whether the citizens wished to live in a federation, in a free association, or whether they preferred independence.

While the MDS seemed to assume that the Federation would continue for some considerable time, Klaus expressed the fear that the negotiations might acquire their own uncontrollably heavy dynamic; the public would not accept prolonging the insecurity, which was severely damaging economic development. "The fact that MDS continuously ties further steps to a referendum doesn't mean that the Czech side will wait for its result."[14]

Mečiar himself did not take part in the press conference but "vanished" in the direction of Bratislava, and Klaus alone went to Hradčany Castle in response to the president's invitation addressed to both sides. At 1:00 A.M. Havel's talks with Klaus were still in progress. The president, it was said, assumed that Mečiar was too exhausted, and the invitation remained open.[15] Considering Mečiar's well-known endurance, the excuse was obviously intended as a graceful way of avoiding open friction.

The following day, June 12, Mečiar, breaking his silence, held a press conference in Bratislava for invited reporters: the MDS used the term "economic-defense community" only once in Brno, and since that time the CDP has emphasized it unnecessarily. The MDS has a program of confederative coexistence, but it supports the preservation of federal organs until the

---

13. *Ibid.*

14. PROSTOR, June 13, 1992, p. 1. The remark led M. Kňažko to ask: "What other way does Mr. Klaus imagine to achieve the so-called cultured division of the state?" NO, June 13, 1992, p. 1, 6.

15. LN, June 12, 1992, p. 1 and back page. Mečiar and Klaus subsequently again consulted other parties. Thus, the chair of the Party of the Democratic Left, P. Weiss, gave Klaus a detailed description of a "free cooperative federation" as conceived by his party, and they both agreed on the need to calm the hectic atmosphere. *Ibid.* In a meeting with Klaus, the CDA, Christian Democrat Party, LSU, CDU-CPP, Czech Social Democrats, and the Moravian group agreed to support current negotiations with the key objective of an agreement on the composition of the federal organs and election of V. Havel. At a press conference, the LSU, Czech Social Democrats, and CDU-CPP insisted strongly that the Slovak model of a defense-economic union was not a common state while the others didn't take a clear position. PROSTOR, June 13, 1992, p. 1.

citizens of the Slovak Republic decide on the form of the constitutional arrangement.[16] Mečiar appreciated the responsiveness on the Czech side, particularly on the part of Klaus, who is "immensely constructive though he doesn't hide his temperament."[17] "In one instance," Mečiar is quoted as saying, "I used [in coalition negotiations] as an example the possibility of Slovakia's membership in the UN. That circumstance was immediately torn out of context and interpreted as Slovakia's insistence on UN membership, which is not our practical politics for the next months."[18]

A number of Czech and all foreign reporters were refused admission to the Mečiar press conference. A committee of the association representing foreign newspaper reporters published a statement criticizing the exclusion of foreign reporters as an inadmissible suppression of the principle of the freedom of the press, "reminiscent of the manners of the former Central Committee of the Czechoslovak Communist Party."[19]

On June 15, Mečiar called on the president at the Castle and they talked in private for almost an hour.[20] After the meeting, the president said that, although general understanding existed in many areas, in the most important field there was no agreement; the discussion covered the "technology" of a possible transition from a federal to another formation based on two states. The president urged that the process be peaceful, and MDS agreed. He thought an early referendum in both Republics should be the first step and that unilateral steps should be avoided. On the last point, Mečiar insisted on the MDS constitutional program, which he had described to the president before the elections.[21] He was ready to accept single defense, the current state of the currency, "the entire system of financial relations," and a single economic policy, but he insisted on "two international legal subjects." The existence of these subjects,

---

16. LN, June 13, 1992, p. 1.

17. PROSTOR, June 13, 1992, p. 1.

18. "Slovakia must first become a body with its own international subjectivity, achieve international recognition and only then can it apply for admission to the UN." Both he and his deputy Kňažko asserted that in reality it was the Czech side that sought the breakup of the Federation; the party that posed unacceptable conditions also carried the responsibility. Kipke and Vodička, *supra*, note 8, 93, citing PRAVDA of June 13, 1992, pp. 1, 2.

19. LN, June 13, 1992, p. 1. Reporters of only two Czech papers were admitted (RUDÉ PRÁVO and PRÁCE, both left oriented) while the representatives of the official press agency, Radio Free Europe, LIDOVÉ NOVINY, SLOVAK DAILY, MLADÁ FRONTA DNES, and TELEGRAF were excluded. *Ibid.* Mečiar refused to answer questions from the Czech reporters and on leaving declared that "Czech newspapermen dramatize, spread tales, are malicious, and they disinform." PROSTOR, June 13, 1992, p. 1. Mečiar's attitude was interpreted as a reaction to an incident at an earlier press conference in which he refused to answer a question of a reporter for MLADÁ FRONTA DNES and insulted him, whereupon a group of reporters left the press conference. *Ibid.*, p. 3.

20. After the private meeting, they were joined by M. Kováč, M.A. Húska, and M. Kňažko. LN, June 16, 1992, p. 1, back page.

21. *Supra,* chap. X, 2.

he declared later, "means in substance a confederate arrangement." Mečiar also confirmed that while his party would not support Havel's candidacy it would not offer its own candidate because that position should be held by a Czech. He also declared that from then on he would inform the president regularly of the negotiations to insure that the president received the picture from both sides.[22] Still, on June 15, 1992, Michael Žantovský, the president's spokesman, said that Mečiar might accept Havel as a Czech president who would then rotate with the Slovak president in the office of the federal president.[23]

At the statue of Saint Wenceslas on the Prague square of the same name where the crowds had shaped the November 1989 revolution, the organizers of "the Czech Initiative" collected more than 50,000 signatures in support of a petition for a referendum on an independent Czech Republic to be held if a functional federation proved impossible. According to the president's spokesman, Havel thought the petitions "were not of a massive dimension . . . they are one direction of opinion . . . there are also other directions."[24]

c. Round Three: Crossing the Rubicon

The two delegations met again in the headquarters of the Civil Democratic Party in Prague on June 17.[25] Mečiar's "closest" advisors (if anyone could be said to be close to him) at the time were two economists, A.M. Húska and the avuncular Michal Kováč (both determined supporters of Slovak independence), and briefly Milan Kňažko, all three "creating a strongly antifederalist atmosphere." R. Filkus and M. Čič inclined toward a compromise with the Czechs.[26] In this six-hour session, the parties were said to have crossed the Rubicon.

Klaus offered the Slovak side what was described as a "Marshall Plan" of economic assistance within a federal framework, but this was rejected as running counter to the immutable aspirations for "visibility" on the international scene.[27] The CDP was determined to make the MDS side choose un-

---

22. LN, June 16, 1992, p. 16. M. Kováč said after the meeting: "The president explained the reasons for his positions, but I don't think that we have a ground for changing our views." *Ibid.*, back page. The same day, CDP published a strong statement in which it noted the emerging all-nation consensus and accused the Communist Party, as a leader of the Left Bloc, of misusing the situation by efforts to destabilize political life and by renewed propagation of socialist and collectivist utopias. The Czech Communist Party chairman rejected these allegations and claimed that the CDP exceeded the mandate for consultations on composition of the federal government, which it received from the president. *Ibid.*

23. LN, June 16, 1992, p. 3.

24. LN, June 13, 1992, p. 2; LN, June 16, 1992, p. 3.

25. ČSTK, June 17, 1992; Kipke and Vodička, *supra,* note 8, 93–95, citing LN, HN, PRAVDA, MFD, SMENA, and RESPEKT, all of June 18, 1992.

26. Conversation with J. Moravčík.

27. *Ibid.*

equivocally between a federal coalition government for a functional, decentralized state or a temporary federal government charged with preparing a dissolution. As Klaus's side saw it, the Slovaks had opted for the second alternative: first, because Mečiar rejected Klaus' proposal that they both enter the federal cabinet, and, second, because Mečiar insisted that each Republic had to cover its full budget exclusively from its own income—an explicit sign of a confederative course. Klaus is said to have reproached the Slovaks for wanting independence financed by Czech money, to which Mečiar responded: "Each one on its own."

In the subsequent, relatively simple negotiations, the parties reached an understanding on the structure of the federal government, including a Czech-Slovak parity representation in a ten-member cabinet, and on a preliminary allocation of ministerial positions. It was indicative of the Slovak priorities that they laid claim to the Ministry for Foreign Affairs (not, as was expected, to the Interior Ministry) and the Defense Ministry. The choice of defense was interpreted by the Czechs as revealing Mečiar's intent to strengthen the future Slovak army and build military airports in Slovakia from federal funds.[28] The Czech side, anxious to shorten the transition period as much as possible, suspected the MDS of wanting to use the new federal government for a long-term transfer of funds from Prague to Bratislava. Mečiar, speaking at the subsequent press conference, appeared to confirm this suspicion when he predicted that the new federal government would remain in office for a year and a half or longer—an estimate that Klaus sharply rejected as "too optimistic, lest the evolution of constitutional relations gain its own dynamic."[29]

Klaus and Mečiar announced that they would present their candidacy for the office of prime minister of their respective Republics. Lauding Klaus's decision, Mečiar commented: "It is a wise decision, and I hope it will lead to a friendly cooperation of both cabinets." If there still was any doubt about the fate of the Federation, this development should have dispelled it.

Although neither party said so openly, it was obvious that they accepted the inevitability of the separation and the consequent need for an agreement on the composition and program of a transitional federal government.

d. Round Four: The Political Agreement

In preparation for the fourth encounter at Bratislava on June 19, representatives of the MDS and CDP worked on a draft of a program for the new government. The principal controversial points were, it was reported, the date for the refer-

---

28. Respekt, June 15–21, 1992, p. 3.
29. HN, June 18, 1992, pp. 1, 2.

endum in Slovakia and the modalities for the temporary budget on the basis of the "each on its own" principle. A crucial question was the continuation of the economic reform in Slovakia.

At the same time, detailed negotiations were in progress in Bratislava and in Prague among the prospective coalition parties for structural and personnel changes in the federal as well as the Republic governments to reflect the postelection constellation of political forces.[30]

President Havel continued his conversations with political leaders. After his talk at the Castle, Dr. Čarnogurský (about to resign as Slovak prime minister) confirmed that his Christian Democratic Movement supported Havel's candidacy and that he, Čarnogurský, did not wish a breakup of the Federation because Slovakia could get into economic difficulties as a result of an "unreasonable policy of the MDS."[31] He acknowledged, however, that the negotiations appeared to lead to two independent states within the next few months. The chair of the Czech Social Democrats appealed to the president to take a more active role in the effort to save Czechoslovakia. The left-center Liberal Social Union was—according to its chair—also for the preservation of the current state but saw possible advantages of a confederation. The chair of the Czech Christian Democratic Party similarly urged maintaining the common state with common defense, currency, foreign policy, and a single international personality.[32]

When Václav Klaus arrived in Bratislava at the Bôrik Hotel on the morning of June 19, he was greeted by a crowd of reporters with a bouquet of flowers for his fifty-first birthday as well as with loud exclamations of "shame on Prague" from a tiny group of some eight demonstrators.

The session of expanded delegations[33] lasted for 13 hours during which Mečiar's spokesmen at regular intervals assured the impatient journalists that the discussions were proceeding "in a constructive spirit and without emo-

---

30. LN, June 19, 1992, pp. 1, back page.
31. LN, June 19, 1992, p. 8. The same day, Dr. Čarnogurský said in Bratislava that in a referendum held in Slovakia today a majority would vote against independence, but he was not sure a referendum would materialize and he questioned the form of the questions proposed by MDS. He stressed that his governments had introduced a calmer atmosphere, no major demonstrations or strikes had occurred, and there was full freedom of the press, steady prices, and currency, but also deep depression, drops in production, 11.3 percent unemployment, and a deficit budget. LN, June 20, 1992, p. 8.
32. LN, June 19, 1992, p. 2.
33. On the Slovak side, Mečiar was joined by M. Kováč, I. Gašparovič, M. Kňažko, A.M. Húska, R. Filkus, J. Moravčík, M. Čič and J. Laluha. The Czech delegation consisted of V. Klaus and deputy party chairs J. Kovář, P. Čermák, M. Macek, J. Zieleniec, and in addition Czech Republic ministers K. Dyba and I. Kočárník, Deputy Chair of the Federal Assembly F. Šedivý, and federal Prime Minister J. Stráský. Experts worked for many hours on drafts of the documents. LN, June 20, 1992, p. 1; June 22, 1992, pp. 1, back page; MFD, Sept. 23, 1992, p. 7; conversation with J. Moravčík.

tions." In the end, the negotiators produced two documents that in effect sealed the fate of the Federation: a political agreement between the two parties signed by the two leaders, constituting a road map toward dissolution; and a draft of a program for the new federal government.

The first document read as follows:

The Political Agreement CDP And MDS

The leadership of CDP and MDS

1. aware of the high political responsibility in a situation that has arisen after the 1992 elections in the Czech Republic and Slovak Republic, propose to solve it in a constitutional way,
2. with the objective of assuring the continuity of all constitutional organs and of all processes initiated in November 1989, have agreed on the formation of a federal government and on its programmatic declaration which forms a part of this agreement,
3. take notice of the differences in their election programs and political goals in the area of the constitutional arrangement,
4. consider it, in this situation, a common objective by all lawful means to initiate a process that will lead by September 30, 1992 to an agreement between the National Councils on the solution of the constitutional arrangement,
5. if it comes to the creation of two states with international legal subjectivity, CDP and MDS consider it appropriate, in the interest of good, friendly neighborliness, to seek such forms of coexistence between the two states and such framework for cooperation that would correspond to the traditions and to the current and expected needs,
6. they will propose that in case of the extinction of the ČSFR, the National Councils should enact laws by which the deputies of the Federal Assembly would be made members of the legislative organs of the Republics,
7. the principles of the programmatic declaration of the federal government are binding for both subjects. On that foundation both parties will inform each other regularly and consult at the level of the Federal Assembly. Chairpersons and the leadership of both parties will gather for regular meetings as the situation evolves.
8. This agreement does not affect the relations of CDP and MDS with other political parties.
9. CDP and MDS obligate themselves to conclude an agreement on further central organs of government administration by July 31, 1992.

Vladimír Mečiar, Václav Klaus[34]

---

34. PROSTOR, June 22, 1992, p. 1.

The second document, the declaration of the government program for the transition period, was reduced by Klaus on his way to Bratislava from the original 13 to three pages.[35] The economic section of the program strongly embraced Klaus's policy. He produced his draft after 12 hours of negotiations and prevailed in a group exhausted by heat and fatigue.[36]

After the meeting, at half past one in the morning, the protagonists held a press conference on the rain-swept Bôrik terrace. They rehearsed the highlights of the outcome, including the agreements on reducing the number of federal ministers and bureaucracies, on the candidates for federal prime minister, and others. Klaus noted that final approval of the constitutional decisions would take place in the federal institutions, although this was not stated in the political agreement.[37] He had mentioned earlier the concern on the part of world financial institutions and may have had in mind the statement of the President in Office of the Council of Ministers of the European Community, viewing the dissolution from the international perspective as "very bad news," which "the politicians will regret," and entailing—according to a member of the European Community Commission—a review of the legal foundation of last year's Association Agreement between Czecho-Slovakia and the Community.[38]

President Havel, who originally planned to travel to Bratislava, was given a detailed briefing about the session by telephone by both Mečiar and Klaus. He commented on the two documents in his regular Sunday broadcast. He saw four advantages in the documents. The first clear "plus" was the prospect

---

35. Its preamble illustrates the tenor of the full document. It provided that the federal government viewed it as its temporary mandate, without changing in principle the current status, to secure an orderly continuity of the government organs and of the post-1989 reforms, to contribute to the solution of the constitutional arrangements, to make possible a further transfer of powers in the direction of the citizen, and, if so authorized, to prepare conditions for the smooth building of two sovereign states with an international subjectivity. *Ibid.*

36. MFD, Sept. 23, 1992, p. 7.

37. Klaus said that language in the agreed document envisaging the division of the Federation by agreement of the National Councils did not prejudice other modes of division: "The referendum method is neither ordained nor excluded." Klaus also stressed the exceptional importance of the person of the federal minister for foreign affairs, who was to represent the country during the difficult time of transition. LN, June 22, 1992, pp. 1, back page.

38. LN, June 20, 1992, p. 1, 8; LN, June 22, 1992, p. 1; Kipke and Vodička, *supra,* note 8, 95–96. On a positive reaction to the agreement by the political clubs of the MDS, PDL, and SNP, see RP, June 29, 1992, p. 1. Regarding Klaus's response to the question on the referendum, a Slovak writer commented that behind that position was the "on the whole correct consideration," that the legislators would not be able to agree on the manner, timing, or formulation of the question for a referendum and whether it was to take place in Slovakia only or in both Republics." "Klaus's asserted faith in maintaining the Federation is only an obligatory rhetoric aimed at softening the emotional reactions at the outset of the split." P. Schutz in RESPEKT, June 22–28, 1992, p. 2.

for an agreement on the new federal government, thus avoiding the danger of a collapse of the state administration and a constitutional crisis. The second "plus" consisted of the commitment to continue the great economic and democratic reforms, privatization, and the opening to Europe, even though limited to the duration of the Federation. The third "plus" was the fixed timetable set for a final decision, and the fourth was "naming things [the two options] in clear language": one common state with a single legal subjectivity or two states that would seek an optimum of neighborly coexistence." "I dare say that I have contributed modestly to this clarification . . . during my long negotiations with the MDS delegation. . . . The true situation is identified and the deadline set for September 30." The president saw a problem, however, in the ambiguous formulation, which admitted the possibility of the exit of the Republics without a referendum, the only constitutional mode available. He intended to enter into "very intensive negotiations" with political parties: "It appears that next week I shall enter somewhat more actively into the current development and will play a role corresponding to my constitutional position." In a defensive tone, he added that contrary to possible appearances he had not been "ambushed" by the "dramatic events of today. . . . All my life I was accustomed to meet new and difficult situations. I try to behave wisely . . ."[39]

A week later, the president was less positive about the course of the discussions. He was disturbed that the negotiations at times exceeded the mandate, as exemplified by the suggestion that if the Czechs held the office of prime minister a Slovak would be chair of the Supreme Court.[40] Similar concerns regarding the appropriate scope of the negotiations began to be voiced by parties on the left, with an emphasis on the need for a referendum.[41] On the other hand, "representatives of 14 right-wing parties and movements" voiced full support for the legitimacy of the talks.[42]

In the wake of the fourth round, the ministers of the interior of the federal and Republic governments agreed to have eight expert commissions work on the smooth separation. The six-member commissions (two from each of the

---

39. LN, June 22, 1992, back page.

40. This, the president felt, was contrary to the principles of division of powers, judicial independence, and stability of the judicial system. He also rejected any system of some "understandings or subunderstandings" on who may or may not be a journalist or director of the means of communication. For that there are laws and regulations. . . . The task [for political parties] is to submit a proposal for the composition of the federal government and a programmatic declaration." LN, June 29, 1992, p. 8.

41. For example, the Czech Communist Party in ČSTK, July 23, 1992; Democratic Party, LN, June 23, 1992, p. 3; and chair of the PDL in Slovakia, Peter Weiss in ČTK, Aug. 18, 1992, complaining that people were not being informed.

42. ČTK, Aug. 10, 1992.

three ministries) were to deal with legal questions of the transfer of competences, property inventories, treatment of archives, termination of the federal counterspy services, documentation on the frontiers between the Republics, the handling of refugees from third countries, and coordination of police
actions.[43]

2. The Context

a. The Three New Governments

The newly instituted government of the Czech Republic, headed by Václav
Klaus with CDA's Jan Kalvoda as one of the deputy premiers, was composed of four right-of-center parties: Klaus's own CDP, the CDA, and the
two Christian Democrat parties.[44] In Slovakia, as expected, Vladimír Mečiar
was returned to the office of prime minister from which he had been removed
the previous year; in his government, 11 ministers came from his own MDS,
one was a nonparty general officer, and one a member of the Slovak National Party.[45] The caretaker federal government (reduced from 16 to ten)
was sworn in by President Havel on July 2. It was based on a coalition between
the CDP and the MDS. CDP's technocrat Jan Stráský replaced Marián
Čalfa as prime minister. "With us," Čalfa told the press, "departs the federation."[46]

---

43. LN, Aug. 21, 1992, p. 1.

44. The government commanded a majority of 105 votes of a total of 200 in the new Czech
National Council. Jan Obrman, "Czechoslovakia's New Governments," RFE/RL RES. REP. July
17, 1992, 1, 3–4.

45. On June 23, 1992, Prime Minister Mečiar presented to the Slovak National Council a
program of his government: civil society, respect for the Charter of Basic Rights, market economy
and privatization, liberation of prices and foreign trade relations, stable currency and thrift in
budgetary expenses, and full respect of minority rights in harmony with international norms.
"Stenogr. Správa o ustanovujúcej (1.) schôdzi Slovenskej nár. rady konanej 23. júna 1992, X.
volebné obdobi [Stenographic Record of the Constitutive (First) Session of the Slovak National
Council, June 23, 1992, Tenth Election Period]," 5, 6; Jiří Pehe, "The New Slovak Government
and Parliament," RFE/RL RES. REP., July 10, 1992, 32. Only five parties gained representation in
the new Slovak National Council: the MDS (74 seats), the PDL (29 seats), the CDM (18 seats), and
the Coexistence/Hungarian Christian Democratic Movement coalition (14 seats). *Ibid.,* LN, June
25, p. 1.

46. M. Čalfa. Of the ten members of the federal cabinet, four (including the Prime Minister Jan Stráský, with a reputation of an effective and hard-working administrator) were members of the CDP, four of the MDS, one of the CDU, and one independent. Jan Obrman, *supra,*
note 44, 1.

b. Havel Resigns (July 1992)

In the second round of the federal presidential election held on July 16, President Havel failed in his bid for reelection due to Slovak opposition.[47]

On July 17, the Slovak National Council finally approved the long delayed and much touted Slovak Declaration of Sovereignty as the first of the trinity of measures promised by the MDS campaign platform. The declaration asserted the Slovak nation's natural right of self-determination and choice of the form of national and state life and promised to respect the rights of national minorities and ethnic groups. It was adopted in a celebratory mood by 113 of the 150 members of the Council after Mečiar and others had made it clear that it was meant as a symbolic political statement and not as a constitutional act or a declaration of independence. In fact, as I suggested earlier, the existing federal Constitution already viewed the Republics as "sovereign," raising the question, particularly among the Czechs, of the purpose of the exercise.[48] Opposition came only from just resigned Prime Minister Ján Čarnogurský's Christian Democratic Movement and the Hungarian coalition.[49] When the deputies who voted against the document asked for police protection from a crowd of nationalists who were celebrating in front of the Parliament Building, Mečiar tried to calm the crowds by saying that "we know who voted against the declaration. Let them leave; they are walking into the past."[50] The Slovak Catholic bishops officially welcomed the declaration, thus—as a Czech writer put it—"betraying" the Christian Democratic Movement of Ján Čarnogurský.[51]

---

47. See also *infra,* chap. XI, 2b. Explaining the Slovak opposition, Mečiar said that the president committed several mistakes. His program for rebuilding the Federation is "nobody's program" since, although he was very popular, he lost all political influence. The parties on which he relied lost the election and in reality expressed no confidence in him by defeating his proposals. He can't deny responsibility for the negative state of the Czech-Slovak relations or for his advisers. Today his person is misused for inciting the Czechs against the Slovaks. He suggested "to Czech political parties" to change the law on the election of the president so as to have both Republics elect their presidents and "then we shall fix the reciprocal relations" for electing the president and vice-president of the common body. The president of the Czech Republic might become also president of the confederation. SP, July 24, 1992, p. 3.

48. As seen by a Slovak commentator, the move was bound to strengthen "the designs" of the Czech right. S. Bombík in NO, July 15, 1992, p. 3.

49. Dr. Čarnogurský called the adoption of the declaration "a dangerous political game, cynically playing on the emotions of our nation, a game pointing toward political destabilization of this part of Europe." NO, July 18, 1992, quoted in Jan Obrman, "Slovakia Declares Sovereignty: President Havel Resigns," RFE/RL RES. REP., July 31, 1992, 25. The second item in the MDS program, the adoption of a Slovak Republic constitution, was accomplished in the Slovak National Council on Sept. 1, 1992 (ČSTK, Sept. 3, 1992), while the third item, the election of the Slovak president, took place only after the Republic became an independent state.

50. Jan Obrman, *supra,* note 49, 25, 26.

51. František Schildberger in LN, Aug. 7, 1992, p. 3.

Minutes after the adoption of the declaration, President Havel announced his resignation from his current term, which was to end three months later, in October of the same year.

The newly organized federal government appeared before the Federal Assembly on July 16, 1992, with a request for a vote of confidence and approval of the declaration of its program.[52] In an extended discussion—which necessitated special late evening transportation arrangements for the deputies—the program was heavily criticized by the opposition on the left for being much too short, general, and contradictory, proposing steps based both on the continuation and the termination of the state.

In a statement that articulated a standard theme of the opposition, Social Democrat Professor Z. Jičínský, a lone survivor of the Czech "first team," declared that "the parties that won the elections but failed to gain a majority obtained rightfully the mandate for the formation of the government but not a mandate to decide the fate of the state."[53] A series of proposed amendments to the program, aiming primarily at increasing the role of the Federal Assembly in the constitutional negotiations, was voted down, and the confidence motion together with the program declaration were approved by a large majority. A substantial part of the opposition while expressing "categoric reservation" with respect to the program voted affirmatively in order to avoid "further unconstitutional decomposition" of the state.[54]

3. Round Five: A New Political Agreement

It was in this atmosphere that Klaus and Mečiar—now the prime ministers of their respective Republics—faced each other in Bratislava from the evening hours on July 22 through the small hours of July 23, this time in the decorous halls and pleasing gardens of a Bratislava palace, the seat of the Slovak govern-

---

52. For a summary of the program, see Prime Minister J. Stráský, in Zpráva a 2. společné schůzi Sněmovny lidu a Sněmovny národů, 2. část, 16.července 1992, VII. volební období. [Report of the 2d Common Session of the Chamber of the People and the Chamber of the Nations, 2d part, 7th election term], July 16, 1992, 103–8.

53. *Ibid.,* 181. Alexander Dubček, now a deputy also for the Social Democratic Party, urged a referendum and another alternative solution combining elements of a federation and confederation. *Ibid.,* 203, 206. Seeking to rebut the criticism, the new Federal Prime Minister Stráský said that it was "not compatible for a government to uphold and simultaneously liquidate a federation, for this very reason it fixed the time horizon [for the program to apply until September 30 only] that it selected." *Ibid.,* 243, 245.

54. *Ibid.,* 283–84 (the vote), 152 (Slovak Party of the Democratic Left Deputy M. Benčík). On the subject of asking the government to prepare an analysis of the economic, cultural, and legal consequences of the split, Prime Minister Stráský opined that no one was capable of undertaking such a task. *Ibid.,* 247.

ment.[55] After some preliminary sparring,[56] the two men managed relatively promptly to agree on an agenda: to trace the optimal course for a termination of the Federation. The outcome was a three-part new political agreement between the CDP and MDS in which the two parties undertook to press a series of far-reaching measures in the executive and legislative organs of the Federation and the Republics.

The first part dealt with a scheme for the operation of federal bodies, including further transfers of competences to the Republics, reorganization of the Federal Security and Information Service and of Czecho-Slovak television and radio, the restructuring of the Academies of Sciences, and so on. In the second and third parts, addressing the constitutional arrangements, the parties pledged themselves to push for the adoption by the Federal Assembly of legislation on the manner of ending the Federation and on settling the property relations by September 30, 1992.[57] Both sides would contribute to the completion of the constitutions of the two Republics and begin to prepare bilateral cooperation agreements on mutual relations in areas of mutual interest. The third part outlined the principles of future cooperation between the two independent states. Agreements in the economic sphere would provide for a customs union, for free movement of goods and factors of production, and institutions for coordination of tax and monetary policies. The parties would

continue searching for ways to coordinate their budget (fiscal) policies, which is the essential prerequisite for maintaining a common currency. Should this not be possible, the separation of currencies must not lead to the depreciation of citizens' savings in either Republic. A separation of currencies will be partially compensated by the formation of a reasonable and effective payments union.[58]

---

55. MfD, Sept. 23, 1992, p. 7. On the CDP side, Klaus was accompanied by Josef Zieleniec, Miroslav Macek, Jiří Kovář, and František Houska. The MDS delegation headed by Mečiar included Milan Kňažko, Michal Kováč, and Augustin Marián Húska. ČSTK, July 22, 1992.

56. Mečiar first urged Klaus that since a Slovak constitution was to be approved shortly, the counterpart Czech constitution should be adopted at the same time—but at that point Klaus was not prepared to agree: the Czech Republic, he said, did not need a constitution—it preferred, after all, the federal model. Kipke and Vodička, *supra,* note 8, 96. Yet later in the same round Klaus did agree. The exchange illustrates the pervasive motive on both sides to avoid being left holding "the black jack," the responsibility for splitting the state.

57. The law would allow a flexible choice between four modes of termination: a declaration of the Federal Assembly, a bilateral agreement of the two National Councils, a referendum, or a unilateral act by one of the Republics. In case none of these steps should be realized, the parties promised to exert maximum control of the breakup process so as to ensure "a calm, civilized, and unchaotic manner." *Ibid.*

58. ČSTK, July 23, 1992. *See also* the report on the Klaus-Mečiar press conference in NO, July 24, 1992, p. 3.

In the civil sphere, agreements would assure "to the maximum extent" equal status for the citizens of the two Republics in each other's territory, and they would settle the questions of social benefits, work-related issues, and execution of court judgments. The parties agreed "on the coordination of a joint approach to foreign policy and also on the possibility of joint representations abroad in some countries and organizations." As a short term defense policy, the parties will proceed from the existing deployment of the Czecho-Slovak army and from the technical and organizational potential for change, in order that both Republics' defense capabilities not be affected.[59]

Four days later, representatives of the newly constituted presidia of the National Councils met also in Bratislava in a show of studied friendliness to explore ways of implementing the agreement reached by their party leaders.[60] Docent Ivan Gašparovič (MDS), who had replaced František Mikloško as chair of the Slovak National Council, gently prodded his Czech counterpart, Milan Uhde (CDP), who had taken the place of Dr. Burešová, to speed up work on the Czech constitution so as to assure coordination with the Slovak document.[61] With equal tact, and anxious to avoid any impression of imposing on his partners, Uhde proffered the idea for the Slovak side to initiate a government commission of all parties' representatives, which would deal with a corresponding body set up on the Czech side, and a series of joint expert minicommissions. The Slovaks readily accepted. Both sides then easily agreed on a common strategy in the Federal Assembly: the deputies of their respective parties would jointly propose a constitutional law on the mode of "extinction" of the Federation and on the settlement of property and other ties within the agreed deadline.[62]

---

59. ČSTK, July 23, 1992. A year earlier, according to Federal Defense Minister Dobrovský, Armed Forces were already being redeployed to Slovakia (39 percent were to be deployed there), ČTK, July 24, 1991.

60. "Stenografický protokol z rokovania predstaviteľov národných rád v Bratislave 27. júla 1992 [Stenographic Protocol of the Deliberations of the Representatives of the National Councils in Bratislava, July 27, 1992]," in the Library of the Czech Parliament.

61. Uhde's response was that not even a working draft of the Czech constitution existed since the Czech government rejected the draft of the Constitutional Commission. Ibid., 1–2. Before becoming a deputy in the Slovak National Council, Docent Gašparovič, a specialist in criminal law at the Comenius Law Faculty in Bratislava, was federal procurator general in Prague. Uhde was a writer and dissident journalist before 1989.

62. In case the Federal Assembly failed to accept the legislation, it would be for the two National Councils to agree on the extinction. Communiqué, ibid., 72–73. In an early comment on the outcome, CDP Deputy Prime Minister Josef Zieleniec (the future first Czech foreign affairs minister) hailed the abandonment by the MDS of a confederation "because it has realized that this would end in chaos." ČTK, July 23, 1992. Applause came from CDA Deputy Chair Daniel Kroupa and from the CDU-CPP. According to the chair of the Hungarian party Együttelés, "in the present situation it would be inappropriate for our deputies to strive hard to preserve the Czechoslovak

4. In the Federal Assembly, Again Referendum?
(August 1992)

A new phase of the debate on a referendum opened with a proposal in the Federal Assembly by three Slovak deputies of the Christian Democratic Movement, led by Ivan Šimko, for a plebiscite to be held throughout the federal territory.[63] In an indirect response to this proposal, Václav Klaus saw no sense in a referendum: "Even if 51 percent vote for maintaining the common state, we shall not have moved even a millimeter further since the centrifugal tendencies will persist."[64] At the same time, Mečiar declared that a referendum at

Federation"; they would not vote for ending the Federation, "but if constitutional separation . . . is the only possibility of preserving calm, they will support it." ČTK, July 24, 1992. On a similar note of resignation, the Slovak Christian Democrat chair and former prime minister Ján Čarnogurský saw the political agreement as a logical consequence of the political development, and in Slovakia, as a consequence of the MDS policy. ČTK, July 23, 1992. Rudolf Filkus, a deputy chair of MDS and the federal first deputy prime minister, warned that the decision of the European Parliament to stop the ratification process for Czechoslovakia's Association Agreement with the European Community because of the impending split was bound to have a serious impact on Slovakia's economy: "It is said that we'll have to get in line behind Romania and Bulgaria to wait for an association accord." Filkus was linked to a group of alleged dissenters within the MDS. ČTK, Aug. 2, 1992. The federal deputy minister for foreign affairs commented, however, that negotiating new agreements with the Czech and Slovak states could be "quite easy." ČTK, Aug. 4, 1992. Mečiar, now again head of government, informed Slovak deputies of the course of his negotiations. The Czech-Slovak constitutional crisis, he said, was only a part of the all-European movement giving rise to a new quality of the European region. It was part of the general crisis in all postcommunist states resulting from the revival of democratic structures and a new shape of freedom not only for the citizen but also for the nation. Here the crisis was deepened by the differences between the Czech Republic and Slovakia, which were due to the 74 years' evolution. "The common state was not a goal, but a means. The goal was coexistence with the Czechs in a new qualitative form." "The process of disintegration proceeds," Mečiar asserted, "regardless of what Klaus or Mečiar want or do not want. At most we can just correct it, make it peaceful, cultured, and not chaotic. But we did not originate it, and we would not know how to block it." In the negotiations, Mečiar continued, thus far MDS had met its program as regards the substance—with the exception of a common currency—but not as to the form, which was to be a confederation. To this Ján Čarnogurský observed that "all you agreed on is the end of the common state, all that you talk about beyond this is your notion, your wish . . ." PRAVDA, Aug. 6, 1992, pp. 1, 2. Mečiar reported a dispute with the Czech side over the rights of succession and warned of any improvident Slovak move, which could be interpreted as secession. KORIDOR, Aug. 11, 1992, p. 3.

63. The Federal Assembly should call for a plebiscite throughout the federal territory on the question: "Do you favor the preservation of the federation and new parliamentary elections in the three legislative bodies?" If the majority in both Republics responded affirmatively, the vote would be held by December 1, 1992. If a majority in one or both voted in the negative, the state would terminate at the end of December, and both Republics would hold elections with the new parliaments taking over the power. PRAVDA, Aug. 10, 1992, p. 5. In a curious statement, Jan Kalvoda distinguished between constitutional solution and division, the first only being subject to a referendum. LN, Aug. 18, 1992, p. 16.

64. Interview with NO, Aug. 5, 1992, pp. 1, 3, reprinted in LN, Aug. 6, 1992, p. 3.

that point was contrary to Slovak interests since it would make possible a unilateral withdrawal [of Slovakia]—a disadvantage from the viewpoint of successor rights.[65]

A month later, Havel, a private citizen but meeting with representatives of the CDP, saw no sense in a referendum on the country's division since Slovakia had decided to proceed along its own path and there would be even less sense to hold it in the Czech Republic since "if Slovakia wants to go along its own path, the Czech Republic must do the same."[66] However, the former president, like Mečiar, favored a "confirmation" referendum, either ratifying a federal constitutional law on the separation or ratifying the constitutions of the two Republics "as intended in Slovakia."[67]

While the "CDP was on vacation," the MDS complained that the federal government had failed to follow the Klaus-Mečiar political agreement in devolving competences to the Republics and respecting the parity representation in international organizations.[68]

5. Round Six: Setting the Date

After the summer vacation, two events that threatened to disrupt the process of separation preceded the sixth meeting. The first incident was a skirmish that at the outset appeared more serious than it turned out to be in the end.

a. A Stumble

At the center was the question of the staff of the Federal Security Information Service (FSIS) and its head, "the hard persecutor" of Vladimír Mečiar.[69] When Mečiar's party deputies in the Federal Assembly, joined by the Czech left, attempted to elect their "leftist" candidate as chair of the organ controlling the counterspy service, CDP parliamentarians walked out crying "leftist putsch." With the Assembly blocked for the lack of a quorum, the CDP with the support of the other Czech coalition parties moved in the federal government to appoint

---

65. "Referendum yes, but not now, today it is politically impossible. We shall not correct referendum with new elections." PRAVDA, Aug. 6, 1992, pp. 1, 2. "Even if a referendum should take place and confirm the Federation, there was no need for new elections since MDS had in its program five modes for a constitutional solution. LN, Aug. 6, 1992, p. 1.

66. The Czechs would either "vote to maintain the common state, which is impossible, or vote for a separation, which will happen in any case." He also spoke against calling an early general election: "In such a complicated state we cannot afford losing three months by an election struggle." ČSTK, Sept. 30, 1992.

67. Ibid.

68. LN, Aug. 3, 1992, p. 1; Aug. 4, 1992, p. 3.

69. PRAVDA, Aug. 25, 1992, pp. 1, 2.

its own candidate as deputy director of the service. Charging a violation of the political agreements, Mečiar refused to appear at the scheduled sixth round and demanded an apology for the "leftist" slur.[70] He addressed a sharply worded letter to Klaus,[71] and Klaus responded in a measured statement to the Czecho-Slovak Press Bureau.[72] The incubus of a breakdown stimulated an outpouring of speculation regarding Mečiar's motives. Was his implied threat to break off the negotiations a ploy commonly used in bargaining? Did he want to counter the accusations of the Slovak nationalists of being "a slave" of Klaus? Was he bent primarily on personal retaliation? Did he contemplate a frontal retreat from a confederation back to a "common state" under the impact of a pessimistic report that one of his economists had brought from Washington about his dealings with the international financial institutions? Or, finally, did he decide to change his tactic and pose as the weaker of the two men, an "insulted honest underdog" entitled to an apology?[73] He was reported to be "a different person," bereft of illusions and listening now to his government officials rather than to the "fairy tales" of his party economists.[74]

Klaus was asked by a reporter whether he had a "counterweapon" to Mečiar's refusal to negotiate. He would not betray the secret, Klaus replied by way of an implied counterthreat, but "we made it absolutely obvious already in

---

70. PRAVDA, Aug. 25, 1992, p. 2; LN, Aug. 25, 1992, pp. 1, 16; ČSTK, Aug. 24, 1992. Mečiar claimed to have information that four FSIS members were seen in the building of the Assembly searching for some parliamentary documents. In early August, CDP and Christian Democratic Party deputies walked off the Federal Assembly floor in protest against what they called a misinterpretation of a previous agreement on electing the chairmen of supervising parliamentary bodies. When the obstruction continued the following day, Chair Michal Kováč ended the second joint session. ČTK, Aug. 9, 1992. *See also* ČSTK, Aug. 3, 1992; LN, Aug. 8, 1992, p. 1; and PRAVDA, Aug. 10, 1992, p. 2.

71. Mečiar charged that the CDP, while questioning the MDS implementation of its own program, itself had failed to comply in federal organs with "concrete and precise accords" and particularly that the party was unwilling to remove the FSIS director. "As long as the CDP does not convince us of its will to realize honestly the compliance with the accord we consider our further negotiations inappropriate." However, he appealed to Klaus "as the only politician in contemporary Czech lands whom the Slovak side can still trust." Letter to Klaus in LN, Aug. 25, 1992, p. 3.

72. Klaus restated the agenda for the aborted meeting. He expressed his disappointment at Mečiar's refusal to attend the scheduled meeting "because it indicates a new phase of the MDS attempt at an inconsequent solution of the constitutional question. The Czech side acceded after the June elections to the weakening and factual liquidation of the common state only under the pressure of the Slovak emancipation process, but today it is no longer prepared to assist inactively in the silent transformation of a federation [into a different form], which—as any other form of a Czechoslovak union—is absolutely unacceptable for the overwhelming majority of the Czech public." *Ibid.*

73. LN, Aug. 25, 1992, p. 1 ("Záminka [A Pretext]," by Jiří Horák); MFD, Sept. 23, 1992, p. 7.

74. MFD, Sept. 23, 1992, p. 7.

the first encounter . . . in Brno that we did not accept this game. And it is clear we shall not accept it now." He too wondered about Mečiar's motives.[75]

In the end, the new federal prime minister, Jan Stráský, acknowledged that there was indeed an "obligation" of sorts regarding the FSIS personnel, while Michal Kováč admitted in a private setting that his party's reproaches against the CDP were not entirely justified.[76] When Mečiar refused to resume negotiations without an apology, Kováč declared that the MDS delegation would go to the meeting without him. This was the beginning of Mečiar's aversion for Michal Kováč, which ultimately matured into deadly enmity.[77] The federal government gave in to the strong pressure of its Slovak members and agreed to the immediate removal of the official particularly obnoxious to Mečiar and his replacement by a Mečiar man.[78] The stage was thus set for the next round.

b. A "Union" Again: A "Trial Balloon"?

"Unexpectedly and mysteriously a text was discovered"[79] in Slovakia purporting to be a working version of a treaty for a Czech-Slovak "union."[80] The spokesman for the Slovak government, MDS member Bohuslav Géci told the press that this was indeed a working document prepared by MDS, which it planned to submit in the next round of negotiations with the CDP. This statement was confirmed by Slovak Minister of International Relations M. Kňažko.[81]

---

75. He saw two explanations for Mečiar's conduct. First, Mečiar might be satisfied with the present state having succeeded in loosening the Federation and was willing to stay in this unclear situation indefinitely. The second, an exactly opposite hypothesis, suggested that under pressure the Slovak side was "opening the door for an accelerated way toward unilateral, single-direction, asynchronic steps—and these are difficult to take while negotiations are in progress." On the other hand, Klaus did not see "a frontal retreat [on the part of the MDS] from a confederation to a common state." *Ibid.* Jan Kalvoda, of the CDA, by then deputy chair of the Czech government, took an essentially identical view, stressing Mečiar's internal political problems and his concern about the reaction of the international community. LN, Aug. 26, 1992, pp. 1, 8.

76. LN, Aug. 27, 1992, p. 3; MFD, Sept. 23, 1992, p. 7.

77. Přemysl Svora, "Kováč prezidentem nikoho [Kováč Nobody's President]," LN, Oct. 8, 1995, p. 5.

78. LN, Aug. 27, 1992, pp. 1, 3, 12. A compromise was reached on the Czech deputy to the FSIS director.

79. PRAVDA, Aug. 25, 1992, p. 1.

80. The text in SMENA, Aug. 24, 1992, p. 6.

81. LN, Aug. 21, 1992, p. 3; Aug. 22, 1992, p. 3. The draft provided in very general terms for the succession of both Republics to the Federation and for common citizenship, protection of basic human rights, commercial union, common or coordinated foreign security policy, and mutual recognition of public documents and decisions; significantly, the underlying treaty would have priority over the constitutions and laws of the two Republics. Another treaty was to establish an economic union in the image of the European Community. Igor Cibula in NO, Aug. 20, 1992, pp. 1, 3.

As seen by a Slovak commentator, the Czech side reacted with "bagatelizing and inappropriate arguments" and rejected the draft before it came on the agenda of the next round.[82] In fact, CDA's Jan Kalvoda spurned "the manipulation [*alibismus!*] of the type of proposals of a Czecho-Slovak Union," but Deputy Chair Zeman of the Czech Social Democrats welcomed the draft as a first step toward a new type of union.[83] A leading member of the MDS, Milan Čič, deputy chair of the federal government and a key person in the legislative preparation of future Czech-Slovak relations, denied any connection with the proposal or any knowledge of its authorship.[84]

Mečiar himself denied that the draft originated in his party.[85] In the end, Michal Kováč, the new MDS chair of the Federal Assembly, revealed that the preparation of the draft had been arranged by the Slovak government at the request of a working group at the Slovak National Council. It was one of the working versions without an official standing and—moreover—it would not be offered at the upcoming meetings with the CDP. He also agreed with the CDP spokesmen that some of the articles in the paper could lead to even closer ties between the Republics than prevailed in the existing Federation.[86]

The dénouement confirmed the suspicion voiced in the Slovak daily *Pravda* that the draft was indeed a trial balloon, sent up to smoke out not only the reaction of the CDP but of the Slovak parties as well, with the idea that if the balloon were shot down by the Czech side, it would not harm the prestige of

---

82. Igor Cibula, citing a controversial Czech adviser to the chair of the Federal Assembly in NO, Aug. 24, 1992, reprinted in LN, Aug. 28, 1992, p. 7.

83. LN, Aug. 26, 1992, pp. 1, 8. "Klaus's lieutenant Macek" also confirmed unmistakably that the idea of the union was dead. Jiří Hanák in LN, Aug. 28, 1992, p. 1. On the other hand, Deputy Chair of the Czech Social Democratic Party Kuča, commenting on the draft, called for the abandonment of the concepts of "federation" and "con-federation," which "provoke mutual distaste on both sides," as the first step toward building a new type of a union whose "unfilled concept may be completed by a positive content." Jaromír Kuča in LN, Aug. 22, 1992, p. 3. In a curiously ambiguous reflection, Federal Prime Minister Jan Stráský discerned recent "signals of a retreat" of the MDS with words that could be interpreted better in terms of a common rather than a divided state. Although this could be a tactical move, in his view it was still possible to retreat to a functional federation, "but this would not be a long-term historical solution; instead it should be possible to establish treaty relations between independent states that would be firmer than a federation and that would entail—whether the Slovak side likes it or not—even a greater relinquishment of sovereignty than exists in today's Federation" (sic!). LN, Aug. 21, 1992, p. 16. In Slovakia, Jozef Prokeš, chair of the SNP, termed the union proposal "a negation of the emancipation efforts of the Slovak Republic and of the hopes of its citizens . . . a genie released from a bottle." LN, Aug. 21, 1992, p. 3; Aug. 25, 1992, p. 3.

84. LN, Aug. 22, 1992, p. 3.

85. *Ibid.* Asked about who was the author, Mečiar said that he knew but would not say—expert groups working with the government "take positions" on the subject and these "materials are only with me and I did not give them to anyone." Moreover, talks about a union are superfluous, "because Václav Klaus in his articles explained several possible variants of economic unions."

86. LN, Aug. 24, 1992, p. 1.

the MDS.[87] Judging from its outcome, the experiment achieved its purpose. It left, however, a bitter aftertaste of a game, a "duel" between two players in which the powerless citizen was relegated to the position of "a second."[88]

c. Return to the Plane Tree

Finally, during the night of August 26–27, "the two lonely men" met again under a plane tree of the villa in Brno, the scene of their first encounter.[89] "Why again at night?" asked a Czech writer—a question relevant to the methodology of negotiation. Was it a fashion of the political season, she wondered, a political necessity, a tactic? Both men, Republic prime ministers and heads of the leading parties with heavy agendas, must have had a sense of their priorities, yet they convened on matters of first priority at the end of a working day. "Press conferences are never held in daylight, night rain magnifies the drama of the moment, the protagonists—modestly smiling—declare that they will continue their labor until the cock crows at dawn while we, ordinary mortals, sleep undisturbed. Indefatigability is indeed a part of a politician's image, but some members of the 'state-splitting' delegations are aged, mildly overweight gentlemen . . ." Why carry such important negotiations to a point where fatigue prevents the signing of a communiqué? "Does the partner wait for our fatigue, for our fatal mistake made when we concentrate on the comforting vision of the horizontal position? After nightly negotiations, is not the morning wiser than the evening?"[90] Recalling the working habits of Churchill and Stalin, a less ominous explanation might be that the two men, workaholics known for their exuberant energy, preferred to do their important work at night.

During an intermission in the eight-hour meeting, Klaus told the reporters that the first two and one-half hours were devoted to a tête à tête between the two leaders, which "renewed the confidence and cooperation between the CDP and the MDS about which the journalists raised so many doubts and which is the guarantee of further cooperation in the future."[91] A Czech source reported that the subject was again the federal spy agency (FSIS) about which Mečiar had the strongest negative feelings.[92]

During the next two hours, the two sides agreed on a detailed timetable for further action, including—for the first time—naming January 1, 1993, as the

---

87. Pravda, Aug. 25, 1992, p. 1 (by Štefan Hrčka).

88. *Ibid.,* p. 2.

89. Jiří Hanák, "Dočasná unie, [A Temporary Union]," LN, Aug. 28, 1992, p. 1.

90. Eva Martínková, "Noční seriál, [A Night Serial]," LN, Aug. 28, 1992, p. 3.

91. Pravda, Aug. 28, 1992, p. 2; LN, Aug. 27, 1992, pp. 1, 12.

92. The authors of the report linked Mečiar's aversion to FSIS with his enmity against Václav Havel, whom he suspected of having directed the agency to collect compromising information against Mečiar prior to his ouster in 1991. MfD, Sept. 23, 1992, p. 7.

effective date of the dissolution. This was the primary objective of the Czech side, but surprisingly it was Mečiar who pronounced the date before the television cameras.[93] Mečiar explained that the success of the timetable was conditional upon the timely action of the respective federal and Republic institutions. More specifically, the deadlines were set for the adoption, by the end of September or mid-October, of the federal law on the mode of extinction of the Federation that would replace the current law on referendum as the only available means of separation, the law on the division of property and successor rights, and the conclusion by the National Councils of agreements on future coexistence. The entire complex of legal relationships leading to the emergence of two independent states was to be solved in the following months. According to Mečiar, the two parties, "aware of the overwhelming emotional ties of Czech and Slovak citizens to the Federal Republic," sought to moderate the impact of the breakup by pointing out the impossibility of maintaining the prevailing situation because the development proceeds so that it could get out of control—and so it is better to look the truth in the eyes and accept it.[94]

Klaus then reported on the substance of the prospective cooperation between the two Republics. In addition to a customs union and a monetary union,[95] negotiators explored proposed agreements on the status of citizens of one Republic in the other and on social and foreign affairs. The defense problem was viewed by both sides as the most difficult one, requiring close cooperation and gradual solution so as not to prejudice the defense capability of either Republic. Finally, the participants undertook, prior to each session of the Federal Assembly, to discuss the possibility of a common posture on pending bills with a view toward preventing deadlock.[96]

Public reaction to the announcement of the date for the division was relatively muted. Except for certain reservations by the CDA, the Czech coalition parties responded favorably, but the opposition was critical.[97]

Some critics argued that the modalities of the separation should be determined by the people[98] or by institutions at the federal level rather than the level

---

93. CDP Deputy Chair Miroslav Macek in LN, Aug. 27, 1992, p. 12; MFD, Sept. 23, 1992, p. 7.

94. PRAVDA, Aug. 28, 1992, p. 2.

95. Common currency was utopia, according to Petr Husák, LN, Aug. 25, 1992, p. 6.

96. *Ibid.;* ČTK, Aug. 26, 1992.

97. *See,* for example, Chair of the CDU Josef Lux, in LN, Aug. 28, 1992, p. 3, who supported the acceleration of the development, "deplorable as it may be." For the opposition Social Democrats, Alexander Dubček welcomed the resumption of the negotiations and the result, which, surprisingly, he viewed "not as a breakup of the state but as a new process of a quantitative transformation of the Federation to a new level of relations." LN, Aug. 29, 1992, p. 3. His own party's spokesmen, however, criticized the process as "contradictory and illogical, designed solely to accelerate the division." PRAVDA, Aug. 29, 1992, p. 2.

98. The LSU.

of the Republics,[99] or that other political parties should be included in the bilateral talks.[100] The Czech Communist Party representative spoke of a new "Munich Crisis."[101]

A newspaper commentator observed: "It may be a union, perhaps long-term-temporary or just short term. . . . Perhaps just a safety belt, thrown by a richer to a poorer, before he emerges from the waves of independence and regains his breath. That would make sense."[102] No popular demonstrations against the fiat of the two men (speaking for two parties) were reported in either Republic despite the opinion polls consistently showing a majority for the common state.

6. Summing Up: Spotlight on "the Heroes-Villains"

I suggested earlier that the Czech-Slovak negotiations might be seen as a two-party, multi-issue, bargaining process for a contract, which was to embody the new constitution.[103] Perhaps as late as fall 1992, the parties were still committed to a common state, although they increasingly differed on its nature and shape. The Milovy face-off was in reality the last episode in this phase of bargaining. Some feel, however, that even there the common objective was in doubt and the final consensus illusory. After the rejection of the Milovy text in the Slovak Presidium, and with the nationwide elections only three months away, the public understanding was that following the elections the constitutional negotiations would resume both in the newly elected Federal Assembly and between the two Republics. President Havel spoke along these lines.

After the elections, however, the negotiations, although still multi-issue and two party, started in an entirely different and unforeseen forum. The two-party nature of the negotiations came into even sharper relief because the federal government was finally relegated to the sidelines and also because of the distinct role assumed by the two individual leaders, our "heroes" (or villains) within a structure that had undergone a radical mutation. The two men

---

99. The CPP.

100. CDA's Kalvoda and the Movement for Self-Governing Democracy/Society for Moravia and Silesia.

101. On the above critical views, see LN, Aug. 27, 1992, p. 3; and Aug. 28, 1992, p. 3 (J. Svoboda, Czech Communist Party). Skepticism was voiced about the monetary union and concern about possible customs frontiers between the two Republics and loss of GATT trade advantages. LN, Aug. 25, 1992, p. 6; LN, Aug. 28, 1992, p. 1; CDA Minister Vladimír Dlouhý in PRAVDA, Aug. 29, 1992, p. 2; LN, Aug. 29, 1992, p. 3. Predictably, Jozef Prokeš of the SNP feared that a customs and monetary union might endanger Slovak economic sovereignty and suggested as an alternative mutual payments in dollars. LN, Aug. 28, 1992, p. 3.

102. Jiří Hanák in LN, Aug. 28, 1992, p. 1.

103. This section draws primarily on private conversations with persons, some of whom held high government positions at the time of writing this book.

alone or joined by delegations drawn exclusively from the two parties constituted the new forum. Power interests of the two men, their lieutenants, and their parties came into play prominently. For Klaus, personal political power was grounded in the Czech lands, his party having fared poorly in Slovakia, and from that perspective at any rate the Federation had become dispensable if not outright burdensome. In fact, Klaus, having refused to serve as federal prime minister, reserved his most trusted collaborators for service in his own Republic government. But power considerations, as I shall suggest shortly, could not have been his only motivation. In the comfortable party-to-party setting, and in contrast to the divided Czech side in the past, Klaus's CDP was able to speak with one voice, his!

Mečiar did not seek a federal position in a "hostile Prague" and preferred the Bratislava castle where he could rule "supreme." While there is evidence that some of Mečiar's collaborators would have been prepared to make some concessions in order to preserve the common state, the fear of Mečiar's wrath kept them from going public. From the viewpoint of personal interests, the prospect of new positions in the structure of an independent Slovak state (particularly in diplomatic missions abroad with salaries paid in hard currencies) must have been alluring to Slovak politicians.[104] Tension within the MDS became noticeable even before the elections, but Mečiar sought to minimize the "deviant" statements.[105] When it came to selecting the Slovak representation for the federal organs, Mečiar sent to Prague those prominent party members whom he felt posed a potential challenge to his power—and in fact they turned against him not long after the end of the Federation.[106]

Klaus's mandate from the president had no connection with the prior constitutional negotiations and called for a new phase different from that which ended in the post-Milovy deadlock: the object was the formation of a federal government and the drafting of its program for approval by the competent federal institutions. Understandably, in contrast with the previous phases from Kroměříž to Milovy, the emotional legal and pseudolegal argumentation on the nature of the Czech-Slovak "treaty" vanished without a trace. For a brief period at an early point, the bargaining was back on the post-Milovy track and turned quickly into a face-off with the Czechs insisting on a "functional federation"

---

104. Kipke and Vodička, (*supra,* note 8, 111) point out that some 80 embassies with an average of 20 posts and 1,600 further jobs plus commercial and cultural representation paid in desirable hard currency were to open up.

105. NO, Aug. 11, 1992, p. 9, concerning statements by R. Filkus, then the MDS federal deputy prime minister. An early source of tension arose from the position of Mečiar's assistant, Anna Nágyová, who "controlled access" to the party chairman. Conversation with J. Moravčík.

106. This group included Michal Kováč, who became chair of the Federal Assembly; R. Filkus, the federal deputy prime minister; and J. Moravčík, federal minister of Foreign Affairs. M. Kňažko refused "the exile" to Prague. Conversation with J. Moravčík.

and the Slovaks on a confederation or a union with "full international subjectivity" for the Republics. With no room for further bargaining, the negotiations turned toward new objects for a "contract" in which there were common interests, the peaceful liquidation of the state. Here again, the strong attachment to conformity with the Constitution that appeared so poignantly earlier, reinforced the search for an orderly, calm process.

It is widely assumed both among the Czechs and the Slovaks, including the actual participants in the negotiations, that Mečiar in the first round decided to press claims he knew the Czech side could not accept—a bargaining ploy about which he earlier publicly boasted to the irritation of Czech public opinion. A prime example was the demand for an independent Slovak membership in the United Nations, which he later sought to fudge. Again, while envisaging a coordination on foreign policy issues, he saw competing interests in the wider market and foreign investment acquisition where coordination would be possible only at the price of satisfying the Czech interest.[107] Paradoxically, the Milovy text went some considerable distance in recognizing the partial international personality of the Republics by according them their own treaty powers, representation in international organizations, and representatives in foreign states within the areas of their internal competences. Mečiar might have gained additional minor concessions to enhance the much vaunted "international visibility" had he urged further strengthening of specific aspects of foreign relations of the Republics' powers. Nor did the Czech side attempt to concretize the issue, since it invoked abstractions such as "an indivisible international personality" to fortify their opposition to any confederate variant.

Mečiar—and here also Czech and Slovak informed observers agree—did not have in mind ending the common state. Indeed, to hold his popular support and affirm his political power—and this, according to the Slovak political scientist Professor Miroslav Kusý and others, has been the primary motivation of his career—Mečiar needed the common state, first as an enemy, the "Pragocentered" bully imposing a socially "disastrous" economic policy on Slovakia, and, second, as a source of federal funds required for the conversion of the obsolete arms industry and for economic transformation generally. His tactic was predicated on a continuing negotiation and the belief that the Czechs, Klaus included, would blink when finally faced with the prospect of a complete split.

Nor did Mečiar take seriously Klaus's position that the reelection of Václav Havel was a nonnegotiable item for the Czech side. Mečiar was not interested in the office of federal president, which he recognized would have to go to a Czech. At one point, he hinted that Klaus would be eminently suited for this office. It was the more influential position of federal prime minister that he

---

107. NO, Aug. 11, 1992, p. 9.

intended to assure for the Slovak side. By offering not to run a Slovak candidate for the presidency and (by implication) not to oppose any Czech other than Havel, by floating the possibility of some Slovak-Czech rotation in the presidency, Mečiar assumed, again mistakenly, that he could get Klaus to jettison Havel. Havel gave as the reason for his resignation from the short remainder of his first term his determination to prevent any bargaining with his office. Slovak blocking of Havel's reelection was considered by the Czech public as a further convincing signal that coexistence with the Slovaks was not possible. In this sense, Havel, "the hero," contributed unintentionally to the breakup. Although Havel and Klaus marched to a different drummer, Klaus's hand was greatly strengthened in the Czech constituency by his loyalty to the widely respected Havel, and on that issue at any rate he had all the political forces and public opinion in the Czech lands behind him, with the exception of the extreme left and the neofascist fringe. Although Havel ranked only in fifth place on the list of politicians most trusted in Slovakia, he was still respected by a substantial sector there.[108] Yet Mečiar's unrelenting opposition to Havel did not affect his popularity among his Slovak supporters.

Several participants on the Czech side told me that, as they saw it, Klaus entered the negotiations with the belief that the common state would, and should, continue in the form of a decentralized federation but with the possibility of a division in mind. Some critical voices on the Czech left suspected Klaus of aiming at a split ever since his appointment as prime minister. In any case, if nothing else, his statements I quoted earlier confirm that he was prepared for that alternative. The Slovaks who were close to the negotiations saw Klaus from the outset as an unyielding "unitarist," willing to accept a common state only as long as economic and financial policy was directed from the center. In fact, for Klaus, who showed little patience for institutional niceties, unobstructed economic transformation and speedy access to the European Union were overriding objectives that he pursued with a religious zeal. For his party to accept the MDS scheme, he said, would be to sign a death sentence for the Czech economy.[109] Whatever may have been his state of mind in the first round in Brno, once he concluded that the Slovak vision of the Slovak state with "full international subjectivity" would endanger his primary goals, he refused "to play" further. During the negotiations, Mečiar repeatedly affirmed his admiration and friendly feeling for Klaus as the only trustworthy Czech partner. Yet a high official in Mečiar's government told me in 1993 that but for Mečiar there would have been a chance for an agreement with Klaus. Some Czechs wondered whether a less single minded person in Klaus's position might have made a difference.

---

108. ČTK, Aug. 25, 1992.
109. SMENA, June 12, 1992, p. 2.

After the decision on the separation, the negotiations slid easily into a new phase with new objects for "the contract." Klaus conceded readily on reducing the temporary federal government to five essential ministries and accepting parity representation despite the Czech two-to-one population prevalence, and eventually, in the face of Mečiar's threat, he accepted the dismissal of the top federal security official. Here Mečiar's tactic of refusing further meetings and thus threatening a crisis produced the desired "payoff."

Klaus was no doubt aware of the option of manipulating the Slovak side toward a unilateral secession, in which case the Czech Republic could claim to be the sole successor of the Federation, leaving Slovakia in the position of a new state in the international arena. Divisive issues of "historic guilt" and potential losses and gains would have come into play. There is, however, no evidence that Klaus, intent as he was for a quick and smooth separation, ever seriously considered such an alternative. This may be seen as another concession by Klaus, since it was the Slovak emancipation drive that was at the origin of the crisis. Both Klaus and Mečiar, as we have seen, playing to their respective galleries, intermittently indulged in half-hearted attempts to leave the "black jack" of responsibility for the split with the other partner.[110]

The parties agreed quickly on a common approach to the Federal Assembly in order to obtain its blessing for the division. Both parties preferred parting in conformity with the Constitution. It was, however, Klaus's goal to bring about the split as quickly as possible, while Mečiar played for time and later boasted that he had gained it.[111] Klaus conceded the relatively short delay obviously in the realization that an earlier date would hardly be feasible in practice. Here, again, the time parameter proved significant. Many believed that the pre-1992 election negotiations had failed because the two-year term of the Federal Assembly proved woefully insufficient to reach an agreement on a new constitution. Similarly, in the post-1992 election period the time constraint played a significant role. On the one hand, both sides worried that during an extended transition period an incident, an act of provocation, might lead to a conflict, possibly involving armed forces, as in Yugoslavia.[112] Others on the Czech side saw an advantage in stopping the flow of federal funds to Slovakia at the earliest possible date. Klaus, not known for his patience, was determined

---

110. Commenting on the passing of the Slovak Constitution, Slovak Democratic Left Party leader Peter Weiss saw in the delay in the adoption of the corresponding Czech Republic Constitution "some game . . . for the Czech Republic to become a universal successor of the Czech federation. . . . Looking for who is to blame only on one side should be stopped as this crisis has its historical and political reasons." ČSTK, Sept. 2, 1992.

111. DIE WELT, Jan. 18, 1993, p. 7, cited in Kipke and Vodička; *supra,* note 8, 110.

112. According to a Prague Public Opinion Research Institute poll, in July 1992, 54 percent of Czechs and 59 percent of Slovaks believed that the Yugoslav conflict could never happen in Czechoslovakia. ČTK, July 28, 1992.

at all costs to prevent a resumption of the unpopular, protracted negotiations, which, he feared, would cause a power vacuum and endanger the economic reform. Yet respectable opinion holds that the Federation, albeit in a reduced form, was quite functional and had the negotiations been allowed to continue over a period of time without unrealistic deadlines—as was the case in Belgium and Canada over decades—a consensus might have emerged.

President Havel, although still supported by a substantial majority in the Czech lands,[113] had little influence on the negotiations, except perhaps for having contributed—as he put it—to the clarification of the issues. He had a chance, even after his resignation, to try to save the state by coming out in favor of a confederate solution. This would have meant crossing swords with Klaus, the CDP, and its allies, with questionable impact on the outcome. As it was, moving into the shadow of his future prime minister, Havel continued his consultations with opposition parties but went along with the Klaus-directed current, limiting himself to gentle criticisms of selected aspects of the Klaus-Mečiar discussions.

---

113. In Slovakia—according to an opinion poll of the Slovak Statistical Office—Havel was in fifth place on the list of most trusted politicians with 8.7 percent of respondents, after Mečiar (50.3 percent), chair of the PDL P. Weiss (28.3 percent), A. Dubček (15.1 percent), and Klaus (14.7 percent). PRAVDA, Aug. 26, 1992, p. 2.

XII

The Deed Is Done (Fall 1992)

1. An Overview

Late summer and fall of 1992 were marked by frantic political activities in the federal as well as the Republic institutions.[1] Day after day, politics—constitutional politics—dominated the first pages of the press while the public watched with a mixture of bewilderment, concern, resignation, and ultimately some relief at the prospect that the seemingly endless negotiations might finally come to an end.

a. At the Federal Level

After the failure of Václav Havel's candidacy, the newly organized Federal Assembly went through the motions of attempting to fill the vacant top office of the rapidly vanishing Federation. Lack of interest manifested by mass absences and abstentions of the deputies marked this futile exercise. In the second of a series of rounds prescribed by the Constitution, the sole candidate, Dr. Miroslav Sládek, chairman of the Czech neofascist Republican Party, received a handful of votes. This enfant terrible of Czech politics, accused at the time of criminal libel because of his vicious attacks against the president and the state, caused consternation among the deputies when he appeared at a session dressed in blue jeans and a T-shirt with his party's logo; in spite of that, he was elected a member of the Czecho-Slovak delegation to the Council of Europe Assembly, an act termed shameful by a Christian Democrat deputy.[2] The

---

1. On this section, *see generally* Jan Obrman, "Czechoslovakia: A Messy Divorce after All," RFE/RL RES. REP., Oct. 16, 1992, 1–5.
2. Zpráva o 2. společné schůzi Sněmovny lidu a Sněmovny národů, 2. část, VII. volební období, 16. července 1992, [Report on the 2d joint session of the Chamber of the People and Chamber of the Nations, 2d part, VIIth election term, July 16, 1992], 81–85; LN, Sept. 25, 1992, pp. 1, 16. In the third vote, round two, other candidates and a woman deputy supported by the Movement for Equality of Women failed at election, the first two receiving only one or two votes. Report of the 2d joint session, 3d part, VIIth election term, July 30, 1992, 373, 393. A similar fate befell the candidacy of Jiří Včelař-Kotas, chair of the Council of the Conservative Party, proposed by a deputy of the LSU. LN, Sept. 25, 1992, p. 1, 16; RP, Sept. 25, 1992, p. 2.

Assembly refused to lift Sládek's immunity from criminal prosecution.[3]

The federal government, in addition to reviewing the bills left by its predecessors, had to prepare legislation on further reducing its size and transferring additional competences to the Republics (the devolution legislation) as well as implementing the political agreements for the termination of the state. In the first days of September, the government passed some 13 bills to the Federal Assembly. Eventually, the caretaker Assembly had before it more than 50 bills to be dealt with presumably before the end of the year.[4]

b. At the Republic Level

The Slovak Constitution, drafted under considerable time pressure was approved by the Slovak National Council on September 1, 1992.[5] It was signed two days later in the Hall of the Knights at the Bratislava castle by the chair of the Slovak National Council, I. Gašparovič, and by Prime Minister Mečiar. A large crowd, assembled in the castle court, sang the Slovak national anthem and a 21 gun salute resounded from the banks of the nearby Danube. The new Slovak flag was raised, and fireworks lit the river. In the "unexplained" absence of Czech Prime Minister Klaus, J. Stráský, the federal prime minister, termed the act of signing and the proclamation of the Constitution a very nice and festive moment, and he wished the Slovak nation "that this step be a happy one." In his view, Slovakia did not split from the Federation by this act.[6] According to Deputy Docent L'ubomír Fogaš, one of its drafters, certain provisions of the Constitution were suspended in order to avoid a conflict with the federal constitutional order.[7] The election of the Slovak president was also deferred until full independence.

The hurriedly concocted new Czech Constitution was approved on December 16, barely a fortnight before the proposed termination of the Federation. I shall return to both constitutions in some detail in the next chapter. In addition to the constitutional activities, the governments of both Republics were greatly occupied by the drafting of agreements intended to govern the relations between the two independent states. This also I shall consider in some detail later.

---

3. In another prank, a Republican deputy submitted a formal proposal (actually accepted for the agenda by the baffled presiding officer) for an Assembly resolution that deputies appear at the next session in swimming trunks ready to be driven by the voters into the river Vltava. RP, Sept. 21, 1992, pp. 1, 3, where the deputy chair of the Assembly, Pavel Jajtner, mused about his experience in the Assembly.

4. Deputy Chair of the Federal Assembly Pavel Jajtner in RP, Sept. 21, 1992, pp. 1, 3.

5. 460/1992 Sb.; Pravda, Sept. 2, 1992, p. 1. See also infra, chap. XIV, 1a.

6. LN, Sept. 4, 1992, pp. 1, 16; Pravda, Sept. 4, 1992, p. 1. Prime Minister Mečiar, asked whether he would attend a ceremony of the proclamation of the Czech Constitution, replied that he might be traveling at that time.

7. Pravda, Sept. 2, 1992, p. 2. See also infra, chap. XIV, 1a.

2. The Defiant Federal Assembly
(September–October 1992)

a. The "Extinction" Bill: Legitimate Process or Treason?

The federal government draft of the Law on the Extinction of the Czech and Slovak Republic ("the extinction law") was under the scrutiny of the committees of the Federal Assembly during the first week of September. The bill, consisting of four brief sections, followed the Klaus-Mečiar model by offering four alternative modes of terminating the federal state without making a choice among them: a declaration of the Federal Assembly approved by a constitutional law, an agreement between the two National Councils, a referendum, or the "exit" of one of the Republics by an "otherwise constitutionally manifested will" of one or the other National Council. A constitutional law or an agreement between the two Republics was to determine the transfer of competences to the successor states as well as the mode of the transfer of federal property to those states.[8]

The federal government decision allowing the Klaus-Mečiar agreement to proceed in conformity with the federal Constitution—still in the interest of continuity and "constitutionality"—entailed a calculated risk of obstruction and delay in the Federal Assembly. The problem was that, although the CDP-MDS coalition was able to muster a simple majority in the Assembly, it needed opposition votes to meet the three-fifths majority required for passing a constitutional law. A Czech international law expert questioned the need for taking the constitutional route.[9] "A law on the split is quite exceptional," wrote a Slovak observer, for states "usually do not contemplate their own extinction."[10] Citizen Havel criticized the bill as a luxury when so little time was left, "a partial step" that only described the constitutional possibilities for termination of the state, and he advocated more flexibility.[11]

---

8. Both Republics were authorized in the bill to negotiate with each other on the settlement of their relations in matters within their competence even before the end of the Federation. Full text in LN, Sept. 8, 1992, p. 2.

9. "It is debatable to say the least, whether the origin of a state is a process that can be controlled by law." Later he suggested that the state may be divided de facto by passing key powers over to the Republics. ČSTK, Oct. 1, 1992. Vladimír Balaš; "The Relations between the Two Republics from the Point of View of International Law" (manuscript). Balaš became ultimately dean of a new Law Faculty in Pilsen and director of the Institute of State and Law of the Czech Academy of Sciences.

10. Štefan Hrčka in PRAVDA, Sept. 11, 1992, p. 3.

11. ČSTK, Sept. 26, 1992. Some suspected a plot: once the four-option constitution law was passed, the government would interpret it as an authority for the Assembly to enact the selected one alternative by a simple majority. The government spokesman denied such intentions. *See generally* Obrman, Czechoslovakia, *supra,* note 1, 2.

Another risk facing Klaus and his allies in resorting to the Federal Assembly was the possible defection of the MDS from the political agreements reached with the CDP (which in fact did occur). Mečiar, with other MDS functionaries, embarked upon a round of regular consultations not only with the influential Slovak left but with almost the entire Czech opposition, from the Communists to the extreme right.[12] Klaus, on the other hand, avoided official contacts with the Slovak opposition to avoid embarrassing Mečiar. In fact, the tactical, if not the strategic, goals of the opposition coincided with those of the Slovak MDS: to slow down the disintegration of the state with a view toward a transformation rather than a breakup. For Klaus, on the other hand, delay was the enemy: for him, time was of the essence since he viewed any postponement of the separation as damaging to the image of both Republics abroad,[13] a hindrance to the critically needed economic reform, and a danger of chaos in what he saw as a disintegrating federation. Mečiar, in contrast, under no time pressure since he wanted to prolong the process, found himself in a stronger bargaining position. The results of Mečiar's wide-ranging consultations would become obvious when the Assembly convened.[14]

The government extinction bill was received favorably in most of the Assembly committees[15] but there were strong rumblings in the opposition on the left. In a historic first, the idea of a Czech-Slovak Union resounded in the august halls of the Federal Assembly for the first time ever,[16] championed this time by the Czech Social Democrats. It was the senior statesman, Professor Zdeněk Jičínský, and the younger, ambitious Miloš Zeman, on the way to claiming the chairmanship of his party, who opposed separation without a referendum and urged a union in the image of the Maastricht Treaty, a confederate type of arrangement generally conforming to Mečiar's vision.[17] He was supported by M. Čič, federal deputy prime minister and a high-ranking MDS member.[18]

A bitter debate on the floor disclosed a formidable array against the government bill, encompassing the strange alliance of the entire Czech and Slovak left as well as the Moravian party and the Slovak Christian Democratic

---

12. *See generally* RP, Sept. 22, 1992, pp. 1, 2.
13. The Vienna-based Economic Intelligence Unit reported that, while Czecho-Slovakia ranked first among Central European States in a 1991 economic survey, in 1992 it trailed behind Hungary and Poland. Obrman, "Czechoslovakia," *supra*, note 1, 1.
14. On the fourth MDS–Czech Left consultations, see RP, Sept. 22, 1992, p. 1.
15. LN, Sept. 11, 1992, pp. 1, 12.
16. Pavel Dostál in RP, Sept. 24, 1992, p. 2.
17. On Zeman's statement in a committee, see LN, Sept. 17, 1992, p. 12.
18. RP, Sept. 22, 1992, p. 1 ("Bud'-anebo [Either Or"]).

Movement.[19] On the extreme left, the Czech Communists called for mass demonstrations against the breakup while the notorious Dr. Sládek on the right fringe announced that his party had asked the procurator general to institute a criminal proceeding against Klaus for treason against the federal state. The coalition deputies were accused of violating their oaths of loyalty to the Federation.[20]

Proposals were offered (and rejected by the coalition parties) to amend the referendum law, to require a constitutional law on the division of federal property to be adopted before the extinction law, and to modify the government bill so as to eliminate three of the four options, leaving the Assembly's own constitutional law as the sole mode of terminating the state.[21]

Seeking to stem the opposition tide, Federal Prime Minister Jan Stráský submitted a government report on the state of the preparation of the constitution laws aiming at the smooth functioning of the two independent states. He warned that the probable consequences of

an obstinate clinging to a referendum [would mean] a campaign un-leashed in advance of the referendum under current conditions, a lack of political preparation to enforce the results of a referendum if it did not confirm the development in course. All that could draw our society dangerously close to the Yugoslav situation.[22]

Prime Minister Klaus, speaking on behalf of the CDP deputies, emphasized two points of interest to the Czechs: Civilized division and preservation of everything that was positive in the Czech-Slovak past. If the citizens voted for the preservation of the state in a referendum, the Federation would disintegrate anyway. "The moment the Federal Assembly failed," he added as an undisguised threat, "we shall have to consider a different approach."[23] After six hours of acrimonious debate, there was "no sign of even a foot bridge, not

---

19. On the presession positioning, see RP, Sept. 8, p. 3. The Moravian party joined the left in exchange for a promise of support for the internal organization of the Czech Republic, based on the "historic" lands. *Ibid.*

20. LN, Sept. 14, 1992, p. 8; HN, Sept. 14, 1992, p. 1.

21. LN, Sept. 9, 1992, p. 2; RP, Sept. 10, p. 2 (on Slovak PDL); RP, Sept. 30, 1992, pp. 1, 2.

22. HN, Sept. 14, 1992, p. 1.

23. Supporting the federal government, Josef Lux of the Czech CDU–CPP, thought that "there was nothing to vote on in a referendum" after the 1992 elections, and he called for "common language on the way to the creation of the two independent states." LN, Sept. 12, pp. 1, 8.

232   Czecho/Slovakia

to speak of a bridge across the abyss."[24] The Assembly leaders, preparing for
the session scheduled for the last week of September, even failed to agree on
whether the government bill on the split should be included in the agenda.[25]

b. The Opposition Triumphs: A "Union"?

The Assembly debate on the government bill during the last two days of
September was resonant again with the opposition's call for a referendum,
which was rejected by the coalition spokesmen as liable only to prolong the
agony of a dying state.[26] Citizen Václav Havel told the press agency that a
referendum about the state's future was impossible but that it would make
sense to hold a referendum ratifying the process of division.[27] After a meeting
with the Social Democrats, a CDP member implied that his party might accept
a ratification referendum but doubted whether the MDS would.[28]

On October 1, contrary to the expectations of most observers, the government bill on the mode of extinction of the Federation failed to obtain the
required three-fifths majority.[29] It did not pass in any of the components of the

24. A somewhat jaded Czech commentator speculated about the motivation of the players:
for Klaus and his CDP, the division of the state was more convenient while its preservation would
play in the hands of the leftist opposition (by offering possibilities to slow down the abhorred
radical economic reform); a referendum by which the citizens would reject the Klaus-Mečiar
constitutional policy would make new elections unavoidable. The left and center left might
calculate that they would gain new votes (due to the eventual impact of the bankruptcy law, for
instance), but this prospect, although alluring, might not materialize considering the growing
private sector in the Czech lands, which would support Klaus. Alena Slezáková in LN, Sept. 12,
1992, p. 1.

25. HN, Sept. 16, 1992, p. 2. An agreement on the inclusion of the bill on the agenda of the
fourth common session was reached only on Sept. 24, 1992. RP, Sept. 25, 1992, p. 1. On the third
common session, see Pravda, Sept. 23, 1992, p. 2; LN Sept. 23, 1992, pp. 1, 8; and LN, Sept. 25,
1992, pp. 1, 16. Another attempt to elect a Federation president failed. The Assembly discussed the
1991 budget and other matters and adopted two pieces of legislation. See also Pravda, Sept. 26,
1992, p. 1.

26. Obrman, "Czechoslovakia," supra, note 1, 2.

27. Havel said that Slovakia, represented by the parties victorious in the elections, decided
to proceed along its own path, and as a result the Czech Republic must do the same: "I do not quite
see what the Czechs should decide in a referendum: either they would support a common state,
which is impossible, or vote for a separation, which will happen in any case." He also opposed
calling early general elections in case of a split since at such a complicated stage as a construction
of a new state "we cannot afford loosing three months by an election struggle." ČSTK, Sept. 30,
1992.

28. Filip Šedivý, first deputy chair of the Federal Assembly, in ČSTK, Sept. 30, 1992. The
Assembly began discussing the amendments to the government bill on the devolution of further
powers to the Republics. Ibid.

29. F.A. Print 72 (federal government proposals) and 99 (proposals of the committees of
the Chamber of the People and the Chamber of the Nations); Report of the 4th joint session, VIIth
elec. term, 5th part, 5th day, Oct. 1, 1992, 6th day, Oct. 2, 1992, vote on Print 99 at pp. 912–13.

Federal Assembly, although the margin of defeat (seven votes) was narrow.[30] Significantly, the MDS deputies were not instructed how to vote on the bill and the majority joined the left in voting against it.[31]

The vote was marred by a technical mistake, which was corrected later after a long and confused procedural skirmish.[32] At that point, when some deputies had left the Parliament Building, Miloš Zeman requested a vote on his "procedure proposal" for a resolution that he previously had submitted to the Assembly. The resolution would call upon the Assembly to establish a commission that would prepare a constitutional law on the transformation of the Federation into a "Czecho-Slovak Union," described in terms somewhat similar to the MDS "trial balloon" of last August. With the view to an accelerated accession to the European Union, the resolution read, the Czech and Slovak Union was to coordinate economic, social, ecological, foreign, and defense policies while respecting the sovereignty of both Republics; powers delegated to the Union by the Republic would be exercised by a union president, Council and Parliament, and other organs; its budget would be provided on a parity basis by the Republics, and union laws would apply throughout its territory when ratified by the Republic Councils; and the union would expire when the Republics entered the European Union, with its competences passing to the European Union.[33]

The Assembly deputy chair, Roman Zelenay, an MDS member, agreed that according to a previous understanding the draft would be considered at this point of the proceedings. Both reporters of the Assembly committees then recommended against the adoption of the resolution on strictly technical legal grounds, which recalled the legal wrangles at Milovy and before. The first reporter could "not imagine sufficiently well a transformation of one international legal subject into a union, which should in reality be created by two international legal subjects" and thus "could be created only after the two international subjects had really been in existence, which for the time being, pending the existence of the Czech and Slovak Federative Republic, is not the case."[34] According to the second reporter, a transformed federation is just that and not a union.[35]

Deputy Zeman responded that if a reporter were unable to imagine a point it would evidence a lack of imagination—an observation that excited applause

---

30. *Ibid.* at 913; Obrman, "Czechoslovakia," *supra,* note 1, 2.

31. Slovak government spokesman Bohuslav Géci in ČSTK, Oct. 1, 1992; ČSTK, Oct. 6, 1992 (quoting Klaus).

32. Report of the 4th session, *supra,* note 29, 925–47.

33. Obrman, *supra,* note 1, 3. An earlier text was leaked to Pravda, Sept. 23, 1992, p. 3. For Zeman's comments, see RP, Sept. 28, 1992, p. 1.

34. Report of the 4th session, *supra,* note 29, Oct. 1, 1992, 922.

35. *Ibid.,* 923.

in the house; he also noted that the deputy chair of the federal government, a leading MDS member, Čič, had "publicly identified himself" with the substance of the resolution, although he had reservations about the procedure. Zeman viewed his proposal as "the last chance" for the Assembly to preserve its work.[36]

No debate followed, only some "factual remarks," one by Czech Communist Deputy Ransdorf, drawing attention to the recent political accord between the two nations in Belgium as a possible inspiration for the Czecho-Slovak union project, and an observation by Slovak Christian Democrat J. Mikloško, noting that the Zeman proposal was an overdue effort to bring the Assembly into the constitutional negotiation process with a view toward preparing "something beyond the law, which we didn't approve."[37]

In a vote on the "procedural" resolution requiring a simple majority, the Zeman proposal was adopted.[38] Following the failure of the extinction law, this was a second startling defeat for Klaus in a single day, engineered by the left with the support of Mečiar's own MDS: 45 of the 56 MDS deputies voted in the affirmative, including all three MDS ministers in the federal government. Klaus, visibly surprised and even distraught, gave the impression of having suffered a shock. "This is the end" he was heard to murmur.[39] Ironically, the adoption was made possible—of all things—by one CDP deputy who left the hall before the vote.[40]

c. The Reaction: Tension Grows

The reaction to the Assembly vote was predictable. While its chair, "the chubby, avuncular"[41] Michal Kováč of the MDS, sought to pour oil on the troubled waters by denying any danger that the Assembly would stop its work, the Czech CDA chair Jan Kalvoda saw "an offensive of the left."[42] Václav

---

36. *Ibid.*, 923–24.

37. *Ibid.*, 924, 928–29.

38. *Ibid.*, 949–50.

39. RP, Oct. 3, 1992, pp. 1, 2.

40. There were 139 deputies present in the Chamber of the People, with 70 votes constituting a majority. That was exactly the number of votes cast for the resolution. Had deputy Michael Malý remained, 71 (of 140) votes would have been needed and the proposal would have failed. LN, Oct. 2, 1992, p. 16.

41. Timothy Garton Ash, "Journey to the Post-Communist East," N.Y. REV. OF BOOKS, June 23, 1994, p. 13.

42. He said that "all parties flirting with liberal or left-center stands when confronted with the public, will have to decide whether they want to follow a line of obstruction and destruction of the consensus." He was not certain whether the Federation still existed after the Slovak Constitution had come into effect. Another CDA spokesman thought that Slovakia completed the process of an independent state, and he questioned the legitimacy of the Federal Assembly. ČSTK, Oct. 2, 1992; LN, Oct. 3, 1992, p. 2; Deputy Chair of the CDA Daniel Kroupa in ČSTK, Oct. 5, 1992.

Havel considered any union, such as that contemplated by the Zeman resolution "a utopia with no chance of working." He advocated a "more liberal" (extraconstitutional) approach rather than insisting on constitutional purism: the Czech National Council should declare that the two Republics were each setting out on a path of their own and would conclude with each other a network of essential agreements, with the Federal Assembly simply noting this fact. He considered it useless for the Assembly to debate devolving legislation that would apply for about a month only.[43]

The spokesman of the left-oriented Liberal Social Union explained that the Czech opposition had reached an agreement on the terms of a Union with Vladimír Mečiar the preceding week: in the Assembly vote, the political culture of the opposition was victorious over the political arrogance of the CDP (which refused any compromise).[44] Czech Prime Minister Václav Klaus declared that passing the Zeman resolution with the majority of the MDS, including its ministers, constituted "a basic and threatening shift" from which he would draw "explicit conclusions."[45]

Rumors circulated about the impending resignation of the MDS federal ministers and a possible Czech unilateral action.[46] Klaus refused any consideration of the common budget beyond January 1, 1993, which the Slovak side viewed as a violation of the previous political agreements. Sharp differences appeared within the CDP-MDS coalition on the proposed formula for dividing federal property. Thus, in a session of the Federal Defense Council, Mečiar called for the continuation in some form of a common army after the split—an idea apparently favored by the federal military establishment—but that suggestion also was flatly turned down by the Czech side. At that point, Mečiar walked out of the meeting, "slamming the door behind him, . . . got in his white BMW with a Czech license and took off."[47] Added controversy arose from a government proposal on the regulation of the press, which was eventually withdrawn. Serious dissention appeared on the Czech side concerning the internal administrative division of the Czech Republic after independence, which had some effect on the Czech stand. Tension between the Mečiar government, the Hungarian minority in Slovakia, and the Hungarian government

---

43. ČSTK, Oct. 5, 1992. This, according to Milan Ftáčnik of the PDL, was not a responsible view since it incited a unilateral Czech Republic step and it indicated Havel's preference of the Czech interest as his personal interest. ČSTK, Oct. 15, 1992. When asked who should be president of the Czech Republic, in July 1992, 60 percent of the Czechs named Havel, in September only 51 percent. RP, Oct. 3, 1992, p. 3.

44. HN, Oct. 6, 1992, p. 2.

45. ČSTK, Oct. 6, 1992.

46. This and the following statements are based on extensive reports in the Czech and Slovak press, late September and early October 1992.

47. RP, Sept. 29, 1992, p. 1.

affected the general atmosphere. Stories in the Czech press predicted a mass influx of Roma (gypsies) from Slovakia into the Czech lands (which never materialized).

Prime Minister Mečiar, in the wake of a meeting with the Bavarian premier in Nuremberg, declared that the Slovakian state would propose a new treaty with Germany to replace the laboriously negotiated and only recently ratified treaty between Germany and the Czech-Slovak Federation. The new treaty, Mečiar said, would deal with all the historic questions, including the issue of possible compensation for the Carpathian Germans expelled by the Beneš government along with some three million Sudeten Germans after World War II. The organization of Sudeten Germans had been calling for discussion of this delicate topic, and Mečiar's pronouncement, spread over the lead pages of the Czech press, struck at a most sensitive spot on the Czech side. Klaus, present at the same conference, promptly denied any need for a new treaty with the Czech Republic.[48] It was not surprising that the baffled foreign observers saw the acute danger of a "wild separation."[49] Finally, the Slovak government announced a postponement of the scheduled meeting with its Czech counterpart until the Assembly passed the law on further devolution of powers to the Republics, a move that Klaus characterized as "the last straw" in the new political situation.[50]

All three governments took advantage of the Assembly's adjournment to review the state of affairs and continue their work on the preparation for the split. In a special session at the Koloděje castle, the Czech government poured over drafts of some 15 treaties with Slovakia. It decided to insist on the principle of separate citizenship for the two Republics, which threatened to turn into a bone of contention with the Slovaks. At the usual late night press conference, Klaus rejected any possibility of negotiations for a union. He could not understand the reasons for the Slovak side's insistence on the prior adoption of the devolution law—and saw it as "a pretext." He denied that the Czech side was on the defensive; on the contrary, the Slovak side found itself in a very complex situation by playing several games that it would find difficult to control. He also disavowed any design for a unilateral action: "I always say it is important to stay away from unilateral steps, slamming of doors, walking out of negotiations, cancelling meetings." This explains his repeated telephone talks with Mečiar.[51]

---

48. RP, Sept. 25, 1992, p. 1; HN, Sept. 25, 1995, p. 1. *See* additional comments by the Slovak Foreign Affairs Minister Milan Kňažko in Pravda, Sept. 28, 1992, p. 2.

49. Austrian Die Presse quoted in LN, Oct. 3, 1992, p. 4.

50. ČSTK, Oct. 6, 1992.

51. "We left all our negotiations with the MDS with the impression that its top representatives understood—and will not anger and provoke us with this concept. We practically never

The Slovak cabinet convened in Trenčianske Teplice to consider both internal matters and the preparation for the meeting with its Czech counterpart. Prime Minister Mečiar told the press that he was "sincerely looking forward to a meeting with the Czech government," but, in view of the putting aside of the law on devolution and Prime Minister Stráský's questioning the right of the three Slovak ministers to continue in the federal government [because of their vote for the union], it might be preferable as the next step for the political leaderships of the CDP and MDS to get together first. The two governments would meet only after the devolution law had been adopted.[52]

The federal government also reviewed the political situation with a view to completing an extended government program for presentation to the Assembly. According to Prime Minister Stráský, there were "complications [during the meeting] in communicating with the MDS representatives" on the question of appointing the "Zeman commission" for a union; all cabinet members would have to state clearly their position on the union, he said. Stráský himself categorically rejected the idea of a union and thought (as adumbrated by Havel) that the division of the Federation could be decided by the institutions of the Republics.[53]

After a series of telephone calls between the two prime ministers, the CDP accepted Mečiar's demand to replace the planned session between the two Republic governments with a get-together limited to their two parties. However, according to the CDP deputy chair, Miroslav Macek, "we shall be much more circumspect in our future negotiations with the MDS" and "require much surer and certain guarantees."[54]

In anticipation of his meeting with Klaus, Mečiar said in Bratislava (with a touch of magnanimity) that he did not see the recent events in the Assembly as Klaus's defeat but as "an occasion for a historic success of unifying all political actors on the common starting point concerning the termination of the Czechoslovak Federation." The MDS paved the way by means of its negotiations with the opposition and even a single insubstantial concession by the

---

talked about a union because the MDS understood it is a thing that the Czech side does not take. The idea that we might return in our negotiations to some union does not come into consideration and I suspect the Slovak side knows it as well as we do." RP, Oct. 5, 1992, pp. 1, 2; LN, Oct. 5, 1992, p. 2.

52. PRAVDA, Oct. 5, 1992, pp. 1, 2; HN, Oct. 5, 1992, p. 1.

53. HN, Oct. 5, 1992, p. 2; PRAVDA, Oct. 3, 1992, p. 2; LN, Oct. 3, 1992, pp. 1, 8. One of the MDS ministers concerned, Jozef Moravčík, commented that the proposed law on transformation into a union could be viewed as a way toward the termination of the Federation, but he added, echoing Stráský's suggestion: "I trust in an accord between the National Councils . . . they will decide whether there will be only a customs union, or some other one." He did not view the interruption of the communications within the federal government seriously. LN, Oct. 3, 1992, pp. 1, 8.

54. ČSTK, Oct. 6, 1992.

Czech coalition would have sufficed for the proposed law to be accepted almost unanimously both by the Slovak side and by an overwhelming majority on the Czech side. He did not specify the type of concession. However, Mečiar continued, "Klaus's appearance in the Parliament ended all understandings, including those between the CDP and MDS [a threat]." The "union" commission was not contrary to the political agreement, but the refusal to support the devolution law was such a violation. "If CDP doesn't want us as a partner, we shall survive and seek cooperation at a different level [a threat again]."[55] Asked to comment on Mečiar's pronouncement, Klaus refused on the ground of not having seen the text.[56]

d. Klaus v. Mečiar Again: The Seventh Round—Jihlava

For the first time since the August 26 meeting in Brno, Klaus and Mečiar, accompanied by the usual coterie of party dignitaries and federal ministers, faced each other on October 6, 1992, this time in the "Golden Star" at Jihlava, a small Moravian town. A Czech commentator not known for his love of Mečiar suspected that the prime minister insisted on the party-to-party meeting at this difficult juncture in order to have with him the one leading expert economist, Michal Kováč, and also R. Filkus, when he faced the rich array of macroeconomists on the Czech side.[57]

Arriving on a pleasant fall afternoon, Klaus was welcomed by several hundred locals (2,000 according to a Czech report)[58] with applause, while Mečiar and his party were greeted with "whistles and derogatory exclamations."[59] At the opening of the session, the Czech side presented a draft of a communiqué in which the MDS would obligate itself in writing not to press for a union or a confederation; in case of a Slovak refusal, the Czech side made it clear—borrowing a leaf from Mečiar's book on tactics—it would leave the negotiations. After more than an hour's consultation within the Slovak group, in which Mečiar was subjected to the "concentrated argumentation" of his colleagues, led by the chair of the Federal Assembly Michal Kováč, and following several hours of joint discussion, the two sides signed a compromise

---

55. PRAVDA, Oct. 6, 1992, pp. 1, 2.

56. *Ibid.,* 2.

57. The Czech economists Klaus, Dlouhý, Zieleniec, Dyba, and Kočárník vs. the Slovaks Černák and Tóth with experience in enterprises, that is, microeconomists only. Karel Kříž in LN, Oct. 6, 1992, p. 3.

58. LN, Oct. 7, 1992, p. 1.

59. PRAVDA, Oct. 7, 1992, pp. 1, 2, also listing the participants on both sides. Klaus told the press that this was not an "either-or" occasion but a "somewhat more sharpened" situation; CDP could not continue to give in and the MDS must adhere to "elementary truthfulness, decency, and generally behavior that is current among normal people." *Ibid.*

text in which, according to Klaus, "each word was weighed on laboratory scales."[60]

In this document, based on the modified CDP draft,[61] the positions of the two parties were once more sharply defined: the CDP "respects" the MDS opposition to the continuation of the Federation and disagrees with transformation into a confederation but does not insist on a federation. Similarly, the MDS respects the CDP's disagreement with a union and with the effort at a transformation into a confederation. Finally, both parties agree to proceed in these questions exclusively on the basis of a common understanding; together they will press for partial accords such as customs, currency, and payment agreements to come into force on January 1, 1993. It was the last clause that made Mečiar proclaim with satisfaction: "A union with a capital *U* was replaced by several unions with a small *u*."[62] Yet he appeared dejected at the early hour press conference.[63]

Following this "break in the logjam," which was viewed as indispensable for further negotiations, the parties got down to business to plan a common strategy in the Assembly on the bills for the extinction of the Federation, the division of federal property, and on the devolution law demanded by the MDS. At an early morning press conference following a total of eight hours of negotiations, Klaus saw "a new chance for further constructive cooperation" and the functionality of the Federal Assembly, but there was no breakthrough on the division of property issue. Mečiar confirmed that the Federal Assembly should determine the mode of the termination of the Federation. It was of no object that the Slovak side abandoned the idea of a common budget for 1993, he said, passing over the dropping of one of his major demands.[64]

e. Jihlava Afterglow

Czech as well as Slovak columnists had a great time speculating about who had "won" and "lost" at Jihlava.[65] While the coalition voices applauded the out-

---

60. Jiří Leschtina and Zdeněk John in MFD, Oct. 8, 1992, p. 6.
61. Text in LN, Oct. 7, 1992, p. 8.
62. MFD, Oct. 8, 1992, p. 6.
63. See *infra,* note 65.
64. RP, Oct. 8, 1992, pp. 1, 2.
65. Under the headline "Mečiar Cornered," a Slovak columnist observed that Mečiar's dejection at the press conference in Jihlava was due not only to fatigue and the early hour of the day but to a sense of defeat. The final communiqué revealed, the comment continued, that Klaus forced Mečiar to accept the despised "black jack" of responsibility for the split, even though it was the objective of the radical part of the Czech side, including Havel. More importantly—Klaus finally cured Mečiar of any illusion of a confederation or union. By renouncing the union proposal, Mečiar betrayed his alliance with Klaus's Czech opposition and thereby abandoned any chance of

come,[66] the left, as expected, was critical.[67] After Jihlava, the leadership of the CDP and the other coalition parties were reported ready to support the adoption of the devolution law demanded by MDS as the next move in the Assembly—having obviously overcome the fear that the MDS would plot to continue the slimmed-down Federation beyond the end of the year. Klaus commented that in fact the competences in question had already passed long ago to the Republics, so it made no sense to hold back the process.[68]

In a session marked by tactical maneuvers and the search for compromises, the Assembly finally adopted the devolution law (technically an amendment to the 1990 law on devolution) on October 8.[69] The new law,

---

realizing the constitutional program of his movement. František Meliš in PRAVDA, Oct. 8, 1992, p. 1. *See,* to the same effect, RP, Oct. 8, 1992, p. 1.

Yet the preceding day, in the same first-page column, another Slovak observer wrote that, while it appeared on the surface that it was Mečiar's MDS that had retreated, the opposite was true: both sides retreated from their election promises (of a functional federation and confederation respectively) to a position that before the elections they had branded as "nationalist," "separatist," and "militant" and as a program advocated by parties that had failed in the elections. Vladimír Jancura in PRAVDA, Oct. 7, 1992. p. 1.

According to a Czech comment, skeptical and ironic as could be expected, Klaus's CDP got in the Jihlava communiqué "a bit more than nothing, seen nevertheless as a win. . . . It is sad to expend greatest energy to get to a spot we had been before. It is depressing, it is exceedingly tiresome." It was obvious that Mečiar's MDS would fight up to the last moment for its unchanged objective: independence with (Czech) "appanage" (perquisites). Before Jihlava, Klaus looked like a cornered man—possibly due only to fatigue. "In reality it is the other one who is driven into a corner. He sold independence cheaply, he will not get any appanage. He knows it, and his voters begin to suspect it as well." Jiří Franěk in LN, Oct. 8, 1992, p. 1. For another Czech comment, *see* RP, Oct. 8, 1992, p. 3: "Mečiar retreated, Klaus got what he wanted, the opposition lost . . ."

66. PRAVDA, Oct. 8, 1992, p. 2.

67. *Ibid.,* citing Z. Jičínský (Czech Social Democrat), I. Šimko (Slovak CDM), and others. In fact, earlier the chair of the Czech Social Democrats, Professor Jiří Horák, clearly distanced himself from the "union" as essentially Zeman's own idea. He was not sure whether the Maastricht model was applicable "to our Republic," and, seeing the breakup as "almost unavoidable," he did not want to play "a destructive role." He again mentioned a ratification referendum and added, after a talk with Klaus, that the latter reacted "altogether positively" to Horák's idea for a new text of the "extinction" law. RP, Oct. 6, 1992, pp. 1, 2. On Horák's disavowal of Zeman, see also HN, Oct. 7, 1992, p. 2, 5th column. Yet Zeman announced that the Social Democrat deputies supported his resolution, which was still a valid act, and that the expected complications in further negotiations might yet render his proposal for a union actual. HN, Oct. 9, 1992, p. 1; ČSTK, Oct. 9, 1992. A Czech commentator concluded, however, that following "the logic of the development," the Czech opposition leaders obviously judged that their political arena in the future would be only the Czech scene, and thus they decided not to get any further into a risky fight for a transformation of the Federation. Kateřina Perknerová in RP, Oct. 8, 1992, p. 3.

68. LN, Oct. 8, 1992, pp. 1, 12.

69. Const. Law 493/1992 Sb. On the allocation of treaty powers in that law, see *supra,* chap. IX, 2b.

approved by a large majority, reduced the number of federal ministries to five (finance, foreign, defense, interior, and economics).[70]

3. Toward a New Form of Coexistence: Bilateral Treaties (October–November 1992)

a. Kolodĕje: "Trust Restored" and Treaties Discussed

The meeting between the two Republic governments, postponed at Mečiar's request, took place—after the detour in Jihlava—on October 10 in the Kolodĕje chateau near Prague, which appeared at the very beginning of our story. It was to be the first of three such sessions charged with preparing a network of bilateral international agreements that would define the new relationship between the two independent states. Most of the agreements would require ratification by the Republic National Councils to be given before the end of the year so that they could come into force on January 1, 1993.[71]

In preparation for the first session, the Czech government sent to Bratislava drafts of ten such agreements, a file of some hundred pages. The Slovak government carrier left Bratislava with the Slovak material only on the eve of the Kolodĕje session, so that the Czech side did not have the chance for a prior study. The documents included—mirabile dictu—an old proposal for a Czech-Slovak Union! In what was described as a dadaist episode, Klaus vehemently chided Mečiar, who apologized, claiming that the paper was added through an unfortunate oversight of a functionary who would be removed.[72] After that incident, "in the glow of the Indian summer," the converse proceeded for eight long hours at a lively pace.[73]

---

70. The Federal Ministry of Control was retained. The second amendment to the same 1990 law, which limited the Federation power in the areas of internal order and security, was approved only after a conciliation procedure between the two chambers. A bill concerning mass media was not approved. ČSTK, Oct. 8, 1992; LN, Oct. 9, 1992, pp. 1, 16; RP, Oct. 9, 1992, p. 1. Earlier, Assembly Chair Michal Kováč (MDS) sought to reassure the CDP that the Slovak side would not want to maintain the devolution level of allocation of powers contrary to the agreement on the termination of the Federation. LN, Oct. 8, 1992, p. 12. Only a part of the Czech Left Bloc and most of the Hungarian coalition deputies opposed the devolution law. The Czech Christian Democrats voted for it in one chamber and against in it the other. The Assembly then approved a resolution asking the government to bring in promptly a bill on the transfer of the remaining competences to the Republics.

71. The final texts of the treaties that were negotiated and came into force, along with both Czech and Slovak commentaries, are set forth in Docent JUDr. Vladimír Mikule et al., Mezinárodní smlouvy mezi Českou republikou a Slovenskou republikou [International Treaties between the Czech Republic and the Slovak Republic] (Codex Bohemia, Praha, 1995).

72. "A good excuse," wrote a Czech columnist: "It is rumored in well-informed circles that the Slovak government tried to slip into Kolodĕje negotiations documents strikingly similar to the idea of a union. So for the last time?" Robert Dengler in RP, Oct. 12, 1992, p. 2.

73. Roman Krasnický in LN, Oct. 12, 1992, p. 1; PRAVDA, Oct. 12, 1992, p. 1.

The Slovaks submitted drafts of six treaties corresponding in substance to the Prague texts and suggested broadening the scope to include environment, schools, culture, and privatization. "A certain passivity" among the Slovak participants was due—according to a Czech writer—to the precise argumentation of the Klaus team of economic experts. "The Slovaks do not move on this ground with self-confidence and do not trust the views of the other side."[74] The focus of the discussion conducted primarily on the basis of the Czech drafts was on the customs union, the monetary union, and a series of agreements on cooperation in health, social affairs, access to courts, use of own languages, legal protection, security, delimitation of the frontiers, and other matters. Both prime minsters emphasized that no territorial disputes existed between the parties. Working groups, chaired by ministers, were to prepare final versions of the treaties to be approved at the next meeting in Slovakia.[75]

The only clear disagreement related again to the problem of citizenship. According to Mečiar, the Czech side preferred a regime treating citizens of the other Republic as aliens, while the Slovaks were for the "unitary principle" (a single common citizenship).[76] According to the 1991 census, there were 314,877 Slovak citizens living in the Czech Republic, while 52,884 Czechs lived in Slovakia.[77] On the Czech side, Mečiar's pressure for a unitary citizenship was viewed as another attempt to salvage some form of a "union."[78] A suggestion was made for another, third variant: "dual citizenship" inspired by the Maastricht Treaty for the European Union, which contemplates the continuation of national citizenship with limited additional rights derived from the union "citizenship."[79]

In a comment on Koloděje, the British *Guardian* wrote that "the velvet divorce" was "back on its insecure tracks."[80] Václav Havel, at this juncture, saw merit in CDA's proposal for a declaration by the Czech National Council

74. The Slovak contribution in effect amounted to comments on the Czech text and the broadening suggestion was in effect a face-saving move. Krasnický in LN, Oct. 12, 1992, p. 1. PDL Chairman P. Weiss was sorry that the negotiation was conducted primarily on the basis of Czech documents since the Slovak government missed the deadline. RP, Oct. 12, 1992, p. 3. R. Kováč thought that the Czech materials were more thorough but some Slovak texts were of better quality. PRAVDA, Oct. 10, 1992, pp. 1, 2.

75. LN, Oct. 12, 1992, pp. 1, 8. On the substance of negotiations, *see also* HN, Oct. 12, 1992, pp. 1, 3.

76. RP, Oct. 12, 1992, p. 2.

77. Roman Kováč, a deputy chair of MDS, presaged the ultimate acceptance of the Czech position when he told the press that "we might create an alien regime on the assumption that it would be supplemented by a full series of treaties ensuring that relations between the citizens of both states remain uninterrupted." RP, Oct. 12, 1992, pp. 1, 2; LN, Oct. 27, 1992, p. 2. See also Milan Kňažko in LN, Oct. 19, 1992, p. 2.

78. Kateřina Perknerová in RP, Oct. 21, 1992, p. 3.

79. LN, Oct. 13, 1992, p. 2.

80. Quoted in LN, Oct. 13, 1992, p. 16.

that would identify the current state of affairs and—like the Slovak Declaration of Sovereignty—express the will of the Czech Republic to build an independent state. Shortly thereafter, that proposal failed dismally in the Czech Parliament.[81] Evidently, Havel as a private citizen did not possess any more influence than he had as the head of state.

During the weekend following Koloděje, the Executive Board of Mečiar's MDS came out in support of a ratification referendum to be held in Slovakia in mid-December, which a Czech editorialist dubbed as the last attempt to push through a confederation or a union solution.[82]

On October 15, while Mečiar was visiting Germany, the authorities there reportedly received a telephone threat of assassination against him. The incident was never explained[83] and—as might have been expected—the Czech press indulged in all sorts of speculation about the "so-called attempt."[84] Speaking to the Italian daily *Corriere della Sera,* Mečiar was quoted as foreseeing a peaceful division: the only source of tension in Central Europe could be Hungarian nationalism; he again charged Havel with a large share of responsibility for the constitutional crisis.[85] In what could be viewed as a reply to Mečiar, Havel said in a press interview: "It is likely that in the policy toward Slovakia I committed various mistakes. . . . However, I am not aware of a basic or fatal mistake."[86] The former president, now definitely back in politics, continued his talks with Czech political parties in order, he said, to explore the differences between the coalition and the opposition and—as we shall see—to

---

81. The proposal was defeated with only 16 deputies voting for it. The CDP opposed it on the ground that gestures or escalation were not necessary. RP, Oct. 22, 1992, p. 2. *See also* "Sloupek," *ibid.,* p. 1.

82. The Slovaks would be asked the question: "Do you agree with the constitutional arrangements according to the treaties between the Czech and the Slovak sides?" LN, Oct. 19, 1992, p. 2; PRAVDA, Oct. 19, 1992, p. 2. A Czech editorialist saw a "last, serious attempt of the MDS to push through a confederative or unionist solution." If a majority voted yes, Mečiar would be vindicated. If a negative vote prevailed, it would mean that the Slovak people rejected the split and wanted a union or confederation as promised in the MDS election program. The negative vote was quite possible in view of the change in the Slovak press in which the initial rejoicing over independence was replaced by comments on "the cunning Czechs who want to get rid of us." Karel Kříž editorial in LN, Oct. 19, 1992, p. 1.

83. RP, Oct. 17, 1992, p. 1; LN, Oct. 20, 1992, p. 1.

84. LN, Oct. 21, 1992, p. 3.

85. Havel was "a visionary with entirely unrealistic political thoughts," who inflamed the tension between the Czechs and the Slovaks; Klaus, on the other hand, was a "difficult but correct partner." HN, Oct. 19, 1992, p. 7.

86. "I have also endeavored to assert democratic approaches and warned of the danger of their violation—in the Slovak as well as in the Czech Republic. But I have always reflected Slovak emancipation efforts and respected them. These efforts have asserted themselves in the last elections. . . . Only a fool can ignore them. The second thing is to what extent the election victors in Slovakia incline toward undemocratic methods." LN, Oct. 20, 1992, pp. 1, 8.

influence the shape of the Czech constitution and the position of the president under it. On his far flung travels abroad, he was received by heads of state.[87]

b. Javorina: Treaties Agreed

The next encounter of the two Republic governments, the second after Koloděje, took place in Hotel Polana, another "luxury" establishment built for the former party nomenclature in Javorina, high in the Slovak Tatra Mountains.[88] After arrival on Sunday morning, October 25, most ministers took the occasion for a leisurely walk to preview the upcoming negotiations. Klaus, accompanied by a mountain guide, embarked on a "grand tour." Mečiar struck out in another direction. For a time the 30 shivering newspaper reporters and numerous television crews were kept out of the hotel by the Slovak security personnel, but after a vociferous protest they marched in a body through the ranks of the guards.[89]

The participants tackled three groups of subjects. First, they dealt with several federal bills that came before them as part of the legislative process before they could be considered by the Federal Assembly. Consensus was reached on a new version of the extinction law, stating simply that the Federation would cease to exist on December 31, 1992, and on related provisions for the treatment of federal employees and deputies of the Federal Assembly after that date. However, the ministers continued to disagree on the bill for the division of federal property, even though the Slovaks accepted the principle of "two to one" to govern the division of certain types of property.

The most important items in the second group were the agreements prepared by expert commissions, including treaties for a customs union and monetary cooperation, which were approved without much discussion. The customs union treaty envisaged a single customs territory without customs duties and nontariff barriers, with free movement of goods and services, with a common external tariff, and with a common customs and trade policy in relation to third countries. Agricultural products were included, and agricultural policies (export subsidies and market regulation) were to be coordinated. Coordination would be assured by a Customs Council with parity representation and a permanent secretariat. Any dispute was to be settled by an arbitration commission. The council would represent both Republics in relation to foreign states

---

87. LN, Oct. 17, 1992, p. 3; RP, Oct. 24, 1992, p. 22.

88. On this section, *see generally* Jiří Pehe, "Czechs and Slovaks Define Postdivorce Relations," RFE/RL RES. REP., Nov. 13, 1992, 1–11.

89. The material in this section is based on ČSTK, Oct. 26, 1992 (a memorandum handed to journalists in Javorina); and reports in HN, Oct. 27, 1992, p. 1; RP, Oct. 26, 1992, pp. 1, 2; PRAVDA, Oct. 26, 1992, pp. 1, 2; LN, Oct. 26, 1992, pp. 1, 8; RP, Oct. 27, 1992, pp. 1, 2; ČSTK, Oct. 30, 1992. A number of federal ministers were also in attendance.

and the European Union. The treaty was subject to unilateral termination on 12 months' notice—a provision to which Mečiar initially strongly objected.[90]

In this connection, the two sides resolved to ask the European Community to extend the validity of the temporary trade agreement concluded between Czecho-Slovakia and the Community in 1991 and indicated the intention to assure all the rights and obligations of the Federation by the successor states. The succession was to be confirmed by an exchange of notes as of January 1, 1993. The Custom Union Council was to assure compliance with the commitments stemming from the agreement—a condition previously articulated by the Brussels Commission. In the interest of a smooth transfer, the governments divided between themselves all export and import quotas.[91]

It was only somewhat later that the problem of physical customs controls at the new Czech-Slovak frontier raised its head. On one hand, the Slovak side argued strongly against building customs offices there, but on the other hand Slovak Finance Minister Julius Tóth made it clear that the income from the added value taxes on imported goods, an essential component of the Slovak budget, could be lost by tax fraud in the absence of effective border checks.

The monetary agreement also approved at Javorina called for the use of the common currency to continue, with each party free to cancel when specified indications disclosed major divergence of the two economies or when the Monetary Committee established by the agreement was unable to agree on fundamental questions of monetary policy.[92] The parties pledged themselves,

---

90. ČSTK, Oct. 30, 1992. For a full text, see HN, Nov. 2, 1992, p. 8. Was the customs union "a true international organization" and what was its initial impact on the agreements with the European Union? Pieter Jan Kuyper, "The Community and State Succession in Respect of Treaties" in Rick Lawson and Mathis de Blois (eds.), The Dynamics of the Protection of Human Rights 619, 636–38 (Martinus Nijhoff Pub., Dordrecht, Boston, London, 1994).

91. For a full text of the memorandum that was handed to British Prime Minister John Major, the current president in office of the European Community Council, see PRAVDA, Oct. 30, 1992, p. 2.

92. That is, when the deficit of the economy or the budget of one of the parties exceeds 10 percent of the budget revenue and the hard currency reserve level sinks below the level of monthly imports in freely convertible currencies or, finally, in case of a major speculative capital movement from one Republic to the other with fundamental impact on the banking system (over 5 percent of the bank deposits). A Monetary Committee, composed of the governor of the Central Bank and two senior Central Bank officials appointed by each party, was to decide all questions relating to the functioning and stability of the common currency. The parties undertook to ensure the application of the committee decisions, which were to be taken by a simple majority. In case of a tie, the two governors would decide. Both Republics would pass laws concerning the Central Banks before the end of 1992. The finance ministers would decide on conditions of the preparation of separate, independent currencies after consultation with the Central Bank governors. ČSTK, Oct. 30, 1992; HN, Nov. 4, 1992, p. 9 (text of the monetary agreement). Josef Tošovský, Governor of the Czech National Bank, is reported to have began preparing a law on the division of the currency as early as August 1992. Jointly with the minister of finance he ordered stamps to be attached to the

however, to coordinate their economic and financial policies in such a way as to preclude any reasons for cancellation before June 30, 1993.[93] In a press conference, Klaus sought to explain the indeterminate cancellation provision by pointing out that the stability of the currency depended not only on the decisions of the governments but on the extent to which 15 million people would move their funds from one Republic to the other.[94] As it happened, the common currency survived only a few weeks into 1993, but a clearing agreement, designed to replace it, lasted for two more years.

To mitigate the rigor of the "alien regime" for Slovak citizens in the Czech Republic, the Czech side offered a series of agreements, including a treaty on free movement of workers. No work permit would be required, only a notice by the employer to the labor office. "This is the first step of our two Republics toward Maastricht," said Czech Minister of Labor and Social Affairs J. Vodička (CDP),[95] and his Slovak counterpart pointed to the Scandinavian model.[96] Payment of pensions from one state to the other was to be assured, and work periods prior to the separation were to be taken into account. Diplomas were to be mutually recognized and the question of students studying in the other Republic was resolved in an ingenious way.[97] Since health administration was in both Republics already almost separated, the agreement reached was to assure medical treatment to citizens from the other Republic essentially on the same financial basis.

Eight treaties on internal security and order dealt with confirming the validity for five years of federal personal documents and of passports (with the seal of the new state added), entry without visa requirement, common treatment of citizens of third states, determination of common frontiers (along current administrative frontiers between the Republics), protection of the environment, and coordination in the fight against drugs, terrorism, and financial

---

banknotes "for reasons of secrecy in the distant Colombia." Marián Leško, Slovenské tango z roku jeden—Dôverná správa o politike a politikoch [Slovak Tango of Year One—Confidential Report about Politics and Politicians] 4, (Perex, 1993).

93. An early Czech draft would have set that day as a terminal date unless earlier cancellation became necessary, but the Slovak side objected. As a compromise, the Slovak side proposed a 30-day notice as a prerequisite to a cancellation, but it dropped this request when the Czech Central Bank governor pointed out that in case of currency movement damaging the economic interest of a party, decisions must be made in a few days time. LN, Oct. 29, 1992, p. 3. For the text of the Treaty on Currency Arrangements, see HN, Nov. 4, 1992, p. 9, with a Special Understanding between the Two Governments. Agreement for Cooperation on Education (HN, Nov. 5, 1992, p. 8).

94. HN, Oct. 27, 1992, p. 2.

95. RP, Oct. 27, 1992, p. 2.

96. Pravda, Oct. 29, 1992, pp. 1, 3.

97. In elementary and middle schools students would be free to answer in Czech or Slovak, and for three years teachers would not be able to fail a student in the language of the other Republic.

crimes.[98] Some days earlier, however, Klaus had emphatically rejected a Slovak idea for a "global treaty," above and beyond the partial agreements, that would provide a foundation for a de facto union.[99] The Czech side was prepared to enter only into a standard treaty of friendship and cooperation such as is traditionally concluded between friendly states. This issue was not raised at Javorina.

The third and last subject was the smoldering controversy over the citizenship question. Mečiar offered a compromise according to which the Slovak side would abandon the unitary single citizenship for the concept of dual citizenship. This Klaus rejected, pointing out that a number of states do not recognize dual citizenship. At Czech insistence, it was agreed that there would be no treaty on citizenship and the matter would be left to each Republic's competence. Mečiar told a press conference that in Slovakia Czech citizens would be able to hold dual citizenship, as would, under Slovak law, Slovak citizens in the Czech Republic who acquired Czech citizenship.[100] A Slovak writer speculated that—paradoxically—the resulting situation clearly favored the treatment of Czechs in Slovakia and corresponded to the Slovak interest in retaining Czech experts in Slovakia.[101]

The specter of a sharpening controversy with Hungary over the Gabčíkovo hydroelectric works hovered over Javorina, but the topic was studiously avoided by the participants. With the imminent threat of the final diversion of the Danube on the Slovak side of the frontier, some envisaged a possibility of violent incidents between the Slovaks and the Hungarians.[102]

According to Klaus, Javorina was a success: 15 of the 22 draft treaties were approved, while from the perspective of everyday life "nothing will immediately change." Travel will be possible without visas or passports (only a personal document), federal currency will continue, and an entrepreneur will be able to transport goods across the new frontier without special customs

---

98. LN, Oct. 23, 1992, p. 3.

99. RP, Oct. 24, 1992, p. 2 ("Glosa ke dni [A Gloss on the Day]").

100. See the statement by the Czech minister of the interior, J. Ruml, in RP, Oct. 27, 1992, p. 1. See the Czech Law of Dec. 29, 1992, on acquisition and loss of citizenship, 40/1992 Sb. (Czech), and the Slovak law on state citizenship of Jan. 19, 1993, 40/1993 Zb. (Slov.). After the breakup, the application of the Czech law was criticized internationally as discriminating against Roma.

101. František Meliš in Pravda, Oct. 29, 1992, p. 3; Aleš Gerloch, "Theorie federalismu a rozdělení Československa [The Theory of Federalism and the Division of Czechoslovakia]," in 1995 Politologická Revue 13, 23–24 (June 1995).

102. With the dispute about to be submitted by the Hungarian government to the International Court of Justice, Klaus said that the matter "is not a Czech problem, and in the end I hesitate a bit to say that it is a federal problem, because in fact, the Federation doesn't exist," implying that the burden was on the Slovak government. RP, Oct. 24, 1992, p. 2. *See generally,* Karoly Okolicsanyi, "Slovak Hungarian Tension: Bratislava Diverts the Danube," RFE/RL Res. Rep., Dec. 11, 1992, 49–54.

documents.[103] A Slovak observer was more skeptical. He pointed to the pervasive disagreement on the division of federal property and the doubts "in the corridors" of Javorina about the durability of the agreements, expressed predominantly by Czech participants.[104]

In Prague on the last day of October, the two prime ministers formally signed 16 agreements. Klaus announced that these texts would now be sent to the National Councils for adoption and that at least ten more would follow after the next planned session of the two governments. Mečiar commented that "[t]he extinction of the common state does not mean the end of common interests and coexistence."[105]

Two days after Javorina, October 28, was the anniversary of the founding of the First Republic, which, in the pre-Communist past, was traditionally celebrated as the most important state holiday. This year, also, commemorative assemblies were held throughout the country. In Prague, Wenceslas Square witnessed a nasty clash between several thousand right-wing Republicans and their opponents, with an exchange of raw eggs, firecrackers, and obscene epithets. Some 200 skinheads armed with chains and sticks marched through the streets, and some Romas were beaten up. Forty persons, mostly skinheads, were held by the police. In late afternoon, citizen Havel laid a wreath at the tomb of Saint Wenceslas, the Czech patron saint.[106]

Significantly, in an October public opinion poll, the number of people viewing the split as "certain" rose from 80 percent in September to 90 percent, but only 37 percent of the Slovaks and 51 percent of the Czechs considered it as "necessary." More than a half of the sample favored a referendum as the mode of termination of the Federation, and the same proportion of the Czechs (36 percent of the Slovaks) favored new elections. "The voters evidently feel that something illegitimate has taken place on which they did not count at the time of the elections. Even though the people accept the division, they feel trapped."[107]

c. Židlochovice: Eight More Treaties Agreed

The third—and presumably the last—meeting of the cabinets of the two Republics took place on a sunny, cool November 9 in the castle of Židlochovice, a

103. LN, Oct. 29, 1992, p. 3.
104. František Meliš in Pravda, Oct. 29, 1992, p. 3.
105. RP, Oct. 30, 1992, p. 1.
106. RP, Oct. 29, 1992, pp. 1, 2; LN, Oct. 29, 1992, p. 12.
107. B. Jungmann, director of the Institute for Public Opinion Research, in LN, Oct. 30, 1992, p. 2. For the first time since 1989, Havel was replaced by the economy minister, Vladimír Dlouhý, as number one in popularity in the Czech Republic. The chair of the PDL, Peter Weiss, was the most popular politician in Slovakia, this time ahead of Vladimír Mečiar. *Ibid.*

historic Austrian neoclassic structure located south of the Moravian capital of Brno.[108]

After a eulogy for Alexander Dubček, who had died two days earlier, succumbing to injuries suffered in a road accident, the ministers got down to work in a businesslike atmosphere. This was the last occasion at the Republic cabinet level for a discussion of the federal bill on the division of federal property before its submission to the Federal Assembly. As regards the division of property, the Slovak side proposed combining the agreed territorial principle (each Republic to keep whatever was in its territory) with the "historic" principle based on the property each side had brought to the restored common state in 1945 from the Czech Protectorate and the "independent" Slovak state respectively. Federal Prime Minister Jan Stráský presented a numerical survey and estimated that property, valued at some 600 billion crowns ($20 billion) was to be divided, 11 billion according to the historic principle. However, the historic principle was not viewed favorably and was put aside.

The "umbrella" treaty "on good-neighborly, friendly relations and cooperation"—"a balm for the nervous systems of millions of people in both Republics"[109]—was approved. The scope of the treaty is truly breathtaking since it covers every imaginable aspect of public activities and a host of private concerns as well. However, the substance is formulated in terms of broad principles and objectives, and, except for a few more specific undertakings, the principal normative impact rests in a general obligation to consult regularly at a variety of levels and in mixed commissions. The basic rights of citizens in the territory of the other Republic are defined with some specificity. The current frontiers are confirmed, and both sides agree, in the event of an armed attack on one of the Republics, to consult on the possibility of assistance according to Article 51 of the UN Charter. The treaty postulates a comprehensive system of agreements to implement the broad goals. In its horizontal scope, if nothing else, the treaty exceeds the standard bilateral treaties of friendship and cooperation. It was concluded for 15 years (subject, however, as a Slovak skeptic noted, to one year's termination notice), with an automatic five years' extension in the absence of a notice of termination.

---

108. In addition to the two prime ministers, the participants were chair of the Federal Assembly Michal Kováč, Federal Prime Minister Jan Stráský, Federal Deputy Prime Minister Rudolf Filkus, Chair of the Slovak National Council Ivan Gašparovič, and Governor of the Czechoslovak State Bank Josef Tošovský. PRAVDA, Nov. 10, 1992, p. 1.

109. PRAVDA, Nov. 11, 1992, p. 3 (by František Meliš). For a detailed description, see Miroslav Potočný, "Smlouva mezi Českou republikou a Slovenskou republikou o dobrém sousedství, přátelských vztazích a spolupráci [Treaty between the Czech Republic and the Slovak Republic on Good Neighborhood, Friendly Relations, and Cooperation]," 8/1993 PRÁVNÍK 679–87.

Several traditional-type agreements were approved, including a treaty against double taxation and on the protection of investments. Beyond that, a consensus was reached on accords concerning foreign exchange relations, cooperation in transport and communications, and agriculture, food, forestry, and water management. Experts were to do further work on a treaty dealing with military problems, the division of military archives, the air force and the antiaircraft command, and on a customs and tax frontier that would avoid physical border controls. A new, reformed tax system was to be introduced in both Republics on January 1, 1993.[110]

Both parties assumed—mistakenly, as subsequent developments would show—that this session was the last in the series of encounters of the two cabinets. They worried about the upcoming debate in the Federal Assembly on the pending federal government bills, including, above all, the controversial division of property proposal, and they feared that the sessions of the presidia of the two National Councils, scheduled for later in November, might face an alternative catastrophic scenario for the divorce if the Assembly were unable to act.[111]

---

110. ČSTK, Nov. 9, 1992; PRAVDA, Nov. 10, 1992, pp. 1, 2. *See,* for example, the treaty on personal and travel documents, driving licenses, and arms and ammunition, HN, Nov. 4, 1992, p. 9; agreement on health care, HN, Nov. 5, 1992, p. 8; treaty on cooperation between the services of the Ministries of the Interior and the Coding Service, HN, Nov. 24, 1992, p. 18; treaty on common exploitation of information and archival resources in the field of internal order and security, *ibid.;* agreement on the support and mutual protection of investments, HN, Dec. 10, p. 11; agreements on the cooperation in transportation and communications and in agriculture, *ibid.,* p. 12; and treaty on the avoidance of double taxation on the tax on income and property, HN, Dec. 29, 1992, pp. 11–12.

111. *See generally* PRAVDA, Nov. 10, 1992, pp. 1, 2.

XIII

Back to the Federal Assembly: Facing the Opposition (Fall 1992 Continued)

1. New Federal Government Program

Since the first federal program approved by the Assembly had expired on September 30, the federal government was obliged to ask the Parliament to approve an extended program for the period ending December 31, 1992. This request offered the opposition on the left and extreme right an occasion for an unrelenting attack on the coalition government, marked by acrid personal interchanges.[1] The thrust of the opposition criticism was the charge that the government had proceeded against the will of the people and in disregard of constitutional norms and Assembly responsibilities, presenting it with a fait accompli of the termination of the Federation. The government was accused of having failed to prepare alternatives to a breakup and a 1993 budget, to provide for a referendum, and to help establish the Commission for a Union as decreed by the Assembly. Even the presiding officer was attacked for napping in his chair. No one in the West—the opposition claimed—favored the split, which would weaken the negotiating position of the successor states to the profit of neighboring countries that would gain priority for European Community membership.[2]

Prime Minister Jan Stráský, who first introduced the program with a survey of the government's accomplishments, assumed its defense:

> I often wonder . . . why so many states expire unconstitutionally and so few constitutionally. The logical answer is clear. Unconstitutionally, because the constitutional organs were unable to retain their existence, and because they did not accomplish the way to a successful end. . . . The entire [preceding Assembly] discussion had actually one tone in common. The government acts unconstitutionally because it takes steps in connec-

---

1. Zpráva o 5. společné schůzi Sněmovny lidu a Sněmovny národů, 2. část 3. den–5. listopadu 1992, 4. den–12. listopadu 1992, VII. volební období [Report on the 5th joint session, 2d part, 3d and 4th day, Nov. 5 and 12, 1992, VIIth electin term], 276–323. The text of the programmatic declaration is in F.A. PRINT 119.
2. LSU Deputy L. Dvořák, *ibid.,* 267, 269.

tion with the preparation of the division of the state. . . . I think . . . that the government does indeed proceed unconstitutionally and will so proceed increasingly as long as the Federal Assembly takes this position. . . . Unconstitutionality grows in time, but so does the damage.

He thought that, while a part of the Assembly might derive pleasure from the defeat of the bill on the mode of extinction, that event had caused colossal harm in the economic and international spheres, and it made difficult the negotiations on the association treaty and other agreements with the European Community.[3]

The resolution that would approve the extended program passed in the Chamber of the People, but it failed in the Chamber of Nations. Somewhat disoriented about the consequences of their vote, the deputies proceeded to other business. Prime Minister Stráský said on television that the Assembly's rejection of the government program amounted "to something like a vote of no-confidence" and revived the question of the government's continuance in office. In a government meeting, five Czech ministers were in favor of stopping the damming of the Danube at the Gabčíkovo works as demanded by Hungary while the five Slovak ministers wanted the operation continued.[4] The government was clearly in difficulty.

Next on the Assembly's agenda was the proposed government program on measures against possible unconstitutional termination of the state and related risks.[5] The resolution "to take notice" of the program was approved but only after the federal government agreed to submit to the Assembly information on specified treaties in the process of negotiation between the two Republics.[6] This was another effort on the part of the federal legislature to gain some influence on the processes evolving beyond its control.

---

3. *Ibid.,* 318–19.

4. ČSTK, Nov. 5, 1992.

5. F.A. PRINT 124. Text is in Report on the 5th joint session, VIIth election term, annexes, content, 989–1001. The measures envisaged were in the areas of security, defense, foreign policy, economic policy, government claims and credits, prices, private law, large infrastructure projects, transport and communications, nuclear safety, and legislation.

6. Resolution no. 87, *ibid.,* 988. The original proposal that the government be *required to submit* the draft treaties to the Assembly was abandoned when Prime Minister Stráský pointed out that while the federal government took part in the negotiations and was able to provide appropriate information, "it does not make the treaties" and would not be able to do so. Report on 5th joint session, Nov. 5 and 12, 1992, *supra,* note 1, 404–5. In the section on foreign policy, the government undertook to create conditions for speedy recognition of successor states and establishment of diplomatic relations and for a formal declaration on the termination of the membership of the ČSFR in international governmental and nongovernmental organizations with the understanding that on the date of the termination both Republics would be successor states ready to assume the rights and obligations of the Federation. Report, annexes, content, *supra,* note 5, 994–95.

In the preceding debate on the resolution, the federal defense minister, army general Imrich Andrejčák, described the complexity of the division of the armed forces such as the special strengthening of security in transportation of explosives; some 40 agreements between the two ministries of defense were concluded, and some 30 more were about ready, concerning the prospective cooperation of the two independent armies; a 720-page timetable was prepared for specific division of all types of equipment and supplies; and a joint committee was in charge of effecting the transfers, thus far without any untoward incident. It was said earlier that the relocation of ground forces had already been practically completed. The majority of airplanes and helicopters that were to be moved from Slovakia had been flown already to the Czech Republic.[7]

2. Dividing Federal Property

a. The Government Bill

The coalition spokesmen reported that the three governments had agreed on the substance of the property division bill[8] as it was discussed at the meeting in Židlochovice.[9] There was no model to follow, just a few general principles of international customary law and a proposed United Nations convention that never came into effect.[10] The point was made that the federal property had been greatly reduced by the devolution, privatization, and other legislation, but the division of the remainder still presented a serious challenge.

---

7. Report of the 5th joint session, Nov. 5 and Nov. 12, 1992, *supra,* note 1, 395–99 (Nov. 5). *See also* an interview with Minister Andrejčák in HN, Dec. 17, 1992, p. 11. In the debate on November 12, 1992, Deputy R. Tvaroška, a member of the Defense Committee, reported that the material to be divided was valued at 426 billion crowns (over $14 billion, representing two-thirds of all federal property) and consisted of hundreds of thousands of items (115,000 tank and automobile materials alone) handled by computer techniques. This process would continue through 1993. The December 31 date was "a gallows' date," harmful for the Slovaks. There was a danger of large-scale thefts of weapons, of much too radical shortening of training of specialists, and social problems (apartments for soldiers, employment for spouses, etc.). *Ibid.,* 504–8 (Nov. 12). A press spokeswoman at the Ministry of Defense reported earlier that the air force would not be divided by the two-to-one formula, but account must be taken of the type, age, firing power, accuracy, and so on of the airplanes, amounting to 440 fighter planes and 56 helicopters. RP, Nov. 5, 1992, p. 9.

8. The bill was supported by the CDP–CPP, MDS, the CDM, and the SNP.

9. *Supra,* chap. XII, 3c. The government bill is in F.A PRINT 152 and 155.

10. Vienna Convention on Succession of States in Respect of State Property, Archives, and Debts," UN Doc. A/CONF. 117/14, Apr. 7, 1983, not in force. The Czecho-Slovak Republic did not sign it. JUDr. Josef Mrázek in HN, Oct. 21, 1992, p. 3. See the early draft of the federal constitution discussed *supra* in chap. III, 5. See also *infra,* chap. XV, 2c, i.

In the government text, a sixth consecutive draft, federal property was classified into four categories: movables and immovables, financial credits and debits, currency credits and debits and reserves, and other rights and obligations of the Federation and state organizations.[11] The division was to be made on the basis of two fundamental principles: according to the "territorial principle," each Republic was to keep all federal immovable property within its territory along with the movable property that was functionally linked to it. The same principle was to apply also to obligations that because of their content related only to one Republic.

Other property would be divided according to the "principle of proportionality," that is, on the basis of two to one, reflecting the size of the respective populations. Underlying this criterion, accepted after tough bargaining, was the assumption of an approximately equal contribution by individual citizens to the creation of federal property. This assumption was questioned by some on the Czech side and the two-to-one basis was considered a substantial Czech concession. The Slovaks, on the other hand, appeared to have abandoned the demand for financial compensation as a corrective criterion.[12]

The third principle to be followed would require attention to the preservation of a functional use of the property "in a just property and financial settlement." Obviously, to divide, for instance, the antiaircraft system into two equal parts would destroy its utility, and other ways had to be conjured up. The originally contemplated "historic principle" proceeding from the original contributions of each Republic to the common state was "put aside" because "the proof of the Slovak contribution was in many respects insufficient."[13]

The territorial principle, an Assembly committee reporter pointed out, corresponded to the 1983 Vienna Convention on Succession of States in Regard to State Property, Archives, and Obligations. Although this treaty was not in force—and the Czecho-Slovak Federation did not even sign it—respect for its principles "may be viewed by the European Community in a positive sense." Moreover, it would avoid "a protracted and rather controversial valua-

---

11. Milan Kňažko, who participated in the negotiations on the Slovak side with Jozef Moravčík, and Josef Zieleniec, estimated the book value of the property to be divided at 22 billion Czech crowns (about $730 million). Included were 53 embassies, 3 consulates, and 4 international missions. Archives and libraries were exempted, but free access and copies would be available. Conversation with M. Kňažko.

12. HN, Oct. 20, 1992, p. 3 (Josef Prouza, "Handl"). Milan Čič told me that he did the principal job on the law on extinction and he and R. Filkus on the division of property.

13. Common reporter Deputy A. Daniel (MDS). "It is therefore historically more just to merge the historic and territorial principles." Report of the 5th joint session, *supra,* note 1, 488 (Nov. 12). According to Deputy Prime Minister R. Filkus (MDS), it was not necessary to pay particular attention to this principle, but it might be taken into account in framing the agreements of the two Republics. *Ibid.,* 473; *see also* 547–48. This was agreed in Židlochovice.

tion of immovables. . . . In all the possible alternatives time and the need for justice and consistency stand against each other."[14] Speed was essential to avoid a further contamination of the atmosphere by mutual recrimination.

A commission based on parity representation was to decide on the settlement of any claims.[15] A series of provisions of the bill dealt with special problems; for example, it was left for the International Monetary Fund to determine the division of the Czecho-Slovak membership quota, an unusual function for an international organization.[16] The law was to be implemented by specified federal laws and agreements between the Republics. It was reported that the inventorization of the property and other preparatory work had already made rapid progress.[17]

b. The Opposition

The voices of the opposition ranged from emotional expostulations and constitutional objections to more or less specific criticisms based on concerns about justice and fairness. Some deputies opposed any bill on principle because they did not accept the division of the state. Others deplored the time restraints, the scarcity of information, and the absence of an intelligent public debate. Social Democrat Deputy Z. Jičínský, a constitutional law expert, compared the 1,000-page unification treaty between the West and East German states with the federal bill—"the German thoroughness" with the "Slavic lightness passing over a series of problems." He suggested an amendment designed to preclude action by other than constitutional legislation. He noted the provision in the bill requiring the Republics to conclude an agreement for the reception of the federal property division law into their legal system and to assure its common interpretation[18]—"something unusual" he added, "we shall obviously enrich our legal experience"—and he offered alternative formulations.

Although personally accepting the bill's criteria for the division, Jičínský questioned its broad generality. He noted that only a few specific federal

---

14. J. Danko, *ibid.,* 478.

15. *Ibid.,* 474. See art. 12(2) of the law as adopted, 541/1992 Sb.

16. The text of the law as finally adopted, which follows the government text, is in 541/1992 Sb.

17. A CDP deputy suggested, that, since the conception of the law involved the work of many experts and represented in effect an agreement between the two Republic governments reached after friendly negotiations, the Assembly consideration should have "a ratifying character"—eschewing more substantive incursions into the bill. Deputy J. Mlčák, Report of the 5th joint session, *supra,* note 1, 486 (Nov. 12).

18. Shades of New York v. United States, 505 U.S. 144 (1992), in which the U.S. Supreme Court struck down as unconstitutional a provision in a federal statute designed to force states to take specified legislative or other action.

implementing laws were envisaged to regulate the division for instance of television, radio broadcasting, railways, telecommunications, and scientific institutions, while prime reliance was on agreements between the Republics. This reduced the role of the parliamentary institutions. Even the Republic parliaments were expected to simply rubber stamp the government agreements concluded under international law. Nor would the proposed arbitration commission be subject to direct parliamentary control.

The proposed principles or the way of their application were questioned by Slovak spokesmen as prejudicial to Slovak interests. The idea that there should not be a division of property but rather joint ownership and common exploitation, regardless of the location, resonated from the Slovak left.[19] The territorial principle was questioned on the ground that the Vienna Convention considered an agreement among the successor states the most broadly recognized principle for settlement of mutual claims.[20] The federal government estimates of the value of the property to be divided were attacked as much too low; moreover, the use of the territorial principle was unfair in view of the alleged fact that, although Slovakia contributed 32 percent to the national product, only 25 percent of federal property was located in the Slovak Republic.[21] Countering the Slovak criticism of the two-to-one criterion, the Czech deputies pointed to the massive federal investments in the Slovak health establishment, housing, and so on, contrasting it with the dismal state of the environment in the Czech Republic and the past allocation of funds in the federal budget favoring Slovakia.[22]

A lively debate developed over which federal establishments, such as the oil and gas pipelines, the airline, and former state foreign trade enterprises, should be exempted from the standard criteria and dealt with on a different basis either by a special law or an agreement by the Republics.[23] In response to several queries, the proponents pointed out that industrial and intellectual property rights would be protected and exploited jointly on the basis of an interstate agreement. The exchanges provided an opportunity for special interests to assert themselves but also for law professors to display their learning and, last but not least, for a rare touch of ironic humor when a deputy inquired about the mode of dividing nonexistent spaceflight facilities.

---

19. PDL Deputy M. Borgula, in Report of the 5th session, *supra*, note 1, 503 (Nov. 12).

20. PDL Deputy S. Grohmann, *ibid.*, 520.

21. Deputy J. Šedovič offered these data, explaining that Slovakia produced raw materials and unfinished products that were finally taxed in the Czech Republic. *Ibid.*, 527.

22. Deputy Z. Smělík, *ibid.*, 543–44.

23. Czechoslovak Airlines and the maritime facilities were already privatized and thus excluded from the division, and this was viewed by the Slovak side as an evasion.

3. The Vote

The vote on the bill took place on the following day, November 13. Of the many amendments approved, some were designed to clarify the procedure for dividing enumerated federal facilities. The proposal to omit any reference to the "historic principle" proved to be a controversial point. In the first vote, the bill failed in the Czech part of the Chamber of Nations. After a further consideration of a series of amendments, the bill suffered the same fate, this time in the Slovak part of the Chamber of Nations.[24]

Finally, a conciliation committee appointed to reconcile the conflict between the two Chambers recommended unanimously two insubstantial changes, one of which responding to Jičínský's amendment, mentioned earlier. Both were accepted. The Assembly then voted to approve the bill as amended.[25] Although the enactment of the law was an important step, Federal Prime Minister Stráský warned against overestimating the import of the new law because it postponed the solution of the principal complex problems. For this reason, he reported, the commission of the two Republic governments established in Židlochovice met in Bratislava just a few hours after the Federal Assembly action to organize its work; some 30 subcommissions were to be appointed, one for each "block" of federal property represented by a federal office, with an expert commission working on a draft of the basic treaty. He noted the absence of a "proper confidence" between the two sides: the political parties' talk of "magnanimity" was not easily transferred to the bureaucrats who handled the negotiations.[26] In fact, although agreement was reached on the division of the bulk of the property before January 1, 1993, the unagreed items (such as a major claim of the Czech National Bank and the Slovak

---

24. Report of the joint session, 3d part, VIIth election term, Nov. 13, 1992, 622, 635.

25. *Ibid.,* 665. The constitutional law is, if not unique, at least quite unusual in modern legislation. It was published in the Collection of the Laws as 541/1992 Sb. The same day the Assembly adopted the Law on the Termination of the Security Information Service, according to which information materials in the files of the Federal Security Information Service were to be divided according to a separate agreement between the two Republics, taking account of their security interests (Sb. 543/1992) and the Law Changing and Adding to Law No. 92/1991 Sb., on the Conditions for Transfer of Property to Other Persons, as amended (Sb. 544/1992). See also Pravda, Nov. 14, 1992, pp. 1, 2.

26. HN, Nov. 17, 1992, pp. 1, 3. He identified as target problems the division of the government claims and obligations administered by the Czechoslovak Commercial Bank, of the federal economic organizations, and of the gold and the reserves. The transit gas pipeline should not be mechanically divided because a planned international company would include foreign as well as Czech and Slovak capital. *Ibid.,* 3. See also Pravda, Nov. 16, 1992, pp. 1, 3. The joint commission mentioned above considered rules for sanctions in case one Republic failed to act within the set deadline: an appeal to the prime minister, an independent international commission, and in an extreme case the International Court of Justice. HN, Nov. 16, 1992, p. 3.

demand for the return of an antique altar) continued to cloud relations between the two governments after the breakup.

4. Havel for President and the End of an Era

On November 16, Havel announced officially his generally expected candidacy for the office of president of the Czech Republic. Conscious of his responsibility for the political conditions, he said he wanted to influence them as president if the office was properly defined in the upcoming Czech Republic constitution. He wanted to contribute to the creation of "stability, inspired by the spirit of freedom, mutual trust, and common responsibility. . . . More, however, is necessary. It is needed to inject a certain spirit into the renewed Czech state, to found it on broader and deeper values, and to strengthen the self-confidence of its citizens . . . to revive values . . . such as mutual understanding, good will for shared cooperation, sense of responsibility, tolerance and magnanimity, ability for a wise overview." The division of Czechoslovakia was not only a technical and administrative task, but also a great spiritual, mental, and social undertaking. "The atmosphere in which it will occur will predetermine our life for many years. It is therefore vitally important for us to attempt particularly at this time to search within ourselves and nurture around us solidarity, unity, and humanity . . ."[27]

By an ironic coincidence, on the same day in the "real world" an announcement was made of the dissolution of the torso of the once all-powerful Slovak Public against Violence, the post-1990 election mainstay in Slovakia of Havel and the first federal government.[28] A few weeks earlier, its counterpart in the Czech lands, the Civic Movement, also decimated in the 1992 election, turned from "a movement" into a regular political party of "Free Democrats" facing an uncertain future.[29]

5. At the End: Again the "Extinction" Bill

a. The Overture

On Saturday, November 14, the representatives of both Czech and Slovak political parties met in the Bratislava Bôrik. Only the right fringe Republicans, the Moravian party, and—surprisingly—"the otherwise occupied" Václav Klaus were missing from what proved to be a crucial prelude to the final performance in the Assembly. It remained uncertain who from among the

27. HN, Nov. 17, 1992, pp. 1, 2.
28. Pravda, Nov. 17, 1992, p. 2.
29. LN, Oct. 5, 1992, p. 8.

participants first suggested[30] that the responsibility for the split should be shifted to, or at least shared with, the Republic National Councils. The idea was clearly designed to assuage the opposition. The MDS and CDP were intrigued, since in these councils their position was much stronger than in the Assembly. Even CDA's Jan Kalvoda, who until recently had rejected such an approach, emphatically agreed. "It was possible," he said, "for the Federal Assembly not to carry any responsibility in this case."[31]

It was clear, however, that this move would require a careful coordination of simultaneous decisions in both Republic councils in order to preclude the chance for one Republic to brand the act of the other as a unilateral secession, with all the international consequences—the familiar "black jack problem." The only outcome of the meeting that ended late at night was an agreement to suggest to the respective parliamentary factions the idea that the two councils would recommend to the Assembly to consider again the extinction bill.[32] Prime Minister Mečiar was skeptical about the usefulness of the Bratislava conclave: "The political will is absent," he said, refusing any further comment.[33]

Yet less than 24 hours later, acting with unexpected, extraordinary alacrity, both National Councils followed the Bratislava suggestion and proceeded to approve a resolution that would urge the Assembly to enact speedily the extinction bill.[34] With the action in the National Councils and the approval in

---

30. The two Left Bloc experts, Deputies Josef Mečl and Josef Masopust, are credited by some with the authorship. Jana Havligerová in HN, Nov. 18, 1992, p. 3.

31. PRAVDA, Nov. 16, 1992, p. 2.

32. The chair of the Slovak PDL thought that "such games should not be played" and accused Czech Deputy Minister of Foreign Affairs Bratinka of talking "in favor of the game for universal inheritance rights of one part of the Federation." The chair of the Czech Communist Party, Jiří Svoboda, branded the proposed move as unconstitutional and charged that because of the obstruction by the CDP and the CDM the Presidium of the Federal Assembly was prevented from appointing the Zeman Commission on a union. HN, Nov. 16, 1992, pp. 1, 2. The committee of the presidia of the two National Councils met on Nov. 16, 1992, in Jihlava primarily on the federal government proposal for the extinction law, which the Czech opposition representative continued to oppose because of the absence of a provision for a referendum. The committee also dealt with the proposed treaties between the two Republics. Communiqué, Nov. 16, 1992, Jihlava, Library of the Czech Republic Parliament.

33. *Ibid.*, 2.

34. The Czech National Council dropped the provision authorizing the Republics to enter into international treaties with each other and with third states even before the termination of the Federation, the treaties with third states to come into effect after the termination. HN, Nov. 18, 1992, p. 1. In the Czech National Council the left, supported by the Republicans and the Moravian party, insisted on a three-fifths vote and proposed to tie the validity of the extinction law to its approval by a referendum. When both proposals were voted down, the resolution with the recommendation to the Assembly was approved. A corresponding resolution was adopted with equal promptness by the Slovak National Council. The outcome in the two Republic parliaments is

the Assembly of the law on the division of property, two of the three measures demanded by the major part of the opposition as conditions for its support of the extinction law were fulfilled. The question remained about the third condition, the demand for a referendum.

b. The Revamped Bill: Reaching for a Common Language

Of the four alternative ways for terminating the Federation set out in the original draft,[35] the new bill retained the first one only: a declaration by the Assembly in the form of a constitutional law. Accordingly, the bill, which was eventually approved with several modifications, simply declared that the federative Republic was to end by December 31, 1992, with the two Republics becoming successor states. The preamble indicated that the Assembly acted "respecting" the resolutions of the two National Councils. Provision was made for the termination of the federal organs and armed forces and for the transfer of the legislative, executive, and judicial powers to the Republic institutions.[36] The original bill dealt with the legislative power only; the two other powers were added in the committee as a bow to Montesquieu's triad and the separation of powers doctrine. Similarly, a specific reference to the Constitutional Court was to hint at continuity in the protection of the basic rights of citizens.[37] Bowing to the Slovak National Council, the use of the federal symbols by either Republic was precluded.[38] This provision, I should add, later caused a wave of opposition among the Czechs and was eventually disregarded by the Czech Parliament, another proof of the power of symbols.

The Republic Councils were authorized in the bill to exercise their competences even before the end of the year by enacting appropriate legislation to come into effect beginning January 1, 1993,[39] and to negotiate treaties with each other and with third states, also to come into effect after the termination of

---

reported in Report of the 5th joint session, 4th part, VIIth election term, 6th day, Nov. 18, 1992, 7th day, Nov. 25, 1992, 693 (Nov. 18), 680, 687; and in F.A. PRINT 166. In the Slovak National Council also, a proposal for a referendum, this time advanced by PDL Chair Peter Weiss and Christian Democrat Ján Čarnogurský, failed of approval. Weiss argued for a referendum "from the logic of democracy" and concern for the precedent in future vital matters. However, the Slovak Council added to its recommendation a request that the "extinction bill" be amended to prohibit either Republic from adopting as its own the existing federal symbols (the flag, the seal, etc.). HN, Nov. 18, 1992, pp. 1, 2. The request originated with the chair of the SNP, Jozef Prokeš.

35. Government proposal of Oct. 4, 1992, F.A. PRINT 72. *See supra,* chap. XIII, 5b.

36. Arts. 2, 3(1), 4. References are to the constitutional law as adopted on Nov. 25, 1992, 542/1992 Sb. Also terminated were federal budgetary contributions and subsidies.

37. The common reporter Deputy L. Voleník, Report of the 5th joint session, *supra,* note 34, 677, 683–84 (Nov. 18).

38. Art. 3(2).

39. Art. 7.

the federal state.[40] Finally, the bill undertook to settle the fate of the Assembly deputies elected in 1992 whose terms were to be cut short at the end of the year: they would be made part of the legislatures of the independent Republics with the understanding, prudently added by an amendment, that it was for each Republic legislature to decide its own "internal conditions."[41] This issue was to haunt politics in the Czech Republic for some time after the independence. All this was formulated in nine brief articles.

The debate[42] paralleled the one held in October, with both the Czech and Slovak oppositions insisting on the referendum and the coalition parties rejecting it. Apart from some nostalgic evocations, the impending end appeared accepted as a reality, however bitterly deplored. Introducing the amended version, Federal Prime Minister Jan Stráský set the tone for the coalition approach. He stressed again the need for a peaceful, constitutional termination that would be viewed favorably abroad and would make possible negotiations for association with the European Community.[43]

In an effort to preempt the argument of unconstitutionality, the committee reporter rehearsed the three alternative modes of terminating the state: a "pure referendum" pursuant to the existing federal legislation, a ratification referendum, or the so-called ratihabition, an ugly neologism connoting an approval of the federal extinction law by the National Councils. In support of the fourth option, embodied in the pending bill, he offered as probably "the most convenient thesis" the proposition that the prevailing federal Constitution of 1968 was built on the "treaty" principle in that it constituted in effect a voluntary bond of two national states (as witnessed by the preambular statement affirming their right of self-determination "up to a separation").[44] Consequently, when the National Councils, acting for the Republics, voted to accept the separation, they bestowed on the process of termination through a federal constitutional law "a seal not only of legality and legitimacy, but real [constitutional] purity," and that precluded any possible questions of the legitimacy of the successor states.[45]

---

40. Art. 8.

41. Art. 4 (1–2).

42. The texts debated were the modified government bill F.A. Print 132 of Nov. 2, 1992 (six articles) and Print 168 of Nov. 18, 1992, the text of the constitutional committees of the two chambers, which was ultimately accepted with modifications.

43. Report of the 5th joint session, *supra,* note 34, 674 (Nov. 18).

44. *Ibid.,* 686. But see the PDL's L. Orosz, *ibid.,* 723–25.

45. The committee rejected the interpretation that the termination of the Federation would revive the unitary pre-1968 state. *Ibid.,* 689. The constitutional committees controlled by the coalition did not accept, the reporter continued, the Social Democrat proposal that the validity of the proposed law be made conditional upon holding a ratification referendum and that, if the law failed in one or both Republics, new elections would follow. For a full text of the proposal, see

c. The Confrontation on the Referendum

Ten deputies signaled their wish to participate in the debate. In the name of the Czech and Slovak Social Democrats and the Christian Democrat Union, Deputy Ivan Fišera[46] introduced his proposal for a referendum. Speaking in support of this proposal, the Slovak Christian Democrat, I. Šimko, offered the thoughtful historical review from a Slovak perspective on which I drew earlier in this book:

> The creation of Czechoslovakia was a salvation of my nation. . . . Many people of my nation, despite everything, viewed and even today view Czechoslovakia as their home. . . . There are many common interests! To a great extent it was Czech books by means of which we gained access to the fruits of world culture. . . . Much that divides us is simply the inability to overcome problems of any coexistence, and the independence of both nations will not in substance solve this question. I fear that the difficult experiment of overcoming the totalitarian regime . . . is by far not at an end, and to overcome it separately will be much more difficult. But the reality of the parting is probably here.

The Czechs, he mused, are often depicted as older brothers of the Slovaks. Now they part, but the solution is for both brothers to become adults: "I believe in such growing up."[47]

Spokesmen for the Czech left, the Slovak Party of the Democratic Left, the Slovak Social Democrats, and the Slovak Christian Democrats implied that they would vote against the bill unless the referendum proposal were accepted, although the deputies of the Czech Liberal Social Union (and perhaps of some of the other parties as well) were left free to follow their consciences.[48] Deputy Zdeněk Jičínský and others thought that the National Councils, rather than

---

ibid., 706–12. By their insistence, "obstinate politicians obstinately attempt to stem the already existing chaotic disintegration," even though, in the reporter Voleník's words, Professor Jičínský would prefer chaos if it were linked to the democratic expression of the will of the people in a referendum. *Ibid.* at 688.

46. For a personal attack on Fišera's past under the old regime by his former friend and Fišera's reply, see RP, Dec. 3, 1992, p. 6. For an interesting report, see MfD, Nov. 20, 1992, p. 6, by Jana Bendová and Jiří Leschtina. On the use of referendum for constitutional changes in other countries, *see supra,* Chap. III, 1. In Germany, in constrast to other federal states, a two-thirds majority of both houses of the federal legislature is sufficient for a constitutional amendment.

47. Report of the 5th joint session, *supra,* note 34, 716, 717, 720–22. For quite another historic version, see *ibid.,* 844–46.

48. Deputy L. Dvořák, *ibid.,* 737. A Czech Left Bloc member, declaring herself "not a politician" but "a woman," claimed the privilege of "a bit of sentiment" and contributed a dainty metaphor in defense of the referendum. Deputy H. Dordová, *ibid.,* 729.

adopting a simple resolution, should have used their power of formal legislative initiative by proposing the pending law to the Assembly in the form of a decision requiring a three-fifths majority.[49] In a sarcastic aside, Jičínský observed that "instead of a valid constitution we have had a constitution with a single article—that everything important is decided by Václav Klaus and Vladimír Mečiar."[50] Social Democrat Deputy Zeman repeated his demand that the government produce a quantification of the economic consequences of the split for which there now were materials available, and he termed the government bill "a crime . . . the same crime as the Munich accord of September 1938," confirming the history of the lack of courage of the Czechoslovak Parliament.[51] The opposition complained again of the Assembly's failure to appoint the Zeman Commission on the Union.[52]

An opponent of the referendum argued that "the first shots in Yugoslavia resounded immediately after the publication of the results of the referendum" and "the true referendum" will be the communal elections in 1994 and national elections in 1996.[53] Prime Minister Klaus was attacked on one hand for not offering secession to Mečiar in their first meeting and on the other hand for not relinquishing his original mandate from the president since he was unable to form a government that would sustain the Federation.[54] With his customary vigor, Klaus responded that he had received by far the highest voter support, higher "than any person sitting in this hall," that he had defended the common state in tens of meetings in both parts of the Republic but that in reality "we are a common state only formally." That a referendum would be of any help are "childish thoughts, false . . . bad. . . . [N]ote the tone of voice of those who propose it . . . they themselves do not believe it."

> The last three years were one gigantic referendum . . . all responsible people know that if the will for a common state is missing, the first minute after the completed referendum we would be in precisely the same situa-

---

49. *Ibid.,* 778. Considering the relatively small majorities by which the resolutions were adopted in the National Councils, the required qualified majorities may not have been available.

50. *Ibid.,* 777.

51. *Ibid.,* 800–802. A deputy countered that "the effort to conserve the process of constitutional negotiations equaled a crime as did the effort at a normalization of socialism." Deputy M. Mihalik, *ibid.,* 859.

52. Deputy L. Indruch, *ibid.,* 765.

53. Deputy J. Vodička, *ibid.,* 875; Deputy K. Kalina, *ibid.,* 840. Time restraints were deplored again with examples of the decade-long constitutional negotiations in Belgium, Canada, and Spain; on the other hand, the passage of time while the Assembly hesitated was said to cause great harm. Adherence to German political thought that "makes a fetish of constitutional form issues" the "babylonian captivity of the Czech culture by the German style" were excoriated (deputy M. Ransdorf, *ibid.,* 819), and Hegel and Heidegger were invoked.

54. *Ibid.,* 734, 768–69.

tion as we are today. This state would be uncontrollable, ungovernable, chaotic, and it would draw us into the depths and entice us into a situation close to what we see in the Balkans. . . . Unhappily, there are enough irresponsible people here [referring to "the internationalist comrade," a deputy of the Czech Communist Party]. . . . [T]he cost of dividing the state must be set against the cost of nondividing it, the cost of the nonfunctioning of this country . . . the coexistence of the Czechs and Slovaks does not end, but it is given at a given moment a new quality, and I am not afraid that [their] relations will become worse than in the last three years. I am convinced, on the contrary, that they certainly will be better "and the series of treaties under preparation will guarantee that they will be of an unusual quality, exceptional and different from relations with other countries. . . ." This was why the deputies should vote for the government bill.[55]

A Slovak daily reported that the Klaus contribution evoked "an avalanche of bad will."[56] Sharp words and innuendos were exchanged ("unscrupulous attempt to profit from a difficult situation," "Slovakia is the only Republic in Europe to which communism came from the West," etc.),[57] and Sládek's Republican deputies, true to form, contributed some purple prose.[58] Václav Havel was criticized also by the left for "having fled the sinking ship," a "cowardice" now compounded by the federal government.[59]

The chair of the Assembly, Michal Kováč (MDS), concluded the debate. In a shrewd tactical move, he addressed the opposition's refusal to share the historic responsibility for a split without a referendum:

Today in fact we do not decide on the extinction of the Federation. It does not exist. . . . [In reality, the decision is about the basic conditions of the birth and "brotherly relations" of the twins to be born of the same mother.] I realize that for many of you these are unwanted children and for that reason you do not want to assume responsibility for their birth. I understand and respect it. But the responsibility was assumed by the CDP and its coalition partners in the Czech Republic and MDS and the SNP in the Slovak Republic. We do not force the responsibility upon you . . . but let

55. *Ibid.,* 861–64.
56. PRAVDA, "Márny boj o referendum [Vain Fight for Referendum]," Nov. 19, 1992, p. 2.
57. Report of the 5th joint session, *supra,* note 34, 878, 882.
58. *Ibid:* "The [Assembly] federal crematorium hall in which to bury forever the common state," "spiritual genocide of the nation," "we shall awake as a German federal land with an eternal bayonet of an 'ausländer' in our backs." Their insults were directed not only at a federal minister (a Polish immigrant) but, with particular venom, at Václav Havel (745, 747, 821–24).
59. Deputy D. Malíř, *ibid.,* 761.

us not produce unnecessary obstacles for them. Those of the opposition who would vote "yes" today do not carry responsibility for the inception of these children but only for their peaceful and normal arrival in this world . . .[60]

d. The Final Vote: Part One

As a first step in the voting procedure, the Assembly rejected the Social Democrat proposal on the referendum[61] as well as an amendment by a Republican deputy that would have made it clear that the termination occurred due to the political agreements between the victorious parties. In order to avoid the past embarrassing experience with the malfunction of the voting devices, the deputies then tested the equipment through two dry-run votes. At that point, a member asked that the presiding officer be recalled because he was "too nervous" and "pushing" and replaced with another, more "deliberate" deputy, but this suggestion received only two votes.

When it finally came to the vote on the amended bill, it passed in the Chamber of the People but failed in the Slovak section of the Chamber of Nations by three votes.[62] It has been suggested that the deputies on the left allowed the bill to pass in one chamber by voting for it or abstaining in the hope of obtaining further concessions in a conciliation committee that would have to be established in order to reconcile the conflicting stances of the two chambers.[63] In fact, the Assembly promptly named a 12-member Conciliation Committee, composed of representatives of all factions, and adjourned until November 24.

e. In the Meantime . . . Another Round

Immediately following the Assembly adjournment, the Czech National Council, after a day of bitter debate and prolonged negotiation, approved a resolution declaring that it assumed, along with the Czech government, "full responsibility for the continuity of state power in the territory of the Czech Republic and for the guarantee of the proper interests and needs of the citizens of the Czech Republic."[64] The Left Bloc attacked the move as contrary to the federal Constitution and as undercutting the work of the Conciliation Committee of the

---

60. *Ibid.,* 890–92.

61. *Ibid.,* 913.

62. *Ibid.,* 927–28. Deputy Ivan Sviták commented that a party that did not manage to corrupt two or three opposition deputies to vote with it did not deserve to be in power, nor would a party that could manage to do so. RP, Nov. 20, 1992, p. 1.

63. RP, Nov. 20, 1992, p. 1; MFD, Nov. 20, 1992, p. 6.

64. Text in HN, Nov. 20, 1992, p. 1.

Assembly; except for five of its members, the entire opposition left the Council hall before the vote.[65] According to Prime Minister Klaus, the declaration was a signal for the world as well as the nervous citizens and a call on the Czech organs "to do something."[66] Václav Havel, agreeing with Klaus, approved of the resolution, Deputy Federal Prime Minister Čič (MDS) thought it exceeded constitutional bounds, Slovak Prime Minister Mečiar "was not surprised," and Jan Kalvoda of the CDA was enthusiastic.[67]

In Bratislava, at the same time, the Slovak National Council approved a law on the conduct of a referendum with provisions regulating the use of television during the campaign.[68] The action evidently followed the earlier decision of the MDS Executive Board to support a ratification referendum.[69] Yet Prime Minister Mečiar now spoke strongly in support of the federal extinction bill and chided the opposition for playing into the hands of those bound on suppressing Slovak identity and for jeopardizing the constitutional understandings.[70]

The moves in the two National Councils did not make the work of the Conciliation Committee any easier. However, in a more encouraging development, on November 23 Prime Minister Mečiar and the Czech Finance Minister I. Kočárník (substituting for Prime Minister Klaus, injured in a tennis game) met in another round of government-to-government negotiations in Bratislava and initialed another eight treaties and agreements. The unsettled issues related to customs, tax systems, and the division of certain federal properties. The only incident marring the constructive atmosphere was the appearance of a paper containing a draft of a Czech constitutional law purporting to make the Czech Republic the sole successor and "heir" of the Federation. The draft was branded "a political provocation" by Mečiar and was promptly disavowed by Kočárník as a forgery, prepared by the Czech left with the intent of discrediting the negotiations. When asked about the document, Zdeněk Jičínský admitted that it had originated within his Social Democrat Party and while he was not the author he did not disagree with it.[71]

---

65. RP, Nov. 20, 1992, p. 1.
66. PRAVDA, Nov. 20, 1992, p. 2.
67. RP, Nov. 21, 1992, p. 2.
68. PRAVDA, Nov. 20, 1992, p. 1.
69. LN, Oct. 19, 1992, pp. 1, 2.
70. RP, Nov. 20, 1992, p. 2.
71. Jičínský did not consider the current National Council as a legitimate organ for the independent Republic. Such legitimacy could arise from new elections only. He favored temporary arrangements according to which the deputies elected for the Federal Assembly would join the National Council in adopting a new Czech constitution. PRAVDA, Nov. 25, 1992, p. 1. On the other hand, Mečiar declared that the Federal Assembly was no longer a determining factor and that it was impossible to wait for the uncertain developments there.

Still in Bratislava, Ivan Gašparovič, chair of the Slovak National Council, hinted that only a single Slovak vote was missing for the passage of the extinction bill in the Assembly. Peter Weiss, PDL chair, spoke of "a brutal political pressure."[72] Prime Minister Mečiar speculated that if the bill failed it would come before the Republic Councils and the required three-fifths vote was assured only in the Slovak Council.[73]

The chair of the Assembly's Chamber of the People, V. Benda, disclosed later that a contingency plan was worked out "by some parliamentary functionaries" (obviously including himself) to be put into action if the Assembly failed to approve the bill: a meeting of all 174 Czech Assembly deputies would be called immediately to express support for action by the Czech government and National Council as well as to underwrite Czech Republic independence.[74]

f. The Final Vote: Part Two (November 1992)

The decisive vote in the Assembly was anticipated with understandable public interest. Some 100 people lined up in front of the Assembly building in the early morning of November 24. To their chagrin, the session could not convene because bad weather prevented the attendance of the Slovak deputies. "Oh, the Czecho-Slovak fog," exclaimed one headline,[75] while another read "Merciful fog," implying that more crucial time was gained for political consultation.[76] Klaus criticized the Slovak deputies for choosing air travel instead of a sleeper in view of the importance of the session. He himself would have "limped" into the hall regardless of his temporary infirmity.[77]

The Assembly leaders agreed that the Conciliation Committee would continue to work, with meetings of the factions to follow during the day when the Slovak members arrived; the plenary was to meet in the evening. However, the weather still refused to cooperate. As a result, the Assembly was able to convene only the following day, November 25. At that time, the Conciliation Committee brought in a divided report, elaborated after four days "of martyrdom,"[78] in which it proposed several modifications in the pending bill. A series of quirky exchanges greeted the report on the floor.[79]

---

72. PRAVDA, Nov. 24, 1992, p. 2.

73. *Ibid.* MDS and SNP would vote for such a law, the Christian Democrat Movement against, and the Hungarian parties would abstain. The PDL was undecided.

74. HN, Nov. 26, 1992, p. 2.

75. PRAVDA, Nov. 25, 1992, p. 2.

76. HN, Nov. 25, 1992, p. 1.

77. *Ibid.*

78. Deputy J. Daněk, Report of the 5th joint session, *supra,* note 34 (Nov. 25), 953. In the conciliation committee, seven members voted for the report (including the CDP representative), two were against, and two abstained. RP, Nov. 26, 1992, p. 1.

79. On the quality of the explosive "semtext," the "Munich marasmus," and so on, *see* Report, *supra,* note 34, 954.

In a separate vote, the first proposed amendment, essentially a clarification, was adopted,[80] but the second, obviously a laborious compromise, proved controversial. It provided that the law on extinction to become effective would have to be approved in both Republics either by a referendum or by an act of the National Council—a return to "the ratihabition." The reporters of the committees of the two chambers took an opposite position on this amendment. The MDS was willing to accept it, as was the CDP representative on the Conciliation Committee. But "after the arrival of CDP chairman V. Klaus the situation of course changed," and the coalition voted against it.[81] As a result, the compromise failed, having passed only in the Slovak part of the Chamber of Nations.[82]

The crucial vote on the entire bill without the compromise amendment took place in considerable tension. The outcome was unpredictable until the last moment. The presiding officer had to call for quiet before he was able to announce the result: the bill had passed in both chambers![83] "Thunderous applause" in the hall and in the gallery greeted the announcement.[84] Thus ended the constitutional calvary of the two peoples. Significantly, in meetings starting the day before, both Republic National Councils had approved "in an assembly line" fashion the treaties and agreements negotiated by their respective governments.[85]

In December 1992, the Slovak National Council followed by the Czech National Council adopted proclamations to world parliaments announcing

---

80. The amendment added the sentences in art. 4(1) and 4(2) to the effect that the "internal conditions" of each Republic's legislative body were determined by the law of that body.

81. RP, Nov. 26, 1992, p. 1.

82. Report of the 5th joint session, *supra,* note 34 (Nov. 25), 960; HN, Nov. 26, 1992, p. 1.

83. Constitutional Law 541/1992 Sb. In the House of the People, of the 143 deputies present, 92 voted yes (a vote of 90 was required for passage), 16 against, and 25 abstained, with eight not voting. In the House of Nations, of the 72 deputies elected in the Czech part, 45 voted yes, 7 against, and 11 abstained, with nine not voting. In the Slovak part, of the 72 deputies, 46 voted yes, seven against, and 16 abstained, with three not voting (45 votes were required for the passage). Report of the 5th joint session, *supra,* note 34 (Nov. 25), 962, 963. I follow the figures announced by the chair after the full vote, which differ somewhat from the figures given during the voting. *See generally,* Jiří Pehe, "Czechoslovak Parliament Votes to Dissolve Federation," RFE/RL RES. REP., Dec. 4, 1992, 1–5. The affirmative votes came from the CPD, CDU–CPP Christian-Democrat Party, the breakaway Republicans, the MDS, and the SNP; the required three-fifths majority was obtained from five LSU members, three Slovak Social Democrats, two Czech Social Democrats, and the PDL. HN, Nov. 26, 1992, p. 1.

84. LN, Nov. 26, 1992, p. 12.

85. HN, Nov. 25, 1992, pp. 1, 2; RP, Nov. 25, 1992, pp. 1, 2. For the text of the treaties and agreements, see Vladimír Mikule (ed.), Mezinárodní smlouvy mezi Českou republikou a Slovenskou republikou [International Treaties between the Czech Republic and Slovak Republic] (Codex Bohemia, Praha, 1995), English translation of headings in Sergio Bartole, Viktor Knapp et al., La dissoluzione della Federazione Cecoslovacca 232–39 (Vladimír Balaš) (La Rosa Editrice, Torino, 1994).

their impending emergence as independent, "sovereign" successor states to the Federative Republic, affirming their determination to observe all international law and treaty obligations including their shares of the financial commitments of the Federal Republic, to join the United Nations as legal successor states, and to become full fledged members of the European and worldwide groupings.[86]

g. The Aftermath: A Flood of Words

The enactment of the extinction law caused a river of post mortem reflections. On the positive side, Klaus viewed it as a step facilitating the process of separation but "not an absolute reversal that would solve all the problems with a wave of a magic wand . . . untying one small knot, not the big one."[87] Mečiar, addressing a large crowd in Eastern Slovakia, termed the mode of the split "highly cultured and without precedent in the world." He warned—and this proved a realistic prophecy—that after an initial period of common currency, each side would introduce its own currency exchangeable on a one-to-one basis. The evolution of the exchange rates would depend on economic development in the two Republics. The starting situation in Slovakia was worse than in the Czech Republic, but the Slovak development programs were "more hopeful."[88] The chair of the Slovak National Council, Ivan Gašparovič, although approving of the Assembly action, thought that the new law required an amendment of the Slovak Constitution because it prescribed the inclusion of the Slovak Federal Assembly deputies into the legislature of the independent Republic. "It is no secret," said a commentator in the *Rudé právo,* that the extinction law passed only because of the promise by the chiefs of the CDP and the MDS to incorporate them [the deputies] into both Republics' legislatures.[89] She may have been right.

As could be expected, Ján Čarnogurský, chair of the Slovak Christian Democrat Movement, emphasized that his party's deputies voted against the bill because it failed to provide for a referendum but that they were determined to support a prosperous democratic, "legal," Slovak state. The chair of the Czech Communist Party viewed the adoption of the extinction law as the latest in a line of disastrous historic events, starting with the execution of the Czech

---

86. Resolution no. 86 of the National Council of the Slovak Republic of Dec. 3, 1992; "Stenografická správa o 10. schôdzi Národnej rady Slovenskej republiky [Stenographic Report of the Tenth meeting of the National Council of the Slovak Republic]"; and a corresponding proclamation of the Czech National Council of Dec. 17, 1992, in UN Gen. Ass. A/47/848, Dec. 31, 1992.

87. HN, Nov. 26, 1992, p. 1.

88. *Ibid.,* p. 2. M. Kováč, chair of the Assembly, spoke of "a victory of reason": the opposition deputies, by providing the necessary affirmative votes, with others abstaining or voting against, had manifested their faithfulness to their election programs.

89. RP, Dec. 8, 1992, p. 3 (Kateřina Perknerová).

nobility in 1621; the founding of the common state in 1918 (!); the Munich, Yalta, and Teheran agreements; and the Warsaw Pact invasion of 1968. Citizen Havel on the other hand thought the enacted law "very good," since it offered "a constitutional framework for the division" and strengthened its credibility.[90]

Worldwide reaction was generally positive, stressing the peaceful aspects and avoidance of the danger of a violent split ("happy divorce," "black theater, no tragedy"). The *Frankfurter Rundschau* discovered a "beauty spot" in the division "from above," while Adam Michnik, the well-known Polish intellectual, saw a victory of particularism and nationalism over sound reason.[91]

In a legal opinion, a member of the Czechoslovak Academy of Sciences concluded that from a purely constitutional viewpoint the extinction law was of the same value as a referendum, although an expression of popular will would supply additional "weight." While the question of the legitimacy of the present Czech Parliament after independence was "complex," the new law "legitimated" the present deputies of both the Assembly and the National Council; "nevertheless, a really clean way" would be to hold new elections.[92] This Solomonic interpretation, although not exactly crystal clear, conflicted with the arguments of the opposition, including those of Professor Jičínský in the Assembly debate.

A Czecho-Slovak Committee for a Renewal of Czechoslovakia was constituted in Prague by, among others, the deputy Miloš Zeman and the Left Bloc caucus chair, deputy Ortman: "Don Quixotes of Czechoslovakia, the last Mohicans of the Federation. Or . . . ?"[93]

Since this is a book about the constitutional negotiations ending in the breakup, the narrative should stop here. However, from the ashes of the Federal Constitution rose two new constitutions, and I could not resist adding a brief sketch of the two documents in order to complete the landscape.

---

90. *Ibid.,* p. 2.
91. LN, Nov. 27, 1992, p. 4; HN, Nov. 26, 1992, p. 30; RP, Nov. 27, 1992, p. 30.
92. JUDr. M. Matula in RP, Nov. 30, 1992, p. 3.
93. HN, Nov. 27, 1992, p. 3. For the views of Prof. Zdeněk Jičínský, see also PRAVDA, Nov. 25, 1992, pp. 1, 3.

Fourth Act

XIV

Constitutions for the
Independent Republics

Although the two Republics were authorized to adopt their own basic instruments by the 1968 Federal Constitution,[1] neither took advantage of this empowerment for more than two decades. I delineated earlier the efforts by the commissions appointed by the Republic parliaments, but during the two years following the 1989 revolution their drafts failed to reach the stage of parliamentary consideration.

1. The Slovak Constitution, September 1992:
Montesquieu Bowdlerized?

a. The Process

Some eight drafts appeared in Slovakia and the work accelerated greatly when the adoption of a constitution[2] became the apex of the election program of the

---

1. Const. Law 143/1968 Sb., art. 142(2).
2. Constitution of the Slovak Republic, adopted on Sept. 1, 1992, in effect Oct. 1, 1992, 460/1992 Sb. English translation in XVII Constitutions of the Countries 69 (1993). I. Gašparovič, chair of the Slovak National Council, graciously presented me with an impressive leather-bound copy of the English translation prepared for the Slovak National Council, with his address delivered on September 3, 1992 (Privatpress, Prešov, Slovakia). I want to express here my appreciation. The earlier drafts prepared by the commission established by the Slovak National Council in conformity with art. 142 of the 1960–68 federal Constitution envisaged a constitution of the Republic as a component of the Federation. This perception was gradually modified in subsequent drafts, contemplating a new foundation for the common state to be defined in a treaty, and in the end a "clean constitution" for an independent Republic. See Zdeněk Jičínský and Vladimír Mikule, Das Ender der Tschechoslovakei 1992 in verfassungsrechtlicher Sicht (Teil I) 21–24, 44 Berichte 1994 (Bundesinstitut für ostwissenschaftliche und internationale Studien, Köln, Germany, 1994), also same, Teil II, 45 Berichte 1994, 3–41, a comparative study of the Czech and Slovak Constitutions, hereafter cited as Jičínský/Mikule, part II. Zdeněk Jičínský, Jan Škaloud, "Transformance politického systému k demokracii [Transformation of the Political System toward Democracy]," in Vlasta Šafaříková and others, Transformace české společnosti 1989–1995 [Transformation of the Czech Society 1989–1995] 50–113 (nakl. Doplněk, Brno, 1996). *See also* L'ubor Cibulka, "Constitutional Law of the Slovak Republic," in Stanislav Frankowski and Paul B. Stefan III (eds.),

273

Movement for Democratic Slovakia. After the elections of June 1992, an expert group led by two members of the Comenius Law Faculty in Bratislava was given primary responsibility for drafting the document. The two leading drafters were Docent Milan Čič of Mečiar's MDS, a specialist in criminal law and a man of remarkable survival skills, who served as the minister of justice in the last Slovak Communist government but, after the 1989 revolution, moved directly to a succession of high posts ending as chair of the newly established Slovak Constitutional Court; and Docent L'ubomír Fogaš, an expert in civil procedure, then a deputy in the Slovak National Council and one of the "bright young men" of the inner circle of the Party of the Democratic Left. We encountered both men earlier as lively participants in the federal constitutional negotiations.

The drafting group received, according to Docent Fogaš, 2,630 communications "representing some 20,000 signatures of the expert and lay public." It was an illusion to assume, he mused, that the all-nation debate during 1992 could on its own produce a final solution, but its realization was beneficial in that it signaled the interest on the part of institutions and common citizens.[3] Some of the Hungarian minority questioned the reality of the public discussion preceding the enactment of the government proposal, which took place under great time pressure.[4]

Paradoxically, the new constitution, although anticipating an independent state, was to come into effect—and in fact did become effective—before the termination of the Federation. I mentioned earlier the disagreement over the resulting legal situation, which grew into another media shouting match between some Czech politicians crying a violation of the Federal Constitution by a unilateral Slovak act and the Slovaks accusing the Czech side of another attempt to brand them as secessionists.[5] In fact, the Slovak Constitution, in

---

Legal Reform in Post-Communist Europe: A View from Within 95–115 (Martinus Nijhoff Pub., Boston, Dordrecht, London, 1995); Ernest Valko, "On the Constitution of the Slovak Republic," in Irena Grudzińska Gross (ed.), Constitutionalism and Politics 315 (Slovak Committee of the European Cultural Foundation, Bratislava, 1994); Peter Tatár, "The Circumstances of the Preparation and Acceptance of the Slovak Constitution," ibid., 318. Peter Kresák, "The Regulation of Mutual Relations between The National Council of the Slovak Republic and the Government in the Constitution of the Slovak Republic," ibid., 320; Lucio Pegoraro, "Il sistema delle fonti giuridiche nelle costituzioni dell' Est europeo," XV QUADERNI COSTITUZIONALI 111 (no. 1, 1995), focusing on legal sources as defined in the Slovak, Czech, and other constitutions; and Constitutionalism in East Central Europe 100–45 (Czecho-Slovak Committee of the European Cultural Foundation, Bratislava, 1994).

3. L'ubomír Fogaš, "Aby nám poriadne zostárla [To Make It Age Well]," 39/92 VÝBĚR, p. 7.

4. PRAVDA, Sept. 4, 1992, p. 3.

5. CDA Deputy Chair P. Bratinka in RP, Sept. 5, 1992, p. 3; PDL Chair P. Weiss in RP, Sept. 9, 1992, p. 2. Taking the "Czech" view, see F. Miklóško of the Slovak Christian Democratic Movement in LN, Sept. 3, 1992, p. 3.

order to avoid a conflict with the Federal Constitution, expressly suspended the effect of a series of articles pending the termination of the common state. Yet other provisions that were not suspended appeared, at first sight at any rate, to be incompatible with the federal legal order.[6]

More than 400 amendments were offered in the course of the parliamentary consideration, of which 150 were accepted by the Constitutional Committee.[7] On the day of the voting in the National Council, the Hungarian Christian Democrats and the Hungarian Coexistence coalition left the hall because their proposals for broader minority rights in education, use of language, and self-administration were rejected. Dr. Čarnogurský's Slovak Christian Democrats announced that they would vote against the government text because their proposals, designed to avoid a conflict with the Federal Constitution, were not accepted and also because of some "un-Christian" and "undemocratic" elements of the government text.[8] In a bitter exchange with Hungarian deputies, Prime Minister Mečiar read to them the Copenhagen Document of the Conference on Security and Cooperation in Europe, defining basic rights, and declared that Slovakia, like other states, did not accept the idea of collective minority rights.[9]

---

6. *See,* for example, art. 57 of the new Constitution creating an independent customs territory. The adoption of the Slovak Constitution could be considered as a secession, but "it was probably politically wise" that the Czech side did not press this point. Dušan Hendrych, "Constitutional Tradition and Preparation of New Constitutions in Czechoslovakia after 1989," in Joachim Jens Hesse and Neville Johnson (eds.), Constitutional Policy and Change in Europe 290 (Oxford U. Press, Oxford, New York, 1995). For a detailed argument, see Pavol Holländer, "The New Slovak Constitution: A Critique," 1 EAST EUR. CONST. REV. 16 (no. 3, 1992). Docent Holländer, formerly a Slovak member of the Comenius Law Faculty, eventually became a judge at the Czech Constitutional Court. *See also* J. Král, "K problémom nového ústavného systému Slovenskej republiky [On Problems of the New Constitutional System of the Slovak Republic]," 77 PO 56, 57 (no. 1, 1994). The author, a docent of the Police Academy in Bratislava, believes that the drafters had in mind a variety of possible arrangements, not only full independence. He concludes that on October 1, 1992, when the new Constitution came into effect, the constitutional situation in the Czech Republic continued to be governed by the federal Constitution while Slovakia was governed by the new Constitution (at 57). Yet (at 59) he cites the "reception" article 152 of the Slovak Constitution and holds that "from that viewpoint" the entire federal legislation continued to apply in Slovakia even after the termination of the Federation except for those provisions that conflicted with the Slovak Constitution. For a criticism of the earlier "Plank" draft by a Slovak jurist, see LN, Feb. 11, 1992, p. 8.

7. PRAVDA, Sept. 1, 1992, p. 1.

8. Deputy F. Mikloško referred to the articles dealing with the mandates of the deputies and referendum as well as to article 158 concerning the suspension of specified provisions of the Constitution. LN, Sept. 2, 1992, p. 8.

9. "The time of the *operetného šantenia* [operetta posturing] is irretrievably gone in this organ," said Mečiar as he lectured to the Hungarians, who called his intervention "arrogant." PRAVDA, Sept. 2, 1992, p. 2.

In the end, on September 1, 1992, the Constitution was approved by 114 deputies, with 16 Christian Democratic Movement deputies voting against, the four Hungarian members of the Party of the Democratic Left abstaining, and 16 Hungarian representatives absent.[10] I described earlier the pomp and circumstance surrounding the signing of the new Constitution.

b. "We, the Slovak Nation"—The Institutions

The preamble, opening with the words "We, the Slovak *nation*" and ending with "we, the citizens of the Slovak Republic," was bound to rekindle the abstract debate on the "national" as against the "civic" principle. The state is not based only on the national principle, argued one member of the drafting duo: "[W]e sought only a formulation of how to express that the nation has a right to its own state . . . citizens of the Slovak Republic . . . all have equal rights."[11] For good measure, the two principal commentators contributed a third, "international" principle.[12] I deal in annex II with the "openness" of the new instrument toward the outside world, international law, and the international community, particularly as regards international human rights standards, international treaties, and access to international bodies. Suffice it to say here that these aspects were greatly stressed by the two commentators as imposing a fundamental orientation upon the new state.

From among the available current, basic models, the American presidential system, its modified French version, and the chancellor system of Germany and Austria, the choice went to an "essentially classic parliamentary form,"[13] which corresponded with the Czecho-Slovak tradition. Conceived in 156 articles, the text contemplates a democratic, pluralist, "socially and ecologically oriented market economy" based on a tripartite division of power. The National Council, a single chamber of 150 deputies, is the legislature that "sits in

---

10. LN, Sept. 2, 1992, p. 8.

11. Milan Čič in Constitutionalism in East Central Europe, *supra,* note 2, 135, pointing to art. 12, which speaks of freedom and equality of the citizens.

12. Milan Čič and Ľubomír Fogaš, "Slovo na úvod [A Word of Introduction]," in Ústava Slovenskej republiky 3 (NKV International, Bratislava, 1992). The preamble, while referring to the heritage of the early Christian missionaries and the Great Moravian Realm, purports to include members of national minorities and ethnic groups in the "we" of the opening phrase and calls for peaceful cooperation with other democracies.

13. Milan Čič and Ľubomír Fogaš, "Demokratický charakter ústavy SR z roku 1992 [Democratic Character of the Constitution of 1992]," *ibid.,* 90, 91; *see also generally,* Ľubomír Fogaš and Ľubor Cibulka, Ústava Slovenskej republiky pre školy [The Constitution of the Slovak Republic for Schools] (Slov. Pedagog. Publisher, Bratislava, 1993); and Marián Posluch and a collective, Štátne právo Slovenskej republiky [State Law of the Slovak Republic] (Univ. Komenského, Bratislava, 1993)]. But *see* Peter Kresák, *supra,* note 2, 320–23.

continuous session." Contrary to past constitutions, no other organ (such as the president or "presidium" of the Communist legislatures) has the power to issue norms of legislative character when the Parliament is unable to convene. The National Council elects the president, as was the case in Czechoslovakia.

The relationship between the legislative and executive branches deviates from the traditional continental parliamentary system in that the National Council has the authority to remove the president for political reasons, in addition to the usual power of impeachment for treason.[14] The potential import of this uncommon provision became clear in the subsequent power struggle between Prime Minister Mečiar and the majority of the National Council on one hand and President M. Kováč, his former ally, on the other.[15]

"The head of the Slovak Republic" is the president,[16] endowed with the usual attributes of a head of state, but it is the government that is "the highest organ of executive power."[17] In accordance with the "checks and balances" concept, the president has the customary authority to return bills to the National Council, but—strangely enough—he *must* do so if the government asks him. This means that the government itself was also given an independent power of a suspensive veto.

The president appoints and recalls the prime minister and names other members of the government on proposal by the prime minister. The prime minister, however, has the authority to ask the president to remove a government member. It is, of course, the National Council that holds the ultimate sway over the government since it may dismiss it by a qualified majority vote of no confidence. The division of power between the president on one hand and the prime minister and the government on the other is not delineated in great detail. The premier's power became a lively issue early in the life of the independent Republic when Prime Minister Mečiar broke with another of his

---

14. The president may be removed by a vote of a three-fifths majority in the National Council for "activity aiming against the sovereignty and territorial integrity or toward the removal of the democratic constitutional system" of the Slovak Republic (art. 106). Article 107 provides that the president may be prosecuted for treason only, with the National Council acting as prosecutor and the Constitutional Court deciding.

15. Prime Minister Vladimír Mečiar stated: "The way [President] Michal Kováč performed his function agitated not only me but all Slovak citizens. . . . His steps are at the border of constitutionality and in my view beyond it. A man who violates the Constitution cannot be president. The decision about it, however, belongs to the Parliament, and we are determined to initiate a parliamentary inquiry into his activity . . ." (interview with LN, Sept. 29, 1994, p. 7). At this writing, the prime minister did not control enough votes in the National Council to apply art. 106 against Kováč. *See supra,* note 14; and Spencer Zifcok, "The Battle over Presidential Power in Slovakia," 4 EAST. EUR. CONST. REV. 61 (no. 3, Summer 1995).

16. Art. 101.

17. Art. 108.

close collaborators, the then Slovak minister of foreign affairs, Milan Kňažko, and demanded his removal. The president complied with the request but asked the Constitutional Court to provide an interpretation of the constitutional provision in question. Ironically, the Court held that the president was not obliged to follow the prime minister's demand for dismissal.[18]

The president may act without obtaining the countersignature of a member of the government—a striking departure from a traditional "check" ensuring the government's responsibility toward the legislature. The President is given the authority to require reports from the government and to be present and even preside at the government meetings, a feature apparently copied from the 1920 Czechoslovak Constitution.[19] He may attend sessions of the National Council, but there is no specification of his right to speak. He does not have a right of legislative initiative.

The president may dissolve the National Council, which, as we have seen, can recall him, but his authority to dissolve the legislature is so limited as not to offer an effective means for dealing with a potential deadlock between the institutions.[20] In fact, not unlike the 1960–68 Federal Constitution, the Slovak Constitution lacks an adequate instrumentality for solving a constitutional crisis. While this may not have been a serious defect under the totalitarian government, where disputes were solved within the party structure, it strikes me as a serious omission here unless the provision on the dissolving authority is given a broad, nontextual, teleological meaning. Generally speaking, the president's position is strong in relation to the government but rather weak in relation to the legislature.

Contrary to the practice in parliamentary systems, a member of the government cannot be elected a deputy in the National Council. However, as an interesting innovation, when a deputy becomes a member of the government, his legislative mandate does not cease but "is not exercised,"[21] and it revives when the government appointment is terminated. In the meantime, under the Slovak election law, a substitute performs the functions of the deputy in the National Council. This, it was explained, was a compromise between the principle of division of powers and the need to uphold the will of the voters

18. ÚS 39/93 of June 2, 1993. The provisions in question are arts. 102(f) and 116(4). Slovak Press Agency, July 3, 1993, in Peter Kresák, "Notes on the Form of Government in the Constitution of the Slovak Republic" (manuscript, 1993). Docent JUDr. Kresák is a member of the Komenského University Law Faculty. See also his essay, *supra*, note 2, 322.

19. Art. 82 of the Constitution of the Czechoslovak Republic (121/1920 Sb. z.a n.). Peter Kresák criticized the Slovak provision as incongruous and transplanted from the modified French presidential model. Peter Kresák, "Notes."

20. The president may dissolve the Parliament only six months after the election and only if the Parliament has failed three times to approve the government program. Art. 102(d).

21. Art. 77(2).

manifested in the elections.[22] Yet this feature was criticized as designed to strengthen the political power of the parties controlling the government and also because of a possible conflict with the Constitution itself.[23]

The Constitution contemplates the use of both optional and obligatory referendums. However, the National Council may change or annul the result of a referendum after three years by means of a constitutional law, an uncommon provision questioned by Docent Fogaš himself.[24]

c. Basic Rights and Freedoms

An important component of the Constitution is the chapter on basic rights and freedoms, which follows and expands the 1991 Federal Charter.[25] A Constitutional Court is the ultimate guarantor of these rights. In response primarily to the demands of the Party of the Democratic Left, economic and social rights were strengthened: whereas the Federal Charter laid down the entitlements of employees to "satisfactory working conditions" with details to be set by law, the Slovak Constitution adds that such a law must secure no less than seven enumerated categories of entitlements, including, for instance, an "adequate rest after work" and a minimum length of paid vacation.[26] Moreover, the right on protection of the living environment and cultural heritage was made more specific.[27] One commentator characterized any law guaranteeing "dignified living conditions" as "a fiction, pure political propaganda."[28] The same critic felt that the inclusion of economic rights as well as the unsatisfactory definition of property rights, allowing state ownership of "practically anything," demonstrated "the principle of state paternalism in the Constitution."[29] In answer to the criticism, one of the drafters opined that the comparable pre-1989 rules must be given "new substance" so that, for instance, "the right to work actually

---

22. L'ubomír Fogaš and L'ubor Cibulka, Ústava Slovenskej republiky pre školy [Constitution of the Slovak Republic for Schools] 85 (Slov. Pedag. Nakl., Bratislava, 1993).

23. Pavol Holländer, *supra,* note 6, 17; Peter Kresák, in Constitutionalism and Politics, *supra,* note 2, 321, 322.

24. L'. Fogaš and L'. Cibulka, *supra,* note 22, 86.

25. Const. Law 23/1991 Sb. For the Slovak text of the Federal Charter, see L'ubomír Fogaš and Luboš Cibulka, Listina základných práv a slobôd, ústavný zákon s komentárom [Charter of Basic Rights and Freedoms, Constitutional Law with a Commentary] (Slov. Pedagog. Nakl., Bratislava, 1992).

26. Art. 36.

27. Arts. 43, 44–45.

28. Pavol Holländer, *supra,* note 6, 16.

29. Pavol Holländer, *ibid.,* 16. *See,* for example, art. 4: "Mineral wealth, underground waters, natural healing springs, and waterways are owned by the Slovak Republic." Ernest Valko in Constitutionalism in East Central Europe, *supra,* note 2, 104. On the definition of ownership, see Viktor Knapp, "Poslední dějství národního majetku [The Last Act of National Property]," 6/1993 Právník 453–62.

means the duty of the state to create employment opportunities. If it does not succeed, the state has a duty to secure job training. If even this does not succeed, then unemployment benefits must be granted. . . . . It is not such a dogmatic prescription of a right to work."[30]

The Constitution guarantees minority citizens the right to education in their own tongue as well as its use in "official" contacts and participation in the settlement of matters that concern minorities. On its face, the protection appears to meet the prevailing European requirements, although the Hungarian minority spokesmen denied it because the Constitution spoke of a state "of the Slovak nation" and failed to provide any collective rights for the minorities.[31] They complained that the Mečiar administration ordered removal of the bilingual signs of the names of communities and demanded transliteration of Hungarian names into the Slovak mode for entry into official registers.

d. The Judiciary

Both the Slovak and the Czech Constitutions set forth the court systems to protect rights and enforce the rule of law, with the traditional safeguards for the independence of judges.[32] Both Constitutions provide for Constitutional Courts and Supreme Courts but a Supreme Administrative Court is envisaged only in the Czech Republic. As an interesting variant, Czech judges are appointed by the president for life, while their Slovak colleagues are elected by

---

30. Constitutionalism in East Central Europe, *supra*, note 2, 106 (L'ubomír Fogaš).

31. For example, Miklós Duray, chair of the Hungarian Coexistence, criticized the hasty preparation of the Constitution "in the exclusive presence of the MDS" without any public discussion as well as the violation of the voting rules. The Constitution "rejects the civic principle" and limits minority rights by not respecting the principles of the Copenhagen document on human rights and recommendation no. 1134 of 1990 by the Council of Europe. There are no guarantees of the protection and development of identity, autonomous organs of the minorities, participation in the right of control and in political life through political parties, protection of the "ethnic structure," the right to "homeland," to own schools, culture, and territorial autonomy. PRAVDA, Sept. 4, 1992, p. 3. As for territorial autonomy, Docent Fogaš told me in June 1993 that only two counties (*okresy*) have a Hungarian majority population with a possibility for territorial autonomy. Without advising the Slovak official delegation to the Council of Europe, the Hungarian parties addressed a letter to the Council demanding the abrogation of the so-called Beneš decrees of 1945, which ordered the confiscation of the property of collaborators with the fascist-Nazi Slovak government, demanding bilingual rights for names of communities, free choice in using Hungarian personal names (without transliteration), and respect for minority representation in drawing up the boundaries of counties.

32. Head seven of the Slovak and Head four of the Czech Constitution. Jiří Přibáň, "The Constitutional Court of the Czech Republic and a Legal-Philosophical Perspective on the Sovereignty of Law," in Istvan Pogany, Human Rights in Eastern Europe 135 (Edward Elgar Pub. Ltd., Aldershot, England, 1995); Ústavný súd Slovenskej republiky [Constitutional Court of the Slovak Republic] (with an introduction by the chair, Prof. JUDr. Milan Čic, DrSc) (Košice, Slovakia, undated).

the National Council on the advice of the government for one four-year term, at the end of which they can be reelected also for life.[33]

e. The Major Influences—A Postscript

The sources of some of the features of the Constitution may be identified with a degree of certainty while others are subject to speculation. The choice of the parliamentary democracy pattern and the indirect election of the president follow the first Czechoslovak Constitution of 1920. The indirect form of election of the president fitted also the power interest of Prime Minister Mečiar, as did the stronger than traditional status of the head of the government and of the government itself in relation to the legislature. The left in Slovakia, although at the time in opposition, was in a substantially stronger position than in the Czech Republic, as was its prospect for an entry into a future government. This may explain in part why, unlike its Czech counterpart, it did not mind seeing the balance of power tilt toward the government.

Some aspects, such as the abolition of the Presidium of the legislature with its lawmaking authority, reflect the revulsion against the past Soviet pattern, but it left a gap that was not filled. The extensive chapter on basic rights and freedoms and the "opening up" to the international community follows worldwide trends, signaling a harmonization of basic values. However, the unquestioned embrace and the widening of economic and social rights, although reflecting a trend in Western Europe, was clearly aided by the confluence of the populist-social goals pursued by the two leading parties, the Movement for Democratic Slovakia and the Party of the Democratic Left. Their posture was in sharp contrast to the position of the parties controlling the government in the Czech Republic.

The Slovak Constitution, with all its real or imaginary faults discerned by its critics, cannot be blamed for the sad state of political instability that has haunted the new Republic from its inception. In spring 1994, Prime Minister Mečiar was dismissed for the second time essentially for the same reasons as in April 1991, following a bitter conflict with his closest collaborators and a scandalous affray with the president. Seventeen deputies left MDS and created a new party, and a new government was installed. Yet, after all the evidence of Mečiar's congenital inability to work within a government even when it is composed of his own party, and after charges of corruption publicly vented by the president himself, in the 1994 elections Mečiar's MDS emerged again as the largest party (albeit with fewer votes than in 1992) and he became prime minister for the third time.[34] Many on the Czech side point to the situation in

---

33. Special rules govern the elections of members of the Constitutional Courts.
34. "Slovakia," 2–3 EAST. EUR. CONST. REV. 23–24 (1993, 1994).

Slovakia as a confirmation that a coexistence in a common state was not feasible owing to the fundamental differences between the political cultures of the two peoples.

2. The Czech Constitution, December 1992: Back to 1920?[35]

a. The Process

During the fateful talks in late summer of 1992, Prime Minister Mečiar pressed the Czech side to hasten the adoption of a Czech constitution parallel with that of the Slovaks, but Prime Minister Klaus demurred. Nevertheless, the preparatory work by the new team got under way in Prague, albeit at a somewhat leisurely pace, in August of that year. The newly appointed deputy prime minister, CDA's Jan Kalvoda, who was placed in charge of the government legislative office, was given primary responsibility to supervise the drafting work.

Two bodies were appointed: a government committee headed by Prime Minister Klaus, with Kalvoda as his deputy, composed exclusively of coalition representatives;[36] and a committee of legislators selected by the Presidium of the National Council from all factions represented in the Council, including the opposition, and chaired by the chair of the National Council, CDP's Milan Uhde. I should note here that under the prevailing Federal Constitution any

---

35. 1/1993 Sb. (Czech), English text in V Constitutions of the Countries, Czech Republic, 117–49 (1993). Charter of Fundamental Rights and Freedoms, *ibid.*, 152–64. In a Resolution of Dec. 15, 1992, 5/1993 Sb. (Czech), the Czech National Council reaffirmed the continuity of its legislative power. Const. Law of the same date, 4/1993 Sb. (Czech) on measures connected with the extinction of the Czech and Slovak Federative Republic provided for a continuing application of the federal legislation, which is not in conflict with Czech Republic laws and transfers federal powers, property, and rights and obligations to the Republic. *See* Václav Pavlíček, "The Foundation of the Czech Republic and the Czechoslovak Continuity," 1994 Home Rule & Civil Society 91 (no. 5, Mar. 1994); Aleš Gerloch et al., Ústavní systém České republiky [Constitutional System of the Czech Republic] (Prospektrum, Praha, 1994); Jiří Grospič, "Some Constitutional Problems of the Czech Republic," in Irena Grudzińska Gross (ed.), Constitutionalism and Politics 220 (Slovak Committee of the European Cultural Foundation, Bratislava, 1994); "Czech Constitutionalism," in Constitutionalism in East Central Europe, *supra,* note 2, 84–98; Helmut Slapnicka, "Die Verfassungsordnung der tschechischen Republik," 40 Osteuropa Recht 28–63 (1994), including a German translation of the Constitution; Bernard H. Siegan, Drafting a Constitution for a Nation or Republic Emerging into Freedom 31–32, 65–68 (2d ed., George Mason U. Press, Fairfax, Va., 1994).

36. Each party represented in the Council received a number of members proportionate to the number of seats it held in the Council. Vojtěch Cepl, "Constitutional Reform in the Czech Republic," 28 U. of San Francisco L. Rev. 29, 31 (1993).

Republic constitutional law required the acceptance by a three-fifths majority in the National Council, which meant, in practical terms, that at the time the governing coalition needed 15 opposition votes for a positive outcome.[37] After an initial tension between them, the two committees settled down to a "ping-pong" interaction:[38] The deputies eschewed creating their own draft, but they flooded the government committee with comments to be taken into account in its drafting work. To improve the lagging cooperation[39] between the two committees, one member of each committee was appointed to attend the sessions of the other.[40] The government committee produced promptly a set of basic principles, which was transmitted to the National Council committee and published on September 15.[41] It was widely debated and criticized. The opposition complained that the government sought to force the approval of a text that was like "a cake patched together by a dog and a cat," hastily sewed together "with a hot needle."[42]

With the rapidly approaching end of the Federation, the threat of a legal vacuum became real. In an effort to find a broader forum, a "committee of 13" was organized, composed of leaders of the coalition parties and top government members, which produced another draft of principles.[43] A complete working text emerged from a meeting at Karlovy Vary of the expanded government committee. According to one of the participants, the principal work was done by a group composed of two judges, three law professors, and four deputies of the National Council,[44] which labored in the total isolation of the villa Titania for four long days.[45] The government revised the text in several sessions. The draft was criticized and stripped down by Prime Minister Klaus himself. Finally, the text was taken up by the standing Constitutional Committee of the National Council, joined by the reporters of the other legislative committees concerned. That group, after struggling with 306 proposed amend-

---

37. There was some criticism of the fact that no academic specializing specifically in constitutional law was included in the drafting process. Václav Pavlíček, "Problémy práv občanů v ústavě České republiky [Problems of Citizens' Rights in the Constitution of the Czech Republic]," 4/1993 PRÁVNÍK, 349, 353. Prof. Pavlíček has been professor of constitutional law and head of the constitutional law department of the Charles University Law Faculty.

38. Chair of the Czech National Council Milan Uhde in RP, Sept. 16, 1992, p. 1; LN, Sept. 19, 1992, p. 3.

39. Jan Kalvoda in RP, Sept. 16, 1992, p. 2; LN, Sept. 19, 1992, p. 3.

40. Vojtěch Cepl, *supra,* note 36, 31, 32.

41. HN, Sept. 16, 1992, p. 2.

42. LN, Oct. 10, 1992, p. 8; RP, Sept. 19, 1992, p. 2 (Social Democrats, LSU, and the Moravian Movement).

43. RP, Oct. 15, 1992, p. 2 ("Glosy ke dni [Glosses of the Day]").

44. Vojtěch Cepl, *supra,* note 36, 29, 32; HN, Oct. 20, 1992, p. 2.

45. LN, Oct. 20, 1992, p. 3; V. Cepl in LN, Oct. 23, 1992, p. 3.

ments, settled the remaining controversial points at a session in the castle of Lány, the traditional residence of the president.[46]

More than 30 speakers took part in the debate of the plenary National Council. Late in the evening of December 16, the Lány text was overwhelmingly approved.[47] Under the headline "Without Pathos," an observer reported that no fireworks illuminated the night over Prague and the soothing buzz of the old town pubs continued as usual.[48] Unlike its Slovak counterpart, the Czech Constitution was to come into effect only upon the extinction of the Federation.

During the drafting process, leading parliamentarians received a host of proposals from a great variety of organizations.[49] An interesting aspect of the constitution making, to which I shall return shortly, was the highly visible role played by citizen Václav Havel, since November 16 a presidential candidate, pressing his own views in consultations with politicians of all parties and in the press and on television.

b. The Issues—Criticism

i. "We, the Citizens"

The instructions from the highest quarters were to follow generally the 1920 Constitution of the First Republic. In case of a dispute—an insider reported— the easiest agreement in the end was to follow that Constitution.[50] Although that model was basically adopted, the new Constitution embodies modifications reflecting a compromise between the prime minister's priority for an untrammeled free economy on one hand and the social concerns pressed by the opposition on the left. Unlike the Slovak Constitution, the Czech one does not have a section on the economy. It takes into account the modern developments in the human rights field, but—unlike its Slovak counterpart—it fails to provide instrumentalities for joining international organizations and for a recep-

---

46. LN, Dec. 8, 1992, pp. 1, 16; RP, Dec. 15, 1992, p. 2; HN, Dec. 14, 1992, p. 1.

47. "Těsnopisecká zpráva o schůzi České národní rady [Shorthand Record of the Meeting of the Czech National Council]," 16–17, Dec. 1992, 10th meeting, VIIth election term, p. 182 (Dec. 16, 1992); LN, Dec. 17, 1992, pp. 1, 12; HN, Dec. 17, 1992, p. 1. Of the 198 deputies, 172 voted yes, 10 abstained and 16 voted against (10 Republicans, four Moravian Movement, 1 LSU, 1 Left Bloc). *See generally* Pavel Mates, "The Czech Constitution," RFE/RL Res. Rep., March 5, 1993, 53–57.

48. LN, Dec. 17, 1992, p. 1.

49. These organizations included a group of city mayors, the bishops' conference, the Federation of Locomotive Engineers, ecologists, the Planned Parenthood Association, societies of artists and architects, the royalist movement, and so on. *See* material in the Library of the Czech Parliament.

50. Vojtěch Cepl, "Cesta k právnímu státu [The Road to a Legal State]," 37/1993 Ekonom 15.

tion of international law that by now are standard features of modern constitutions.[51]

Also in contrast to the Slovak text, the Czech preamble opens with "We, the citizens," and—as in the U.S. Constitution—the words *nation* and *national* are absent. The difference is more than symbolic: it illustrates the different developmental levels of the idea of nationalism. Yet the then head of the Constitutional Law Department of Charles University repeatedly complained of the failure "at least to mention the existence of the Czech nation."[52] As another interesting difference from the Slovak text, in the Czech "Basic Provisions," "state power derives from the people." This conforms to the concepts of the United States and the continental constitutions. Yet the corresponding article in the Slovak Constitution identifies "the citizens" as the source of state power. The understandable allergy in postcommunist societies to the term *people,* systematically abused by the old regime, is evidently stronger in Slovakia than in the Czech lands. A Czech constitutionalist concluded that such aversion leads to a distortion of the historic concept of the sovereignty of the people.[53] The Czech preamble, instead of a "Czech nation," speaks of a renewal of an independent Czech state, the inviolable values of human dignity and freedom, civil society, rule of law, and identification with the family of the European and world democracies.

ii. The Legislature: A Senate? The Voting Procedure

As in Slovakia, the institutional scheme is generally in line with the continental concept of a parliamentary democracy. It also was strongly influenced by the 1920 Constitution. However, in contrast to the Slovak unicameral Parliament, the legislative branch is composed of two chambers, the House (*sněmovna,* the Assembly of Deputies), elected by a proportional voting system, and a Senate, elected under a "first to the pole" majority vote, which introduces significant innovation. The length of the mandates, the eligibility requirements, and the functions of the two chambers differ.[54]

The question of the Senate proved to be one of the four most controversial issues. The proponents invoked the precedent of a Senate in the First Republic, its role as a filter or "an insurance policy" against hasty legislation, as a welcome deviation from the unwieldy proportional electoral system, "as a way station to a Hayek utopia" in which the Senate would be responsible for private

51. See *infra,* annex II.
52. Pavel Peška, "Nedůstojná preambule [Undignified Preamble]," *LN,* Nov. 24, 1992, p. 9; *ibid.,* Mar. 18, 1993, p. 9.
53. Vladimír Klokočka, "Dvě rozdílné ústavy [Two Differing Constitutions]," *LN,* Sept. 25, 1992, p. 8, commenting on an early Czech draft.
54. The new Senate differs significantly from that of the First Republic not only in composition but in its function and powers as well.

law with the House concentrating on public law. They pointed out that of the 19 Western European states only six have a "true" unicameral structure.[55] The opponents, primarily on the left side of the political spectrum, argued against a Senate as a costly luxury for a small state that is neither a federation nor ethnically heterogenous; they claimed that the insistence on a second chamber was motivated by the political objective (and a deal) of some coalition parties to find a place for the Czech deputies elected in 1992 for the Federal Assembly with a mandate extending until 1996 who would become unemployed after January 1, 1993.[56]

In the end, a political compromise, described by one of its progenitors with some hyperbole as "a triumph of transitional constitution making,"[57] resulted in postponing the issue.[58] According to the final text, the House assumed the functions of the Senate pending the adoption of a new constitutional law, which was to determine the composition of the "Provisional Senate"; during that period the House could not be dissolved,[59] making it possible for the House alone to adopt promptly whatever legislation was urgently needed for the nascent independent state but creating a most unusual situation of an nondissolvable legislature. The Provisional Senate envisaged by the conundrum has never been organized and the very existence of the second chamber was a subject of continuing controversy until September 1995 when the Parliament decided that it should be activated.[60] Special elections for that purpose were held in November 1996 and the Senate was finally organized.

55. Denmark, Greece, Luxembourg, Malta, Portugal and Sweden. Finland, Iceland, and Norway are said to have a "false" second chamber, elected by the first chamber. Andrea Baušová, "Senát se neosvědčil [Senate Did Not Prove Itself]," LN, Oct. 6, 1992, p. 9. It was said that the opposition against the second chamber on the part of the parties on the left existed during the First Republic and elsewhere in the world. That chamber had stood in the way of the "persistent dream to change the world radically," as seen in the experiment of the Swedish socialists installed only after the abolition of the second chamber. Andrej Gjurič in LN, Oct. 1, 1994, p. 5.

56. There were divisions within parties as well as within the coalition. Some in the CDA and among the Christian Democrats favored the Senate as a way to decrease presidential powers. Klaus and Kalvoda were not enthusiastic for it, but when the Social Democrats insisted on a single chamber the coalition lined up behind the Senate. Conversation with Professor Dušan Hendrych, dean of the Charles University Law Faculty in 1995. The opposition as well as the CDA were strongly against filling the Senate with Federal Assembly deputies. HN, Nov. 4, 1992, p. 2. The vice-chair of the Civic Movement, V. Žák, thought that a Senate had sense only in federations. In all other countries, it is a "historic hangover" without political significance. LN, Oct. 17, 1992, p. 3.

57. Vojtěch Cepl and David Franklin, "Senate, Anyone?" 2 EAST EUR. CONST. REV. 59 (1993). See interview with Vojtěch Cepl, "Bojím se nové federace [I Am Afraid of a New Federation]," by Ivana Vajnerová, in MFD, Nov. 26, 1992, p. 6.

58. V. Cepl and D. Franklin, ibid., 59.

59. Art. 106(1–3) of the Constitution.

60. LN, Sept. 28, 1995, p. 1. Only two days after the adoption of the Constitution, the Czech National Council rejected a proposal that federal deputies be transferred to the Senate. Pavel Mates, supra, note 47, 55. See, for example, the proposal of the 21 deputies of the Czech Social

As in Slovakia, the legislature is in continuous session with the possibility of a limited temporary adjournment, but the Senate is given the important power to enact emergency legislation if the House is dissolved.[61] This fills the gap (left open in Slovakia).[62]

The voting procedure for the adoption of constitutional legislation and approval of international treaties proved to be another bone of contention. The government, apparently traumatized by the experience with the minority veto ("prohibition of majorization") under the 1960–68 Constitution,[63] initially proposed the formula of a simple majority of *all* members of the House.[64] The opposition in unison cried foul play since the current coalition controlled an absolute majority and thus would be free to shape the constitutional order at will. Václav Havel endorsed the opposition's view.[65] Following a critical showdown, the government relented, accepting the traditional three-fifths majority requirement.[66]

Contrary to the Slovak solution, a member of the Czech legislative branch who becomes also a member of the government retains his right to active participation and voting in the Parliament except that he or she may not serve as a chair or vice-chair of a parliamentary committee or of an investigating commission. This provision—as well as the authority of the government to give an opinion on any legislative proposal, appears to strengthen the position of the government, which is termed (as in Slovakia) "the supreme organ of executive power."[67]

Democratic Party, one LSU, and one Left Bloc deputy for a constitutional amendment to abolish the Senate altogether, in LN, Oct. 7, 1993, p. 3; Oct. 15, 1993, p. 3; Nov. 6, 1993, p. 3; and Jan Štětka in LN, Sept. 9, 1994, p. 5. A proposal to abolish the Senate was rejected, LN, Nov. 28, 1994, p. 3. On the outcome of first Senate elections, *see* "Senátní volby '96 [Senate Elections '96]," Supplement to LN, Nov. 25, 1996, p. I–VII.

61. Art. 33(1).

62. In the summer of 1994, with the "provisional state" still continuing, President Havel warned of a possible constitutional deadlock should the coalition break up, while Prime Minister Klaus saw no real danger in the "temporary" absence of the possibility to dissolve the House. "Hovory z Lán [Talks from Lány]," LN, June 13, 1994, p. 16.

63. LN, Nov. 3, 1992, p. 1.

64. LN, Nov. 3, 1992, p. 1 ("Šance [The Chance]").

65. RP, Nov. 10, 1992, p. 2.

66. A deputy described the arduous negotiations between the coalition and opposition representatives: every day until one or two hours of the night facing a skimpy government proposal, each of us with many amendments, without any leading experts of constitutional law, which was a "fundamental error." Jiří Vyvadil, "Naplňování ústavy [On Completing the Constitution]," LN, July 18, 1994, p. 8.

67. Art. 67(1). It takes a written proposal by at least 50 deputies and a majority of all deputies for the House to vote a motion of non confidence in the government (art. 72[2])—a provision viewed as also strengthening the position of the government. Eva Broklová, "Vláda silnější než parlament [The Government Stronger than the Parliament]," LN, Dec. 1, 1992, p. 8.

iii. The President and the Government

A second cause for disagreement concerned the mode of electing the president. It marred the relations between Václav Havel and the prime minister. Havel, a declared candidate for the office, urged direct election by the people, and he had the support of a broad political spectrum as well as the prevailing trend in post-Communist Central and Eastern Europe. Only the CDP and its ally, the minuscule Christian Democratic Party, were opposed. The CDP Executive Board took the position that "[a] direct election would result in constituting a second, competing center of the executive power. Both centers could easily come into conflict."[68] Ultimately, it was Klaus and the First Republic tradition that prevailed: the Constitution provides for the election by both chambers (rather than the lower House only), a solution Havel viewed eventually as an acceptable compromise.[69]

Clearly in line with the prime minister's concepts, the powers of the president in the new Constitution were substantially reduced in comparison with his status under the 1920 instrument. The vital plenary power to dissolve the House that the president enjoyed in the First Republic was confined to enumerated situations.[70] He remains free to select the prime minister, but his power to appoint and recall other members of the government requires a proposal by the prime minister.[71] "The president must do what the premier proposes," Havel said, but this does not make the head of state "an automat for signing." True to form, he explained in detail his concept of a prudent, structured interaction between the two actors in a variety of scenarios, which only a talented playwright could conjure up.[72] Still, Havel's interpretation runs counter to the holding of the Slovak Constitutional Court on a corresponding text in the Slovak Constitution to the effect that the president is not bound by the prime minister's proposal.

In sharp contrast to the Slovak solution, the Czech president cannot be recalled by the legislature. It is the government that is responsible for specified presidential acts which, in contrast to the Slovak Constitution, require gener-

---

68. RP, Nov. 4, 1992, p. 1. Klaus was quoted as "not having given the direct election a single thought" and as having said that the coalition never dealt with it. RP, Nov. 2, 1992, pp. 1, 2. By early December, he denied that there was a serious dispute and blamed the media.

69. According to Havel, the election by both chambers, as distinguished from the power to vote no confidence in the government given to the lower House only, adds "a certain different character to the political position of the President." He opposed the idea of the Parliament's power to recall the president. LN, Sept. 23, 1992, pp. 1, 8.

70. Art. 35. Compare with art. 31(1), (2), of the Constitution of the Czechoslovak Republic of Feb. 29, 1920, 121 Sb. z.a.n.

71. Art. 62(a) in conjunction with art. 68(2) and (5).

72. Havel added that this interpretation applied to the recall of a minister while a case of the nomination of a new minister was not as clear (?). LN, June 21, 1993, p. 8.

ally the countersignature of one of its members.[73] The president's suspensive veto power over legislation is limited to ordinary laws and excludes constitutional legislation. In part, this solution met Václav Havel's objection to an earlier draft.[74] The Senate enjoys the power of a suspensive veto as well. A simple majority of *all* deputies of the House may adopt the law returned by either the president or the Senate.[75]

The president as the "head of state" is "the supreme commander of the armed forces" and wields the standard foreign relations powers, although here also subject to approval of certain of his actions. Critics, obviously with some justification, complained of the failure of the Constitution to state clearly who has the final say in the conduct of war.[76] The U.S. Constitution, I may recall, did place the power to declare war explicitly in the hands of the Congress, but the tug of war between the president and the legislature over the use of American troops abroad has proved one of the most controversial issues between the two branches of the federal government.

The president has no right of legislative initiative, but he appoints (in some instances subject to the consent of the Senate) the judiciary and the Supreme Audit Board and Central Bank officials, an important authority that in Slovakia is generally entrusted to the Parliament, tipping the balance there toward the legislative branch.[77] As in the Slovak instrument, the president may be present at the meetings of the government. I was told that President Havel in fact appeared at one such meeting, listened in silence, and left.

The new text, also inspired by the 1920 Constitution, grants immunity "forever" from criminal prosecution to the president and (if the chamber refuses to lift the immunity) to the members of the legislature, and it even broadens it to comprise judges of the Constitutional Court.[78] This concept

---

73. Art 63(3) and (4). See also art. 62 and 54(3).

74. In that draft, the president's suspensive veto was limited to constitutional laws only. Havel argued that the suspensive veto, a substitute for legislative initiative, should cover ordinary legislation as well because constitutional laws were very rare and usually well prepared, and without such a right the president "would be cut off from the legislative process." LN, Nov. 18, 1992, p. 3.

75. *See generally* Vojtěch Cepl and Mark Gillis, in "Survey of Presidential Powers in Eastern Europe," 2–3 EAST. EUR. CONST. REV. 64–68 (1993, 1994).

76. V. Cepl and M. Gillis, *ibid.*, 66–67. In the Slovak Constitution, the president, "on proposal by the government," declares a state of war and declares "war by a resolution of the National Council" in the event of aggression or where international obligations require joint defense. Slovak Const., art. 102(k).

77. Cf. art. 62 (e), (f), (j), (k) of the Czech Constitution with art. 86 of the Slovak Constitution.

78. Arts. 27, 65, 86. It was the Committee of the National Council that reportedly proposed a permanent immunity for deputies. LN, Sept. 26, 1992, p. 3. This accorded with the 1920 Czechoslovak Constitution, art. 24 (on members of the Parliament).

exceeds the rationale for an immunity based on the functional theory, and it was justly criticized as creating a privileged group placed above the law.[79]

On the other hand, the provisions of the 1920 Constitution directed against conflicts of interest of public officials, such as a prohibition barring government members from serving on company boards, are omitted, perhaps on the understandable assumption that such matters should be confined to ordinary legislation. In the face of a number of scandals, an earlier legislation was made more stringent in 1995.[80]

The weakness of the president's authority in comparison with his power under the 1920 Constitution is in large part attributable to the strong position of Prime Minister Klaus during the drafting of the Constitution. At that time, there was no Czech Republic president to counteract Klaus, and even the federal presidency was vacant. This left citizen Havel to speak in favor of his prospective office. It was up to President Havel, despite the weak formal powers, to "breathe life into his office" by capitalizing on the precedent of the "monarchical presidency" of T.G. Masaryk and on his own significant popularity.[81]

iv. The Charter of Basic Human Rights and Freedoms
The question of whether the federal Charter of Basic Rights and Freedoms should be made a part of the new Czech Constitution, and if so in what form, turned out to be the third divisive issue between the coalition and the opposition. The debate was a replay, in a new context, of the 1990 controversy centering on the wisdom of including economic, social, and cultural "rights" in the federal constitution.

Prime Minister Klaus apparently was too busy as the federal minister of finance to pay attention to the federal Charter when it was adopted in January 1991.[82] "When we read it"—he told the press two years later—"we were horrified that something of this sort was possible."[83] He would not allow the new constitution to be "sowed with weeds" of declaratory, unrealizable, and unenforceable "rights."[84] The chair of the National Council, Milan Uhde, also a CDP member, urged against following the Communist practice of "beautiful words" devoid of any chance of keeping the promises.[85] Jan Kalvoda of the

---

79. V. Pavlíček, *supra,* note 37, 349, 351–52. *See* in this connection Vladimír Sládeček, "K otázce imunity bývalých poslanců Federálního shromáždění [On the Question of Former Deputies of the Federal Assembly]," 9/1993 PRÁVNÍK 795–99.

80. Law 328/1992 Sb. as amended by Law 287/1995 Sb. For a criticism, see V. Pavlíček, *ibid.*, and also the position of the Czechoslovak Helsinki Committee, 4/1993 PRÁVNÍK 354–55.

81. V. Cepl and M. Gillis, *supra,* note 75, 67.

82. 23/1991 Sb.

83. LN, Sept. 12, 1992, pp. 1, 8.

84. RP, Dec. 8, 1992, p. 1.

85. LN, Oct. 16, 1992, p. 3.

CDA declared that, although the majority of the government supported the inclusion of the federal Charter, he belonged to the minority, which wanted the Charter stripped of the "proclamatory provisions" and adopted apart from the Constitution.[86] The entire opposition on the left, as well as the labor unions, fiercely disagreed and insisted on integrating the entire unchanged Charter directly into the Constitution. When the committee of the National Council set up a subcommittee to deal with the problem, the Left Bloc and the Social Democrats refused even to participate.[87]

Invoking modern trends in defining basic social rights, Václav Žák, vice-chair of the original Civic Movement and of the pre-1992 National Council, cited the "declaratory" articles such as "the right to work" in the constitutions of nine Western European states, all members of the European Community. Žák assailed the "educated and intelligent people who speak of the Charter with a contemptuous smile, who never read the Charter, never read any other constitution"; without including the Charter in the Czech Constitution "we could compete for the worst constitution in Europe."[88]

Considering the time restraint, it was clearly not practicable for the coalition to seek a change in the text of the federal Charter. A compromise was reached at a late stage of the negotiations, according to which the Charter would not be included in the Constitution itself but would be adopted, albeit without any change, as a separate constitutional act and made a component of the "constitutional order," a newly invented term defined in the Constitution itself.[89] Whatever the newfangled concept may mean (as Professor Knapp put it, "only the devil alone knows what it means"), in practice presumably the Charter could be changed by a three-fifths majority only. There is, I assume, a

---

86. RP, Sept. 16, 1992, p. 2; LN, Nov. 10, 1992, p. 3.

87. LN, Oct. 10, 1992, p. 8. Only the LSU and the Republicans agreed to join with the coalition members.

88. Václav Žák, "Plevel v ústavě [Weeds in the Constitution]," LN, Dec. 18, 1992, p. 8. Avoiding a possible conflict with international obligations was cited as one reason for the ultimate compromise solution. Václav Benda, chair of the Christian Democratic Party, in Constitutionalism in East Central Europe, *supra,* note 2, 92.

89. Art. 3 of the Constitution: *Ústavní pořádek* rather than the common term *ústavní řád.* Article 112 of the Constitution provides that the "constitutional order" is composed, in addition to the Constitution (1/1993 Sb. [Czech]) and the Charter, which was proclaimed again by a resolution of the Presidium of the National Council (2/1993 Sb. [Czech]), of constitutional laws enacted on the basis of this Constitution and of specific other federal and Republic constitutional laws, and it abolishes the then extant federal Constitution and related constitutional laws as well as the Czech law on state symbols. Other constitutional laws valid at the effective date of the new Constitution have the force of ordinary law. For a specific list of the constitutional laws that form the "constitutional order," see Jiří Hřebejk, "Ústavní pořádek České republiky [Constitutional Order of the Czech Republic]," 5/1993 PRÁVNÍK 441–42. For some questions of interpretation, see Zdeněk Jičínský and Vladimír Mikule, part II, *supra,* note 2, 35–36.

symbolic meaning in separating it from the Constitution, and precedents exist for such an arrangement.[90]

The Czech Constitution makes international human rights treaties, accepted by the Republic, directly applicable in Czech courts and superior to ordinary legislation.[91] The Constitution does not state expressly that the Czech Republic accepts all treaties concluded by the Federation, but the National Council so decreed in a separate constitutional law.[92] This means that the obligations concerning the entitlements embodied, for instance, in the UN Covenant on Economic, Social, and Cultural Rights, to which the Federation was a party,[93] also bind the Czech Republic and could be changed in the domestic order by a qualified majority vote only. The Czech constitutional provision incorporating human rights treaties is similar to the Slovak text.[94] In Slovakia, the Constitution itself contains the principle of succession to the rights and obligations arising out of all treaties to which the Federation was a party.[95]

v. The Territorial Division

To an outside observer, it may come as a surprise that the fourth and most fiercely contested issue concerned the internal administrative organization of the Republic. Yet the issue was important because it concerned the vertical division of powers. Everyone agreed that municipalities should be the basic autonomous units. The dispute was over the size and number of the higher units projected between the municipalities and the central government. At the core of the controversy was the status of Moravia and Silesia, the eastern part of the Republic which historically enjoyed a degree of autonomy. Some 1.3 million

---

90. Mostly for historical and systemic reasons, some other constitutions do not contain special chapters on basic rights, for example, the French, Austrian, Norwegian, and Dutch constitutions. Vladimír Klokočka, "Renesance práv člověka [Revival of the Rights of Men]," LN, Dec. 11, 1992, p. 9. Professor Viktor Knapp, an internationally known member of the Charles University Law Faculty, writes that the Charter, although a part of the "constitutional order" ("the devil alone knows what this means") is "by itself not a law (even less a constitutional law)," but it was published in the Official Gazette. Viktor Knapp, "Poslední dějství národního majetku [The Last Act of National Patrimony]," 6/1993 Právník 453, 456. The Constitution did not include the introductory law to the Charter, and that created problems of overlapping provisions.

91. Art. 10 of the Czech Constitution. *See* annex II, *infra.*

92. Const. Law on Measures Connected with the End of the Czech and Slovak Federal Republic, 4/1993 Sb. (following the federal constitutional law 542/1992 Sb.), arts. 4, 5; Vladimír Mikule and Vladimír Sládeček, Ústavní soudnictví a lidská práva [Constitutional Judiciary and Human Rights] 27–28 (Codex, Prague 1994). *See also* annex II.

93. 120/1976 Sb. *See generally* Václav Pavlíček, "Listina základních práv a svobod a problémy přeměny právního řádu [Charter of Basic Rights and Problems of Transformation of the Legal Order]," 5/1992 Právník 365.

94. Czech art. 10 and Slovak art. 11. *See* annex II, *infra.*

95. Art. 153 provides that the Slovak Republic shall be the successor to the Federation's rights and obligations "to the extent determined by constitutional law of the Czech and Slovak Federative Republic or to the extent agreed between the Slovak and the Czech Republic."

people living in the area consider themselves of "Moravian nationality," and a small group of local politicians, demanding a federal arrangement, even created an "Assembly" with pretensions to lawmaking powers.[96]

Most of the coalition, obviously under the incubus of the experience with the Slovaks, opposed—as the prime minister put it—"any hint of dualism" in the Constitution.[97] Some of the opposition, with the Communists particularly articulate, urged the recognition of the Moravian and Silesian "lands." Václav Havel considered "Moravia a serious problem that would require sufficient time for quiet thought," but on the other hand he warned against a postponement. Within the coalition—he told a press conference—there was a distaste for responding to Moravian aspirations because of the fears of elements smacking of federalism; Moravia is becoming "a weapon in the hands of one side against another" and "within the ranks of the opposition there are people who wave the Moravian flag only to differentiate themselves from the coalition." His proposal was for five "regions" in the Czech part and the two Moravian and Silesian lands, all with the same status and competences[98] but preserving the symbolism of the "lands." His idea was in direct conflict with the government scheme, which envisaged more numerous "regions" in both parts of the Republic and no "lands."

With no consensus on the horizon and all the other controversial matters settled, a last minute compromise was reached, postponing the matter for action by the Parliament of the new Republic.[99] By the time of this writing, the issue was still embroiled in an acute controversy, a threat from time to time to the cohesion of the coalition.[100] The Slovak Constitution leaves the question of higher territorial units to an ordinary rather than a constitutional law,[101] in principle a more sensible approach, which, however, was beyond the realm of possibility in the Czech political landscape of the day.

vi. On Referendum and Constitutional Amendment
In the negotiations, the opposition on the left, clearly mesmerized by the prevailing political power situation, sought to create a counterweight against the "rightist" government and Parliament by strengthening the president and introducing a referendum. The coalition, on the other hand, reflecting Klaus's distinct preference for "a representative democracy," objected in principle to

---

96. LN, Dec. 7, 1992, p. 8.

97. HN, Dec. 9, 1992, p. 2.

98. LN, Sept. 23, 1992, pp. 1, 8; LN, Oct. 20, pp. 1, 8; LN, Nov. 18, 1992, p. 3. The government proposed regions of one to three million people in both parts.

99. Art. 99, confirming the status of municipalities as the basic territorial self-administrating units, provides that "the higher territorial self-administrating units are lands or regions."

100. LN, June 15, 1994, p. 5.

101. Art. 64(3).

"direct democracy," but as a concession to the opposition it agreed on a text to the effect that a constitutional law may determine when "the people exercise public power directly."[102] This, and other references to future constitutional legislation[103] evidence the expectation that the pernicious practice of spreading constitutional-level provisions in a succession of separate laws would continue in the new Republic. During the admittedly exceptional period between 1989 and the end of 1992, the Federal Assembly adopted 43 constitutional acts—a "veritable Communist-like constitutional goulash."[104] Clearly this legislative vice reduces the transparency of the constitutional system as well as the weight of the Constitution itself.[105] Indications are that the Slovak Republic will not be immune to the same practice.[106]

Even those who criticize aspects of the Czech Constitution consider it as a good "point of departure" for the development of a tradition of modern democracy.[107] But Professor Jičínský, ever the censorious Cato, rejected the hasty process, dominated by "a conservative ideology," and even questioned the very legitimacy of the National Council elected under the Federation to adopt a constitution for the independent state.[108] And the chair of the small Moravian National Party complained that the Constitution "degraded Moravia to the level of a mere region; . . . the nascent state creates a source of instability and discontent."[109]

vii. The Lion and the Lamb: A Mismatch Made in Heaven?
The constitution making provided the cauldron within which the relationship between the prime minister and the future head of state began to take shape. Klaus never belonged to Havel's cotery of friends, and there are reports that, already during the days of the revolution, Havel sought to keep Klaus from crucial political posts. Moreover, some tension was inevitable between the two

---

102. Art. 2(2). No such constitutional law has been adopted, and "its adoption in the near future is improbable." Jiří Grospič, *supra,* note 35, 225.

103. *See* art. 9(1): "The Constitution may be supplemented . . . by constitutional laws only"; and art. 100(3).

104. Prof. Pavel Peška, criticizing the practice, in LN, Mar. 18, 1993, p. 9; Martin Daneš in LN, Sept. 2, 1994, p. 8.

105. Actually, in September 1993 the government rejected a proposal by a group of deputies purporting to introduce a referendum or, as Klaus put it, "to superimpose the referendum over everything else, to introduce a . . . direct democracy." This was an attempt, he said, at a significant amendment of the Constitution, not a supplement to it." LN, Sept. 30, 1993, p. 1.

106. *See,* for example, art. 102(1) of the Slovak Constitution.

107. Pavel Peška, in LN, *supra,* note 104; V. Pavlíček, *supra,* note 37, 354, praising particularly the contribution of the Constitutional Committee of the Czech Parliament.

108. Filip Hanzlík, "Vědecká konference o české ústavě [Scientific Conference on the Czech Constitution]," 6/1993 PRÁVNÍK, 535, 537.

109. I. Dřímal in RP, Dec. 19, 1992, p. 3.

popular political figures slated to perform two distinct, if not adversary, constitutional roles.

After his resignation in July 1992, citizen Havel withdrew to his country "hut" for "summer meditation." In early fall, however, he returned to Prague, and to general surprise he hurled himself into the churning political waters with what a sympathetic commentator described as "convulsive activity" of meetings and informal and formal media happenings.[110] Although he spoke up on federal issues, his principal focus was the debate on the Czech Constitution, which he sought assiduously to influence. Even before he announced his widely expected candidacy for the presidency, he made it clear that his interest in that office was conditioned upon the status accorded to it in the Constitution. He had in mind, no doubt, that the first Czechoslovak president, T.G. Masaryk, rejected a draft of the 1920 Constitution that would have made the president a ceremonial figure only. Accordingly, Havel spoke up for direct election of the president and on other issues I mentioned earlier, which brought him into direct conflict with Klaus and his CDP. At one point, Havel's harmless aside about Klaus's CDP elicited an irate public rebuff by Klaus. The press eagerly focused on the exchange, but the misunderstanding was quickly clarified during a widely popular television program.[111] On his part, Havel took every care, when disagreeing with the coalition or with Klaus's own public views, to articulate his dissent in nonadversarial terms, to pose the issue, explore the options, and then, almost tentatively, adumbrate his preferred solution. Although he met repeatedly with almost the entire gamut of the coalition and opposition parties, he saw Klaus in private sessions as well.

On a number of important constitutional issues, as we have seen, Havel's views were ultimately disregarded. Where the coalition modified its position in the direction of Havel's ideas, it was difficult to gauge whether it had done so in response to Havel's views or in order to gain the necessary opposition votes. Naturally, Havel's frantic exploits caused a flurry of speculation. Having tasted and enjoyed power, was he now motivated primarily by a quest for returning to "the Castle?" Would the famed playwright become a puppet in "director" Klaus's hands? Had he finally learned that politics is more than public statements and that he must build a solid bases with the political parties of the day

---

110. LN, Nov. 5, 1992, p. 1.

111. In the course of the telecast, when a reporter suggested that the prime minister disagreed with Havel, Klaus declared with an unaccustomed humility: "That I would not allow myself to do, that is not possible." RP, Nov. 2, 1992, p. 1. This dénouement was the result of an understanding the two men reached three days earlier in Havel's apartment "[t]o release as much as possible common signals to the public" in order to surpass particular interests and seek common areas. RP *ibid;* PRAVDA, Nov. 7, 1992, p. 3. A rumor initiated in a Czech periodical and spread on the Czech television about Klaus abandoning Havel's candidacy outraged Klaus and eventually led to a shakeup at the TV administration. RP, Nov. 5, 1992, p. 1.

and in the institutions? In responding with sympathy to a number of demands of the opposition, did he seek to reduce his dependence on Klaus's favor?

The personalities, talents, and ways of thinking, as well as the priorities of values, of the two men differ: "I would not describe our relationship as mutual dependence," Havel told the reporters. It is rather a question of a will to cooperate. "We both are different, and perhaps for that very reason we should supplement each other"; he realized that his candidacy depended substantially on Klaus as the leader of the victorious party, but "assuredly my destiny as such is not dependent on them. . . . We are both adults, we respect each other's views, and I believe we are capable of understanding each other."[112]

The two men have established a delicate but apparently stable working relationship. The prime minister, because of both his constitutional position and his assertive ways, has been the undisputed leading force. By mid-1995, the president invoked his prerogative with respect to the Parliament by vetoing several bills. Unlike the German federal president, who keeps aloof from daily squabbles, he has commented with abandon on any issue before the public, regardless of its importance, which, some believe has trivialized the high office;[113] he has not hesitated to criticize the government at the risk of exacerbating divisions within the coalition. This evidently has posed a challenge to the prime minister's self-restraint. Yet the people at large applaud, and Havel remains the most popular public figure in the Czech Republic. In 1994, he was deluged by 27,000 petitions and complaints.[114]

A Comparative Parenthesis

The American historian Edmund S. Morgan observed that a distinguishing mark of American politics has been the absence of irreconcilable differences between the two parties that successively dominate the federal government: "Each party rests on a coalition of interests so diverse and inclusive as to prevent the formulation of any program that the other party will find intolerable." The obvious exception was the one issue "that eventually erupted into civil war." But American politics did not begin with the placid interplay of the two parties. The public debate preceding the adoption of the Constitution in 1789 had been "extraordinarily rational," but the majority favoring it had been narrow in most component states. Consequently, hardly anyone, Morgan continues, expected it to last for long. Although those in charge of the new federal government were concerned about the fragility of the Constitution, their fears

---

112. LN, Oct. 20, 1992, p. 8.
113. For example, he castigated the bureaucrats for overcharging an American film crew of Tom Cruise for a day's rent of a palace in Prague. MfD, May 3, 1995, p. 3.
114. MfD, May 6, 1995, p. 2; LN, July 26, 1996, p. 2.

proved groundless and subsequent criticism was aimed not at the Constitution but at the policies and politicians in the federal government.[115]

It is fair to say that the debates on the Czech and Slovak Constitutions were also rational, despite complaints directed particularly at the haste and time constraint. But, unlike the American basic document, both the Czech and Slovak Constitutions were adopted by overwhelming majorities. This suggests that a broad consensus at least on fundamental issues is possible within the two societies, which have been in the process of an unprecedented transformation. In Slovakia, the vehement dissent of the Hungarian minority of course is a reason for concern. As in the young American Republic, public criticism after the adoption of the two new Constitutions has been muted, with the political personalities and politics of the day bearing the brunt of disapproval.

---

115. Edmund S. Morgan, "Pioneers of Paranoia," N.Y. REV. OF BOOKS, Oct. 6, 1994, 11.

Epilogue

XV

An Overview: Some Answers and Some Reflections at the End of the Day

1. Sources of Ethnic Conflict and Causes of Separation

In the opening pages of this book, I quoted Donald L. Horowitz's question about the source of ethnic conflicts: is it "cultural difference" or "ignorance or realistic divergence of interests?" I would conclude from the Czech and Slovak story that both cultural differences and ignorance are indeed the core of the conflict and the cause of the separation—along with significant subsidiary factors closely connected with, if not actually derived from, the cultural differences. I shall return to the divergence of interests promptly.

a. The Primary Cause

In the second chapter of this book I dealt with the relationship between the Czechs and Slovaks within the framework of three broad categories of environmental, historical, and social conditions. These conditions, I have suggested, formed the underpinning of the interests, real or perceived, of the two components of the Federation in their relationship with each other as well as with the federal state. The relative harmony or disharmony of these interests determined the position of the federal state on an imaginary continuum between an ideal symmetrical model and "a complete conflict potential" of the asymmetric model. My analysis disclosed significant similarities between the Czechs and the Slovaks, such as an almost identical language and similar living standards, but important differences as well, first and foremost a diverse history that exposed them to profoundly divergent influences. Both peoples experienced the evolution of the nationalist idea from the revival of folklore and the local language to the formulation of nationalist ideologies and a political movement.[1] In this development, however, due to the oppressive Hungarian regime, the Slovaks remained some half a century behind the Czechs, and this caused a

---

1. However, the eighteenth-century Czech "*risorgimento*" contained a political element from the onset due to the memories of the long history of the Czech Kingdom and the role of the Czech nobility. Conversation with Professor P. Piťha.

distorted, almost colonial, type of relationship with the Czechs at the time of the formation of the first Czechoslovak Republic in 1918. The perception of the Czech dominance reinforced by the two-to-one Czech population majority, continued in some sectors of the Slovak society during subsequent decades, culminating in the fatal events of 1939 when German power destroyed the Republic and sponsored a separate Slovak state, and again after 1948 when a reunited Czechoslovakia became a part of the Soviet empire. The situation prevailing after the collapse of the Communist regime has been vividly described by a noted Slovak writer:

> A Czech with an average education knows nothing about Slovakia. He does not read Slovak literature, nor does he get around to Slovak papers. . . . Vacation outings to Slovakia are equally fruitless as regards getting to know the nation. . . . A Czech has the feeling of civilizational superiority and is not aware of the basic things that burden our life. The Slovak nation has an entirely different mentality . . . a different historical experience, it finds itself in an entirely different economic, political, and cultural situation. As long as the Czech citizen fails to take these matters into account, he will live together with an unknown nation without understanding its complexes. The Slovaks are a minority nation in the Republic, and are hypersensitive to Czech ignorance and nationalism. That is not the only one, but one of the principal reasons of the contemporary crisis.[2]

This statement illuminates the factors of ignorance, ressentiment, and "contempt" leading to the divergence of interests, even though in my judgment it overstates the weight of the actual differences in the conditions prevailing in 1989. However, the statement correctly recognizes the existence of other, albeit unspecified, factors, which I shall identify in the following section. I should signal that some of these factors, although often intertwined with the past, emerged only after the collapse of the Communist regime.

b. Subsidiary Factors

i. Structure and "Heroes"
Two structural barriers are readily identified as having contributed to the breakup. One was the inherent fault of a Federation composed of only two component units in which demands for parity ran sharply counter to the significant disparity in the size of their populations. The other was the Communist Constitution, which, although amended, remained in force and proved largely dysfunctional in the new setting.

---

2. Ladislav Mňačko in LN, June 27, 1992, pp. 1, 8.

Related but distinct were several subjective factors: the insistence on "continuity" and "constitutionality" of the process of change, the lack of understanding of federalism and the absence of the minimal trust required for its working, the lack of political experience of the actors, and the fatigue from the exhausting constitutional negotiations.[3]

However, perhaps the most important subsidiary factor was the massive structural change in the political system that began shortly after the first free elections in 1990 and was completed by the 1992 elections. The post-1989 federal political structure disintegrated and new power bases emerged in the two Republics with radically different constellations of political forces and leaders. Some of the political elites in both Republics, but notably in Slovakia, stirred and exploited nationalist feelings with a significant impact on the constitutional discourse. This development also had its roots in the "primary cause," the cultural differences.

What of the fascinating dichotomy between "the structure" and the individual actors and their acts of will? In Friedrich Nietzsche's world of disconnected individuals, it is the heroes or villains, rather than the structure, that determine the outcome.[4] Lev Tolstoy, on the other hand, passionately rejected "the heroic theory of history" in favor of "inexorable historic determinism."[5] Taking a different view on "what is meant by acts of will and their freedom," a gestalt psychologist wrote:

> In a functioning structure, acts of will are something better than arbitrary intrusions and coercions. They are vectors deriving by necessity from unresolved tensions that interfere with the equilibrium of the whole. These tensions call for appeasing of unsatisfied needs. As such they [the acts of will] are lawfully determined rather than "free" in the popular sense of arising as gratuitous acts from nowhere.[6]

The Czech-Slovak case confirms that, although the structure does not dictate outcome, individual actors, far from being freewheeling and unconstrained, act

---

3. Aleš Gerloch, "Československá federace: uzavřená minulost? [Czechoslovak Federation: Closed Past?]," in Vojtěch Šimíček (ed.), Česko-slovenské vztahy a střední Evropa [Czecho-Slovak Relations and Central Europe] 71, 72 (Mezinár. politol. ústav právnické faculty Masarykovy university v Brně, Czech Rep., 1994); Aleš Gerloch, "Teorie federalismu a rozdělení Československa [Theory of Federalism and Division of Czechoslovakia]," 1995 POLITOLOGICKÁ REVUE 13 (June 1995).

4. Friedrich Nietzsche, Der Wille zur Macht, sec. 70 at 57, sec. 770 at 512–13 and *passim* (Alfred Kröner Verlag, Leipzig, 1930).

5. Isaiah Berlin, Russian Thinkers 41, 43 (Penguin Books, New York, 1979).

6. Rudolf Arnheim, "The Split and the Structure," 1992 MICHIGAN QUARTERLY REVIEW 195, 204. See, however, Gertrude Himmelfarb, On Looking into the Abyss: Untimely Thoughts on Culture and Society (A.A. Knopf, New York, 1994).

within the confines of the structure. They have real choices, real responsibilities. They may act in arbitrary, artless, or self-serving ways involving
important political stakes, but they cannot ignore the historical-social realities
any more than the constitutional framework. Constitutional issues, infused
with politics of power and other interests, are significant. Even in Bosnia,
where nationalist leadership has loomed so prominently, "to ascribe the
courses of the war to unscrupulous leaders . . . is to ignore the historical and
cultural sources of hatred."[7]

In a revolutionary period, individual personalities play a more significant
role than in subsequent phases when conditions tend to stabilize and the hands
of individuals become progressively tied by the structure.[8] If the first leaders in
power after 1989 may have been in the position to restructure the state with a
lasting effect, that opportunity evaporated quickly with the mutation of political forces and the rise of the institutions. In the last phase, two individuals, the
Czech Republic Prime Minister, *homo economicus* (Adam Smith), and his
Slovak counterpart, *homo sociologicus* (Emile Durkheim), articulating the new
"vectors," sealed the breakup. "Of these, the former is supposed to be guided
by instrumental rationality, while the behavior of the latter is dictated by social
norms."[9]

I shall return to this theme in the concluding analysis of the constitutional
negotiations.

ii. The Economic Component
In my judgment, economics and the divergence of economic interests, while
present in the Czech and Slovak conflict—as they are in most ethnic clashes—
did not play more than a secondary role in the breakup. Four sets of factors
might be distinguished: first, the differences in the economic structures of the
two Republics as they still existed in 1989; second, the divergent impact of
post-1989 federal economic policies on the two economies; third, the results of
the diverging economic policies in the two Republics, particularly after the
1992 elections; and last, but not least, the diverse perceptions and expectations
of the economic impact of the dissolution of the state.

The Slovak economy underwent a radical modernization over the last
decades under the Communist regime with living standards rising due to substantial (and often unwise) investments. According to the Czech-American
economist, Professor Jan Švejnar, the basic macroeconomic data were quite
similar in both Republics in 1989. With one important exception—the unem-

---

7. Conversation with Ján Budaj.
8. Misha Glenny, "Why the Balkans Are So Violent," N.Y. REV. OF BOOKS, Sept. 19, 1996,
pp. 35, 39.
9. Jon Elster, The Cement of Society: A Study of Social Order 128 (Cambridge U. Press,
Cambridge, New York, Port Chester, Melbourne, Sydney, 1989).

ployment rate three times higher in Slovakia than in the Czech lands—these data have continued generally on a parallel course after 1989 and, surprisingly, also in the years following the breakup.[10] I am in no position to evaluate the economy-based reasons for the striking divergence in the unemployment figures. However, the most common explanation points to the structure of the Slovak economy and particularly to the fact that a major part of the arms industry and large Soviet style establishments were located in Slovakia, and they suffered disproportionately after 1989 from the loss of the eastern markets and the critical early decision of the federal government to terminate weapons production. These enterprises required large funds for conversion and were particularly difficult to restructure, with the result that the federal radical transformation policies had more severe social consequences in Slovakia particularly for the employment. This objective fact—the so-called Slovak "economic specificity"—had an understandable impact on Slovak voters but it also lent itself readily to nationalist campaign exploitation with Prague being represented as the convenient enemy. In the same vein the Slovaks blamed centralist Prague—perhaps with some justification—for influencing the flow of foreign investment to the Czech part of the federation, to the prejudice of Slovakia.

The split of the common state, although enabling the Slovaks to frame their own economic policies, meant among other things the end of regular transfers of substantial resources from the Czech side to Slovakia. Owing to the intentional camouflage in the budget, it was virtually impossible to determine the size of these annual transfers, estimated by the Czechs at more than $800 million, an amount vigorously challenged by the Slovaks. This factor and the general economic cost-benefit issue of the split were barely explored in the media and in the campaign oratory. Citizens of both parts of the country agreed that separation would have negative economic consequences.[11] It is undisputed that the principal actors decided on the dissolution convinced that both economies would suffer, although for different reasons and to a different degree, with Slovakia carrying the heavier burden in the short run at any rate.[12] This expectation was confirmed by a drop of about one-third in the volume of trade between the newly independent states immediately following the split. However, the collapse of the Slovak economy predicted by some in the course

---

10. Jan Švejnar, "Economic Transformation in Central and Eastern Europe: The Task Still Ahead," in Economic Transformation—The Task Still Ahead—A Symposium, Jan Švejnar, Oleh Havrylyshyn, Sergei K. Dubinin 4–8 (Per Jacobsson Foundation, Washington, D.C., 1995). See also *supra*, chap. V, text at notes 59, 60.

11. Public opinion survey of mid-1992 in Sharon L. Wolchik, "The Politics of Transition and the Break-Up of Czechoslovakia," in Jiří Musil (ed.), The End of Czechoslovakia 235–36 (Central European U. Press, Budapest, London, New York, 1995).

12. Conversation with Docent Robert Holman, adviser to Czech Republic Prime Minister Klaus.

of the constitutional negotiations did not materialize, and, two years after the dissolution, the gross national product in both Republics grew at the healthy rate of about 4 percent.

One would assume that the economic benefits from a larger state would have worked in favor of the continuation of a common state. As Ellen Comisso has pointed out, however, this condition is effective only when there is a commercial group able to capitalize on the advantages of a larger market and press for its preservation. No such group existed in the Czecho-Slovak state at the time of the dissolution decision. Moreover, the increasingly liberalized international economy has reduced the allure of the larger domestic market,[13] and there was also "the model" of a small successful economy (Austria and Switzerland). Finally, the issue was defused in part by the network of treaties between the two Republics designed to reduce, as much as possible, the negative economic impact of the separation, including a customs union, which has endured despite some frictions, and a monetary union, which collapsed after some six weeks.[14]

On the Czech side, economic considerations favoring a larger market obviously did not prevail over Prime Minister Klaus's determination to shield his concept of economic transformation from possible impairment by the Slovak divergent policies even at the price of a separation. Economists dominated the influential Civic Democratic Party[15] if not the Czech government. Like the Italian supporters of the Northern League, tired of carrying the poorer south, some Czechs welcomed the end of "subsidizing" their neighbors. This view reduced the perceived need for the common state, and, although it may not have influenced noticeably the final decision, it may have accounted in part for the passive attitude toward the impending split on the part of the Czech population at large.

The Slovak valuation of economic interests confirms—to paraphrase Adam Smith, whom I quoted earlier—that it is status in society that "is the end of half of the labors of human life" and that it prevails over economics. This conclusion applies as well to another possible economy-based "rival" of nationalism—class interest.[16] The Czech opposition on the left, presumably a

---

13. Ellen Comisso, "Federalism and Nationalism in Post-Socialist Eastern Europe," unpublished paper for a symposium on "Federalism for the New Europe," Benjamin Cardozo School of Law, New York, Sept. 10–12, 1992.

14. The monetary union was replaced by a payments treaty (text in 64/1993 Sb. [Czech], providing a clearing system based on the European Currency Unit, which, however, was scheduled to end (as a result of the Czech notification) in October 1995.

15. Conversation with Jiří Weigel, adviser to the Czech Republic prime minister.

16. "To be sure, there are class realities, but ethnic realities are there as well. Increasingly they are the *dominant* realities." Daniel P. Moynihan, "Elitland" 4 PSYCHOLOGY TODAY 70 (no. 4, 1970).

primary advocate of such interest, toned down the unpopular class argument reminiscent of the old regime, even when it criticized the adverse social impact of the government reform, and ultimately, albeit reluctantly, it supported the termination of the common state. Nor was class rhetoric prominent in the public discourse in Slovakia, where populist nationalism ruled supreme, feebly challenged, and at times even seconded, by the reorganized, former Communist left.[17]

iii. The Media
In a thoughtful piece on "Nationalism and the Marketplace of Ideas," two American scholars suggest that during incipient democratization, when civil society is reviving but democratic institutions are not fully entrenched, the suddenly emerged openness of public debate often fosters nationalist myth-making and ethnic conflict because opportunistic governmental and non-governmental elites exploit partial monopolies of supply, segmented demand, and the weakness of regulatory institutions. Moreover, journalists, public intellectuals, and public-interest watchdogs tend to perform poorly in the initial stages of the expansion of press freedom.[18]

The well-known Czech writer Jan Urban confirmed this perception. Speaking to a Slovak audience in 1993, he declared that if the journalists had acted as independent professionals the Czech-Slovak split would not have occurred: they copied the politicians, adding selected pieces of history to the statements of the ministers; they failed to distinguish facts from opinions and were unable to look beyond the confines of a single story. Urban's conclusion overstates the case, but with the memories of the First Republic freedoms faded, the concept of an independent, free press was in fact a novelty for which the journalists were not trained, and the general quality of reporting was low. The media discourse was uninformative and tended to magnify and sharpen the differences of views rather than explain them in a calm way. Above all, there was little effort to explore objectively the prospective consequences of the separation. The press was almost invariably in the service of a certain political orientation, did not seek to form independent public opinion, and was replete with inciting speculations of "who subsidizes whom." It helped to radicalize public opinion, which, even in Slovakia, was less nationalist than that of some of the elites.[19]

---

17. Some suspected the left of actually favoring the split because of the turn to the right in the Czech lands perceived as a threat to the left's influence in a common state and in Slovakia as well.

18. Jack Snyder and Karen Ballentine, "Nationalism and the Marketplace of Ideas," 21 *International Security* 5, 24, and *passim* (no. 2, 1996).

19. *See generally* Jiří Pehe, "Czechoslovakia," RFE/RL Res. Rep. Oct. 2, 1992, 34, 37.

iv. External Influence

A distinction must be made between the "intervention" of outside forces into the internal processes on one hand and on the other hand the impact of external events on the thinking and actions of the principal internal actors.

In the past, the fate of the Czechs and Slovaks was almost invariably determined by foreign powers. In fact, extraneous forces triggered even the 1989 revolution. However, the decision for the dissolution of the Federation was made without any intrusive intervention, in fact against friendly advice from other states, including the United States and members and institutions of the European Union, all of which uniformly favored the continuation of the common state.[20] Their bottom line interest was the preservation of peace and stability in an area of some geopolitical importance, and that concern appeared satisfied in the short run by the peaceful character of the separation. As for foreign private intervention, there is evidence that associations of Slovak emigrés, particularly in Canada, West Germany, and Australia, supported the militant nationalist circles in Slovakia.[21]

If there was no direct intervention from the outside world, world events had a noticeable influence on the thinking of the elites. With the collapse of Soviet dominion, "the eggs of Versailles and Brest Litowsk" resumed "hatching."[22] In world of drastic change and uncertainty, with the Soviet-erected structures (the Warsaw Pact, COMECON) in liquidation, the prospect of joining the European Union and NATO was a lodestar of federal foreign policy supported by all mainstream movements and parties.[23] It was immensely important for the government, concerned about security, and for the people as a hopeful goal during the early travails of the transformation. Advanced democracies offered compelling political-economic alternatives to the Communist system. In Slovakia, the quick, in effect unconditional, recognition of the new, post-Communist states by the international community contradicted any assumption that world opinion was opposed to fragmentation.[24] If Croatia, Slovenia, and Moldova, why not Slovakia with its memory of "independent" statehood in 1939–45? The Slovak proposal for a "treaty" to replace a federal constitution was inspired by the compact for the establishment of the Com-

20. Jacques Rupnik, "The International Context," in Jiří Musil (ed.), The End of Czechoslovakia, *supra,* note 9, 276.

21. Vladimír V. Kusín, "Czechs and Slovaks: The Road to the Current Debate," RFE/RL RES. REP., Oct. 5, 1990, 4, 5.

22. E.J. Hobsbawm, Nations and Nationalism since 1780: Programme, Myth, Reality 164 (2d ed., Cambridge U. Press, Cambridge, New York, Melbourne, 1992).

23. Regina Cowen Karp, Central and Eastern Europe: The Challenge of Transition 7 (SIPRI, Oxford U. Press, New York, 1993).

24. Germany led the move for recognition. See "Recognition of the Yugoslav Successor States," position paper of the German Foreign Ministry, Bonn, March 10, 1993, in Statements and Speeches, German Information Center, vol. 16, no. 10.

monwealth of Independent States of the former Soviet Union. A "union" between the two independent Republics, modeled after the Maastricht Treaty for a European Union, was the goal advanced ultimately by the Slovaks with the support of the Czech "moderates" and the left. Again, the idea of a "Europe of regions," which reemerged in the Western discourse over the Maastricht Treaty, was embraced by the Slovak Christian Democrats in support of an independent membership of the two Republics in the European integration structures.

2. On Eliminating Differences: A Taxonomy Applied

a. Neither Genocide nor Mass Population Transfer

One useful study offers a taxonomy of four methods for eliminating ethnic differences and resolving ethnic conflicts.[25] The first two, genocide and forced mass population transfers, did not come under consideration in the Czech-Slovak conflict. Both, I may say parenthetically, have been tolerated by the international community in the Serb-Croatian-Bosnian conflict, with some 3.5 to 5 million displaced since 1991.[26] Although some 300,000 Slovaks reside in the Czech Republic and a few thousand Czechs live in Slovakia, the only problem in this respect related to the Czech citizenship legislation as applied to Slovak residents. The fact that no measurable displacement of population was anticipated reduced the cost of the separation significantly. Yet a sort of "ethnic cleansing" occurred in Czecho-Slovakia, first by the German wartime deportation of the Jews and then, after 1945, by the expulsion of some 3 million Sudeten Germans and some thousands of Hungarians. For the Czechs, at any rate, the split completed the process by the separation not only from the Slovaks but also from the Hungarian minority of some 600,000 in Slovakia.[27] The Czechs, it was said, are now "finally alone."

---

25. John McGary and Brendan O'Leary (eds.), The Politics of Ethnic Conflict Regulation: Case Studies of Protracted Ethnic Conflict 8–22 (Routledge, London, New York, 1993).

26. THE ECONOMIST, Aug. 19, 1995, p. 42.

27. Ondřej Neuman in LN, Aug. 2, 1996, p. 3. Apart from the Slovaks residing in the Czech Republic, only a few thousand Germans, Poles, Ukrainians, and Vietnamese remain, along with several hundred thousand gypsies (Roma), most of whom, however, do not claim Roma nationality. A prominent Czech Social Democrat speaks of "a principle of exclusion" and asks whom the new state will exclude in the next crisis ("Will [the Czechs] not rather get rid of the burdensome state?"). Miloš Zeman in RP, Oct. 17, 1992, p. 4. For a criticism of the Czech Government minority policy, see Ján Mlynárik, LN, Aug. 6, 1996, p. 11. See also Petr Pithart, "Paradoxy rozchodu: filosofická a právní hlediska a evropské paralely [Paradoxes of the Parting: Philosophic and Legal Views and European Parallels]," in Rüdiger, Kipke, Karel Vodička (eds.), Rozloučení's Československem [Parting with Czechoslovakia] 215, 220 (Český spisovatel, a.s. Praha, 1993).

b. Integration/Assimilation/Multicultural Policy?

The question is whether integration and/or assimilation or multicultural policies might have succeeded in bridging the Czech-Slovak differences if given adequate time. T.G. Masaryk, president of the first Republic, said in the late 1920s:

> I think we need some twenty, thirty more years for safeguarding the Republic. Afterwards, I am not afraid for it any more. . . . At that time a new generation will be there, born in freedom. Surely, that generation won't let anyone take the freedom away.[28]

E.H. Carr, on the other hand, with the easy benefit of hindsight, disputed the viability of the First Republic from its very birth.[29] Yet, despite the controversial minority policy of the Czech-Slovak state and the Czech indifference toward Slovakia, economic, cultural, and professional interactions between the two people intensified over the years, and their mutual relations, although conflicting in some respects, were certainly closer than with any other country or community.[30] In that sense, an assimilation process was under way, but it was drastically shaken by the split even though a deeply divisive issue was eliminated by it. Another common state is nowhere on the horizon, but for the optimists, the prospective membership in the European Union is likely to advance "integration," albeit within a regional regime.[31]

c. Self-Determination/Separation

i. The Successor States in International Law

With the extinction of the Federation by a federal constitutional law, the two component Republics declared themselves independent successor states and the international community recognized them as such.[32] Except for some tacti-

---

28. Karel Čapek, Čtení o TGM [Reading about TGM] 18 (Melantrich, Praha, 1969).

29. See *supra*, "A Framework," 2.

30. Zdeněk Strmiska, "Quelques remarques sur 'Le divorce tchéco-slovaque,'" 26 REV. D'ÉTUDES COMPARATIVES EST OUEST 183, 193 (no. 2, 1995).

31. According to a public opinion poll taken in the Czech Republic three years after the breakup, more than half of the Czechs consider the relations between the Czechs and Slovaks as good; 43 percent would welcome more intensive relations, and 50 percent believe that cooperation with Slovakia should be parallel to that with other states. LN, Feb. 28, 1996, p. 3.

32. McGary and O'Leary speak of "Partition and/or secession (self-determination)" (*supra*, note 22, 11). There are no generally accepted categories: the principal distinction is between cases in which the original state continues to exist within its diminished territory after the "separa-

cal maneuvers, neither side made a serious effort to force the other into a position of unilateral secession. The specific aspects of the solution relevant to the uncertain international law of succession of states may be summarized in a greatly simplified manner as follows:

> The two Republics met the prerequisites of statehood, had to receive recognition by other states, and had to be admitted as new members to international organizations.[33]
>
> They agreed to continue to observe their obligations toward other states under the bilateral and multilateral treaties concluded by the predecessor Federative Republic and to notify the respective parties and depositories.[34]

---

tion" and those instances where it ceases to exist. Based on a study by the U.S. Department of State, Williams lists the following cases of "separation": Greater Colombia (1829–31), Union of Norway and Sweden (1905), Austro-Hungarian Empire (1918), United Arab Republic (1961), Union of Iceland and Denmark (1944), and Federation of Mali (1961). Paul R. Williams, "The Treaty Obligations of the Successor States of the Former Soviet Union, Yugoslavia, and Czechoslovakia: Do They Continue in Force?" 23 DENVER JOURNAL OF INTERNATIONAL LAW AND POLITICS 1, 13–16 (1994); Michael P. Scharf, "Musical Chairs: The Dissolution of States and Membership in the United Nations," 28 CORNELL J'L OF INTERNATIONAL LAW 29, 66 (1995); Mahulena Hošková, "Die Selbstauflösung der ČFSR—Ausgewählte rechtliche Aspekte," 53/3 ZAöRV 688, 715–31 (1993); Joelle de Morzellec, "Nástupnictví států: Příklad rozdělení České a Slovenské Federativní Republiky [Succession of States: The Example of Division of the Czech and Slovak Federative Republic]," 9/93 PRÁVNÍK 777 (1993); Vladimír Balaš, "Některé mezinárodní aspekty dělení státu [Some International Aspects of the Division of States]," 11/92 PRÁVNÍK 996 (1992).

33. The Czech and Slovak Federative Republic belonged to some 50 international organizations.

34. Some 2,000 bilateral and 800 multilateral treaties concluded by the Federal Republic were involved. See also Const. Law 4/1993 Sb. of the Czech National Council, adopted on Dec. 15, 1992, on measures connected with the extinction of the Czech and Slovak Federative Republic, arts. 4 and 5. Treaties not relating to the territory of the Czech Republic are excluded from these obligations. According to a Czech expert, rights and obligations deriving from international customary law are included; principles of the Vienna Convention on state succession in respect of treaties "received a strong endorsement." Václav Mikulka, State Succession in Respect of Treaties—Czech Republic (National Report) in my file. *See also*, for example, exchange of notes with the German Federal Republic on continuing observation of treaties "until both sides agree otherwise," BUNDESGESETZBLATT 1993, part II, p. 762.

See art. 153 of the new Constitution of the Slovak Republic. Dean Kenneth J. Vandevelde, who advised the Slovakian Ministry of Foreign Affairs on an assignment by the American Bar Association's Central and East European Law Initiative, reported in June 1994 that Slovakia was a party to about 3,300 treaties. Since a case by case consideration of each treaty would take some years, Slovakia declared that it will honor its obligations under all treaties. Having established this presumption, the Ministry of Foreign Affairs would then determine the advisability of pursuing modification or termination of particular treaties. A major problem would relate to the many

Each Republic alone determined who were its citizens, but a simplified
procedure for changing citizenship was made available to citizens of
one Republic living in the other. In contrast to the Czech Republic,
Slovakia recognizes dual citizenship.

Federal immovable property was divided on the territorial principle, the
movable on the two-to-one key, reflecting the size of the population,
with a number of special provisions and agreements.

Special agreements determined the disposition of archives, taking into
account their links to the institutions concerned and mutual access.[35]

The two Republics concluded with each other a dense network of treaties
designed to establish a regime exceeding the traditional links between
friendly states including a customs union.

The new relationship between the two Republics is a child of a compromise representing the remainder of the common interests as perceived by
the political powers of the day: the Slovak side seeking to salvage the debris of
their cherished dream of a "union" or "confederation," the Czech side interested in preserving the advantages of a common state, particularly a wider
trading area, without institutional restraints. A pragmatic approach of this sort,
eschewing "boilerplate normative responses" and tailor made for concrete
circumstances, may offer an opportunity for dealing with other ethnic conflicts
in which separation proves unavoidable.[36]

ii. On Self-Determination and Referendum
The ideological underpinning of the Slovak claim was the much discussed
notion of self-determination, which the International Court of Justice has reaffirmed lately as "one of the essential principles of contemporary international
law" with the important "*erga omnes*" (valid against everyone) character.[37]

---

reservations to multilateral treaties. "Interim Report on Technical Assistance to Slovakia," June
24, 1994.

"The Vienna Convention on Succession of States in Respect of Treaties" (UN Doc.
A/CONF/80/31 [1978]) is not in force.

35. *See,* for example, Treaty between the Government of the Czech Republic and the
Government of the Slovak Republic on the joint use of reserved information and archival materials
from the Ministries of Interior in the field of internal order and security. Vladimír Mikule et al.,
Mezinárodní smlouvy mezi Českou a Slovenskou republikou [International Treaties between the
Czech Republic and Slovak Republic] 317–21 (Codex Bohemia, Praha, 1995).

36. Gideon Gottlieb, Nation against State: A New Approach to Ethnic Conflicts and the
Decline of Sovereignty 122, also 3–5 and *passim* (Council on Foreign Relations Press, New York,
1993).

37. East Timor (Portugal v. Australia), Judgment 30 June 1995, I.C.J. Reports 1995, p.
13, par. 29.

Whatever may be the disputed dimension of the concept of "peoples" entitled to self-determination,[38] the qualification of the Slovak people on that score was not at issue.[39] Even the often controversial problem of territory was not in question, since, subject to only a minimal adjustment, the administrative frontier between the two Republics in the expired Federation was accepted as the new international frontier. Nor was there at the time a problem in regard to another prerequisite, the observance of basic human rights in the nascent Republics.[40] Finally, a free expression of "the peoples" concerned is generally envisaged for the application of self-determination, but in the Czech-Slovak case no popular referendum was held. However, the dissolution decision was blessed by the Federal Parliament on recommendations from both Republic legislatures, with broad acquiescence of the population at large. No authoritative international voice was raised to question the legitimacy of the process.

Referendum is not a necessary condition for an expression of the right of self-determination under either general international practice or UN principles. "The minimum requirement seems to be the existence of some kind of representative procedures," which in the Czecho-Slovak case was clearly met.[41]

On the domestic scene, calls for a referendum resonated throughout the constitutional negotiations; it was available under the prevailing Constitution and demanded by a major part of the political representation in both Republics.[42] Some writers thought that "this is one of the rare cases where a referendum might have made it possible for a country to stay together."[43] There was indeed a lively internal controversy over whether the two "peoples" desired to achieve their right of self-determination in the form of independent states rather than in some variant of a continuing common state. Some on the Czech left argue that had the referendum been allowed and had it come out

---

38. The UN Charter (art. 1) and the UN instruments on self-determination, including the Covenants on Human Rights, speak of the right of "peoples."

39. See *supra,* chap. II, 2.

40. Thomas M. Franck, "The Emerging Right to Democratic Governance," 86 AJIL 46 (1992). The Slovak Hungarian parties complained about the Slovak government minority policy during the proceeding for admission of Slovakia to the Council of Europe, but their complaint did not affect its outcome.

41. Markku Suksi, Bringing in the People: A Comparison of Constitutional Forms and Practices of the Referendum 247, 268–69 (Martinus Nijhoff Publishers, Dordrecht, Boston, London, 1993). *See generally* Robert J. Thompson, "Referendums and Ethnoterritorial Movements: The Policy Consequences and Political Ramifications," in Robert J. Thompson and Joseph R. Rudolph Jr. (eds.), Ethnoterritorial Politics, Policy, and the Western World 181 (Lynne Rienner Pub., Boulder and London, 1989).

42. See *supra,* chap. VII, 3 e; XI, 4; XIII, 4c.

43. Henry E. Brady and Cynthia S. Kaplan, "Eastern Europe and Former Soviet Union," in David Butler and Austin Ranney (eds.), Referendums around the World: The Growing Use of Direct Democracy 212 (AEI Press, Washington, D.C., 1994).

against the dissolution, the leadership—facing a complex and uncertain situation—could not have ignored popular opinion. However, the Federal Parliament failed to agree on questions to be submitted to the people. In fact, widespread dislike of the "Prague-centered" Federation in Slovakia and the lack of popular understanding and consensus in both Republics regarding the possible alternative forms of a common state would have made it difficult to compose meaningful questions for a referendum. In the end, Czech Prime Minister Klaus and his party opposed the referendum because it would delay the split and cause chaos in "the ungovernable state." The Slovak premier abandoned the idea in the face of this determined resistance, perhaps also bearing in mind the ambiguous state of Slovak public opinion with regard to a complete separation. There was indeed a possibility that the outcome of a popular vote would be inconclusive or even ignored by the elites. The final proposals for holding a referendum were rejected in the Federal Parliament.

In contrast to Czecho-Slovakia, which had no tradition of direct democracy, referendums proliferated during and after the collapse of communism in Central, Eastern, and Southern Europe: "All in all, referendums in this part of the world have been much better at ripping apart than tying together."[44] In the West, they sanctioned the split of the Sweden-Norway Union in 1905, but they did not prove helpful in Canada[45] and have posed serious problems on the way to European integration. A referendum may be a helpful device for advancing legitimacy but it is a risky tool for dealing with complex constitutional arrangements, particularly in times of transition and disorientation.

I cannot deal here with the current outpouring of learned literature seeking to define a rational basis for self-determination claims. Suffice it to say that the Slovak demand might be justified under the theories stressing the right to territory[46] under the "liberal theory of secession" (and its exceptions)[47] as well as pursuant to the doctrine postulating historical grievance, "discriminatory

---

44. Henry E. Brady and Cynthia S. Kaplan, *ibid.* at 215.

45. In the Swedish-Norwegian case, an overwhelming majority supported the dissolution of the union in a referendum, which was required by Sweden as a condition for the dissolution. The vote was 368, 208 in support of the dissolution, 184 against. Karen Larsen, A History of Norway 491 (Princeton U. Press, Princeton, 1948). In the October 30, 1995, referendum, the Quebecois rejected sovereignty by the slim margin of 50.6 to 49.4 percent. Fifteen years earlier the separatists lost 60 to 40 percent. N.Y. TIMES, Oct. 31, 1995, p. 1A. In early 1996, with the popular separatist Lucian Bouchard appointed provincial premier, the polls indicated that the support within Quebec for independence was even higher than in October 1995. N.Y. TIMES, Jan. 30, 1996, p. 4A. See also *supra,* chap. I, note 28, and *infra,* note 49.

46. Lea Brilmayer, "Secession and Self-Determination: A Territorial Interpretation," 16 YALE J. INT'L L. 177 (no. 1, Winter 1991).

47. Harry Beran, "A Liberal Theory of Secession," XXXII POLITICAL STUDIES 21–31 (1984).

distribution," or the need to preserve the distinctive conception of a community.[48]

All domino theories are inherently suspect, but there is, for the time being, no danger of a domino effect of new claims for self-determination within one or both Republics. A movement for autonomy among the 1.3 million who claim Moravian nationality in the Czech Republic has been muted since independence; however, the extent of the eventual claims of the large Hungarian minority in Slovakia is unpredictable. Although other separatist movements, as in Belgium, Quebec, and most recently northern Italy, look to the Czech dénouement as a model,[49] is difficult to say whether a "new virus" of peaceful separation is on the loose.

In one view, "excessive self-determination" works against democratization in nondemocratic countries and threatens democracy in countries that have already attained it.[50] Others offer "overwhelming" evidence that "democracy almost never works in societies that are highly divided along linguistic and

---

48. Allen Buchanan, "Toward a Theory of Secession," 101 ETHICS 322, 323 (January 1991); Allen Buchanan, Secession: The Morality of Political Divorce from Fort Sumter to Lithuania and Quebec (Westview Press, Boulder, San Francisco, Oxford, 1991). *See generally* Holly A. Osterland, "National Self-Determination and Secession: The Slovak Model," 25 CASE WESTERN RESERVE JOURNAL OF INTERNATIONAL LAW 655 (no. 3, Summer 1993).

49. Lionel Vandenbergh, head of the Flemish separatist movement: "Walloon friends, we have lived for 160 years together and we have not been happy. Let's now get a divorce before a notary, as did the Czechs and Slovaks." "Obava z čs. syndromu [Fear of the Czs. Syndrome]," HN, Oct. 20, 1992, p. 30. Former Czech Prime Minister Pithart "now finds himself being invited to Belgium and Quebec, to tell them how you make a velvet divorce." Timothy Garton Ash, "Journey to the Post-Communist East," N.Y. REVIEW OF BOOKS, June 23, 1994, 13, 17. The leader of the Italian Northern League, Umberto Bossi, suggested "a Czecho-Slovak solution" and the league organized a "Parliament of the North" and a "shadow government" for "Padania." N.Y. TIMES, May 12, 1996, p. 8; May 13, 1996, p. A5. In Quebec, the Prime Minister with an unblemished pro-independence record took the helm of the Provincial government after the referendum vote rejecting session by the slimmest of margins. His strategy has been to "say as little [about the secession] as his radical supporters will allow" while seeking federal help for a recovery of the ailing Quebec Province economy, hoping for a referendum victory after 1999. The Economist, June 15, 1996, p. 43. With one important exception, his design is similar to Ján Čarnogurský's plan for Slovakia to enjoy the advantages of a federation with the Czechs until both Republics join the European Union as independent states. The important difference was that Čarnogurský proclaimed his goal frankly and openly from the outset. When the Slovak Prime Minister Mečiar was asked in Strasbourg by Luciano Lorenzi of the Italian Lega Nord whether he had any suggestions regarding the independence of "Padania," he responded with unaccustomed self-restraint: "We have no advice to offer you," he said, but proceeded to enumerate the many difficulties requiring solution in cases of separation. In the case of Slovakia, he added, the benefits outweighed the disadvantages: two states that cooperate are better than a state in a disequilibrium. EUROPE, no. 6762 (n.s.), July 3, 1996, p. 4.

50. Amitai Etzioni, "The Evils of Self-Determination," 1992–93 FOREIGN POLICY 21.

cultural lines."⁵¹ Current developments do not sustain any concern for the free institutions in the Czech Republic, but in the short run, at any rate, democracy in independent Slovakia appears less firm than within the late federal system.⁵²

As I noted earlier, outside powers played no appreciable role in the Czecho-Slovak solution, nor did the United Nations provide "midwife" ministration as it did in the post–World War II decolonization wave of self-determination claims. In the absence of pervasive national interests of other states (oil in "Desert Storm") or international community concerns (breach of peace, humanitarian aid, protection of human rights or democracy), this was clearly not a case for outside "conflict management."

Although the Slovaks sought to invoke the right of self-determination as a revolutionary principle applicable extraconstitutionally, the Czechs balked and prevailed with their insistence on continuity and a constitutional route even when it came to the modalities of the dissolution.⁵³ Moreover—and this perhaps is the most valuable contribution to self-determination practice—the dissolution occurred without the slightest sign of a threat of force from either side.⁵⁴

I have wondered why the Czecho-Slovak outcome was so different from the situation in former Yugoslavia and the Soviet Union. A major reason— Professor Petr Piťha suggested—was the fact that the Slovaks and the Czechs had never gone to battle against each other; there was no compulsion to

---

51. The evidence listed includes Cyprus, Lebanon, Sri Lanka, Sudan, and "increasingly" India but curiously also the Soviet Union, Yugoslavia, and Czechoslovakia, where the absence of democracy had little, if any, connection with the cultural or ethnic differences. Michael Lind, "In Defense of Liberal Nationalism," 13 FOREIGN AFFAIRS 87, 95 (No. 3, 1994).

52. The U.S. government and the Parliament of the European Union expressed formally their concern about observances of democratic principles by the Mečiar government, and there was some criticism in the Council of Europe and among U.S. senators of the discrimination against the Roma by the Czech government's application of the citizenship legislation. "Slovakia-Madness," THE ECONOMIST, Dec. 2, 1995, pp. 54–55; "Czech Government Eases Citizenship Restrictions," OPEN MEDIA RESEARCH INSTITUTE DAILY DIGEST II, no. 28, Feb. 8, 1996, p. 3.

53. *See* on this Jiří Boguszak and Luboš Tichý in LN, July 28, 1992, p. 8.

54. Even in the eventually peaceful dissolution of the Norway-Sweden Union in 1905 an armed conflict was a possibility. The last straw for its breakup was Norway's insistence on fully independent consular offices to represent its interests abroad, shades of the Slovak peremptory demand for their own representation abroad. The Czech side, during the negotiations, accepted separate treaty-making powers of the Republics and their own diplomatic representation within the federal foreign affairs framework. It rejected, however, separate membership in international organizations, arguing the concept of "indivisibility" of the international personality of the Federation. The Union of Norway and Sweden, which lasted 90 years, was a much looser association than the Czecho-Slovak Federation. Karen Larsen, *supra,* note 45, 484–87. It has been suggested that Norway's refusal to join the European Union might be "a consequence of Norway's relatively recent independence from Sweden." Christine Ingebritsen, "Norway and European Union," 7 ECSA NEWSLETTER 16 (no. 3, Fall 1994).

revenge the blood spilled in such a conflict.[55] Another reason, identified by Ivan Gašparovič, chair of the Slovak Parliament, was the absence of any territorial dispute.[56] The humanist experience of Masaryk's First Republic may have had a role in taming militant nationalism in both parts of the Federation. For the last three centuries, the Czechs have been averse to taking up arms, and they were certainly not ready to fight for a common state that had lost its appeal for Czech leadership. Still in the Czech Republic, the elimination of most of the minority populations removed the most convenient motivation and target of extreme nationalism. In Slovakia, also, where a more pristine, "earlier stage" nationalism is seen as still prevailing, even the most aggressive nationalist rhetoric eschewed any implications of outright belligerent action. Finally, a major factor for the peaceful resolution of the conflict was the protodemocratic political environment in which the process took place.[57] This confirms the general thesis postulating a correlation between democratic regimes and peaceful behavior.[58]

d. Separation as an Alternative: Geopolitics and Legitimacy

Two scholars correctly conclude that the merits of separation as against integration had to be decided by political argument and pragmatic considerations such as feasibility and estimates about long-run efficacy. They suggest that there is no obvious moral hierarchy that would place separation over other alternatives such as integration.[59] However, if the international system is viewed as exclusively state based, fragmentation by separation would appear an inferior choice in principle. That system "relegates ethnic groups to the status of dependent variables or policy problems."[60] If, on the other hand, one perceives the international system in the process of change with individuals, groups, "regions," and a great variety of international regimes joining the

---

55. *See also* Sharon L. Wolchik, "The Politics of Ethnicity in Post-Communist Czechoslovakia," 8 EAST EUROPEAN POLITICS AND SOCIETIES 153, 174 (no. 1, 1994). The army was not an "independently functioning power factor." Vladimír Kusín in XXII LISTY 18, 20 (no. 2, 1992).
56. Conversation with I. Gašparovič. A miniscule territorial adjustment was approved by Slovakia but it was still before the Czech House in mid-1996.
57. Ted Robert Gurr and Barbara Harff, Ethnic Conflict in World Politics 85 (Westview Press, Boulder, San Francisco, Oxford, 1994).
58. Bruce Russett, "Politics and Alternative Security: Toward a More Democratic, Therefore More Peaceful, World," in Burns H. Weston (ed.), Alternative Security: Living without Nuclear Deterrence 107, 111 (Westview Press, Boulder, San Francisco, Oxford, 1990).
59. John McGary and Brendan O'Leary, *supra,* note 25, 6.
60. Cynthia H. Enloe, Ethnic Conflict and Political Development 7 (Little Brown and Co., Boston, 1972).

"sovereign" states as actors ("subjects" or players) in the international arena, then the stance may be less negative. Fuming against the "stabilitarians" and mistaken prophets of the postnationalist world, some see less interstate conflict in a world of relatively homogenous nation-states than in a world of intrastate conflict between ethnic groups within multinational states. Even if a dozen or two new nations are added in the next few decades, "through peaceful or violent partition . . . the very inequality of power among states would prevent too great a degree of disorder."[61] This, the stabilitarians rejoin, would indeed increase the potential for global disorder, if the number of states of doubtful viability is raised dramatically and power vacuums result.[62]

As for the geopolitical impact of the Czech-Slovak separation, historic experience in Central Europe (for instance the Munich 1938 episode) suggests that one small larger states might not be necessarily less vulnerable than two small states. Two economically viable Republics coexisting peacefully may be preferable to a common state rent by ethnic conflict, even if arguably they might have done better economically together as a larger state.

As in the past, the policies of the West and of Russia will be the essential factor. Except for some voices in Slovakia, the "bridge role" between the East and West is generally rejected as a viable security option. The "buffer" idea behind the post–World War I Little Entente did not work either. Some see chaos in Russia overflowing to its neighbors; others—harking back to recent history—fear that Russia, unable or unwilling to cooperate with the West, might seek to "finlandize" the region under its own surveillance or, worse still, to restore its former empire, in which case—so goes the prophecy—it might attempt to establish a foothold in Slovakia. Disappointed with the Conference on Security and Cooperation in Europe and other European security schemes, the governments of both Republics are still looking toward a close association with the European Union and NATO although the depth of public support for NATO membership is uncertain. The Slovak government has been making a determined effort to build political and economic ties with its Eastern neighbors, including a free trade area with the Russian Federation. Both Republics are parties to the fledgling Central European Free Trade Agreement. The tension between Slovakia and Hungary over the status of the Hungarian minor-

---

61. Michael Lind, "In Defense of Liberal Nationalism," 73 FOREIGN AFFAIRS 87, 89, 90–91 (no. 3, 1994). *See generally* Timothy Garton Ash, "Bosnia in Our Future," N.Y. REV. OF BOOKS, Dec. 21, 1995, p. 31.

62. Another writer offers a third alternative to separation and independence in the form of regimes not based on territoriality such as functional zones granting limited exercise of national rights beyond established frontiers, loose unions, and so on. Gideon Gottlieb, "Nations without States," 73 FOREIGN AFFAIRS 100 (no. 3, 1994). I deal with these suggestions in the context of the Czecho-Slovak negotiations elsewhere.

ity in Slovakia is likely to continue despite the conclusion of a significant treaty. The controversy over the claims of the expelled Sudeten Germans has marred the Czech-German relations and some in the Czech Republic fear the growing German economic influence. The treatment of the thousands of Roma in the Czech Republic has been the subject of international concern.

Although at this juncture Central Europe—unlike Eastern and South Eastern Europe—appears relatively stable, the entire area experiences the aftermath of the disintegration of the Soviet empire, which is likely to have long-term destabilizing effects not unlike the breakup of other imperial structures in Europe's history. If nothing else, the pressure of substantial ethnic minorities in all states of the region is likely to contribute to the instability.[63]

One view heard particularly among the members of the first post-1989 government elite warns that the separation will eventually prove a heavy burden on those responsible for it and that the lack of a manifested consent of the people will undermine the legitimacy and the consciousness of the "stateness" of the two Republics. Unlike the states emerging from the former Yugoslavia or Soviet Union, the two Republics—the critics argue—are "unwanted children," like the post–World War I Republic of Austria in 1918; in Central Europe's environment, hostile to small states, they will be absorbed in one form or another by their powerful neighbors. Yet the newly independent Czech Republic seems to have slid smoothly into the shoes of the former Czechoslovakia with its tradition, history, and reputation, having appropriated its symbols, including the flag, the main state holiday, and the capital with its apparently irresistible lore. The Slovak "stateness" is viewed as a natural culmination of a historic process for assertion of national identity, although many Slovaks feel that full independence was neither a logical nor the most desirable option. Whatever it may be worth, in the fall of 1993, less than a year after independence, 60 percent of the Slovaks interviewed in an opinion poll

---

63. An Oxford University scholar paints the following picture: "In every one of the new democracies, there are large national minorities. Even Poland, normally thought of as a homogeneous state, contains around 250,000 Germans, while roughly the same number of Poles live in Lithuania. In every state bordering Hungary, except in Austria, there is a large Hungarian minority, amounting to two million in Rumanian Transylvania. Indeed, almost 30 percent of the Hungarian-speaking population of Central Europe live outside Hungary. Similarly, 1.8 million Albanians live in Kosovo, a region of Yugoslavia, while Bulgaria contains around one million Turkish-speaking Muslims, amounting to 10 percent of the population. The Baltic states contain large Russian minorities, and indeed there are 25 million Russians living outside Russia, while Bulgaria, the Czech Republic, Hungary, Rumania, and Slovakia contain large gypsy populations, and Hungary has a substantial Jewish minority. The internal divisions within the states formed from the former Yugoslavia are too painfully obvious to need recital." Vernon Bogdanor, "1. Overcoming the Twentieth Century: Democracy and Nationalism in Central and Eastern Europe," in Istwan Pogany (ed.), Human Rights in Eastern Europe 4 (Edward Elgar, Aldershot, England, 1995).

indicated that they would vote against the separation, while only 23 percent would support it.[64]

Returning to the conceptual framework suggested in the first chapter, one might conclude that on the continuum "symmetric-asymmetric systems," Czechoslovakia moved from the state of "latent succession" to separation. In other terms, the structure suffered from "tension-producing faults," which led to the split.

3. On Multiple Transformations

a. The Priorities

It has become a cliché in the literature on contemporary Central-Eastern Europe to expatiate upon the uniqueness of the simultaneous transformations at the societal, political, and economic levels. In fact, no precedent or theory exists for a transition from a Communist regime to a free market democracy. One scholar saw as the closest parallel natural or man-made disasters: floods, earthquakes, famines, or wars.[65] In contrast with unitary states such as Poland and Hungary, the political transformation in the Czecho-Slovak Federation was greatly complicated by still another "transformation" directed at the form of coexistence between the two peoples and ultimately by the painful process of dividing the state into two independent entities.

The necessary interaction between the political and economic transformation processes raised questions of priorities in the allocation of resources. Some writers, including Professor Bruce Ackerman, felt that in Eastern Europe political democracy and constitution writing should precede, and provide conditions for, the establishment of the free market, while others argued that a certain level of economic stability was an indispensable precondition for

---

64. Sharon Fisher, "Slovakia: The First Year of Independence," RFE/RL Res. Rep., Jan. 7, 1994, 87, 91. This a posteriori expression of feelings does not say much about how the Slovaks might have voted in a referendum prior to the dissolution. *See* James F. Brown, Hopes and Shadows: Eastern Europe after Communism 63–66 ("Alone in the World") (Duke University Press, Durham, 1994).

65. Michael Mandelbaum, "Introduction," in Shafigul Islam and Michael Mandelbaum (eds.), Making Markets: Economic Transformation in Eastern Europe and Post-Soviet States 1 (Council on Foreign Relations, New York, 1993). *See generally* James F. Brown, *supra,* note 60; Georg Brunner, Politischer Systemwandel und Verfassungsreformen in Osteuropa (Verlag Josef Eul, Bergisch Gladbach–Köln, 1990). Christopher G.A. Bryant and Edmund Mokrzycki (eds.), The New Great Transformation? Change and Continuity in East-Central Europe (Routledge, London, New York, 1994). Robert A. Dahl, in Democracy and Its Critics (Yale U. Press, New Haven, London, 1989), sees two historical transformations toward democracy: the birth of democratic city states in ancient Greece and Rome; and the emergence of large-scale representative democracies in the eighteenth century, multiplied in the nineteenth and twentieth centuries. He asks whether the present marks the third democratic transformation.

democracy. Judge Richard A. Posner, although disclaiming any expertise about European law and politics, had no doubt that the "priority for Eastern Europe" should be economic rather than political.[66] Jon Elster perceived a possible parallel with Latin American states but wisely warned that vital distinctions among the various countries could not be ignored in this context.[67] President Havel "did not agree with the view that the constitution is not the principal matter and that it can wait."[68] In the Czech-Slovak case, at any rate, the Slovaks saw to it that the fundamental constitutional issue defining the relation between the two peoples had to be tackled along with, if not before, economics.[69] As for some other Communist states, Bulgaria and Romania adopted their constitutions as early as in 1991, but Poland and Hungary, after years of transformation, in mid-1996 still do not have a new constitution in the formal sense, and the Ukrainian parliament adopted one as late as June 1996 only after the president threatened to call a popular referendum. In reality, these countries have enacted a veritable mass of constitutional laws amending the communist constitutions, with the effect that in Hungary, for instance, almost all of the vital components of a new basic document have been in place for some time, with the post-Communist Constitutional Court undertaking to assure some coherence within the system. Even the Czecho-Slovak Federal Assembly adopted some 43 such constitutional laws before it went out of business. It follows that priority has never been a real issue: constitution-making has been pursued after the fall of the old regimes with vigor but, as an eminently political process, it has been subject in different countries to widely different forces and outcomes.

b. On Free Societies

A transformation from the atomized and passive to an active civil society postulates a certain constitutional and legal framework, but it cannot do without a change in individual behavior. As Ralf Dahrendorf told a Prague audience, the new civil society envisages "a broad scale of associations, organi-

---

66. Richard A. Posner, "Review of the Future of Liberal Revolution by Bruce Ackerman" (Yale U. Press, New Haven, 1992) in I E. EUR. CONST. REV. 35 at 37 (Fall 1992).

67. Jon Elster, "The Necessity and Impossibility of Simultaneous Economic and Political Reform," in Douglas Greenberg, Stanley N. Katz, Melanie Beth Oliviero, and Steven C. Wheatley (eds.), Constitutionalism and Democracy 267, 268 (Oxford U. Press, New York, Oxford, 1993).

68. "I felt on the contrary that we could not solve successfully any of the great problems with which our society was struggling, from the political to the economic to the social, without responding first to the question in what kind of a state do we want to live." Václav Havel, "Projev ve Federálním shromáždění, Praha, 3.12, 1991 [Address in the Federal Assembly, Prague, Dec. 3, 1991]," in Vážení občané—Projevy, červemec 1990—červemec 1992 [Esteemed Citizens— Addresses, July 1990–July 1992] 123 (LN, Praha, 1992).

69. Ilja Šetlík in LN, Sept. 3, 1993, p. 5.

zations, and institutions independent of the government (at least of the central government) and fulfilling the real lives of real people."[70] Two American sociologists distinguish civil society from both the political society of parties, political organizations, and political publics (in particular parliaments) and an economic society composed of organizations of production and distribution (firms, cooperatives, etc.); political and economic societies generally arise from civil society.[71]

i. The Civil Society

"There is an enormous difference," wrote Ernest Gellner, "between longing for civil society . . . and being able to take it for granted," which was the condition at the time of the American Revolution. "The collapse of [the Marxist] system has left a moral vacuum. . . . The American Revolution by contrast . . . was not a collapse of a moral order. The moral order remained intact and the revolution was its expression, not its violation."[72] And Václav Havel, returning from his first voyage to the United States as Czech president, waxed enthusiastically over "the tremendously developed American civil society" with "millions of nonprofit organizations."[73] Clearly, at times a comparison enlightens by bringing into view not the similarities but the differences between the compared phenomena. Some American writers, however, take a less sanguine view of the current state of civil society in the United States.[74]

The Czechs have been known as inveterate joiners—a tradition revived with a vengeance after 1989. Over 50,000 associations functioned in the First

---

70. Ralf Dahrendorf, in his lecture in Prague, in LN, March 15, 1994, p. 1.

71. Jean L. Cohen and Andrew Arato, Civil Society and Political Theory viii, ix (MIT Press, Cambridge, Mass., London, 1992). Michael Walzer points to the disagreement on what the concept of "civil society" includes and excludes. "It is enough to say," he writes, "that the civil society incorporates many of the associations and identities we value outside of, prior to, or in the shadow of state and citizenship." Michael Walzer (ed.), Toward a Global Civil Society 1 (Berghahn Books, Providence, Oxford, 1995).

72. Ernest Gellner, "Innocents Abroad: The Future of Liberal Revolution by Bruce Ackerman," NEW REPUBLIC, Nov. 30, 1992, 38, 39.

73. Havel complained that "at home" people confused the concept of civil society "with direct democracy" or "a chaotic rule of thousands of associations and civic initiatives." In America, the citizens voluntarily take over uncounted social, ecological, health, cultural, and education functions that can be better performed by them than by the state, in what can be described as "citizens' self-care" with millions of nonprofit organizations. It is a part of human self-realization because man is a social creature. LN, Oct. 10, 1994, p. 16.

74. Jean Bethke Elshtain, Democracy on Trial (Basic Books, New York, 1995). In the United States, participation in traditional voluntary associations declined between 25 and 30 percent, because, it is said, of television. Other data indicate, however, that the voluntary activity in other areas has risen substantially. Anthony Lewis, "An Atomized America," N.Y. TIMES, Dec. 18, 1995, p. A11; Frank Riessman, "America's Still a Nation of Joiners," N.Y. TIMES, Dec. 21, 1995, p. 28.

Republic, but only 1,400 were counted in 1990–91, a testimony to the impact of the Communist regime. By 1994, in the Czech Republic alone there were more than 20,000 associations and clubs, about 3,000 foundations, 1,500 church organizations, 171 professional "chambers," and over 50 interest groups. The "economic society" counted some 55,000 companies.[75] A major part of the working population moved from the public to the private sector. Thousands became property owners through restitution of property confiscated by the Communists, and some six million became shareholders through privatization, a development toward a revival of the historically strong Czech middle class.

Unlike the Czechs, the Slovaks typically do not feel the need for association with others of the same persuasion except in religious organizations. Moreover, joining was risky under the old regime, and the distaste for it continues along with a fear of change and relapse to poverty, suspicion of authority, and a respect for power.[76] Privatization in Slovakia has been slower and was at times suspended. One Slovak view attributed the substantially higher unemployment in Slovakia in part to the inflexibility of the work force and a lack of entrepreneurial spirit among the people. Current statistics show a disproportionately smaller number of individual entrepreneurs and new small enterprises in Slovakia.[77]

Professor Robert Putnam has concluded, drawing on his study of differences between the societies of Italy's North and South, that good government and political-economic progress depended on the existence of a civil

---

75. Sociologist Lubomír Brokl, quoted in Přítomnost, 4/1992, p. 2. LN, Aug. 1, 1994, p. 3. *See generally* Michael Walzer, "Political Actors and Political Roles in East-Central Europe," in Michael Waller and Martin Myant (eds.), Parties, Trade Unions and Society in East-Central Europe 21–35 (Frank Cass, Illford, Essex, Eng., Portland, Ore., 1994).

76. Petr Příhoda in LN, June 5, 1992, p. 8; conversations with M. Leško, Slovak editor in chief, Pravda.

77. Number of enterprises with up to 100 employees in 1991:

Cz. Sl. Fed. Rep. 12, 975, employing 130,640
Czech Rep. 9,936, employing 99,181
Slovak Rep. 3,039, employing 31,459

Of these in the private sector:

Cz. Sl. Fed. Rep. 9,318, employing 62,014
Czech Rep. 7,390, employing 47,677
Slovak Rep. 1,928, employing 14,337

Number of small private entrepreneurs:

	March 31, 1991	December 31, 1992
Cz. Sl. Fed. Rep.	655,023	1,338,353
Czech Rep.	495,670	1,058,504
Slovak Rep.	159,353	279,849

society marked by a traditional tendency to form small-scale associations.[78] I have asked myself whether the divergence between the Czech and Slovak societies might confirm this theorem. The newly independent Czech Republic continued to experience a stable, democratic government with favorable macroeconomic data including sizable economic growth, low unemployment and relatively moderate inflation, along with moderate social-economic tensions endemic to rapid post-Communist transformation.[79] In Slovakia, as I mentioned earlier, economic revival has paralleled and even somewhat surpassed the growth rate in the Czech Republic but the government and politics are a different story. In sharp contrast with the Czech Republic, where differentiation of political parties along the traditional West-European left-right spectrum was essentially completed even before the breakup, the scene in Slovakia has been dominated by the populist-nationalist movement of Vladimír Mečiar. Mečiar, dismissed twice before from the office of prime minister, nevertheless regained it for the third time in 1994. In that year's election his movement, supported widely in the rural areas, retained its plurality despite an unseemly conflict between Mečiar and the president of the Republic, the efforts to exclude the opposition from any participation, a series of scandals, and serious charges of abuse of governmental power. As for the civil society, the Slovak Parliament has adopted legislation making it substantially more costly for private nonprofit foundations to be recognized. The European Union and the United States took the unusual steps of expressing official concern about the state of democracy in

---

Statistická ročenka [Annual of Statistics], Czech and Slovak Fed. Rep., p. 537 (SEVT, Praha, 1992). There are roughly twice as many people living in the Czech Republic than in Slovakia.

Another set of figures on the situation in the Czech Republic was made available by the Czech Bureau of Statistics:

	Business associations	Associations of natural and legal persons
1991	23,112	11,558
1993	60,376	28,446
1994	88,424	33,618

Pavel Machonin, Milan Tuček, "Genese nové struktury v České republice a její sociální aktéři [Genesis of the New Social Structure in the Czech Republic and Its Social Actors]," in Vlasta Šafaríková et al., Transformace české společnosti 1989–1995 [Transformation of the Czech Society], (Doplněk, Brno, 1996), report (at 27) that the number of registered private entrepreneurs in the Czech Republic rose from 65,000 in 1989 to approximately one million in 1993. See also Jan Švejnar, supra, note 10, 5 and passim.

78. Robert D. Putnam with Robert Leonardi and Raffaella T. Nanetti, Making Democracy Work-Civic Traditions in Modern Italy (Princeton U. Press, Princeton, NJ, 1993).

79. In the 1996 election, the ruling right-of-center coalition lost its parliamentary majority in the face of an unexpected, dramatic rise of support for the left-oriented reconstructed Social Democratic party. A new minority government composed of the same coalition once again headed by Václav Klaus may find it more difficult to govern but there is no evidence that either the pluralist democracy or the basic economic reforms are in danger.

the country. Slovakia was dropped at least for the time being from the first group of candidates for admission to NATO and the European Union.

Obviously, more empirical work on the region is called for, but the data appear to support Putnam's correlation between a civil society of vibrant private groupings and good government. Clearly, in the Czech-Slovak context, the degree of progress toward a civil society, or lack of it, has had an impact on the political and economic transformation process, but it was also reflected in the postures of the elites conducting the constitutional negotiations, in the tone of the public discourse and the political culture generally, and in the attitudes and votes of the people at large.

ii. The Political Society

As for the "political society," it was the political "movements" and parties that played a central role in the regime change generally and—as I stress throughout this book—in the constitutional negotiations in particular.[80] In some measure, these negotiations made more difficult the process of a differentiation of the parties along the traditional left-right spectrum. The rapid pace of regrouping and the lack of clarity of their programs impaired the role of the parties as instruments of integration of the political will of the people. They served as a natural vehicle for advancing not only party interests but individual ambitions as well.

As a result of the political fragmentation, the Slovak representation in the negotiations was not in a position to evolve a common strategy; it offered always a continuum of postures ranging from "mildly" federalist to extreme separatist. Only the "federal Slovaks," such as Federal Prime Minister Marián Čalfa, and whatever remained of the original Public against Violence stood for a strong Federation, and in the end they had little influence. The negotiations were complicated by the significant role played by the Christian Democratic Movement, which for a time was the strongest party in the Slovak National Council, and its founder-leader Dr. Ján Čarnogurský. Dr. Čarnogurský had in mind—and he said so at the outset—the independence of Slovakia not at once but in a number of years when both Republics would enter the European Union as separate members. In the negotiations, he and his colleagues supported any move that would loosen the Federation, so that at the time of accession to the European Union the separation would be a logical step since the structure of the common state, or what was left of it, would be too weak to ensure confor-

---

80. *See generally,* Michael Waller and Martin Myant (eds.), Parties, Trade Unions, and Society in East Central Europe (Frank Cass, Illford, Essex, Eng., Portland, Ore., 1994); Sten Berglund and Jan Åke Dellenbrant (eds.), The New Democracies in Eastern Europe: Party Systems and Political Cleavages (2d ed., Edward Elgar Publishing Ltd., Aldershot, Eng., Vermont, 1994); and Hans-Ulrich Derlien and George J. Szablowski (eds.), Regime Transition, Elites, and Bureaucracies in Eastern Europe, 6 GOVERNANCE, Special Issue (no. 3, July 1993).

mity with the European Union rules and discipline: thus, the two Republics would form a bloc of two votes in the Union councils. This stance was consistent with Dr. Čarnogurský's vision of a growing role of "regions" within the integrating Europe, but it appeared thoroughly disruptive to the Czech side.[81] The Slovak Party of the Democratic Left, although supporting a strong role for the Republics in line with nationalist aspirations, did not aim at the destruction of the Federation, but it was hampered by its Communist heritage. At times reluctant to take a clear stand, it sought to avoid a collision with the influential Mečiar's populist Movement for a Democratic Slovakia, which played the nationalist card for a confederation or "union."

On the Czech side, the breakup of the original majority Civic Forum and the emerging new factions and parties created divisions within the negotiating group, which, however, were gradually overcome by the ascending influence of the new "right wing" parties and their leaders, insisting on a "functional federation or nothing."

4. "Strategic Elements" of Constitutional Negotiations

At the beginning of this book, I referred to Howard Raiffa's empirically derived criteria, which, adjusted to the subject of this book, provide a convenient grid for an analysis of the negotiation issues, parties, strategies, and tactics.

a. The Time Dimension

The time factor was one of the strategic elements highlighted by Raiffa. Günther Winkler, an Austrian legal philosopher, has challenged the sacred canon that "at the beginning was the Word": neither the Word, nor Faust's existentialist "action," but Time was at the beginning of all things.[82] The importance of the time dimension for human affairs was brought out amply by the Czech-Slovak case. I stressed earlier the role of the time element in the potential assimilation or integration of the two societies. Whether or not an integration of the two peoples was feasible had more time been allowed for it remains a question.

In a less hypothetical context, time restraints haunted the constitutional negotiations of the 1990s from the outset. President Havel is blamed for the

---

81. If this were a society amenable to pragmatic solutions—which of course it is not—one might take a charitable view that over the years preceding the admission to the European Union, contrary to general expectation, the Federation would prove useful, if not indispensable. On the personality of Ján Čarnogurský, *see* Petr Nováček in MFD, May 27, 1992, p. 7. *See also* Čarnogurský's lecture at Oxford in PIATOK, Jan. 3, 1992, p. 12.

82. Günter Winkler, Zeit und Recht 569–70 (Springer Verlag, Wien, New York, 1995).

decision to limit the term of the first freely elected Federal Assembly (and of his presidency) to a mere two years, a period too short to allow for a consensus to have been reached on a new federal constitution.[83] There is some force in this argument, since the second elections after the lapse of this period marked the death knell of the state. Yet, even before the expiration of the first two-year term, with the swift disintegration of the ruling profederalist movements, the leadership in charge of the negotiations was losing its legitimacy and new elections confirming the realignment of political power appeared appropriate. Behind the decision on the shortened first term was no doubt the idea that the postrevolutionary euphoria offered the magic moment for achieving a constitutional consensus.

The succession of arbitrary deadlines for completing the constitution making both reflected and fed the growing impatience on both sides, with the media contributing to an atmosphere of irritation and peevishness. In the end, the fatal, short deadline for the dissolution of the state was set by the chafing Czech side with the grudging acquiescence of the Slovaks. This last time limit was employed to compel the opposition in both Republics, under the threat of an impending chaos, to abandon any delaying moves (such as proposals for a confederate scheme and a referendum) and support the termination of the state.

Finally, in the broadest sense, the length of time required for the realization of the transformations in Central-Eastern Europe has imposed a severe test of patience on people suffering an abrupt deterioration of living standards against an uncertain promise of a better life in the future. It took the West generations (perhaps two centuries) to achieve a working model of democracy with a free market, an objective that the countries of Central-Eastern Europe have hoped to reach in one decade.

b. Issues and Parties

Vladimír Kusín has suggested a chronological scheme to analyze the process of disintegration of the "national-unitary" power structures in the former Soviet Union and Yugoslavia, as well as in Czechoslovakia, "the only multinational European [unitary] state formation remaining after the end of the First World War." He offers a three-phase perspective that I have found useful for thinking about the complex, multi-issue, Czech-Slovak negotiations in which both the main issues and the party constellations changed over the period of some three years.[84]

---

83. Havel strongly supported that decision in a speech of February 25, 1990. Václav Havel, Projevy [Addresses] 68 (Vyšehrad, Praha, 1990).

84. Vladimír V. Kusín, "O novém pojetí česko-slovenské vzájemnosti, [On a New Perception of the Czecho-Slovak Mutuality]," 22 LISTY 18, 19–20 (no. 2, 1992). The author is a former Czech emigré on the staff of the Radio Free Europe–Radio Liberty. He observes that Ireland separated from Great Britain in 1921.

The first two phases at any rate were conducted under the spell of the "naive realism" described by two American scholars: "It is I who sees the things as they 'really' are (including history) so that other rational and fair people will share my responses, and any failure [on the part of the other party] to do so must be due to lack of information, ignorance, laziness, irrationality, unfairness or bias."[85] For the Czechs, indifferent and mostly ignorant of Slovak history and sensibilities, only a strong federation could successfully accomplish the multiple transformations, but for the Slovaks "self-determination," until now "unfairly denied," had to be finally realized now.

i. The "Reform" Phase

Issues: In this phase, the two basic issues were the transfer of powers from the center to the component Republics and "strengthening national symbolism" such as the change of the name from the "Czechoslovak" to the "Czech and Slovak" Federative Republic. The constitutional negotiations encompassed the entire spectrum of issues of federalism, constitutionalism, and democracy and led to the adoption in early 1991 of the Charter of Basic Rights and Freedoms and a host of other constitutional and "quasi-constitutional" legislation. The primary focus, however, was the devolution discourse.

The Czech side believed that a solution might be found in the form of "a moderate, enlightened, supranational centralism," a "functional federation," which would preserve a uniform economic and foreign policy, while the Slovaks signaled a growing, albeit not articulated, dissatisfaction. Neverthe-less, the parties engaged in an essentially cooperative interaction: while seeking their own "payoffs" on the basic issues of power distribution and other aspects of the successive drafts of the federal constitution, they were prepared to cooperate in a solution that would preserve the federal state.

Parties: Nominally, there were three parties to the negotiations, the Federation and the two Republics, represented by spokespeople drawn in this phase primarily from the executive branches. However, all three legislatures became involved through their respective Constitutional Commissions working on various drafts of both the federal and Republic constitutions. With the governmental and parliamentary structure only slowly coming to life in late 1989 and early 1990, President Havel, armed with strong support and prestige, exerted during this brief phase a great, if not controlling, influence, along with the leaders of the two large movements victorious in the 1990 elections, which, however, had already begun the process of differentiation into conventional political parties. The discredited labor unions had scarcely begun to show signs

---

85. Lee Ross and Andrew Ward, "Naive Realism: Implications for Social Conflict and Misunderstanding," unpublished, 1994. See also, by the same authors, "Naive Realism in Every-day Life: Implications for Social Conflict and Misunderstanding," in Kenneth Arrow et al. (eds.), Barriers to Conflict Resolution 103, 110–11 (W.W. Norton and Co., New York, London, 1995).

of revival, and there were no other special interest groups pressing on the political leadership with a noticeable effect. This meant that in this proto-democratic system basic policy was made between the president and the organs of the political parties influenced by individual actors in crucial government positions. The three-party negotiation pattern quickly turned into a two-party face-off, with the Czech Republic representatives generally joining the "federals" in the defense of the federal scheme against Slovak pressure for change.

This phase ended with the adoption, under strong Slovak pressure, of the 1990 federal devolution law, which restored in effect the allocation of powers as it was originally made in the 1968 constitutional law, before the "recentralization" ordained in 1970 as an aspect of the Soviet imposed "normalization."

ii. The "Restructuring" Phase

Issues: In this phase, the Slovak side pressed beyond devolution and symbolism for a new contractual foundation of the state in the form of a "treaty" between the two "sovereign" Republics that would determine both the power allocation and the constitutional structure and would be embodied in the new constitution; the powers of the center would be limited to foreign affairs, defense, and the single market. The treaty would legally bind both Republics and would oblige the central legislature to incorporate it in the federal constitution. The hardest bargaining, however, centered on newly introduced issues regarding the legal nature of the treaty:

> The treaty, the Slovaks proposed, should be binding under international law, in effect an extraconstitutional instrument. After the initial shock on the Czech side, which branded the proposal as unconstitutional and revolutionary, a compromise was reached, with the majority of the Czech spokesmen accepting the treaty idea and the Slovaks conceding that the treaty would be an internal rather than an international instrument. However, the question of the status of the treaty remained highly controversial.

> The Slovaks insisted—and this appeared to be a point closest to their hearts—that the "sovereign" Republics must as such be the parties to the treaty, while the Czechs considered that absurd since the Republics were components of the Federation: only the Republic parliaments, acting on behalf of "the people," could be the contracting parties. This, in reality a largely symbolic issue, turned out to be a major reason, or at least a pretext, for the ultimate defeat of the draft treaty in the Slovak Parliament's Presidium.

> The Slovaks demanded that the treaty be legally "binding" on the Federal Assembly, but the Czechs refused this claim as well as a constitutional

amendment to that effect because it would impair the position of the Assembly as the highest constitutional organ. Although formulated in terms of a compromise, the Czech position, based on strict adherence to the 1960–68 Constitution, prevailed.[86]

Finally, the Slovaks claimed that the new constitution embodying the treaty, after adoption by the Federal Assembly, must be ratified by the two Republic parliaments, a demand that the Czechs reluctantly accepted, although they viewed it as an inappropriate "confederative element." They refused, however, to agree that any subsequent constitutional amendments would likewise be subject to such ratification.

As regards the issue of "international visibility," so close to Slovak hearts, a compromise solution recognized the treaty-making power of the Republics in the areas of their legislative competence to be exercised "in harmony" with federal foreign policy (the modalities of assuring such harmony to be left to future legislation), as well as the authority of the Republics to send their own representatives abroad and receive foreign representatives.

Parallel to the Republic-to-Republic negotiations on the treaty, the Federal Assembly debated proposals for the core parts of the constitution that defined the three branches of the central government. The prevailing constitutional provisions for the protection of the Slovak minority and the guarantees of Czech and Slovak parity representation were to be retained or strengthened and consociational elements added to assure the participation of Slovak representatives in central decision making. The bill, based in part on President Havel's draft, failed in the Federal Assembly by four votes.

Parties: As regards the negotiating parties, this phase progressed in two distinct stages. First, the president assembled the representatives of the three executive branches and leaders of the two majority movements in no less than 18 meetings to deal with the treaty proposal. When this elaborate effort failed, due mainly to Czech intransigence, the negotiations were taken up by delegations of the two Republic parliaments, bringing in the opposition parties—a development that was viewed as "a catastrophe" by some and as the only possible alternative by others. The idea was that the Republic organs should shape the treaty content, relieving by the same token the president, whose influence on the negotiations faded rapidly. However, in what was supposed to be a Republic-to-Republic discourse, federal officials continued to loom large, if for no other reason because of the unique expertise of the federal establishment. The Czech Republic organs, although seeking with some hesitation to assert their own independent stance, found it difficult to extricate themselves

---

86. See *supra,* chap. IX, 2.

from a position of serving as a "regional extension of federal organs and personalities."[87] Although the deputies of both the Czech and Slovak parliaments shared the feeling that federal parliamentarians looked down on them, the Slovaks identified federal "arrogance" with the Czechs. As both Republics proceeded to exercise their competences, enlarged by the new devolution law, frictions with federal organs occurred. The disintegration of the ruling pro-federalist movements in both Republics into competing political groupings led by regional politicians changed the power interests and priorities on both sides. The rhetoric surrounding the negotiations fanned the rising Slovak nationalism, which in turn impacted the Slovak posture and evoked a negative response on the Czech side. The approach of national elections burdened the negotiations greatly. Against all odds, in February 1992 an agreement appeared to have been reached on a draft text of a treaty to be submitted to the Republic parliaments. The formal issues regarding the treaty seemed either resolved or intentionally left ambiguous, and a solution was found for the most vexing items of allocation of powers, including a single central bank, joint "protection of frontiers," and the division of foreign affairs powers. However, the Slovak Parliament Presidium rejected the draft. Thus, the Slovaks were the defectors at this critical juncture of "the game." It was likely that the Czech Parliament would have endorsed the agreement, although some observers on the Czech side doubt it.

iii. The "New Form of Coexistence" Phase

After the 1992 elections had sealed the radical restructuring of the political scene in the two Republics, a face-off persisted for a brief period between the Slovak demand, now formulated in terms of a "union" modeled vaguely on the Maastricht Treaty for the European Union, and a resolute Czech insistence on "a functional federation." The deadlock came to an abrupt end with the two leaders of the newly victorious parties quickly agreeing on the division of the common state into two successor states.

Issues: An entirely new phase, based on newly defined common interests, turned on the following two sets of issues.

> The modalities of the separation, including
>> the date of the split and budgetary implications for the period preceding it,
>> the dismantling of the federal establishment,
>> the constitutionality and legitimacy of the separation process, including a possible referendum and the role of the Federal Assembly and the Republic parliaments,

---

87. Kusín, *supra,* note 84, 18.

the division of federal property and other rights and obligations of
the Federation, and

the stance toward the outside world.

The forms of the future coexistence of the two states. The Slovaks, eager
to salvage as much as possible of the "union" scheme, pressed for a
joint coordinating organ, but the Czechs were ready only for a dense
network of bilateral international treaties between independent states.
The Czechs prevailed, and some 40 such treaties or agreements were
negotiated.

The negotiations at this stage proceeded with surprising speed under the
Damoclean sword of the imminent date set for the split and in the new realization of the strong common interest in assuring an orderly, peaceful separation.

Parties: It is no exaggeration to say that in this episode the basic decisions
were made essentially by two men, the prime ministers of the two Republics.
Their decisions were blessed by their parties and coalition allies, by the Republic organs, and finally, after tumultuous debates, by the Federal Assembly.
Both men first employed only small teams of close advisers, but, after the basic
decisions had been made, the circle of participants broadened with the inclusion of many ministerial officials and experts who worked with considerable
skill and efficiency on the maze of innumerable, overwhelming problems.
There still was no evidence of special interest groups intruding in any significant way into the negotiations, although the top industrial management in
Slovakia was said to be particularly close to Prime Minister Mečiar. The labor
unions generally kept their distance from political involvement.[88] I may add,
parenthetically, that after only a few months of Slovak independence most of
his closest advisers in the negotiations turned against the Slovak prime minister
in an unseemly squabble.

5. Forums and Tactics

All the tactical devices conjured up by Raiffa were employed.

The Slovak prime minister's ploy, of which he publicly boasted, to ask
consistently for more than he knew he could expect and offer minimal concessions, built his home reputation as the only fighter who could stand up to the
Czechs, but it provoked the charge of Slovak "extortion" and handicapped the
moderates in the negotiations. Following this tactic, in an early encounter with
newly appointed Czech Prime Minister Klaus, the Slovak premier demanded
independent membership of the Slovak state in the United Nations, and Klaus

88. Martin Bútora and Zora Bútorová, "Slovakia: The Identity Challenges of the Newly
Born States," 60 SOCIAL RESEARCH 705, 718–20 (no. 4, Winter 1993); Martin Myant, "Czech and
Slovak Trade Unions," in Michael Waller and Martin Myant (eds.), *supra,* note 75, 59.

promptly accepted, thus sealing the split. It was at this point that Klaus was able to make a showing that there was no longer any room for "splitting the difference." For a long time, perhaps until the final stage of the negotiations, Klaus believed, consistent with his economic view of the world and Mečiar's tactics, that the Slovaks, although engaging in a bargaining game, were not prepared to give up the financial benefits of the common state. Mečiar on the other hand might have labored under the misapprehension that the Czech side was so deeply wedded to the common state that in the end it would compromise to save it.[89] Thus, each leader may have misconceived the limits of the other's negotiating position. One is struck by the personal relationship between the two "strong men." Even at the height of the controversy, Mečiar professed his admiration of, and confidence in, Klaus as "the only trustworthy person" on the Czech side, while Klaus, although uncompromising on the merit of the issues, went out of his way to avoid any show of personal animosity.[90]

The negotiations in all three phases—excepting, of course, the proceedings in the parliaments—were conducted in secrecy. Although the final communiqués were mostly bland, considerable information became available. The expectation that secrecy would make it easier for the parties to make concessions did not materialize; it made it easier for the participants to "reinterpret" or deny any alleged agreement, and it played into the hands of demagogues.[91] This does not mean that secrecy would not have been appropriate in preparatory stages.

The Czech side appeared stronger not only because of its demographic and economic superiority but also because of the Czech-federal alliance and federal expertise, particularly in financial and other technical matters, confirming the Slovak underdog feeling. On the other hand, it was the Slovaks who had the initiative, but their way of gradually raising their claims contributed to the Czech inflexibility.

The effort to commit the participants to their negotiating positions by having them answer questionnaires or formally signing communiqués proved uniformly unsuccessful. This made it possible for the participants either to

---

89. Jiří Weigel, economic adviser in the office of Czech Republic Prime Minister Klaus, asserted that there was no prior intent for a separation. I have noted, however, as early as March 1991, Klaus made it clear that a breakup would be preferable to any constitutional arrangements that would endanger the reforms. When he perceived an actual threat (e.g., two banks of emission), he acted accordingly. LN, Mar. 13, 1991, p. 2.

90. While Mečiar "never loved" Klaus, he stressed that the Czech leader "has never criticized us, never offended, when we come to negotiations [presumably before Klaus became Czech prime minister], he is the only one to keep silent. We view it as a tactical variant for the future . . ." SMENA, Jan. 29, 1992, p. 3.

91. Czech historian Jaroslav Valenta, XXIII LISTY 107, 108 (no. 4, 1993).

avoid any commitment or disavow any previously given or perceived agreement.

The "bulldozer" tactic by which negotiators concentrated in each session on issues that appeared tractable, "sweeping" the more controversial items out of the way to be considered in the future, worked to some degree in the initial stages only.

Appeals to common interest, rational principles, and fairness were made on both sides. The Slovaks insistently recalled the history of Czech broken promises of equality and autonomy. The "restructuring phase" was complicated by theoretical altercations regarding the meaning of "sovereignty," international subjectivity or personality, "confederation" versus federation, and national as against civic principles. The participants employed sometime questionable legal arguments and categories in support of their negotiating positions. Ignorance of modern legal thought and attachment to obsolete positivist ideas hampered the discourse.[92]

More or less veiled threats of unilateral action or retaliation were employed by both sides, more frequently, however, by Mečiar, who repeatedly feigned leaving the negotiations. He would walk out, "slamming the door," demand an apology, set preconditions to resuming negotiations, and make exuberant statements to strengthen his negotiating position. Klaus eschewed emotional reactions and pursued his main objective aggressively while generally willing to concede on nonessentials.

In the final phase, disregarding the agreement on the split, the Slovak side repeatedly attempted, in alliance with the Czech opposition, to resuscitate the idea of a "union" in open moves within the Federal Assembly as well as by employing an "anonymous" trial balloon and a mysterious document slipped into the negotiation files. The Czech coalition remained unified under Klaus's iron hand.

Both sides, although in reality agreed on the two new states as equal successors, maneuvered intermittently to pass the "black jack" of a secessionist to the other side.

6. The "Intervenor"

When Raiffa speaks of an "intervenor," "facilitator" or "mediator," Václav Havel's role in the negotiations comes naturally to mind. Yet the position of the last federal president bristled with paradoxes relating both to his private and political persona. One of his advisers, a high functionary in the Civic Forum, told me that, although not impartial, he was always reasonable. His

---

92. I dealt with the specific arguments previously, particularly chap. VI, 4c, chap. VII, 3c, chap. IX, 1 and 2a–b, and chap. XV, 4, b, ii.

performance—and his writings—disclose a deep ambiguity about power. As a product of the Czech bourgeoisie who enjoys the small pleasures of the "little Czech man," and as an artist at heart, he denies "any desire for power or love of it" and is horrified by its temptations.[93] Yet power holds a fascination for him, a gate to a great adventure in which a simple lad of the Czech folktale becomes a powerful king. Yet again, during a university ceremony at which he was given an honorary degree, he confessed expecting at any moment one of the familiar men from Kafka's "castle" to enter, wrench his freshly acquired diploma from his hand, and evict him from the aula as an impostor. Although he appears from the outside as the very "antipode" of Josef K., his sense of nonbelonging and self-doubt is, he suggests, the motor propelling him into the most unlikely exploits such as the presidency.[94] Yet again—and finally—this alienated modern intellectual believes strongly in a transcendental being as a measure of all human values and individual responsibility; any societal change in his view must come from within the individual.[95]

With great personal courage, he was able to confront the old regime and after its collapse to artfully articulate the ideals and ills of his evolving new society and of modern democracy in general. He emerged after 1989 with great prestige but with the sole experience of a dissident totally excluded from the public political process, confined to the world of samizdats, secret get-togethers of kindred souls, and seminars and theatrical happenings in private apartments, all under the ubiquitous eye of Big Brother, and in the end—a prison cell. He described this pitiful caricature of "public life" as "anti-" or "nonpolitical politics," which allowed him to preserve his personal integrity but did not prepare him for high office in a democracy.

His critics charged—and he vehemently denied—that he consciously continued to adhere to "nonpolitical politics" in his new environment because of his aversion, on moral grounds, to the normal give and take of the political process. Again, Havel's critics point to his public pronouncements evidencing a degree of diffidence toward traditional political parties, which he explained by the experience in the First Republic in which the ruling political parties, with their own presses, labor unions, cooperatives, and sports and educational

---

93. Marián Leško, "Mysleli sme, že nie je politik [We thought he was not a politician]," Nové slovo bez respektu, Oct. 19, 1992, p. 24. *See also ibid.,* Oct. 26, 1992, p. 20; Nov. 2, 1992, p. 20; Nov. 16, 1992, p. 20; Nov. 23, 1992, p. 20; Nov. 30, 1992, p. 20. This is a "hatchet job" on Havel in which the author confronts Havel's rhetoric with his "deeds." What politician could fare well in such a confrontation? In 1995, Leško, by then editor in chief of the largest Slovak daily, told me with a sheepish smile that he had been carried away by a youthful enthusiasm and today would be "much softer" on Havel.

94. "Jerusalem, April 26, 1990," in Václav Havel, Projevy [Addresses] 100–103 (Vyšehrad, Praha, 1990).

95. *Ibid.* Washington, Feb. 21, 1990, 59, 60.

facilities, exerted excessive influence over the life of the country. This posture, it is said with some justification, must have inspired the election slogan "parties are for partisans, the Civic Forum is for all."

There has been little comment on the way in which Havel orchestrated the first phase of the constitutional negotiations, starting with his meeting in a pub with Slovak Prime Minister Mečiar and extending over the many peregrinations "from castles to manors" in 1990 and early 1991. By definition, as a high federal official and as a Czech, he could not be disassociated from one of the parties to the negotiations. He is blamed, among other things, for having promised Mečiar in that meeting a new competence law in advance of, and separate from, the new constitution because, it is said, he could not conceive that a parliament, elected under the Communist regime, could frame a democratic constitution. With his influence at its peak, he may have been able to force an agreement on a full constitution at that time.[96] However, he was not given enough time to acquire the indispensable skills of working with the fragile, groping institutions that were the ultimate arbiters of the constitutional issues or to strike out on an extraconstitutional route. He never succeeded in forming a good working relationship with Alexander Dubček, the Slovak leader of the 1968 Communist reform movement, the kindly, but not very effective, chair of the Federal Assembly, or with its important committees. As his staff, Havel brought with him to "the Castle" people whom he met primarily as dissident journalists, artists, and musicians, who shared his beliefs and excelled in their dedication and enthusiasm rather than in competence in governmental affairs. Yet, if one listens to his first chancellor, persons with the needed background and training were simply not available, particularly if "the ruling circles" of the old regime were to be excluded. Havel remains fiercely loyal to his "old friends" and collaborators and promotes them to positions for which, at times, they are not suited.

When he first came into office, Havel was impressed by "the unusually extensive powers [of the president], almost as extensive as in the so-called presidential system," and he felt that in a new federal constitution "the power of the president could still be somewhat weakened." Not long thereafter, however, when in the course of his learning process he became aware of the increasing divisions in the Parliament and of the serious threat of an unresolvable deadlock due to the unworkability of the prevailing Communist Constitution, he proposed a series of legislative measures, including a bill for increasing his powers in specified situations. With one exception, all of these proposals failed of adoption. A former prominent deputy in the Federal Parliament and Havel's ardent supporter deplored the president's isolation and described the circumstances of the failure of his legislative initiative:

---

96. Conversation with V. Žák.

Some of the advisers acted as if they did not know (or did not want to know) what they were really expected to defend in parliamentary committees. . . . The high distinction and learnedness of Professor Klokočka [a Czech emigré law professor at the University of Munich, consultant to the president] were for a number of deputies . . . unintelligible talk. Most of the deputies shunned his seminars on . . . the premises of the Parliament.[97]

When the negotiations under the president's patronage ran into the ground and the representatives of the two Republic parliaments took over, Havel continued to "intervene" at the margin. Concerned about the lack of progress in the talks between the parliamentarians, Havel proposed, in November 1991, that the Czech side accept the Slovak demands on the deadlocked formal issues relating to the parties and legal nature of the proposed treaty, but the Czech side almost unanimously recoiled against this suggestion with varied degrees of sincere or feigned horror.

Finally, when another series of his constitutional proposals was in dire distress in the Federal Parliament, he decided to appeal to the citizens over the heads of the deputies. He was encouraged to take this risky route by more than two million signatures (mostly Czech) on a petition urging the preservation of the common state. Some thousands of Prague citizens responded in a manifestation at the historic Wenceslas Square. It was perhaps at this point that the president had to decide whether to come out openly in support of the looser, "confederate" structure of the state demanded by the Slovak negotiators. Such a move would have brought Havel into a direct confrontation with the newly emerging Czech team led by Václav Klaus. Shortly after the first mass meeting, Havel declared that there was no need for further demonstrations, leaving behind a feeling of disappointment and—more importantly—an irritated Parliament, which then proceeded to defeat again his proposals for breaking the constitutional logjam. With the bulk of the Czech population more or less indifferent and the Slovaks generally distrustful of him, it is not at all clear what would have happened if Havel had decided to continue his campaign for popular support.

When the president ran for reelection in the summer of 1992, he was defeated in the Federal Assembly by the Slovak vote. His relationship with Slovakia was not an easy one. His original eight advisers included only one Slovak, who left after six months.[98] At the outset, Havel was no less unaware of the Slovak situation than any other Czech intellectual and no less surprised at the outburst of Slovak nationalist rhetoric during the early parliamentary

---

97. Heřman Chromý, "Politik Václav Havel," XXIV LISTY 11, 13 (no. 3, 1994).
98. Conversation with Milan Kňažko.

debate on the new name for the Federation. On one of his visits to Bratislava, he was forcibly prevented from speaking by Slovak separatists. More importantly, he earned the undying hostility of Slovak Prime Minister Mečiar, first because he was said to have opposed Mečiar's appointment to a high federal office, then because of the alleged involvement of "the Castle" in Mečiar's "first" removal from the office of Slovak prime minister, and finally because in his preelection appeal he abjured the voters by clear implication from voting for Mečiar's new party, which nevertheless came out victorious in the elections. Mečiar, "who never forgets or forgives," tried to use Havel's office as a bargaining chip with Václav Klaus, by then his negotiating protagonist, but Klaus refused.

When in July 1992 Havel resigned the remainder of his term, he was accused of "having left the sinking ship" thereby hastening the breakup because he had already accepted it as inevitable and wished to avoid being placed in a position that might compromise his chances for election to the presidency of the new Czech state. Yet under the circumstances his withdrawal a few weeks before the expiration of his term appeared understandable. This, many of his friends thought, marked the end of the politician and the rebirth of the artist. Yet, after another period of "summer meditations" in his country cottage, private citizen Havel plunged into frantic consultations with both the new coalition parties and the opposition on the left. He sought to facilitate the passage of the constitutional legislation on the termination of the state in the deadlocked Federal Parliament, at one point briefly suggesting an extra-constitutional action, this time not to save the common state but to end it quickly and peacefully. With that objective in mind, he ultimately abandoned his commitment to both the common state and a national referendum.

At the same time, he intervened actively and with limited success in the negotiations for a new Czech constitution, often airing the views of the opposition. Contrary to the position of Klaus's party, he advocated a direct election of the Czech president by the people in order to strengthen the authority of that office. His view did not prevail, but he carefully avoided an open confrontation. Having decided to run for the Czech presidency, he was well aware that Klaus's support was essential. In January 1993, he was in fact elected president of the new Czech Republic by a large majority of the Czech Parliament.

Although sincerely dedicated to the preservation of the common state, Havel was unable to sustain this objective in the capacity of "intervenor" or "facilitator," or for that matter as a member of one of the parties to the constitutional negotiations. This, however, is only one perspective from which to view his role. His is a moving story of a courageous struggle to preserve personal integrity under the old regime, of learning and adapting with some difficulty and mixed success to the post-Communist world, of living with internal conflicts, of coming to terms with his own limitations, and of making difficult judgments of "the reality" calling for often distasteful compromises.

Earlier in this book I speculated about a parallel with Lincoln, the consummate lawyer-politician. Bruce Ackerman has evoked George Washington's decision to lend his immense prestige to breaking the then existing confederate Constitution in order to save the Constitutional Convention from certain failure. Ackerman adds:

> If Mr. Havel had President Yeltsin's courage, he would have broken with the Communist Constitution and used his prestige to call a constitutional convention and a subsequent referendum, in which a national majority could have expressed its will.[99]

Ernest Gellner, a distinguished scholar with a Czech background, strongly disagreed, pointing to the fundamental differences in the relevant conditions.[100] I do not propose "to mock comparison" (Ackerman), and in fact I thrive on it, as evidenced in this book. But it is difficult to conjure up in Czecho-Slovakia a scenario comparable with President Yeltsin's troops storming the parliament building in October 1993. There may have been a magic moment, in the fall of 1990 at the latest, when Havel might have had enough influence to force an extraconstitutional way toward the adoption of a new constitution, such as the calling of a constitutional convention. In fact, Federal Prime Minister Čalfa, the astute, professional politician in a sea of amateurs, raised this alternative in one of the president's confabs but abandoned it promptly as unrealistic[101] since the Assembly never would have agreed to surrender its constitutional power. With the Federal Assembly functioning and the constitution-making process just gearing up, there was no apparent reason to foresee the eventual deadlock and to embark on a revolutionary route so foreign to the local tradition. Havel's prestige as seen from Bratislava or from the parliamentary couloirs in Prague might not have been as immense as it was perceived to be from New Haven. Apart from his lack of political experience, Havel's power position, in a civilized, protodemocratic environment stressing "continuity" and legality as against Communist arbitrariness, was not compar-

---

99. Bruce A. Ackerman, "1787 and 1993," NEW YORK TIMES, April 3, 1993, Op Ed, p. 23. *See generally* Bruce A. Ackerman, The Future of Liberal Revolution (Yale U. Press, New Haven, London, 1992).

100. Ernest Gellner, "Innocents Abroad: The Future Liberal Revolution by Bruce Ackerman," NEW REPUBLIC, Nov. 30, 1992, p. 38. *See* David Golove, "Liberal Revolution, Constitutionalism, and the Consolidation of Democracy: A Review of Bruce Ackerman's The Future of Liberal Revolution," 1993 WISC. L. R. 1591, 1595 (no. 6).

101. *Supra,* chap. VII, c.

able to Boris Yeltsin's. However, the full story of his role as a statesman on the domestic and international scenes remains to be told.

Two separate but related questions will have to be addressed by historians: first, could Havel, in the face of prevailing reality, have done more to save the common state and would his effort have made a difference in the outcome; and, second, was the dissolution a preferred alternative to an uneasy coexistence of the two peoples?

If I were cornered with a demand to answer the first question, I would respond that it was not within Václav Havel's power to avert the breakup. The structure prevailed over the "hero" even though in the final phase the drama was played out by other heroes (or villains, depending on the beholder's view). As for the second question, I have attempted in this book to recount as accurately as I could the factors militating for and against the breakup, including some estimate of the consequences of the dissolution for the two peoples and the international community. Beyond that I feel unable to go, although I am tempted to suggest that the dissolution was not in the interest of the Slovaks and perhaps—in the long run—of the Czechs as well. Both questions call for more empirical work and analytical thought; the second requires a particularly difficult cost-benefit analysis with a heavy dose of futuristic speculation.

According to Arthur M. Schlesinger Jr.: "There is no solution in the last chapter; there is no last chapter. The best the interpreter can do is to trace figures in the carpet, recognizing as he must that other interpreters will trace other figures."[102] In Alan Brinkley's words: "There's never a moment when a historical question is settled, about which over time there is not some debate."[103] This is evidenced by the generation of revisionist historians who have interpreted the American Civil War as an "avoidable conflict," heaping blame on Lincoln and others. I am quite composed to see my story—and my answers—"revised."

7. The Last Afterthought

Ross and Ward suggest that parties in conflict often attribute a stalemate to differences in basic values or incompatibility of basic interests: some conflicts do reflect such irreconcilable differences and have little chance of being resolved by negotiations until one party can impose its will on the other or until objective circumstances change in a way that creates a greater commonality of interest.

---

102. Arthur M. Schlesinger Jr., The Cycles of American History 3 (Houghton Mifflin, New York, 1986).
103. Quoted in James Atlas, "Ways to Look at the Past (or Did It Really Happen?)," N.Y. TIMES, Nov. 13, 1994, E3.

Conflict resolution is not always a desirable goal—sometimes wrongs must be righted, structural changes accomplished, or power redistributed under circumstances where any germane resolution demands that the objectives and interests of one party to the dispute be compromised to a degree that it will deem unacceptable and resist as long as it has any means to do so. But . . . many and perhaps even most conflicts are far more tractable than they seem, . . . disputants are often constrained not by objective circumstances but by cognitive, perceptual and motivating biases, . . . that incompatibility in basic needs, interests, and values [is] often more apparent than real.[104]

Unlike the Serb, Croatian, and Muslim strife, the Czech-Slovak conflict, while much less tractable than it appeared to most observers, falls into the category in which the incompatibilities proved in fact susceptible to a negotiated solution, albeit by a dissolution of the common state.

---

104. Lee Ross and Andrew Ward, "Naive Realism: Implications for Social Conflict and Misunderstanding" (unpublished).

Annexes

Annex I

The International Conference, Bratislava, June 1991

In late June 1991, several members of the international group met with their Czech and Slovak counterparts in the Slovak capital under the sponsorship of Slovak Prime Minister Dr. Ján Čarnogurský and the Charter 77 Foundation of New York. This "Conference on Constitutional Preconditions for a Transition to a Market Economy" convened only a few days after the Kroměříž understanding, which shifted the responsibility for constitutional negotiations to the parliaments of the two Republics. It was thus essential—if the conference was to have direct impact—to ensure the participation of members of the Slovak Parliament. Alas, as Professor Karol Plank, chair of the Slovak Supreme Court observed, it was a pity that relatively few Slovak deputies were among more than 40 participants, due—we were told—to a conflict with the ongoing session of the Slovak Parliament.[1]

On the other hand, the array of Czech parliamentarians and officials was impressive. The more articulate voices on the Czech federal and Republic side came from the faction of the Civic Movement, whose political support was already on the decline; similarly, Dr. Čarnogurský's party, although then at the peak of its influence, was to regress to a minor opposition group in less than a year's time. It is safe to assume that no one in the international group was in a position to anticipate future developments, although the possibility of the *rozpad* (split) of the Federation was already in the air.

Three issues were selected for consideration: the ever present problem of the allocation of powers between the Federation and the Republics, the structure of federal institutions, and the provisions for compliance with international obligations, with particular attention to prospective membership in the European Community. The proposed "treaty" between the two Republics was mentioned only to assure the foreign participants that the idea of an international law treaty had been abandoned in favor of an "internal agreement."

---

1. I had the benefit of the record of the Proceedings of the Conference (hereafter Proceedings) prepared with expert skill by David Franklin. A copy is in my file. Plank observation is at p. 17.

1. The Allocation of Powers

The foreign participants, including the Americans, were generally skeptical about the workability of the December 1990 law allocating powers between the Federation and the Republics, particularly in conjunction with the many possibilities for a deadlock in the legislative process under the prevailing federal Constitution.[2] Although they professed to sympathize with the pervasive distaste for bureaucratic centralism—a heritage from the old regime—and with the affirmation of sovereignty of the Republics, they advocated, as they did in the first series of meetings a year before, a central government strong enough to assure economic transformation at home and integration into the international system; failure of effective action during the difficult transition could undermine the still fragile democratic institutions. Will it be possible— they asked—to preserve the unity of the economy and the market with the Republics wielding wide regulatory and implementing authority over the economy as contemplated in the 1990 law?

According to American University Professor Herman Schwartz, "decentralization can and should take place in cultural, health, safety and even economic matters. . . . Strong central government is not inconsistent with strong constitutional units. . . . American states have separate, and often huge, budgets."[3] "Reinforcing national identity"—Professor Dick Howard of the Virginia Law School said—"does not carry with it the corollary that one must also have an equal autonomy in matters of economic judgement."[4]

Professor Steinberger of the Heidelberg Max Planck Institute reported that since 1948 the move in the German Federation had been toward centralization at the expense of the states (*Länder*), particularly in economic matters. In financial matters, there had been an attempt to find a balance: the power to raise and distribute taxes was divided; and a statute providing for equalization of the burden between economically stronger and weaker *Länder* is modified every five or ten years. But the fiscal policies of the various *Länder* differ widely; the strong ones naturally don't want to finance the profligacy of others—"this complicates matters."[5] There has always been a very strong, single central bank. Federal laws are executed by the *Länder* administrations, unlike in the United States.

A resounding plea for an effective central government was made by Dr. Claus-Dieter Ehlermann, at the time a director general at the Commission of

---

2. Schwartz, Proceedings, 1–2; Cutler, 2.
3. *Ibid.,* 15, 16.
4. *Ibid.,* 13.
5. *Ibid.,* 3.

the European Communities in Brussels.[6] "Brussels legislates," he stressed, but "it does not implement." For the present, the Community legislature was shaped by the Council of Ministers in negotiations mostly by civil servants of the member states, with input from the European Parliament. It was therefore essential for the Federative Republic, when it joined, to be represented in Brussels by delegates from an efficient central government, who would speak with a single voice. Again, only a strong central government would be in position to ensure that Community legislation was effectively implemented in the Republic legal order and, where so indicated, was directly enforceable in local courts on the basis of the principle of supremacy of Community law over national law. It would be desirable for this principle to be enshrined in the new constitution since "the absence of such provision could be a barrier to membership."[7]

In their responses, both the Czechs and Slovaks highlighted "the historic situation" in the country, which pointed in a direction diametrically opposite to central power. Professor Jičínský, deputy chair of the Federal Assembly (at that time still a member of the Civic Forum), recognized that public opinion did not pay sufficient attention to international realities, but—referring to the independence of Slovenia and Croatia—he saw the pendulum swinging away from centralism. He affirmed, however, the need for uniform rules for transition to the Common Market. But he and Dr. Burešová, chair of the Czech Parliament and also a prominent member of the Civic Forum, defended the 1990 law on power allocation, as did a high official of the federal government. The latter felt that the six months' experience confirmed the viability of the new distribution of powers, with problems remaining in transport, energy, and agriculture. I have dealt with the difficulties arising out of the application of the law earlier.[8]

In the view of Docent L'ubomír Fogaš, representing the Party of the Democratic Left in the Slovak Parliament, history had proved that there could be no final division of competences; there should be a certain flexibility—"we could move toward centralization or decentralization," a sensible statement.[9] Chair Plank retorted that, although it was not necessary to specify all competences, the division should be as precise as possible. He stressed the particular challenges of a two-member Federation magnified by the disproportion in the strength of the two units: budget and taxes were the big problems. Centrally collected tax revenues were divided among the Republics, but opinions differed about whether the money was returned equitably to the parties; there

---

6. In his preceding assignment, Mr. Ehlermann had headed the Legal Service of the commission and later was appointed spokesman for its president, Jacques Delors.

7. Proceedings, 5.

8. *Supra,* chap. IV, 3d.

9. Proceedings, 2.

was the question of redistribution of tax revenues to Slovakia to deal, for instance, with the urgent conversion of Slovak arms industries (located there for political reasons), which Slovakia could not accomplish by itself.[10] Still, according to Plank, Lloyd Cutler, the American co-organizer of the international group, may have overstated the value of a strong central state. Elsewhere in the world, federations consist of a number of components, so the role of coordination is much more important. Here in the Czech and Slovak Republic it was possible to solve many questions on the Republic level, and only where joint rules were required should the Federation step in. After all, the Republics needed to function smoothly as well, as there were many matters that should be within their exclusive spheres. In his opinion, some competences were already too broad on the federal level.[11]

The most revealing reaction came from the host of the conference, Dr. Čarnogurský himself:

[W]e are grateful for the time and effort which our Western colleagues have devoted to these discussions, and for the rational arguments they have brought to them. I have the impression, however, that our country is not fully prepared to absorb these rational points. Perhaps we stand mentally as well as geographically between East and West, between a politics based on calculated reason and one more attuned to the emotional dimension. Above all, we find ourselves at a historical moment in which the emotional reaction away from centralized power is very strong, and we must act within this context.[12]

The question was raised, in the wake of Dr. Ehlermann's explanation, that if the Czech and Slovak Federation became a member of the European Union and later on one Republic (presumably Slovakia) decided to secede, under international law would the Czech Republic continue as a successor state (as Pakistan did after the secession of Bangladesh) or would both Republics have to apply for admission as new states?[13]

---

10. *Ibid.*, 1.

11. *Ibid.*, 2–3.

12. *Ibid.*, 13.

13. There was support for the first alternative, even though the argument was advanced that, in the case of a two-unit federation, a secession of one component meant the end of the state as an international person. Dr. Ehlermann recalled two precedents in which territory associated with a member state was separated from the European Community: the status of Algeria was left unclear, while the secession of Greenland from Denmark after its decolonization was the subject of extremely difficult negotiations. In any case, "massive renegotiations" would be required in the hypothetical case of Slovakia's secession after the admission of the Federation to membership, considering the high degree of integration of the Union. If the Czech and Slovak Federation

In line with Dr. Ehlermann's conclusions, Professor Steinberger pointed to the "tremendous legislative power" of the European Union over, among other things, German agriculture; the *Länder* are concerned that they may lose to the Union even those remnants of power that they have under the federal Basic Law (Constitution). One solution would be to require German delegates to the Union to follow decisions of the *Bundesrat,* the upper chamber of the Parliament composed of representatives of *Länder* governments; the other would be to generally include regional representatives at the Union level "at least as a forum for articulation." He asked the Czechs and Slovaks to take into account this European dimension.[14] I may add that the Maastricht Treaty for a European Union provided for the representation of regions, albeit by a purely advisory body.

2. The Institutional Structure: The Parliament

The discussion of the institutional structure revealed the challenge to reconcile the requirements of the separation of powers, the rule of majority, the protection of minorities, and the efficiency of the legislative process.

Chair Plank and Professor Jiří Boguszak, deputy chair of the Commission of Experts of the Federal Assembly, analyzed President Havel's draft, which was designed in part to reduce minority blocking power and the danger of a deadlock, with the modifications made by the commission. The idea that the Assembly would consist of a "conglomeration" of the two Republic parliaments (obviously a "confederate" approach) was put aside, but a wide range of other options was explored, including a unicameral solution. President Havel's proposal for a proportionally elected unicameral Assembly with a Federal Council culled from the two Republic parliaments was changed by the commission: The Assembly would vote as one block rather than separately by nation,[15] but on constitutional acts a "prohibition of majorization"[16] of the minority would remain. The Federal Council, composed of 15 Czechs and

---

acceded, it would sit as such in the Council, and it would be inconceivable for Czechs and Slovaks to be represented separately. Only in the European Parliament could the diversity be expressed by deputies elected in the two Republics:

> Even the idea of a consultative status for regions [such as component states of a federation] is fraught with difficulties, because the Community contains strong central states. Spain's autonomous regions each have tailor-made status and their own constitutions . . . and this has caused problems. So there is no realistic hope of regions having anything more than a consultative role in the Community. (*Ibid.,* 7)

14. *Ibid.,* 3.

15. Half of the 150 deputies in the upper Chamber of Nations was elected from the Czech Republic and half from Slovakia.

16. On "the prohibition of majorization," see *supra,* chap. III, 8 a.

Slovaks delegated from the Republic parliaments would be convened only if a specified number of Czech or Slovak members wished to discuss a given bill; eight of the 15 Czechs or Slovaks would wield a suspensive veto over legislation. The council would have the competence to act on several other matters by simple majority. Some commission members preferred a council in the image of the German *Bundesrat* (Federal Council) composed of appointees of the governments of the *Länder* rather than of their parliaments, while others objected that the council would be too powerful, even though the Assembly, acting presumably by a two-thirds majority, would have a final say on proposed legislation. Referring to the "extraordinary blocking powers" granted to a small minority under the unprecedented "prohibition of majorization," Lloyd Cutler suggested that cases involving international obligations or laws essential for the transformation to a market economy be excluded from this clause. He mentioned the Belgian system, which, although at that time unitary in its appearance, gave representatives of the three language communities the authority to object to legislation on ethnic matters (culture, language, education) on the grounds that it would adversely affect relations between the communities; after receiving the objection, the government makes a report, which is followed by a simple majority vote in the Assembly.

Professor Steinberger recalled that in 1948, a U.S.-style Senate was considered in Germany, but the *Bundesrat* system was chosen. The *Bundesrat* may object to laws yet can be overridden by the lower chamber. In some categories, the assent of the *Bundesrat* is necessary. If the federal legislature wants to provide rules for *Länder* governments, it needs that assent: so the *Länder* parliaments are weakened, but *Länder* governments that control the *Bundesrat* are strengthened. The *Bundesrat* has accumulated "an enormous amount of know-how and experience."[17] As I mentioned earlier, the Czech-Slovak expert commission chose a variant of the *Bundesrat* model, composed, however, of nominees of the Republic parliaments, rather than that of their governments.

3. The President: Back to 1920?

As regards the head of state, "[t]he ideal we are striving toward"—said Professor Boguszak, "is the 1920 Constitution, under which the president was neither too strong nor too weak, as the constitutional committee of those days put it";[18] however, the expert commission's text differed from both the 1920 Constitution and Havel's draft in a number of ways.

---

17. Proceedings, 3.
18. *Ibid.*, 9.

The commission rejected Havel's ideas introducing a variant of a direct election[19] and favored in effect a continuation of the present system of election by the Assembly, requiring a majority of each Republic's deputies. The president's term would be five years as against the Assembly's four. The Austrian, French, as well as American participants, on the other hand, urged direct election of the president as a unifying force, obviously reflecting their experience with that procedure in their own countries:

> You have no federation-wide parties—another reflection of the observation that there is no such thing as Czechoslovakia. If you had a direct election of the President as the Poles and Austrians do [and Bulgarians and Russians], and as Hungary plans to institute, it would mean there would have to be federation-wide parties . . .[20]

Councillor Errera recalled the situation in the French Third and Fourth Republics when presidents were elected by the Parliament and before direct election was instituted in 1962:

> With all respect, the Presidents in those days were average if not mediocre people without the personal will or capacity to make important decisions, especially in times of emergency.[21]

Errera warned against a requirement that the president gain a majority in all or several parts of the country and suggested that the president and the Parliament not be elected at the same time.

According to the expert commission, the president would have a suspensive veto over legislation independent from that of the Federal Council, and a majority of *all* members of the Assembly would be necessary to override it. There would thus be two suspensive vetoes. As in the 1920 Constitution, the president would be unaccountable and unrecallable, but—as in France and Germany—not all his acts would have to be countersigned by a minister. Still, in contrast to the 1920 Constitution, the president's right to dissolve the Assembly would be hedged by a complex set of conditions. Personally, chair

---

19. The president envisaged the first round in the Assembly; if unsuccessful, there would be a direct election by the people. Councilor Errera called this "the worst combination." *Ibid.,* 10. I was told that the direct election was barred back in 1990 for fear that it might be won by the Communist Party, whose strength at the time was difficult to estimate. *See generally* Arend Lijphart (ed.), Parliamentary versus Presidential Government (Oxford U. Press, Oxford, 1992).

20. Cutler, *ibid.,* 7. Hungary first instituted and later abolished direct election of the president.

21. *Ibid.,* 10.

Plank would prefer no veto right for the president (as in the prevailing federal Constitution) since he would participate in the Federal Council, but would accord him the right of legislative initiative, which the commission would deny him. Plank saw the president "stronger than the average," with a mediation role between the two Republics; the Slovak constitution might provide for a president of Slovakia, in which case the relationship between the two presidents would have to be worked out.[22]

Two variants were under consideration as regards the establishment of the government: the government would be appointed by the president or—the president would designate the prime minister, who would appoint the rest of the government—the German "chancellor" concept.

Counselor Errera described the strong position of the French directly elected president and more specifically his power to call a referendum at the suggestion of the Prime Minister but in reality as his own prerogative; this power, which "has its uses, but its dangers as well," "should be a preserve of the President."[23] In this dual-executive system, the president approves and dismisses the prime minister, but the latter is seen as a potential rival and successor to the president, "which is dangerous"—but the system works. Modern countries are run by the executive—"[p]arliamentary rule has never led to happiness or democracy—it has led to unhappiness and dictatorship," Errera added.[24] Lloyd Cutler thought that the president should be given the authority to declare a state of emergency when a deadlock existed on serious matters or to call for a referendum of the people when a decision must be taken—generally in the image of the powers of the French president. "If nothing else works you may consider the system used in Belgium."[25]

The uneasiness about a strong executive, I suggested, might reflect the experience with the centralized Communist regime, and there was a danger of writing a constitution against the past.[26]

4. Ethnic Minorities

Deputy Rozsa, a representative of the Hungarian minority in the Slovak Parliament, declared that the creation of conditions for market reform required stability, which in turn called for legal protection of the rights of ethnic minor-

---

22. *Ibid.*, 11.

23. *Ibid.*, 10. The referenda were used more recently for four purposes: to ratify new constitutions (in 1945 for the provisional constitution, in 1946, and in 1958); to amend a constitution (in 1962 and 1969); to approve the president's powers, as during the Algiers crisis; and to ratify a treaty (in 1972 and 1989).

24. *Ibid.*, 15.

25. *Ibid.*, Cutler, 7, 14.

26. *Ibid.*, 12.

ities (such as some 600,000 Hungarians in Slovakia). These rights to education, language, and information, and to self-governing bodies and political representation, should be set forth in the federal constitution; and the Republic constitutions should be able to widen but not to narrow them.[27] The federal Charter of Fundamental Rights and Freedoms prohibited the use of the national or ethnic identity of any individual to his or her detriment; minorities were guaranteed rights to develop their own cultures, to disseminate and receive information in their languages, the right of association, the right of education in their languages and use of them in official contacts, as well as the right to participate in decisions concerning them. A federal law would settle the details and conditions.[28] The Council of Europe, observed Professor Steinberger, had worked out principles for the protection of minorities, which were reflected in the 1990 Copenhagen document of the Conference on Security Cooperation in Europe (CSCE). The CSCE countries were to discuss this issue, and a draft of a convention was in the hands of the Czech and Slovak ministers of justice.

5. On Impartial Advice

On the second day of the meeting, an independent Slovak daily reported a statement by the chair of the Slovak National Party, Jozef Prokeš, in which he expressed his "immense disappointment" over the activity of our group:

> We view it as an effort to support a certain wing in the Czech and Slovak Federal Republic, which seeks a strong central power and the idea of a single Czecho-Slovak nation . . . the foreign participants proceed from erroneous assumptions when they compare Czecho-Slovakia as a federation with Germany, Austria, and the United States. They forget that these countries are one-nation federations and their central organs act abroad in the name of that nation. In Czecho-Slovakia, however, live two different nations, and one of them is being denied the right to speak in its own name. The Czecho-Slovak Federal Republic should be compared to Canada with all the consequences flowing from it.[29]

We were asked to comment on this statement at a press conference for Slovak journalists. "The characterization," Professor Schwartz replied, "is a bit unfair. We come as impartial experts, having spent a lifetime studying constitu-

---

27. *Ibid.,* 12.

28. 23/1991 Sb., arts. 24 and 25. The Federal Assembly had legislative competence in matters of basic rights and freedoms "to the extent laid down in constitutional laws." Art 37, 103/1991 Sb.

29. "Predseda SNS sklamaný konferenciou [Chair of SNP Disappointed by the Conference]," NO, June 24, 1991, p. 1.

tions and political systems around the world." Dr. Burešová, the chair of the Czech National Council, agreed that "these experts do not have a political agenda and wish to be as objective as possible."

Dr. Čarnogurský noted that many remarks were made about strong central government: "As I said, constitution-making has both a political and legal dimension. The purpose of this conference is to cast light on the preparation of the future constitutions . . . and it fulfilled this purpose. But the political decisions will be taken here . . . with an awareness of all circumstances, including those pointed out by our foreign colleagues."[30]

In the same press meeting, I made a personal comment, which—as I suggested earlier—I subsequently felt was out of place. I include an excerpt because it reveals unabashedly the point of view that informs this book:

I grew up as a young man under the Masaryk Republic. The First Republic wasn't perfect, and the treatment of the Slovaks by the Czechs during the Republic wasn't perfect. But it grieves me to even contemplate the prospect of breaking up the Czech and Slovak union. In a world where the West is integrating and internationalizing while the East is disintegrating into smaller units, the idea that this country, which was my country and about which I feel very strongly, could go the Eastern way, distresses me greatly . . .

The new vision of Europe should not be put in terms of central or local government, but as little government as possible, and government as close to the people as possible. I think the long-range development in Europe will unfold in this way: the main decisions about economy and environment will be taken at a supranational level by consensus of all the nations, while the problems that concern the components . . . will be decided at the level of these components. This is the ideal vision of modern Europe and I fervently hope that Czechs and Slovaks will participate in its realization, because of the great talent and history that support your important role in Europe and in the world.[31]

---

30. Proceedings, 17.
31. *Ibid.,* 16–17.

Annex II

Constitutions and the World

1. The "Opening" Issue

One question facing the Czech and Slovak constitution makers was whether—and in what form—the constitution should include provisions regulating the effect of international law in the internal legal order and the procedure for accession to membership in international bodies such the European Union. This two-pronged issue of an "opening" to the international community surfaced first in the negotiations for the federal constitution.[1]

In the contemporary international system, a state is required to perform its international obligations (treaties and general international law) in good faith, but it is free to choose the modalities of the performance within its internal legal order. A state may allow—by a constitutional or legislative rule or by practice—for a treaty to become directly applicable to individuals, enabling them to invoke it in national courts ("self-executing" in the United States, "direct effect" in European Union law), or it may require a national legislative act "transforming" the treaty into internal law, making its performance subject to the control of the national legislative process. If an irreconcilable conflict arises between a treaty and internal law, the state may provide that a treaty, while conforming to the national constitution, prevails over prior *and* subsequent legislation, or it may make a treaty supersede prior legislation only, according to the *lex posterior* rule. The first of the two alternatives—the more liberal "opening"—is followed by at least six members of the European Union, while the *lex posterior* rule applies in the United States, Germany, and Italy.[2]

Again, a modern state that by necessity must join many international organizations is free to define its internal procedures for that purpose. The question is whether the constitution should specify such procedures for accession particularly to integrated structures such as the European Union and define the effect of normative acts of such bodies in its internal legal order. National

---

1. I deal with this subject in detail in "International Law in Internal Law: Toward Internationalization of Central-Eastern European Constitutions," 88 AJIL 427–50 (1994).

2. For citations to the constitutions of the members of the European Union and other states, see *ibid.*, 431 n. 16.

constitutions of the European Union members contain either a general or a specific constitutional authorization to that effect.[3]

2. At the Federal Level

The successive constitutions adopted since the Czechoslovak state came into existence in 1918 were silent on these matters. There was no general legislation, and practice was not uniform. A number of provisions in international treaties were made applicable in the federal internal order by specific legislation. Scholarly voices called for a constitutional regulation to remedy the state of legal uncertainty. As an important albeit partial step toward a constitutional solution the Charter of Fundamental Rights and Freedoms, adopted by the Federal Assembly in January of 1991, prescribed that "international treaties on human rights and fundamental freedoms, ratified and promulgated by the Czech and Slovak Federative Republic, are universally binding on its territory and supersede its own laws [legislation]."[4] The clear import was that the human rights treaties, which like any other treaties had to conform to the federal Constitution, became directly applicable upon promulgation and superseded any conflicting prior or subsequent federal law and the law of the component Republics. The Federal Constitutional Court was given jurisdiction to enforce this rule.[5]

The action of the federal legislature reflected the post–World War II recognition of the individual as an "international person" endowed with fundamental rights guaranteed by treaties and the evolving customary law. It confirmed the attachment of the newly emerging society to the concept of fundamental rights, which, before the revolution, had served as a rallying program for the dissenters within the Charter 77 group led by Václav Havel. It was also motivated by the desire to establish the eligibility of the Federation for membership in Western European institutions, starting with the Council of Europe in which assurance of basic rights protection is a specific prerequisite. Nevertheless, the innovative provision singling out human rights treaties for special constitutional treatment[6] raised a number of questions applying also to the

---

3. For relevant citations, see *ibid.*, 432 n. 17.

4. Const. Law 23/1991 Sb., art. 2. On the interpretation of this article, see Jiří Malenovský in 11/1992 PRÁVNÍK 931.

5. The Constitutional Court was to declare void any provisions of the federal legislation and of the constitutions and laws of the Republics that it found to be in conflict with such international treaties. These provisions were to cease to be effective upon the ruling by the Court and were to become null and void unless amended within a six-month period. The review proceeding could be initiated not only by specified public authorities but also by an individual complainant and a court. Const. Law 91/1991 Sb., arts. 2(b), 3(1), 6.

6. For citations to similar provisions in other constitutions (Peru, Russia, and Spain) and the status in Austria, *see* Stein, AJIL, *supra,* note 1, 435–36 n. 36.

constitutions of the two independent Republics, which subsequently have embraced the tenor of the federal Charter. For instance, what treaties, in addition to the global and regional conventions aimed specifically at the protection of basic rights, would fall within its parameters? Would the provision apply to extradition treaties or treaties of cooperation, commerce, and investment with guarantees of selected individual rights? The Federal Ministry of Foreign Affairs tentatively took the view that only multilateral treaties dealing with human rights were to be included.[7]

Foremost, however, was the question regarding the status of treaties *other* than those dealing with basic rights. Should the new federal constitution continue the tradition of silence, leaving the solutions to ad hoc legislation and ambivalent practice? The question was considered in the context of the consultations with the international advisory group, and an opinion was addressed to the Commission of Experts on the Federal Constitution. The opinion stressed several points.[8]

A possible solution would be to extend the treatment of the human rights treaties to either certain other important treaties (e.g., arms control, environment protection, and "lawmaking" treaties such as the Vienna Convention codifying the law on treaties) or to *all* treaties that purport to have effect on individuals and are approved by the Federal Assembly and duly ratified and promulgated. The extension to all treaties would have certain advantages.

> As a small state in the heart of Europe, the Czech and Slovak Federation depended greatly upon the stability and faithful compliance with international law by other states. By guaranteeing the supremacy of its international commitments in its constitution, the Federative Republic would join a number of other modern democracies with the same system. It would contribute to a trend that in the long run might lead to a general practice requiring priority of international law over internal law in domestic legal orders.
>
> Only through such a constitutional provision could the Republic protect itself against intentional or unintentional violation of its international obligations by the legislative branch.
>
> In order to guarantee an effective performance of the treaty, the constitution should enable individuals to seek enforcement of their rights

---

7. Letter from the acting director, International Law and Treaties Department, Federal Ministry of Foreign Affairs, dated November 22, 1991.

8. My letter to Prof. Dr. Jiří Boguszak, cochair, Commission of Experts on the Federal Constitution, Office of the Government of the Czech and Slovak Federative Republic, dated July 12, 1991. *See also* my correspondence with the acting director, International Law Department, Federal Ministry of Foreign Affairs, November 1991–January 1992, and statements at meetings in Prague and Bratislava.

derived from the treaty in domestic courts—as has been the experience, for instance, in the United States and the European Union system.

In anticipation of admission to the European Union, such a provision—along with a clause defining the internal procedures for accession to international organizations—would assure the required incorporation of the extensive European Union law into the Republic's internal legal order.[9]

The August 1991 working draft of the experts appointed by the Federal Assembly encapsulated the substance of the opinion.[10] However, the prospect of the impending dissolution of the state made any further effort fruitless.

3. Constitutions for the Independent Republics

a. The Czech Constitution

The Czech Constitution approved in December 1992[11] contains only the federally inspired text on human rights treaties, giving them direct effect and unqualified supremacy over legislation, and it grants the Constitutional Court jurisdiction to enforce it.[12] As for other treaties, the new team that took over the drafting task after the 1992 elections appeared inclined to follow the course outlined in the opinion just described.[13] However, opposition to granting direct effect and superiority to ordinary treaties developed mainly from two sources. The old regime protagonists of the "dualist" system requiring the "transformation" of treaties by legislation were against such a solution on doctrinal grounds. Certain high instances in the new Republic government feared that

---

9. For a full summary of the opinion and counterarguments, see Stein, AJIL, *supra,* note 1, 436–39.

10. Art. 8. No. 1: International treaties approved by the Federal Assembly, ratified and proclaimed in the OFFICIAL JOURNAL destined for the proclamation of laws, from which flow rights or obligations of physical or legal persons, are immediately applicable in the Czech and Slovak Federative Republic and have priority before the law. No. 2: By an international treaty, powers established in this Constitution may be entrusted to international organizations. To be valid, such treaty requires approval by a constitutional law of the Federal Assembly before its ratification. Constitution of the Czech and Slovak Federative Republic, working proposal, head VIII, arts. 8, 129 (Aug. 1991).

11. For previous developments, see Stein, AJIL, *supra,* note 1, 440–41.

12. Arts. 10, 87(1) a and b.

13. My fax letters to Dr. Jiří Payne, chair of the Foreign Affairs Committee of the Czech National Council, dated November 5, 1992, and to Docent JUDr. Vojtěch Cepl, dated November 9, 1992, and my comments on the government proposal for a constitution of the Czech Republic (international and selected other aspects), fax message to the vice-chair of the Czech Republic Constitutional Commission, Jiří Boguszak, dated December 3, 1992.

"Western European socialism," perceived, for instance, in the European Social Charter, might be imposed on the new liberal economic policy.[14]

Thus, nothing is said in the Czech Constitution about treaties other than those dealing with protection of human rights; nor is there any text on accession to integrated organizations, a curious omission in view of the almost ritualistic affirmation by the spokesmen of the new government of the policy to join not only the European Union but NATO as well.[15]

b. The Slovak Constitution

The Slovak Constitution, like its Czech counterpart, incorporates the human rights treaties, albeit in a somewhat different formulation, which may cause additional difficulties of interpretation.[16] The Constitutional Court is given

---

14. See *supra,* chap. XIV, 2b, iv.

15. The proposal of the drafting team included a clause on accession to international organizations, but it was dropped, I am informed, for personal rather than substantive reasons. The Constitution also introduces the much-needed requirement of promulgation, which conditions "the validity" of both legislation and international agreements approved by the legislature. Art. 52. Clearly, since "validity" (*platnost*) in *international* law cannot be made dependent on promulgation, the term may refer to the effect of directly applicable treaties in *internal* law. See Vladimír Mikule et al., Mezinárodní smlouvy mezi Českou republikou a Slovenskou republikou [International Treaties between the Czech Republic and Slovak Republic] 7 (Codex Bohemia, Praha 1995). Docent Mikule suggests that in the light of this silence, a treaty becomes directly applicable by virtue of a specific provision of an individual legislation, which—in his view—was the practice followed in the latest decades. *Ibid.,* 8–9. Article 49 provides that "[i]nternational treaties, which must be approved by Parliament, are passed by Parliament like draft laws." Article 49(2) lists the treaties that require parliamentary approval.

A clause carried over from an early draft enables the Constitutional Court to decide on measures necessary to carry out a binding decision of an international court "if it cannot be carried out in another way." Art. 87(1) I.

16. Article 11 reads: "International treaties on human rights and basic freedoms ratified by the Slovak Republic and promulgated in a manner prescribed by the law shall have priority over laws [legislation] to the extent that the treaties ensure a greater scope of constitutional rights and freedoms." If narrowly read, this variant may raise doubts about the direct applicability of the treaties in question because, if for no other reason, it omits the specific clause to that effect, which was included in other drafts. Moreover, the application of the limitation on the reach of these treaties may well cause difficulties. *See* Pavol Holländer, "The New Slovak Constitution: A Critique," 1 EAST EUR. CONST. REV. 16, 17 (no. 3, 1992). The article quoted above is limited to treaties dealing with those human rights that are protected by the Constitution. It assumes that if the Constitution provides for a higher standard of protection than a treaty, that higher standard will apply. On the face of it, the corresponding text adopted in the Czech Constitution does not so assume. However, a reasonable interpretation would reach the same result, and, in any event, the principal human rights treaties generally safeguard any higher national standard. The Slovak text prevents the possibility that a lower legislative (not constitutional) standard might prevail over a treaty standard.

jurisdiction to pass upon the conformity of "generally binding legal provisions" with duly promulgated international treaties and to declare any conflicting provisions "ineffective."[17] According to another article included in the section on ordinary courts, "judges are bound also [sic] by an international treaty if so provided by the Constitution or a law [legislation]."[18] The Constitution contains no other directly relevant text. Nevertheless, these provisions, read with the law governing the publication of treaties,[19] are apparently interpreted as according the status of legislation to ratified treaties. All treaties, including the human rights treaties, must conform to the Constitution.[20] At any rate, the two principal drafters see the Constitution as characterized by "the reception of generally accepted international pacts and agreements."[21]

Judges, unaccustomed as they are to dealing with cases of this sort, may find it rather difficult to fashion a coherent pattern from this constitutional conceit. Yet, in contrast to the bland silence of its Czech counterpart, the Slovak Constitution, if interpreted as suggested, has taken a significant step toward defining the effect of legal obligations of the new Republic toward the outside world.

In the same vein, one of the "Basic Provisions" of the Slovak Constitution enables the Republic to enter, pursuant to a free decision, into an association with other states. However, the right to "exit" from the association cannot be limited, and treaties on entry or exit must be approved by a constitutional law followed by a referendum.[22] The two main drafters of the Constitution saw

---

17. If the respective organs fail to comply within six months' time, the contested provisions lose their "validity." Slovak Const., arts. 125(e), 132(1). The formulation of articles 125 and 132(1) may raise some question whether the jurisdiction of the Constitutional Court was intended to embrace conflicts between a treaty and legislation. What is meant by "generally binding legal provisions" in article 125(e)? The concept is used in the rest of the article to denote exclusively legal measures *other* than legislation. But that does not seem to be the common understanding of the concept.

18. *Ibid.*, art. 144(2).

19. Law on the Collection of Laws of the Slovak Republic, 1/1993 Zb.

20. "The law [legislation] has superiority over everything. But only such law or other generally legally binding legal provisions that are in conformity with the basic law—the Constitution. That, naturally, applies also to . . . international treaties promulgated in the way determined by the law." Milan Čič and Ľubomír Fogaš, "Slovo na úvod [A Word for an Introduction]," in Ústava Slovenskej republiky [Constitution of the Slovak Republic] 3, 7, (NVK International, Bratislava, 1992).

21. *Ibid.*, 5. What is meant by "generally recognized?" Only multilateral treaties? Only certain multilateral treaties?

22. Slovak Const., arts. 7, 86(c). It has been suggested that since these provisions were formulated at the time of the Slovak campaign for a Czech-Slovak "union," their purpose was to leave open the opportunity for some such new association. Zdeněk Jičínský and Vladimír Mikule, Das Ende der Tschechoslowakei 1992 in verfassungsrechtlicher Sicht (Teil II) 7, Berichte des Bundesinstitutes für ostwissenschaftliche und internationale Studien no. 45–1994, Köln, 1994.

the significance of this provision in broader contexts. It is an effort, on the one hand, to build our own existence as a state, but on the other hand, and this in harmony with the overall developmental tendencies, to fit into the framework of the integrating Europe, which neither denies the right of a nation to self-determination and national identity nor attributes to that right priority significance. This article creates constitutional prerequisites for a new form of relationship between the Czech and Slovak nations . . . based on full equality, cooperation, and mutual advantage . . .[23]

This constitutional text shows a degree of awareness of the new realities facing the new state in the international arena that contrasts strikingly with the Czech instrument. It evidently contemplates an association (*zväzok, a union,* as translated unofficially) closer than a simple cooperative, purely intergovernmental regime. This interpretation is confirmed by the demanding requirement of a popular referendum in addition to legislative approval by special majorities. The two authoritative commentators confirm the underlying effort to reconcile the national assertion of independence with the needs of European integration and the desire for special links with the Czech state.

Neither the Slovak nor the Czech Constitution deals with the effect of general international law.[24]

4. Concluding Thoughts on the "Opening"

Regarding the status and the effect of treaties, the drafts prepared by the original teams prior to the 1992 elections offered more positive formulations. In fact, had the Federative Republic continued, a fair assumption is that its new constitution would have included the comprehensive formula envisaged in the previously cited opinion. The new political forces that came to power after June 1992 on the Czech side, at any rate, manifested less understanding of, or inclination to deal with, the problem. This posture went against the trend marking the recent constitutional documents in post-Communist Central-Eastern Europe and elsewhere.[25]

---

23. Milan Čič and L'ubomír Fogaš, "Demokratický charakter ústavy SR z roku 1992 [Democratic Character of the Constitution of the SR of 1992]," in Ústava Slovenskej republiky, *supra,* note 20, 82. For criticism of the Slovak Constitution, *see* Peter Kresák, "Notes on the Form of Government in the Constitution of the Slovak Republic" (unpublished).

24. On this general problem, *see* Stein, AJIL, *supra,* note 1, *passim.*

25. Of the 15 such post-Communist Constitutions or drafts I have surveyed, most incorporated treaties as an integral part of the internal order, and, although this is not clear in all instances, treaties are to have the status of ordinary legislation. In five (probably seven) cases, treaties are made superior to national legislation, while in three documents this higher rank is reserved to human rights treaties only. Stein, AJIL, *supra,* note 1, 444–46.

The tendency toward a more or less liberal "opening" of national constitutions reflects the profound changes in the international arena the impact of which could escape the attention of only the most parochial of the constitution makers: the massive proliferation of international agreements after World War II, including novel types of lawmaking conventions and treaties specifically designed to affect internal legal orders, the unprecedented growth of international regimes, some with prescriptive authority, and the intensified common security interest in moderating unilateral use of state military power. The pervasive normative changes correspond also with the globalization of the economy and communications. I have signaled earlier the two developments specifically relevant to the post-Communist Central-Eastern European governments with totalitarian histories: the emerging status of the individual in international law and the integrating structures in Western Europe the accession to which forms the cornerstone of the foreign policies of these governments.

In a considerable measure, of course, the trend toward internationalization dilutes the traditional concepts of "sovereignty" and intrudes into areas of "domestic jurisdiction," including the most intimate ties between the state and its citizens. The elites in the states that recently have gained independent status on a platform of ethnic self-determination and national sovereignty find it difficult to adjust to the fact that the concept of absolute and indivisible sovereignty has become a mirage in the political, economic, and the legal senses, owing in no small measure to the emergence of an international law of individual and minority-group rights and the many international organizations.[26] The technical nature of the problem postulating a certain level of sophistication in international law and the domination of extreme positivist doctrines among these leaders posed additional complications.

In the face of the unprecedented challenges of national economic and political reconstruction, the specific issue of constitutional regulation of the internal effect of international law is not a compelling priority. In fact, under the circumstances some might question the need to elevate this subject to the constitutional level rather than leave it to the normal play of the legislative process. Yet five years after independence there is no clue suggesting that the Czech Parliament is prepared to deal with the problem. The result of inaction is continued uncertainty.

Norms grounding international law and institutions in national basic documents are of more than symbolic value, although symbols are important on their own account. These constitutional rules help delegitimize nonconforming conduct of states and enhance the visibility of, and respect for, interna-

---

26. For an effective argument on this subject, *see* Neil MacCormick, "Beyond the Sovereign State," 56 MOD. L. REV. 1 (1993). *See also* José Alvarez, "Positivism Regained, Nihilism Postponed," 15 MICH. J. INT'L. L. 747 (1994).

tional standards. They reinforce the state of legal certainty and political-economic stability in the internal and international legal orders and advance the protection of individuals. In a historical survey, Professor Antonio Cassese has shown a correlation between the "opening" clauses in national constitutions and the efforts to establish democracy following the defeat of an authoritative system.[27] Such clauses, one may conclude, are a manifestation of the will to join the community of peaceful, democratic, "liberal states."[28] In its final, alas still utopian, vision, such a community would encompass transnational civil societies, which—although bound together by novel institutional arrangements—would assure that decisions are made at a level closest to the individuals.

---

27. Antonio Cassese, "Modern Constitutions and International Law," 192 RECUEIL DES COURS 331, 351 (1985 III).

28. Anne-Marie Slaughter Burley, "International Law and International Relations Theory: A Dual Agenda," 87 AJIL 205, 234 (1993).

Selected Bibliography

Only a fraction of the sources is listed here since the references in the footnotes within each chapter provide complete citations to each item. I have drawn with profit on the Research Reports on Eastern Europe of Radio Free Europe–Radio Liberty. Other frequently cited materials are legislation, including preparatory works, records of parliamentary debates, transcripts of shorthand minutes of meetings, official press releases, notes of private conversations, and Slovak and Czech periodicals, including: ČESKOSLOVENSKÝ ČASOPIS HISTORICKÝ, ČESKÝ DENÍK, CZECH SOCIOLOGICAL REVIEW, EKONOM, FORUM, HOSPO-DÁŘSKÉ NOVINY, KULTURNÝ ŽIVOT, LIDOVÁ DEMOKRACIE, LIDOVÉ NOVINY, LISTY, LITERÁRNÍ NOVINY, MLADÁ FRONTA DNES, NÁRODNÁ OBRODA, NOVÁ PŘÍTOMNOST, POLITOLOGICKÁ REVUE, PRÁCA, PRAGUE POST, PRAVDA, PRÁV-NÍK, PRÁVNÝ OBZOR, PŘÍTOMNOST, PROSTOR, REPUBLIKA, RESPEKT, RUDÉ KRÁVO, RUDÉ PRÁVO, SLOBODNÝ PIATOK, SLOVENSKÉ LISTY, SLOVENSKÝ DEN-NÍK, SMENA, STÁT A PRÁVO, STŘEDOEVROPSKÉ NOVINY (enclosed with LIDOVÉ NOVINY), SVOBODNÉ SLOVO, TELEGRAF, TVORBA, VEČERNÍ PRAHA, VEČERNÍK, VÝBĚR, ZEMĚDĚLSKÉ NOVINY, and ZMENA.

Nationalism, Ethnic Conflict, Separation

Anderson, Benedict. Imagined Communities: Reflections on the Origin and Spread of Nationalism. Verso, London, New York, 1983.

Arnheim, Rudolf. "The Split and the Structure." 1992 MICHIGAN QUARTERLY REVIEW 195.

Balaš, Vladimír. "Některé mezinárodní aspekty dělení státu [Some International Aspects of the Division of States]." 11/1992 PRÁVNÍK 996.

Beran, Harry. "A Liberal Theory of Secession." 32 POLITICAL STUDIES (1984).

Breuilly, John. Nationalism and the State. 2d ed. University of Chicago Press, Chicago, 1993.

Brilmayer, Lea. "Secession and Self-Determination: A Territorial Interpretation." 16 YALE J. INT'L L. 177 (no. 1, Winter 1991).

Buchanan, Allen. "Toward a Theory of Secession." 101 ETHICS 322 (Jan. 1991).

Etzioni, Amitai. "The Evils of Self-Determination." 1992–93 FOREIGN POLICY 21.

Frank, Thomas M. "Clan and Superclan: Loyalty, Identity, and Community in Law and Practice." 90 AJIL 359 (1996).

Gellner, Ernest. "Nationalism Reconsidered and E.H. Carr." 18 REVIEW OF INTERNA-
TIONAL STUDIES 285 (Great Britain, 1992).

Gellner, Ernest. Nations and Nationalism. Cornell University Press, Ithaca, London,
1983.

Gottlieb, Gideon. Nation against State: A New Approach to Ethnic Conflicts and the
Decline of Sovereignty. Council on Foreign Relations Press, New York, 1993.

Greenfield, Liah. Nationalism: Five Roads to Modernity. Harvard University Press,
Cambridge, Mass., 1992.

Gurr, Ted Robert, and Barbara Harff. Ethnic Conflict in World Politics. Westview Press,
Boulder, San Francisco, Oxford, 1994.

Hall, John. "Nationalism Classified and Explained." 122 DAEDALUS 1 (no. 3, 1993).

Herzog, Donald L. "A Comparative Theory of Contempt." Unpublished, 1994.

Hobsbawm, Eric J. Nations and Nationalism since 1780: Programme, Myth, Reality. 2d
ed., Cambridge University Press, Cambridge, New York, Melbourne, 1992.

Horowitz, Donald L. Ethnic Groups in Conflict. University of California Press,
Berkeley, Los Angeles, London, 1985.

Hroch, Miroslav. Social Preconditions of National Revival in Europe. Translated by
Ben Fowkes. Cambridge University Press, Cambridge, London, New York, 1985.

Isaacs, Harold R. Idols of the Tribe, Group Identity, and Political Changes. Harper and
Row, New York, 1975.

Judt, Tony. "The New Old Nationalism." NEW YORK REVIEW OF BOOKS, Mar. 26, 1994,
p. 44.

Kuyper, Pieter Jan. "The Community and State Succession in Respect of Treaties," in
Rick Lawson and Mathis de Blois (eds.), The Dynamics of the Protection of
Human Rights. Martinus Nijhoff Pub., Dordrecht, Boston, London, 1994.

Lind, Michael. "In Defense of Liberal Nationalism." FOREIGN AFFAIRS 87 (no. 3, 1994).

McGary, John, and Brendan O'Leary (eds.). The Politics of Ethnic Conflict Regulation:
Case Studies of Protraced Ethnic Conflict. Routledge, London, New York, 1993.

Mikule, Vladimír (ed.). Mezinárodní smlouvy mezi Českou republikou a Slovenskou
republikou [International Treaties between the Czech Republic and Slovak Re-
public]. Codex Bohemia, Praha, 1995.

Montville, Joseph V. (ed.). Conflict and Peacemaking in Multi-Ethnic Societies. Lexington Books, Lexington, Mass., Toronto, 1990.

Moynihan, Daniel P. "Elitland." 4 PSYCHOLOGY TODAY 70 (no. 4, 1970).

Pfaff, William. The Wrath of Nations, Civilization, and the Furies of Nationalism.
Simon and Schuster, New York, 1993.

Ross, Lee, and Andrew Ward. Naive Realism: Implications for Social Conflict and
Misunderstanding. Unpublished, 1994.

Ross, Lee, and Andrew Ward. "Naive Realism in Everyday Life: Implications for Social
Conflict and Misunderstanding." In Kenneth Arrow et al. (eds.), Barriers to Conflict Resolution. W.W. Norton and Co., New York, London, 1995.

Rudolf, J.R. Jr., and R.J. Thompson (eds.). Ethnoterritorial Politics, Policy, and the
Western World. Lynne Rienner Pub., Boulder, London, 1989.

Smith, Anthony D. Theories of Nationalism. Harper and Row, New York, Evanston, San
Francisco, London, 1971.

Suksi, Markku. Bringing in the People: A Comparison of Constitutional Forms and

Practices of the Referendum. Martinus Nijhoff Publishers, Dordrecht, Boston, London, 1993.

Thompson, Robert J. "Referendums and Ethnoterritorial Movements: The Policy Consequences and Political Ramifications." In Robert J. Thompson and Joseph R. Rudolph Jr. (eds.), Ethnoterritorial Politics, Policy, and the Western World. Lynne Rienner Pub., Boulder, London, 1989.

Wolchik, Sharon L. "The Politics of Ethnicity in Post-Communist Czechoslovakia." 8 EAST EUROPEAN POLITICS AND SOCIETIES 153 (no. 1, 1994).

Federalism

Comisso, Ellen. "Federalism and Nationalism in Post-Socialist Europe." 1 NEW EUROPE LAW REV. 489 (no. 2, 1993).

Dehousse, Renaud. Fédéralisme et relations internationales. Bruylant, Bruxelles, 1991.

Delpérée, Francis (ed. and coauthor). La Constitution Fédérale du 5 May 1993. Bruylant, Bruxelles, 1993.

Elazar, Daniel J. (ed.). Federal Systems of the World: A Handbook of Federal, Confederal, and Autonomy Arrangements. Longman Group UK Limited, Harlow, Essex, UK, 1991.

Elazar, Daniel J., and Ilan Greilsammer. "Federal Democracy: The U.S.A. and Europe Compared—A Political Science Perspective." In Capelletti et al. (eds.), Integration through Law, vol. 1, bk. 1. Walter de Gruyter, Berlin, New York, 1986.

Forsyth, Murray. Union of States: Theory and Practice of Confederation. Leicester University Press, Holmes and Merk Pub., Inc., New York, 1981.

Frowein, Jochem Abr. "Konkurrierende Zuständigkeit und Subsidiarität zur Kompetenzverteilung in bündnischen Systemen." In Peter Badura and Rupert Scholz (eds.), Wege und Verfahren des Verfassungslebens. C.H. Beck's Verl., München, 1993.

Inotai, András. "Past, Present, and Future of Federalism in Central and Eastern Europe." 1 NEW EUROPE LAW REV. 505 (no. 2, 1993).

King, Preston. Federalism and Federation. Croom Helm, London, Canberra, 1982.

Knapp, Viktor. "Socialist Federation: A Legal Means to the Solution of the Nationality Problem: A Comparative Study." 82 MICHIGAN LAW REVIEW 1213 (1984.

Knop, Karen et al. Rethinking Federalism: Citizens, Markets and Governments in a Changing World. UBC Press, Vancouver, B.C., 1995.

Krecht, Jaroslav. "Federativní stát a jeho právní systém (Studie zaměřená k ústavní problematice) [Federative State and Its Legal System (A Study Aimed at Constitutional Problematic)]." 9–10/1991 PRÁVNÍK 721.

Majone, Giandomenico. "Preservation of Cultural Diversity in a Federal System: The Role of the Regions." In Mark Tushnet (ed.), Comparative Constitutional Federalism: Europe and America. Greenwood Press, New York, Westport, Conn., London, 1990.

Milne, David. The Canadian Constitution: The Players and the Issues in the Process That Has Led from Patriation to Meech Lake to an Uncertain Future. 3d ed., J. Lorimer and Co., Toronto, 1991.

Tarlton, Charles D. "Symmetry and Asymmetry as Elements of Federalism: A Theoretical Speculation." 27 JOURNAL OF POLITICS 861 (1965).

Post-Communist Transformations

Ackerman, Bruce. The Future of Liberal Revolution. Yale University Press, New Haven, London, 1992.

Bělohradský, Václav. Kapitalismus a občanské ctnosti [Capitalism and Civic Virtues]. Český spisovatel, Praha, 1992.

Bělohradský, Václav, Pierre Kende, and Jaques Rupnick (eds.). Democrazie da inventare: culture politiche e stato in Ungheria e Cecoslovacchia. Edizioni della Fondazione Giovanni Agnelli, Torino, 1991.

Berglund, Sten, and Jan Åke Dellenbrant (eds.). The New Democracies in Eastern Europe: Party Systems and Political Clevages. 2d ed., Edward Elgar Publishing Ltd., Aldershot, Eng., Vermont, 1994.

Brokl, Lubomír, and Zdenka Mansfeldová. "Von der 'unpolitischen' zur 'professionellen' Politik." In Peter Gerlich et al. (eds.), Regimewechsel: Demokratisierung und politische Kultur in Ostmitteleuropa. Böhlau Verlag, Wien, Köln, Graz, 1992.

Brown, Chris (ed.). Political Restructuring in Europe: Ethical Perspectives. Routledge, London, New York, 1994.

Brown, James F. Hopes and Shadows: Eastern Europe after Communism. Duke University Press, Durham, 1994.

Brunner, Georg. Politischer Systemwandel und Verfassungsreformen in Osteuropa. Verlag Josef Eul, Bergisch Gladbach–Köln, 1990.

Bryant, Christopher G., and Edmund Mokrzycki (eds.). The New Great Transformation? Change and Continuity in East-Central Europe. Routledge, London, New York, 1994.

Cohen, Jean L., and Andrew Arato. Civil Society and Political Theory. MIT Press, Cambridge, Mass., London, 1992.

DAEDALUS. After Communism What? (Summer 1994).

Derlien, Hans-Ulrich, and George J. Szablowski (eds.). "Regime Transition, Elites, and Bureaucracies in Eastern Europe." 6 GOVERNANCE, Special Issue (no. 3, July 1993).

Dyba, Karel. O hospodářském optimismu a realismu [About Economic Optimism and Realism]. APP Group, Praha, 1994.

Ebke, Werner F., and Detlev F. Vagts, (eds.). Demokratie, Markwirtschaft und Recht-Democracy, Market Economy, and the Law. Verlag Recht und Wirtschaft GmbH, Heidelberg, 1995.

Elster, Jon. The Cement of Society: A Study of Social Order. Cambridge University Press, New York, Dorechester, Melbourne, Sydney, 1989.

Elster, Jon. "The Necessity and Impossibility of Simultaneous Economic and Political Reform." In Douglas Greenberg, Stanley N. Katz, Melanie Beth Oliviero, and Steven C. Wheatley (eds.), Constitutionalism and Democracy. Oxford University Press, New York, Oxford, 1993.

Gray, Robert D. (ed.). Democratic Theory and Post-Communist Change (Prentice Hall, Upper Sadle River, N. Jer., 1997), particularly chap. 5 and 6 by John Reitz.

Gerlich, Peter, et al. (eds.). Regimewechsel: Demokratisierung und politische Kultur in Ostmitteleuropa. Böhlau Verlag, Wien, Köln, Gratz, 1992.

Gerloch, Aleš (ed.). Aktuální problémy demokratizace postkomunistických států střední Evropy [Actual Problems of Democratization of Post-Communist Central-European States]. Česká společnost pro politické vědy, Praha, 1995.

Islam, Shafigul, and Michael Mandelbaum (eds.). Making Markets: Economic Transformation in Eastern Europe and Post-Soviet States. Council on Foreign Relations, New York, 1993.

Karp, Regina Cowen. Central and Eastern Europe: The Challenge of Transition. SIPRI, Oxford University Press, New York, 1993.

Klaus, Václav. Česká cesta [The Czech Way]. Profile s.r.o., Praha, 1994.

Klaus, Václav. Rok-Málo či mnoho v dějinách země [A Year: Little or a Lot in History of the Country]. Repro-Media, Praha, 1993.

Klingsberg, Ethan. "The State Rebuilding Society: Constitutionalism and the Post-Communist Paradox." 13 MICHIGAN JOURNAL OF INTERNATIONAL LAW 865 (1992).

Mestmäcker, Ernst-Joachim. "Die Wiederkehr der bürgerlichen Gesselschaft und ihres Rechts." Max Planck-Gesellschaft Jahrbuch 1991, 24. Max-Planck-Ges., München, Verlag Vanderhoeck and Ruprecht, Göttingen, 1992.

Raus, Daniel. Politika a ideál [Politics and ideal]. Návrat, Praha, 1992.

Rollo, J.M.C., et al. The New Eastern Europe: Western Responses. Royal Institute of International Affairs, Pinter Pub., London, 1990.

Rustow, Dankwart A. "Transition to Democracy: Toward a Dynamic Model." 3 COMPARATIVE POLITICS 337 (April 1970).

Schöpflin, George. "Post-Communism: Constructing New Democracies in Central Europe." 67 INTERNATIONAL AFFAIRS 235 (April 1991).

Švejnar, Jan, et al. Economic Transformation: The Tasks Still Ahead—A Symposium. Per Jacobson Foundation, Washington, D.C., 1995.

Waller, Michael, and Martin Myant, Martin (eds.). Parties, Trade Unions, and Society in East Central Europe. Frank Cass, Illford, Essex, Eng., Portland, Ore., 1994.

Walzer, Michael (ed.). Toward a Global Civil Society. Berghahn Books, Providence, Oxford, 1995.

Zel'ová, Alena, et al. Minoritné etnické spoločenstva na Slovensku v procesoch spoločenských premien [Ethnic Minority Communities in Processes of Societal Changes]. Veda, Bratislava, 1994.

Constitution Making in Eastern Europe and Generally

Axelrod, Robert. "The Emergence of Cooperation among Egoists." 75 AMERICAN POLITICAL SCIENCE REVIEW 306 (1981).

Brady, Henry E., and Cynthia S. Kaplan. "Eastern Europe and Former Soviet Union." In David Butler and Austin Ramsey (eds.), Referendums around the World: The Growing Use of Direct Democracy. The AEI Press, Washington, D.C., 1994.

Einhorn, Barbara, Mary Kaldor, and Zdeněk Kavan. Citizenship and Democratic Control in Contemporary Europe. Edward Elgar, Cheltenham Eng., Brookfield, US, 1996.

Elster, Jon. "Constitution-Making in Eastern Europe: Rebuilding the Boat in the Open Sea." 71 PUBLIC ADMINISTRATION (1993).

Elster, Jon. "Constitutionalism in Eastern Europe: An Introduction." 58 UNIVERSITY OF CHICAGO LAW REVIEW 447 (1991).

Elster, Jon. "Making Sense of Constitution-Making." 1 EAST EUR. CONST. REV. 15 (1992).

Häberle, Peter. "Constitutional Developments in Eastern Europe from the Point of View of Jurisprudence and Constitutional Theory." 46 LAW AND STATE 64 (Institut für Wissenschaftliche Zusammenarbeit, Tübingen, 1992).

Heckathorn, Douglas D., and Steven M. Maser. "Bargaining and Constitutional Contracts." 31 AMERICAN JOURNAL OF POLITICAL SCIENCE 142 (1987).

Howard, A.E. Dick (ed.). Constitution-Making in Eastern Europe. W. Wilson Center Press, Washington, D.C., 1993.

Kresák, Peter. "Centralizovany a decentralizovany model súdnej kontroly ústavnosti, [Centralized and Decentralized Model of Judicial Control for Constitutionality]," 78 PRÁVNY OBZOR 185 (1995).

Ludwikowski, Rett R. "Searching for a New Constitutional Model for East-Central Europe." 17 SYRACUSE J. INT'L L. AND COM. 155 (1991).

Maser, Steven M. "Bargaining and Constitutional Contracts." 31 AMERICAN JOURNAL OF POLITICAL SCIENCE 142 (1987).

McWhinney, Edward. Constitution-Making: Principles, Process, Practice. University of Toronto Press, Toronto, Buffalo, London, 1981.

Pegoraro, Lucio. "Il sistema delle fonti giuridiche nelle costituzioni dell' Est europeo." 15 QUADERNI COSTITUZIONALI 111 (no. 1, 1995).

Pogany, Istvan (ed.). Human Rights in Eastern Europe. Edward Elgar Pub. Ltd., Aldershot, Eng., 1995.

Raiffa, Howard. The Art and Science of Negotiation. Harvard University Press, Cambridge, Mass., 1982.

Schwartz, Herman. "Innocents and Experience." 1 EAST EUR. CONST. REV. 26 (1992).

Stein, Eric. "International Law in Internal Law: Toward Internationalization of Central-Eastern European Constitutions." 88 AMERICAN JOURNAL OF INTERNATIONAL LAW 427 (1994).

Czech and Slovak History

Ash, Timothy Garton. The Magic Lantern: The Revolution of '89 Witnessed in Warsaw, Budapest, Berlin, and Prague, Random House, New York, 1990.

Bútora, Martin, et al. Slovensko rok po [Slovakia a Year After]. Sociologické nakladatelství, Praha, 1994.

Čapek, Karel. Čtení o TGM [Reading about TGM]. Melantrich, Praha, 1969.

Dahrendorf, Ralf. Reflections on the Revolution in Europe. Random House, New York, 1990.

Dějiny státu a práva [History of the State and Law]. Vols. 1 and 2. Slovak Academy of Sciences, Bratislava, 1973.

Dubček, Alexander. Nádej zomiera posledná [Hope Dies Last]. Národná obroda, a.s., Práca, spol. s r.o., 1993.

Echikson, William. Lighting the Night: Revolution in Eastern Europe. William Morrow and Co., Inc., New York, 1990.

Grospič, Jiří. "Zákonodárná pravomoc a působnost v československé federaci a otázky jejího uplatňování [Legislative Competence and Activity in the Czechoslovak Federation and Questions of Its Application]." 15 Stát a Právo 5 (1973).

Havel, Václav. Do různých stran [To Varied Directions]. Lidové noviny, Praha, 1989.

Havel, Václav. Letters to Olga. Henry Holt and Co., New York, 1989.

Havel, Václav. '94. Paseka, Praha, Litomyšl, 1995.

Havel, Václav. O lidskou identitu [For Human Identity]. Nakl. Alexandra Tomského Rozmluvy, Praha, 1990.

Havel, Václav. Open Letters: Selected Writings, 1965–1990. Vintage Books, New York, 1992.

Havel, Václav. Summer Meditations. A.A. Knopf, New York, 1992.

Hermann, A.H. A History of the Czechs. Allen Lane, London, 1975.

Jičínský, Zdeněk. Vznik České národní rady v době Pražského jara a její působení do podzimu 1969 [The Establishment of the Czech National Council at the Time of the Prague Spring and Its Functioning until Autumn 1969]. Svoboda, Prague, 1990.

Judt, Tony R. "Metamorphosis: The Democratic Revolution in Czechoslovakia." In Ivo Banac (ed.), Eastern Europe in Revolution. Cornell University Press, Ithaca, London, 1992.

Knapp, Viktor. "The Legislative Challenge for Former Socialist States in Europe." 1992 Statute Law Review (Oxford) 97.

Kresák, Peter. Porovnávacie štátne právo [Comparative Public Law]. Vydavatelské oddelenie právnickej Faculty, UK, Bratislava, 1993.

Kriseová, Eda. Václav Havel, Životopis [Václav Havel, a Biography]. Atlantis, Brno, 1991.

Leff, Carol Skalnik. National Conflict in Czechoslovakia: The Making and Remaking of a State, 1918–1987. Princeton U. Press, Princeton, N.J., 1988.

Leško, Marián. L'udia a l'udkovia z politickej elity [People and Little People of the Political Elite]. Perex a.s., Bratislava, 1993.

Leško, Marián. Slovenské tango z roku jeden—Dôverná správa o politike a politikoch [Slovak Tango from Year One—Confidential Report about Politics and Politicians], Perex, 1993.

Lettrich, Jozef. History of Modern Slovakia. Praeger, New York, 1955.

Luers, William H. "Czechoslovakia: Road to Revolution." 69 Foreign Affairs 77 (1990).

Olson, David M. "Dissolution of the State Political Parties and the 1992 Elections in Czechoslovakia." 26 Communist and Post-Communist Studies 301 (no. 3, 1993).

Pavlíček, Václav. "The Foundation of the Czech Republic and the Czechoslovak Continuity," 1994 Home Rule and Civil Society (no. 5, Mar. 1994).

Peroutka, Ferdinand. Začátky Česko—Slovenského soužití [The Beginnings of the Czecho-Slovak Coexistence]. Ed. Sokolova, Paris, 1953.

Rychetský, Pavel. "Vývoj právního řádu po 17. listopadu 1989 a výhled dalších systémových změn právního řádu [The Evolution of the Legal Order after 17 November 1989 and Prospect of Further Systematic Changes of the Legal Order]." 3–4/1992 Právník 185.

Setton-Watson, Robert William. A History of the Czechs and Slovaks. Hutchison and Co., Ltd., London, New York, Melbourne, 1943.
Šimečka, Milan. The Restoration of Order: The Normalization of Czechoslovakia, 1969–1976. Translated by A.G. Brain. Verso Ed., London, 1984.
Šimíček, Vojtěch (ed.). Česko-slovenské vztahy a střední Evropa [Czecho-Slovak Relations and Central Europe]. Mezinárodní politologický ústav právnické fakulty Masarykovy university v Brně, Brno, 1994.
Simmons, Michael. The Reluctant President. Methuen, London, 1991.
Táborský, Edward. Czechoslovak Democracy at Work. George Allen and Unwin Ltd., London, 1945.
Thompson, Samuel Harrison. Czechoslovakia in European History. Princeton University Press, Princeton, N.J., 1953.
Wehrlé, Frédéric. Le divorce tchéco-slovaque: vie et mort de la Tchécoslovaquie, 1918–1992. Ed. L'harmattan, Paris, 1994.
Zpráva poslance akademika Viktora Knappa k zákonu o čs. federaci [Report of Deputy Academician Viktor Knapp on the Law on the Czech Federation]. 1/1969 PRÁVNÍK 66.

Czecho-Slovak Constitutional Choices and Negotiations: The Breakup

Bubílková, Zuzana. Co kamery neviděly [What the Cameras Did Not See]. Lidové noviny, Praha, 1993.
Bubílková, Zuzana, and Ota Černý. Co týden (ne)dal [What the Week Did (Not) Give]. Lidové noviny, Praha, 1993.
Bútora, Martin, and Zora Bútorová. "Slovakia: The Identity Challenges of the Newly Born States." 60 SOCIAL RESEARCH 705 (no. 4, Winter 1993).
Bútorová, Zora. "A Deliberate 'Yes' to the Dissolution of the ČFSR?" 1 CZECH SOCIOLOGICAL REVIEW 58 (no. 1, 1993).
Cepl, Vojtěch. "Constitutional Reform in the Czech Republic." 28 U. OF SAN FRANCISCO L. REV. 29 (1993).
Cepl, Vojtěch, and David Franklin. "Senate, Anyone?" 2 EAST EUR. CONST. REV. 59 (1993).
Cepl, Vojtěch, and Mark Gillis. "Survey of Presidential Powers in Eastern Europe." 2–3 EAST EUR. CONST. REV. (1993, 1994).
Cibulka, L'ubor. "Constitutional Law of the Slovak Republic." In Stanislav Frankowski and Paul B. Stefan III (eds.), Legal Reform in Post-Communist Europe: A View from Within. Martinus Nijhoff Pub., Boston, Dordrecht, London, 1995.
Čič, Milan, and L'ubomír Fogaš. "Ústava Slovenskej republiky [Constitution of the Slovak Republic]." NKV International, Bratislava, 1992.
Cutler, Lloyd, and Herman Schwartz. "Constitutional Reform in Czechoslovakia: E Duobus Unum?" 58 CHICAGO LAW REVIEW 511 (1991).
Fogaš, L'ubomír, and Luboš Cibula. Listina základných práv a slobôd, ústavný zákon s komentárom [List of Basic Rights and Freedoms, Constitutional Law with a Commentary]. Slov. Pedagog. Nakl., Bratislava, 1992.

Gál, Fedor et al. Dnešní krise česko-slovenského vztahu [Today's Crisis of the Czecho-Slovak Relations]. Sociologické nakladatelství, Praha, 1992.

Gerloch, Aleš. "Československá federace: uzavřená minulost? [Czechoslovak Federation: Closed Past?]." In Vojtěch Šimíček (ed.), Česko-slovenské vztahy a střední Evropa [Czecho-Slovak Relations and Central Europe]. Mezinár. politol. ústav právnické fakulty Masarykovy university v Brně, Czech Rep., 1994.

Gerloch, Aleš. Teorie federalismu a rozdělení Československa [The Theory of Federalism and the Division of Czechoslovakia]. 1995 POLITOLOGICKÁ REVUE 13 (June 1995).

Grospič, Jiří. "Some Constitutional Problems of the Czech Republic." In Irena Grudzińska Gross (ed.), Constitutionalism and Politics. Slovak Committee of the European Cultural Foundation, Bratislava, 1994.

Gross, Irena Grudzińska. Constitutionalism in East Central Europe. Czecho-Slovak Committee of the European Cultural Foundation, Bratislava, 1994.

Havel, Václav. Projevy [Pronouncements]. Vyšehrad, Praha, 1990.

Havel, Václav. Vážení občané—Projevy, červenec 1990–červenec 1992 [Esteemed Citizens—Addresses, July 1990–July 1992]. LN, Praha, 1992.

Hendrych, Dušan. "Constitutional Transition and Preparation of New Constitution in Czechoslovakia after 1989." In Joachim Jens Hesse and Neville Johnson (eds.), Constitutional policy and Change in Europe. Oxford University Press, Oxford, New York, 1995.

Holländer, Pavol. "The New Slovak Constitution: A Critique." 1 EAST. EUR. CONST. REV. 16 (no. 3, 1992).

Javorský, František, et al. (eds.). Dialogy Vladimíra Mečiara [Dialogues of Vladimír Mečiar]. HOS, Slovakia, 1992.

Jičínský, Zdeněk. Československý parlament v polistopadovém vývoji [The Czechoslovak Parliament in the post-November Development]. NADAS-AFGH s.r.o., Praha, 1993.

Jičínský, Zdeněk. "Ke ztroskotání československého federalismu [On the Foundering of the Czechoslovak Federalism]." In Rüdiger Kipke and Karel Vodička (eds.), Rozloučení s Československem [Parting with Czechoslovakia]. Český Spisovatel a.s., Prague, 1993.

Jičínský, Zdeněk, and Vladimír Mikule. Das Ende der Tschechoslowakei 1992 in verfassungsrechlicher Sicht (Teil I) Berichte 1994. Bundesinstitut für ostwissenschaftliche und internationale Studien, Köln, Germany, 1994. Also Teil II, no. 45 Berichte 1994.

Kipke, Rüdiger, and Karel Vodička (eds.). Rozloučení s Československem [Parting with Czechoslovakia]. Český Spisovatel, Praha, 1993.

Kirschbaum, Stanislav J. "Federalism in Slovak Communist Politics." 19 CANADIAN SLAVONIC PAPERS 444 (1977).

Klusáková, Jana. Fedor Gál. Nadoraz, Primus, Praha, 1992.

Klusáková, Jana a Jiří Dienstbier rozmlouvají [Jana Klusáková and Jiří Dienstbier Converse]. Nadoraz, Primus, Praha, 1993.

Klusáková, Jana a Karel Schwarzenberg rozmlouvají [Jana Klusáková and Karel Schwarzenberg Converse]. Nadoraz, Primus, Praha, 1993.

Klusáková, Jana. Petr Pithart—Nadoraz. Primus, Praha, 1992.

Knapp, Viktor, and Bartole, Sergio. La dissoluzione della Federazione cecoslovacca. La Rosa Ed., Torino, 1994.

Král, J., "K problémom nového ústavného systému Slovenskej republiky [On Problems of the New Constitutional System of the Slovak Republic]." 77 PRÁVNY OBZOR 56 (no. 1, 1994).

Kresák, Petr. "The Government Structure in the New Slovak Republic," 4 *Tulsa Journal of Comparative and International Law* 1 (no. 1, 1996).

Kresák, Peter. "The Regulation of Mutual Relations between the National Council of the Slovak Republic and the Government in the Constitution of the Slovak Republic." In Irena Gruzińska (ed.), Constitutionalism and Politics. Slovak Committee of the European Cultural Foundation, Bratislava, 1994.

Kubín, L'., M. Velšic, R. Daňo, B. Juhás, D. Balko, and J. Stupaň. Dva roky politickej slobody [Two Years of Political Freedom]. RaPaMaN, Bratislava, 1992.

Kusín, Vladimír V. "The Confederal Search." Res. Rep. on E. Eur. RFL/RL, Inc., Munich, F.R.G., July 5, 1991, 36.

Lijphart, Arend. "Democratization and Constitutional Choices in Czechoslovakia, Hungary, and Poland." 4 J'L OF THEORETICAL POLITICS 207 (no. 2, 1992).

Mikule, Vladimír, and Vladimír Sládeček. Ústavní soudnictví a lidská práva [Constitutional Judiciary and Human Rights]. Codex, Nakl. Hugo Grotia, a.s., Praha, 1994.

de Morzellec, Joelle. "Nástupnictví států: Příklad rozdělení České a Slovenské Federativní Republiky [Succession of States: Example of Division of the Czech and Slovak Federative Republic]." 9/1993 PRÁVNÍK 777.

Osterland, Holly A. "National Self-Determination and Secession: The Slovak Model." 25 CASE WESTERN RESERVE JOURNAL OF INTERNATIONAL LAW 655 (no. 3, Summer 1993).

Pavlíček, Václav. "Problémy práv občanů v ústavě České republiky [Problems of the Rights of Citizens in the Constitution of the Czech Republic]." 4/1993 PRÁVNÍK, 349.

Posluch, Marián, and a Collective. Štátne právo Slovenskej republiky [State Law of the Slovak Republic]. Universita Komenského, Bratislava, 1993.

Potočný, Miroslav. Smlouva mezi Českou republikou a Slovenskou republikou o dobrém sousedství, přátelských vztazích a spolupráci [Treaty between the Czech Republic and the Slovak Republic on Good Neighborhood, Friendly Relations, and Cooperation]. 8/1993 PRÁVNÍK 679.

Škaloud, Jan. "Trojí rozpad Československa a vznik České republiky [Triple Breakup of Czechoslovakia and Inception of the Czech Republic]." 1994 POLITOLOGICKÁ REVUE 78.

Slapnicka, Helmut. "Die Verfassungsordnung der Tschechischen Republik." 40 OSTEUROPA RECHT 28 (1994). Includes a German translation of the Czech Constitution.

Strmiska, Zdeněk. Quelques remarques sur Le divorce tchéco-slovaque. 26 REV. D'ÉTUDES COMPARATIVES EST OUEST 183 (no. 2, 1995).

Valko, Ernest. "On the Constitution of the Slovak Republic." In Irena Grudzińska Gross (ed.), Constitutionalism and Politics. Slovak Committee on the European Cultural Foundation, Bratislava, 1994.

Williams, Paul R. "The Treaty Obligations of the Successor States of the Former Soviet Union, Yugoslavia, and Czechoslovakia: Do They Continue in Force?" 23 DENVER JOURNAL OF INTERNATIONAL LAW AND POLITICS 1 (1994).

Wolchik, Sharon L. "The Politics of Transition and the Break-Up of Czechoslovakia." In Jiří Musil (ed.), The End of Czechoslovakia. Central European University Press, Budapest, London, New York, 1995.

Žák, Václav. The Velvet Divorce: Institutional Foundations. In Jiří Musil (ed.), The End of Czechoslovakia. Central European University Press, Budapest, London, New York, 1995.

Oral Sources

The affiliations indicated are generally as of the time of my interviews. Where several interviews with a person were conducted over time I list the consecutive positions. I am deeply indebted to the persons listed here for their time and assistance.

JUDr. Vladimír Balaš, Dean of the Law Faculty, Czech-Western University, Director of the Institute of State and Law, Czech Academy of Sciences; Ivo Bárta LLM, attorney; Prof. JUDr. Josef Blahož, Director, Institute of Government and Law, Czechoslovak Academy of Sciences; Prof. JUDr. Jiří Boguszak, Charles University Law Faculty, Deputy Chair of the Commission of Experts for Preparation of the Federal Constitution; JUDr. Gabriel Brenka, Acting Director, International Law Department, Ministry of Foreign Affairs, Czech and Slovak Federative Republic; Zuzana Bubílková, journalist and author; Ján Budaj, Deputy for the Democratic Union in the Slovak National Council; JUDr. Dagmar Burešová, Chair, National Council of the Czech Republic, attorney; JUDr. Marián Čalfa, former Prime Minister of the Czech and Slovak Federative Republic, consultant; JUDr. Ján Čarnogurský, Deputy Prime Minister of the Czech and Slovak Federative Republic, Prime Minister of the Slovak Republic, deputy for the Christian Democratic Movement in the Slovak National Council; Doc. JUDr. Vojtěch Cepl Jr., Vice-Dean Law Faculty, Charles University, Professor and Judge of the Constitutional Court of the Czech Republic; JUDr. Brigita Chrastilová, Director of the Legislative Department, Office of the President of the Czech Republic; Dr. Zuzana Chudomelová, Staff, Parliament of the Czech Republic; Prof. JUDr. Milan Čič, Chair, Constitutional Court of the Slovak Republic; Pavol Demeš, Minister of International Relations of the Slovak Republic; Jiří Dienstbier, former Minister of Foreign Affairs of the Czech and Slovak Federative Republic, Chairman of the Free Democrat Party; Luboš Dobrovský, Head of the Office of the President of the Czech Republic; Doc. JUDr. Jan Filip, Law Faculty, Masaryk University, Brno; Doc. JUDr. L'ubomír Fogaš, Deputy for the Slovak Democratic Party of the Left and member of the Presidium, Slovak National Council; Ivan Gabal, Office of the President of the Czech and Slovak Federative Republic; Doc. JUDr. Ivan Gašparovič, Chair, National Council of the Slovak Republic; Doc. JUDr. Aleš Gerloch, Law Faculty, Charles University; JUDr. Jiří Grospič, Senior Research Fellow, Czechoslovak Academy of Sciences; JUDr. Vojen Güttler, Judge, Constitutional Court of the Czech and Slovak Federative Republic; Prof. JUDr. Dušan Hendrych, Dean, Law Faculty, Charles University; Doc. JUDr. Pavol Holländer, Comenius (Bratislava) and Olomouc (Moravia) University Faculties of Law,

Professor and Judge, Constitutional Court of the Czech Republic; Doc. Robert Holman, adviser to Prime Minister Klaus, Office of the Prime Minister of the Czech Republic; JUDr. Jaroslav Horák, Director, International Law Department, Ministry of Foreign Affairs, Czech Republic; Jozef Horal, Editor in Chief, Slovenské listy; Prof. JUDr. Zdeněk Jičínský, Deputy Chair of the Federal Assembly, author and member of the Presidium of the Social Democratic Party; JUDr. Jan Kalvoda, Deputy Prime Minister, Czech Republic, Chair of the Civic Democratic Alliance; Rita Klímová, Ambassador of the Czech and Slovak Federative Republic to the United States; Prof. Dr. Viktor Knapp, Law Faculty, Charles University, Director of the Institute of State and Law, Czechoslovak Academy of Sciences, Vice-President, Czechoslovak Academy of Sciences; Milan Kňažko, former Minister of Foreign Affairs of the Slovak Republic, deputy for the Democratic Union in the Slovak National Council; MUDr. Roman Kováč, Deputy Prime Minister in charge of internal policy, Slovak Republic; Doc. JUDr. Peter Kresák, Law Faculty, Comenius University, Bratislava, adviser to the Chair of the Constitutional Court of the Slovak Republic; Prof. Dr. Miroslav Kusý, Comenius University, Bratislava; Marián Leško, Editor in Chief, PRAVDA, Bratislava; JUDr. Ivan Majerik, Vice-President, Supreme Court of the Slovak Republic; Dr. Herberta and Dr. Anna Masaryk; Helen E. McKee, Public Affairs Officer, American Embassy, Bratislava; Ivan Medek, Deputy Head, Office of the President of the Czech Republik; František Mikloško, former Chair of the Slovak National Council, deputy; Doc. JUDr. Vladimír Mikule, Law Faculty, Charles University; Vladimír Mlynář, Editor, RESPEKT; Doc. JUDr. Jozef Moravčík, former Minister of Foreign Affairs of the Czech and Slovak Federative Republic, former Minister of Foreign Affairs and Prime Minister of the Slovak Republic, deputy in the Slovak National Council and Chair of the Democratic Union Party; JUDr. Otakar Motejl, Chair of the Supreme Court of the Czech and Slovak Federative Republic, Chair of the Supreme Court of the Czech Republic; Doc. PhDr. Ivan Mucha, Dean, Law Faculty, Charles University; Cameron Munter, Deputy Chief of Mission, American Embassy, Prague; Laszlo Nagy, Chair of the Hungarian Civic Party and deputy in the Slovak National Council; JUDr. Dušan Nikodým, Ministry of Justice of the Slovak Republic; Prof. JUDr. Václav Pavlíček, Head of the Department of Constitutional Law, Law Faculty, Charles University; Dr. Jiří Payne, Deputy of the Civic Democratic Party in the National Council of the Czech Republic and Chair of the Foreign Relations Committee, same position in the Parliament of the Czech Republic; Prof. PhDr. Petr Piťha, member of a commission appointed by the President of the Czech and Slovak Federative Republic, Minister of Education, Czech Republic; Doc. Dr. Petr Pithart, former Prime Minister of the Czech Republic, Professor at the Central European University; Prof. JUDr. Karol Plank, Chair of the Supreme Court of the Slovak Republic, Head of the Department of Civil Law, Comenius University, Bratislava; PhDr. Tomáš Pštross, Deputy Director, Foreign Policy Department, Office of the President of the Czech Republic; Elizabeth Richard, Country Officer for the Czech Republic, U.S. Department of State; JUDr. Leon Richter, Minister of Justice of the Czech Republic; Ernö Rozsa, Deputy for the (Hungarian) Coexistence Party in the Slovak National Council; Doc. Dr. Valentin Rufus, Dean, Law Faculty, Charles University; JUDr. Pavel Rychetský, Procurator General, Deputy Prime Minister of the Czech and Slovak Federal Republic, attorney; Timothy M. Savage, Counselor, American Embassy, Prague; Jiří Schneider, adviser to the Minister of Foreign Affairs, Czech Republic; Karel

Schwarzenberg, Chancellor, Office of the President of the Czech and Slovak Federative Republic; Dr. Pavel Seifter, Director, Foreign Policy Department, Office of the President of the Czech Republic; Ph.D. Jiřina Šiklová, Department of Sociology, Charles University; JUDr. Ivan Šimko, Deputy in the National Council of the Slovak Republic and Vice-Chair, Christian Democratic Movement; Dr. Vladimír Sládeček, Secretary of the Commission for the Preparation of the Constitution, Federal Assembly, Doc., Law Faculty, Charles University; Zuzana Szatmary, sociologist, foundation official, publicist; MUDr. Peter Tatár, Deputy in the Slovak National Council; Eric R. Terzuolo, First Secretary, American Embassy, Prague; Doc. Luboš Tichý, Head Department of European Community Law, Law Faculty, Charles University and attorney; Dr. Jiří Weigel, adviser to Prime Minister Klaus, Office of the Prime Minister of the Czech Republic; Ing. Václav Žák, Deputy Chair of the Czech National Council, member of the Presidium of the Free Democrat Party, publicist; PhDr. Milan Zemko, Office of the Prime Minister of the Slovak Republic, Office of the President of the Slovak Republic; JUDr. František Zoulík, Ministry of Justice of the Czech Republic, also Department of Civil Law, Charles University.

Index

Note: The detailed table of contents at the beginning of the book should lead the reader to any phase or major topic of the negotiation process which forms the core of this study.

380   Index